TULANE

TULANE

THE BIOGRAPHY OF A UNIVERSITY

1834–1965

JOHN P. DYER

HARPER & ROW, PUBLISHERS, NEW YORK AND LONDON

To the former students of
Tulane and Newcomb scattered
over the face of the earth

CONTENTS

*Sixteen pages of black-and-white
photographs appear following p. 146.*

Preface

A book about Tulane University has been long in the making.

In the early 1930s the university began preparations looking toward a celebration of its centennial. In the minds of many professors and alumni a necessary part of the program was the publication of a history of the institution, and early in 1931 the Arts and Sciences faculty cooperated with the Tulane Alumni Association in perfecting plans for such a book. It was generally agreed that Richard K. Bruff, Registrar Emeritus, probably knew more about the university and its past than any other man and that he should be commissioned to write it.

The condition of Bruff's health prevented his undertaking the task, however, and in 1932 at President Dinwiddie's suggestion Samuel Lang, a Tulane journalism graduate, was asked to take up the work. A modest sum had been raised by the Engineering and the Arts and Sciences classes of 1905 to be used in the preparation of a history of the university. This gift was supplemented by the university, and Lang was appointed a research assistant with Mrs. Florence Wintz Toppino as his secretary. Lang completed a manuscript in May 1934, two years before he graduated from the law school, but for various reasons this manuscript was never published. Subsequent revisions were made by Professor Mack Swearingen and by Dean Edward Ambrose Bechtel, but still there was no agreement on publication.

For fifteen years the matter was quiescent; then through the efforts of an anonymous alumnus it was revived. In 1950, Arthur B. Nuhrah, a young Ph.D. in history from Tulane, was commissioned to do a thorough research and writing job. At the end of a four-year period he had accumulated an enormous mass of information. Professor Charles Roland of the Tulane history department made a digest of this material, but still no publishable history emerged.

I can thoroughly sympathize with the efforts of my predecessors to produce a readable and at the same time adequate history of the university, for it is difficult. The chief difficulty in a work of this nature is steering a course between a superficial narrative on the one hand, and a ponderous, encyclopedic, and dull work on the other. I have attempted to steer this middle course, but in so doing I have had to sacrifice a great deal of material, particularly with respect to names and personalities. There are people who will be disappointed that I have failed to mention numerous persons who have made noteworthy contributions to the growth of the university. I regret the necessity of these omissions. Hundreds have helped to build Tulane, but it simply is not possible to discuss or even mention all these in the text. The judgment on this matter is mine. No one has told me what to write nor how to write it. Conclusions are my own and do not necessarily reflect the official position of the university.

Nor is it possible to name all those who have helped me in the preparation of this manuscript. Many of my faculty colleagues at the university have read the manuscript as have numerous people from the outside. They know who they are and how much I appreciate their assistance. I must, however, mention these people: Mrs. William J. Griffith and Mr. A. W. Chapman of the manuscript division of the Howard-Tilton Library; Mrs. Robert C. Whittemore, Reference Librarian; Miss Susan B. Kean, retired Reference Secretary of the University; Mr. A. P. Generes, Secretary-Treasurer of the Board of Administrators; Mrs. Florence Toppino, retired Registrar; and Miss Louise Keenan, Reference Secretary. They have been most helpful. I am also indebted to Edison B. Allen, Director of Development for Annual Giving, for editorial advice and proofreading.

I have elected to eliminate footnotes which give citations to sources. Such citations do exist, however, neatly filed away for reference if necessary. There is no scarcity of primary source material for a history of the university. The minutes of the Board of Administrators are invaluable. So are deans' reports, faculty minutes, presidential reports, bulletins and catalogs of the university, minutes of the University Council and the University Senate, correspondence of the deans and presidents, financial reports, and numerous other materials of this nature. New Orleans newspapers and the various university newspapers and yearbooks supply an abundance of material. Important, too, are the recollections of faculty members. I have, of course, drawn heavily on the manuscript histories mentioned above. Two collections of letters and manuscripts in the Howard-Tilton Library—the Johnston Papers and the newly acquired McConnell Papers—are especially valuable.

This history makes its appearance in the one hundred and thirty-second year of the university's life. Those years cover the period from Andrew Jackson to Lyndon Johnson, a substantial span of the nation's history. During this time Tulane was prominently identified with the life of the South. In such an identity the university knew corrosive penury and pestilence and had its life riven by civil war. But there have been many years of the peaceful pursuit of knowledge and of service to society. In latter years Tulane has, through the force of circumstances, changed its nature and

PREFACE

perspective from a local or regional university to one which serves the nation and is rapidly acquiring global dimensions. Perhaps its Alma Mater hymn, after all, does express rather accurately the retrospective judgment that

> Thy hand hath done its work full faithfully.
> The incense of thy spirit hath ascended
> And filled America from sea to sea!

JOHN P. DYER

NEW ORLEANS
JANUARY 1966

TULANE

CHAPTER 1

The Giver and the Gift

SOMETIME IN THE WINTER or early spring of 1881 in Princeton, New Jersey, an aloof, solitary, and dour old gentleman reached a decision. One may conclude that it was neither sudden nor whimsical, for Paul Tulane was never capricious about any matter involving money. Later, when he discussed it with a friend, he said that he had been thinking about the matter off and on since the time when as a young man in his late teens he had stood on the steamboat landing at Paducah and watched planters and their sons from New Orleans disembark from the puffing upriver steamers and start the remainder of their trip overland to one of Kentucky's colleges.

Why, he wondered, did a city like New Orleans not have a college? At that time in his youth he did not know the answer, but ahead of him was more than a half century in which he would find out. He came to New Orleans, became a clever and successful merchant and real estate investor, and in the process accumulated what was for his day a substantial fortune. Always addicted to minor philanthropies he now in early 1881 decided after years of careful deliberation to give a considerable portion of his wealth for the education of the youth of New Orleans.

It was characteristic of Paul Tulane to act promptly once he had made up his mind, and this instance was no exception. On March 27, 1881, he summoned George O. Vanderbilt, his attorney, to his residence and asked him to go to Washington. There he was to get in touch with Tulane's friend, Senator Theodore F. Randolph of New Jersey. Together the two men were to call on Representative Randall Lee Gibson of New Orleans and invite him to come to Princeton for a conference. Always a secretive man, Tulane did not fully reveal even to his attorney exactly what he had in mind. He apparently only gave him a hint.

Vanderbilt and Senator Randolph dutifully called on Mr. Gibson at his office and extended the invitation, but at first the congressman was hesitant. What did Paul Tulane want? Abashedly, the two callers had to admit they did not know precisely, but it had something to do with Mr. Tulane's desire to upgrade education in New Orleans. This clue, however, was enough to interest any congressman on the lookout for the interests of

3

his constituency. "Tell Mr. Tulane," he said in substance, "that I will call on him in a few days just before I sail for my European vacation."

On April 18, 1881, Gibson called on Tulane at his sturdy, roomy stone house at Stockton Place on Constitution Hill just outside Princeton. As the two men sat in the Tulane home and talked, an observer, had he been present, doubtless would have been struck by the contrasts in their looks and personalities. Both men were of medium build, but here all resemblance ended. Gibson, not quite fifty, bore his years lightly. Heavily mustached, with mild eyes and a high brow, he presented an appearance of polite and scholarly gentility. Tulane's clean-shaved and swarthy face with its searching eyes almost always bore an expression of preternatural gravity. Its deep lines drawn downward from a rather low forehead on which rested the velvet skull cap he habitually wore gave him at times an expression of sadness and at other times of acidity. This mien coupled with a natural reticence made him somewhat formidable in his relationships with strangers. Both men were almost stereotypes of their respective milieu. Tulane was the shrewd, austere, calculating tradesman; Gibson the well-educated, urbane gentleman of the planter tradition. The evidence indicates that although both had lived in New Orleans they probably were not well acquainted with each other. Indeed, they may have never met before this April day in 1881. During the period of Tulane's greatest pre-Civil War activity in New Orleans, young Gibson had lived on his father's sugar plantation in Lafourche Parish near Thibodaux, a period in his life interspersed with study at Yale and extensive travel abroad. He had completed his law study at the University of Louisiana, but before he had time to get a practice well established the Civil War came. Immediately he offered his services to the Confederacy, rising eventually to the rank of brigadier general. It was thus not until after 1865 that he may be said to have become a permanent resident of New Orleans, and by that time Tulane was spending less and less time in the city. Tulane had, however, been a friend of Gibson's father-in-law and had known his father. It is a safe bet, therefore, that he knew a great deal about the congressman, for he did not select men for positions of responsibility without most careful investigation.

The exact details of the conference between the two men are not known. However, Mr. Gibson later sketched the essentials. "Upon presenting myself," he wrote, "Mr. Tulane observed that my father had been his esteemed friend in early times in Louisiana, and that my father-in-law, Mr. R. W. Montgomery, had been the best friend he ever had. He invited me into the library and told me he desired to do something for the education of the youth of Louisiana. Taking from his drawer a list of properties in New Orleans, he said, 'I desire to leave this property to you to be devoted to education in Louisiana.' I replied that I could not consent to accept a bequest, as the relations between us did not justify such a trust, and it might be embarrassing, especially as I was in public life. Mr. Tulane observed that he would as willingly give me the property as to will it for that purpose. Thereupon I said that I would accept the trust. The next day I sailed for Europe, and while in Carlsbad, Germany, projected a plan by which the donation was to be put into effect."

The plan which Gibson submitted in a letter to Tulane from Carlsbad was a relatively simple one: Set up a self-perpetuating board of administrators composed of leading citizens and give it the authority to supervise and administer the grant. Stopping off at Princeton on his way home to New Orleans in October, Gibson again talked with Tulane. Although the personnel of the proposed board may have been discussed, it appears that Tulane wished to give the whole matter further consideration before any public announcement of the gift was made and before any persons were asked to serve as administrators.

Thus Gibson came home to New Orleans in the early fall of 1881 with a rather definite idea of what the aged merchant was going to do but with little more knowledge of the man himself than he had had before the two conferences.

The bare facts of Tulane's life and career were not difficult to learn. His ancestors were bourgeois French Huguenots who for generations lived in Touraine. Paul Tulane's father, Louis, was born in 1767 in Rillé, a village some twenty miles northwest of Tours. An ardent Royalist, he fled France during the Revolution and settled in Santo Domingo, where he established a profitable export trade in lumber. In 1791 a violent uprising of the Negroes of Santo Domingo again forced him to flee, and this time he, along with other French families, came to the new country just emerging as the United States of America. Pausing briefly at Philadelphia, Louis Tulane soon moved to Trenton, New Jersey, and then shortly to Princeton, a few miles to the east, where in 1795 he purchased a massive timbered house and a 500-acre rolling estate of orchard and farmland in Cherry Valley, two and a half miles north of Princeton. Here patient, kindly, stolid Maria bore her husband four of their five sons. The first was Louis, Jr., then Victor, then on May 10, 1801, Paul. Two younger brothers, Gershom and Florentine, were born before the mother died in August of 1813.

Life in the Tulane home apparently, from the standpoint of the purely physical, was comfortable. However, it does not appear to have been a very closely knit and happy family. Maria Tulane's death left her husband with five sons, and he displayed no great aptitude for dealing with growing boys. Gershom and Florentine drifted away into obscurity. According to family tradition, the elder Tulane became angered at Louis over his handling of money matters and drove him from home. Louis went to New Orleans and entered business. Later, after Paul settled in New Orleans, Victor joined his two brothers there.

Young Paul seems to have been his father's favorite, possibly because at an early age he showed signs of developing many of the father's traits, especially an aptitude for merchandising and in minor business matters a shrewdness that was impressive. At any rate, after a brief period at a private school in Princeton and a business course at Somerville, five miles away, Paul Tulane entered the mercantile establishment of Thomas White in Princeton. The budding career, however, was interrupted by the visit of a prominent and wealthy cousin from the old Tulane country near Tours. He had come to the United States for his health and proposed to make an extensive tour through the West and to take Paul Tulane, then about eighteen years of age, with him. The trip proved a most important event in the young man's life.

At Nashville the two travelers stopped at the Hermitage, where they were received by Andrew Jackson. So impressed was the young man with "Old Hickory" that he became a lifelong and staunch Jacksonian Democrat. Traveling on, they were likewise received by Henry Clay at his home in Lexington, Kentucky, and then on into the old Northwest. Tulane saw and interviewed pioneers moving into this area. He observed flatboats loaded with grain, whiskey, salt meat, furs, and squealing pigs drifting southward on the yellowish brown current of the Mississippi to New Orleans. He boarded the noisy, vibrating steamboats, so new on western waters, which had brought cargoes of goods up from that city. Everywhere he saw a booming, trade-conscious region linked to the outside world by the city at the mouth of the river. He had once considered settling in the cotton empire of Alabama, but by the time he and his cousin had themselves descended the river to the Crescent City he apparently had made up his mind that this was the place to do business. Even his brother, Louis, who had not been considered much of a businessman by his father, was doing well in the fur business there.

At the end of their travels, late in 1821 or early 1822, he and his cousin returned to Princeton; and in November, 1822, at the age of twenty-one, young Tulane returned to New Orleans where he was to live, off and on, for the next fifty years. With the financial assistance and encouragement of his father the young man promptly went into the wholesale and retail merchandising of clothes, shoes, and hats with his first store at 20 and later at 26 Levee, now North Peters Street. Soon he and his agents were pushing up the river, into the territory he had so recently visited, taking orders; and soon he was standing on the levee watching these goods start their journey up the river. "Paul Tulane and Company" became a well-known firm throughout the Mississippi Valley.

Tulane's career in New Orleans concided with a period of flush times in the city as the steamboat era came into its own. The two-way flow of traffic in raw materials and food from the interior, and of manufactured goods and luxury articles from the East and Europe, enriched many factors and merchants. Ship tonnage and the value of commodities loaded at New Orleans warehouses doubled and trebled in the span of two decades, and although by 1850 the railroads were offering some competition in the Northwest, victory in the struggle for the valley's trade seemed to be securely in New Orleans' grasp. The years from 1825 to 1860 were the most prosperous ones in the city's history, until the boom period of the mid-twentieth century.

Tulane thus had the advantage of adequate financial support from his father, a natural aptitude for business, and a climate of prosperity in which to operate. Rapidly he expanded the scope of his operations, moving from time to time in search of larger and more convenient quarters. Brothers and nephews joined him at various times to work in his store, but this did not always prove a harmonious arrangement, for the kinsmen apparently resented his cold and impersonal, strictly business attitude toward them. Actually he enjoyed greater success in partnership with a man unrelated to him, Isaac Baldwin, a New Orleans tailor who persuaded Tulane to join with him in a scheme for producing ready-made clothing for men. As with his other ventures this one proved successful, so successful that he bought a factory in Plainfield, New Jersey, to manufacture men's clothes, shoes, harnesses, and other leather products. He sent Baldwin north to manage the plant and soon it became a partnership—"Tulane, Baldwin and Company."

In New Orleans the process of moving and opening new stores went on. In 1830 he opened a clothing store at No. 5 Old Levee. In 1834 he had two stores, one at No. 2 Old Levee managed by his brother, Victor, and another at 28 Chartres Street. Two years later he consolidated both stores at the Chartres address, and in 1840 he moved to 16 Chartres. For a brief time he also operated a retail store at 79 Canal Street. By 1859 he had added a store at 38 Magazine Street, and in 1861 he again consolidated his mercantile operations, this time at 74 Gravier Street in the heart of the city's new financial and merchandising area.

Still another venture occupied his energies. In 1859 he began the construction of a "mammoth" five-story office building at 31–33 Camp Street, which he proposed to make his central headquarters. In October 1860, the partially completed structure was severely damaged by a storm. He rebuilt it, however, and from offices in it conducted his increasingly important real estate transactions which were by 1860 becoming almost as extensive as his mercantile activities.

The coming of the war in 1861 caught Tulane in a rather awkward situation, but one which did not seriously affect his fortune. He was in the East on a business trip when Louisiana seceded and war between the sections became a reality. Through the good offices of his friend, Governor Charles Olden of New Jersey, he secured a pass through the federal lines and hurried to New Orleans to look after his interests. He of course suffered heavy losses in income during the war—both from his real estate and from his business, but most of his capital was untouched. For more than two years before 1861 he had been rapidly transferring his liquid assets to the East. Having saved his real estate holdings and safely reinvested his money in securities in the North he rode out the ravaging years of war and emerged with most of his wealth intact. But Tulane's relations with New Orleans were never quite the same after the war. His father had died in 1847, bequeathing to him the farm in Cherry Valley, and now with the bloom gone from New Orleans' prosperous antebellum days he was inclined to spend more and more time at Princeton. He paid winter visits to New Orleans each year until 1873, when he retired to Princeton; not to Cherry Valley, however, for he had sold these ancestral acres and bought Stockton Place, where Gibson visited him in 1881.

Thus it is not difficult to summarize Tulane's career. But what was he like? What sort of man was he? Undoubtedly Gibson asked these questions many times of his friends in New Orleans during the fall and winter of 1881–1882, as the personnel of the new board was being discussed. And a correct estimate probably was as difficult for Gibson as it is for the historian of today, for there was polarity in Tulane's life which makes an accurate appraisal of his true self very difficult. If one had asked a half-dozen contemporary New Orleanians about him, the chances are they would each have given a different characterization and perhaps no one of them would have been entirely correct, and yet all would have contributed something toward a revealing portrait. This polarity, with many intermediate shadings, gave Tulane a dual personality, one for the public and one for his friends. In matters of business and duty he was austere, stern. In personal relationships he was often warm-hearted and affable to the point of fondness for those who came within the circle of his affections.

It is not strange, therefore, to find one man describing him as parsimonious and another as generous. One man felt his harshness in a business deal and another saw the glow of sentiment in his face as he gave money for a secret charity. His friends knew of his deep religious feeling, but others only knew he would not publicly profess his faith and join a church. One would speak of his Spartan simplicity in food and clothes; another that he enjoyed good food and wine and dressed well. And always there was about him the aura of mystery which was bound to surround the dark, brooding, and wealthy bachelor.

This failure of Paul Tulane to get married became more and more of a mystery as he approached middle age, and, as is the case in all such mysteries, numerous theories were whispered around the tea tables; and out of this gossip legends have grown. Some had a simple explanation for his continued bachelorhood: he was too selfish and stingy to support a wife. Others concocted a legend which connected Tulane with the now almost mythical Madame Lalaurie, reputed to have been New Orleans' wickedest woman in the 1840s. According to the story she was so cruel her slaves revolted against her and she had to flee. Paul Tulane, being in love with her, sent her to Paris and then waited for her to return. But she did not come back. She died a madwoman in Paris. Another story not so fanciful connects Tulane with a tragic love affair reminiscent of hearts, flowers, and sisterly devotion. This legend has it that Tulane as a young man of nineteen fell in love with Ruth Olden, Princeton girl and the sister of Tulane's good friend Charles Olden, wartime governor of New Jersey. But, according to the story, Mary Olden, Ruth's sister, was in love with Tulane, and Ruth and Paul agreed they could never get married because it would crush Mary. So Ruth married another man, Mary died, and Tulane was left to carry a torch the rest of his life.

As a matter of fact no one seems to know for sure why Tulane never married. A very intelligent conjecture can be made, however, that among the important reasons, if not the most important one, is the fact that he was too busy. Setting up a home would have forced him to live a life of domesticity, and for this he obviously had little time. He was a restless, dynamic man, always on the go. There were frequent trips to Princeton and Plainfield. For months of each year he traveled over the Mississippi Valley, selling goods and making new business contacts. There were trips to France now and then. Thus the time he spent in New Orleans had to be devoted to his stores. It was much more in keeping with his way of life to take a room at a hotel or maintain a small apartment over one of his stores than to preside over a household.

Tulane was not exactly a recluse, but he seems never to have identified himself with any social group in New Orleans. He was a Frenchman who spoke the language fluently, and it would have been natural to expect that he would identify himself with the Creoles, but he did not. (Tulane, although French, could not be classified as a Creole. A Creole was a Louisiana-born descendant of French and/or Spanish settlers.) Perhaps his failure to associate more with Creoles was due to the fact that he was Huguenot rather than Catholic, but again one suspects he simply did not have time for much social life. He never identified himself with the Americans either. His extrabusiness activities seem to have been civic in nature. He did jury duty, served as a member of the city council, and once ran for the state legislature, but was decisively defeated. He apparently was considered by most people who knew him as an impeccably decorous and conservative businessman whose watchwords were economy, practicality, and shrewd common sense. Yet he somewhat altered this pattern by buying a race horse and racing him. When the news was received that Andrew Jackson was elected President, he further defied decorum by whooping it up with a barbecue for his friends in Jackson Square.

There were those who summed up his paradoxical traits and gave him the label of "individualist." Others classified him as merely eccentric. But the attention he attracted because of his way of life became a matter of pride with him as he grew older. According to his attorney he came to enjoy more and more hearing his friends say, "There's no one like Paul Tulane." He also liked to hear them as they very sincerely characterized him as a man of great integrity, winning confidence, keen at a bargain, shrewd and farseeing.

His minor philanthropies when added up come to quite a sum. Much of it was bestowed upon ministers, churches, and missions often without regard for denomination or sect. In New Orleans he contributed to the building fund of the Napoleon Avenue Presbyterian Church and for the remainder of the minister's life aided him and his family. He donated ground for the old Seaman's Bethel at the foot of Esplanade Avenue and annually gave sums to St. Vincent's Orphanage and to the Little Sisters of the Poor. After he had retired he sent sizable sums each year to his New Orleans agent, P. N. Strong, to be distributed to various charities. Included in his New Orleans charities also were varying amounts to miscellaneous benevolent associations and to yellow fever relief.

Outside of New Orleans he gave to the First Presbyterian Church of Princeton several acres of ground and $27,000 in cash to be used for maintenance and partly as a trust fund. Later he gave $1,000 toward endowment of a Louisiana Chair of Languages at Washington and Lee University. Then, too, there were the needs of his brothers' children for education and, in the case of Victor's widow, for actual support.

In the last years of his retirement at Princeton the mild vagaries which had characterized his earlier life became more pronounced and serious. The people of Princeton knew him hardly at all. His attorney has related how he would have alternate periods of silence and garrulity. During his periods of withdrawal he would read or just sit apparently lost in thought. Then he would suddenly take up a pen and a sheaf of foolscap paper and write thirty-page letters to friends, often taking two or three days to compose a single letter. In his more garrulous moods he would talk to the visitor incessantly for hours about his career and his personal triumphs. But one subject he avoided almost completely. He refused to discuss his business affairs even with his attorneys. He read the financial sections of the newspapers, made his investments in stocks, bonds, and mortgages, and no one knew what or how much he was buying and selling. Apparently he became more suspicious of men and events in general than ever before; but two of his lifelong traits were not dimmed: He never lost the impulse to be charitable nor the ability to recognize a bargain. Secretively he was still giving away small sums of money to what he considered worthy causes. Secretively, too, he had planned his greatest philanthropy.

His first conference with Gibson at Princeton, it will be recalled, was on

April 18, 1881. The Board of Administrators of The Tulane Education Fund held its first official meeting on April 17, 1882. Thus, lacking one day, a year had been spent in conferences and correspondence between New Orleans and Princeton with reference to the personnel of the board and its powers and duties. When the roster was announced it was revealed that there were seventeen members: Randall L. Gibson, Charles E. Fenner, James McConnell, T. G. Richardson, Edward D. White, E. H. Farrar, P. N. Strong, B. M. Palmer, Hugh M. Thompson, Charles A. Whitney, Samuel H. Kennedy, Walter Stauffer, Cartwright Eustis, Henry Ginder, John T. Hardie, R. M. Walmsley, and William O. Rogers.

It was a group heavily weighted with lawyers and businessmen, but two members were clergymen, one was a physician, one a public school administrator, and three were bankers, if one may separate them from the classification of businessmen. The members Tulane himself characterized in his Act of Donation as "wise and good men." Indeed it was a capable, even distinguished, board, not only because of the character and accomplishments of its individual members (Randall Lee Gibson, for example, became United States Senator from Louisiana, Edward Douglass White became Chief Justice of the United States, and Charles E. Fenner was a justice of the Louisiana Supreme Court) but because of the flexibility and good judgment it displayed in the solutions of its problems, not the least of these problems being Paul Tulane himself. The board had hardly been organized when it discovered that it was easier to accept the custody of a large sum of money for educational purposes than it was to determine the wisest and most effective way of using such funds. From the second of May 1882, when Tulane advised the board that he was donating property in New Orleans assessed at $288,700 it was beset by doubts and at times by serious indecision as to what course ought to be pursued; and always there was before it the most nagging question of what would please Paul Tulane.[1] There were, of course, the formalities of organization, of legal donation and acceptance of the gift, of proper expression of gratitude to the donor, and other similar matters, but these were rather quickly disposed of. Tulane himself had requested that General Gibson be made the first president of the board and that Judge Fenner and Mr. McConnell be vice-presidents. An act of incorporation was adopted on May 23, 1882. Tulane's Act of Donation was dated June 10, 1882. Formal acceptance was made by the board on June 12 of that year followed by a dignified expression of thanks to the donor.

These were necessary formalities but they were not, of course, the really

[1] This was the assessed valuation as given in the Act of Donation. Undoubtedly this was far below the market value. The income was about $38,000 per year. This sum capitalized at 7 per cent (a rather low figure for that day) would have made the market value in excess of half a million dollars. The value as given in the Register of Tulane University is $363,000.

important matters for the first board to consider. The all-important and overshadowing question was: What will be done with the money? On this the newspapers editorialized, the administrators debated, and the man in the street speculated.

Actually the board could make one of two choices. It could establish an entirely new educational institution, or it could put the money into a strengthening and rehabilitation of the then-existing University of Louisiana.[2] As a corollary to the first alternative was the question of what type of new institution should be created. Should it be technical, liberal arts, professional, or a combination of all these?

Tulane had written that he had great confidence in the board, but at the same time he set forth, as might be expected, his views on the matter for the administrators' guidance. Briefly summarized, largely in Tulane's own words, these were:

1. The gift was to be used "for the promotion and encouragement of intellectual, moral, and industrial education among the white young persons in the City of New Orleans, State of Louisiana, and for the advancement of learning and letters the arts and sciences therein [sic]. . . . By the term education, I mean to foster such a course of intellectual development as shall be useful and of solid worth, and not be merely ornamental or superficial." He further instructed the board that it "should adopt the course, which as wise and good men, would commend itself to you, as being conducive to immediate practical benefit, rather than of theoretical possible advantage."

2. It was left to the judgment of the board (at least the words said that) whether it should "establish" or "foster" an educational institution.

3. Whatever the decision was, such an institution should be one "of a higher grade of learning" which would give the young people "the benefit of a more advanced degree of educational culture."

4. "Intellectual advancement should be unfettered by sectarianism, but the profound reverence I entertain for the Holy Scriptures leads me to express the hope that the development intended by this gift should never antagonize, but be in harmony with the great fundamental principles of Christian truth, contained in them."

5. "The fact that property donated for educational purposes is at this time liable to taxation in the State of Louisiana, has occasioned me much embarrassment . . . and I earnestly urge that you make immediate efforts to secure the exemption of this property from taxation, and be constant in so doing until your efforts have been successful."

6. Implicit in the Act of Donation was the desire to keep whatever

[2] Not to be confused with Louisiana State University. Louisiana had two state universities at this time; the University of Louisiana in New Orleans and Louisiana State University in Baton Rouge.

institution might be established or fostered out of politics and political control. Later Tulane became much more explicit on this subject.

It is obvious that his educational philosophy indicated in the first point above could be interpreted in more than one way. One could find here a perfectly valid argument in favor of vocational, technical, or professional education. One could find an equally valid argument in favor of the liberal arts, or for a combination of all these. It is small wonder, therefore, in view of this and in view of the fact that several board members themselves believed in a "practical" education that there was a division of opinion on what sort of educational program ought to be emphasized in whatever new institution the board should create, if indeed it was to create an entirely new institution. In its state of disagreement the board did the obvious thing—it appointed a Committee on Education to study the matter.[3]

Meantime, officials of the University of Louisiana let it be known that they were not averse to any sort of reasonable plan which would enable the university to profit from Tulane's gift. As a matter of fact it was generally understood that they were willing to come under full control of the new Tulane board if it took that to relieve the financial distress in which the university found itself. Shortly before the adoption of the Act of Incorporation of the Tulane Educational Fund,[4] Judge John K. Kennard, president of the University of Louisiana board, invited James McConnell, Tulane's attorney in New Orleans as well as board member, who had just returned from a conference with Tulane at Princeton, to a meeting of the entire university board. It is recorded only that McConnell "spoke at length on matters of great importance to the University of Louisiana." Knowing that McConnell favored the use of the Tulane money for strengthening the existing university, it is not difficult to imagine, however, that he impressed upon his listeners the gains that could be realized through a cooperative effort of the two boards. Apparently the university board was not hard to convince, for shortly thereafter Judge Kennard wrote Gibson that much could be gained through a cooperative venture. He offered protection from political interference and stated that if Tulane funds were made available to the University of Louisiana the Tulane administrators could have four positions on the university board.

The matter was being discussed in other quarters, too. The *Picayune* had from the beginning advocated the use of the gift for strengthening the University of Louisiana. Now the *Times* came out in support of its rival's

---

[3] Judge Fenner was chairman of the committee. Its members were Messrs. McConnell, Richardson, White, Farrar, Eustis, Palmer, Thompson, and Rogers.

[4] There are discrepancies in the use of the term. In the charter of Tulane University and in all its official publications today the term "Tulane Educational Fund" is used. Act No. 43 of the General Assembly of Louisiana 1884 creating the Tulane University of Louisiana uses the term "Tulane Education Fund." In early minutes of the Board of Administrators both terms are used.

position. "If necessary to build up this University," it predicted, "no doubt the present Administrators, or a majority of them, would cheerfully resign to allow an equal number of Tulane trustees to be appointed in their places." As a matter of fact, supporters of the plan for aiding the University of Louisiana with Tulane funds were fully aware that such procedure probably would lead eventually to control of the university by the Tulane board, but in view of the precarious financial position of the university and of the fact that upstate political influence was being thrown more and more behind Louisiana State University, the idea of full Tulane board control was not an unwelcome one.

One has but to read the minutes of the Tulane Board of Administrators to realize how serious were the pressures which were upon the members, pressures which produced conflicts in the minds of a group of men trying so hard to determine what the proper course for them really was. They were torn between their desire to do what they themselves felt to be the wise thing and the ever present fear that in so doing they might alienate the affection of the donor and thus endanger further gifts from him. It was with a considerable feeling of tension, therefore, that the board faced the time when its Committee on Education would make its report.

This report was made on the evening of November 22, 1882, with only one member of the board absent. Mr. Whitney had died in October, and his successor had not been named. Actually two reports were made, a majority and a minority opinion. The majority report recommended fostering the University of Louisiana rather than undertaking the task of setting up a new college. As a sort of compromise with those who held different views it was proposed that for purposes of vocational and engineering education a combined manual training–technical school could be established as a branch of the university. "Such a combined institute," it was pointed out, "would be of incalculable benefit to the Southern people, tending to dignify and elevate labor and to equip them for the development of the material interests and resources of their States."

The majority report went on to point out all the advantages which would flow from a cooperative effort with the university. Here was an established, reputable institution with buildings, a student body, and a capable faculty. It had already passed the experimental stage and had survived. To aid it would be to produce immediately beneficial results for youth, results that would gladden Paul Tulane's heart before he died. A combination of resources would do far more for education than could be done for two weak schools separately. And, it was added, adequate safeguards for the Tulane donations could be provided. "If we should conclude to devote our income to the fostering and development of the University," it was stated, "it must be expended by us or under our authority and only for purposes first approved by the Board, and . . . we should have adequate representation in the general administration."

The minority report submitted by Dr. Richardson was much briefer. When reduced to its essentials it made four major points or observations. The minority looked with disfavor on any alliance with a board under political control such as that which existed with the university board. Further, it believed that Paul Tulane himself wanted an independent institution. It pointed out the "pressing demand for an institution which shall afford practical instruction in the application of theoretical studies to the industrial pursuits of life." Finally, it was pointed out that such a course of study was what Paul Tulane really had in mind when he gave the money.

The details of the discussion which went on after these two reports were submitted are not available. The minutes do show that the time allotted to each member had to be extended over and over again by the presiding officer. It is not difficult to imagine, therefore, that the discussion became heated as the evening wore on, for these were men of conscience and conviction, each convinced that he knew the wise and proper way of using the money. In the end when the vote was taken the majority report was adopted by the narrow vote of nine to seven.[5] By such a slim margin Tulane University missed being largely if not wholly a technical school. The board that night had the distinct feeling that it had created a university, and it hoped its action would meet with Paul Tulane's approval.

It seemed unlikely that Paul Tulane ever fully understood that his gift made him the third of a great triumvirate whose wealth came to mean so much to public and higher education in the South. He died before the full import of his philanthropy was evident. But today one can look back and see it all in perspective. In 1867 while the South was entering the dark period of Reconstruction, George Peabody gave liberally of his wealth and as one result of the gift George Peabody College for Teachers emerged out of the old University of Nashville. A few years later "Commodore" Vanderbilt gave a large sum which enabled feeble Central University to be transformed into Vanderbilt University. And now Paul Tulane, a Northerner who had made a successful business career for himself in New Orleans, made it possible for a weak and wobbly University of Lousiana to become the Tulane University of Louisiana.[6]

In retrospect it can now be seen that these three men—Peabody, Vanderbilt, and Tulane—and their pioneering philanthropies not only were of immediate value but immeasurably influenced a climate of opinion which

[5] Voting for approval of the majority report were Messrs. Gibson, Fenner, McConnell, Strong, White, Farrar, Thompson, Kennedy, and Eustis. For the minority report were Messrs. Richardson, Rogers, Palmer, Hardie, Ginder, Walmsley, and Stauffer.

[6] In the opinion of Robert E. Winthrop, president of the Peabody Fund in 1882, the Peabody and Tulane gifts were "correlative parts of one and the same great system and both of them essential to the success of our Republican Institutions." Peabody always hoped, Winthrop wrote, that such a gift as the Tulane one would be made by some public-spirited man who had accumulated his wealth in the South.

grew shortly into a far-reaching movement of Southern "redemption" through philanthropy and education. The "New South" was more than an economic concept as envisioned by Henry W. Grady and the Bourbons. The idea of the New South had aspects of uplift and social reform in it which combined Northern humanitarianism with Southern paternalism and *noblesse oblige*. In the end it influenced almost every phase of Southern life. And, it might be added, the humanitarian aspect had its beginnings earlier than is sometimes thought. The great awakening in Southern education is generally placed in the first two decades of the twentieth century, and this is true of public school education; but it is worth noting that in the last quarter of the nineteenth century seventy-five new institutions of higher learning were chartered in the eleven states which formerly made up the Confederacy. Many of them were privately or church endowed.

For those institutions assisted by Northern philanthropy there was an almost identical pattern. There was first of all the donor whose name often was perpetuated by having an educational institution named for him. Then there were the Southerners who matched Northern millions with the only assets they had—imagination and constructive leadership. These Southern leaders fall into two classifications: the professional educator and the lay board member.

The professional educator has been given at least meager recognition and even today a listing of these resembles the roll call of the faithful in the book of Hebrews. In Alabama there was the venerable old warrior, J. L. M. Curry. North Carolina produced Edwin A. Alderman who was president of three Southern universities in a period of five years—North Carolina, Tulane, and Virginia. In Louisiana there was William Preston Johnston, president of Tulane, and the brothers David F. and Thomas Duckett Boyd, both presidents of the institution which came to be the modern Louisiana State University. To the list one might add Booker T. Washington of Alabama, Charles D. McIver of North Carolina, Rufus C. Burleson of Texas, and scores of others. These men wrought mightily in the early dawn of the Southern educational awakening in the period from 1875 to 1900 before the great foundations were formed or interested themselves in the South's problems.

The forgotten man of the period is the Southern trustee who gave so generously of his time to the administration of the business affairs of these newly created institutions. It would, for example, be impossible to estimate the monetary value of the total man-hours contributed by the members of the board of the Peabody Education Fund. These men and those who served on the boards of many other institutions were ordinarily not educators but business and professional men—lawyers, bankers, merchants, planters. But though largely unknown to the historian they nevertheless were indispensable to the cause of higher education in the South. Such a man was Randall Lee Gibson, in 1882 a member of the Peabody board and president of the Administrators of the Tulane Educational Fund. Such were the fifteen other administrators who walked out to their carriages on the night of November 22, 1882, from the stormy session where the Tulane University of Louisiana was born.

CHAPTER 2

The University of Louisiana

SINCE THE ADMINISTRATORS OF the Tulane Educational Fund had decided to foster the University of Louisiana it seems appropriate to look into its history and to discover what sort of institution it was.

The early history of both elementary and higher education in Louisiana, and in New Orleans in particular, is the record of a series of desultory beginnings and failures. Religious orders, private individuals, and the state at one time or another attempted to provide educational facilities only to meet with partial or, in many instances, complete failure. As far as higher education was concerned the first four decades of the American period (1803–1843) were singularly barren except for a small medical college in New Orleans.

During this period Governor William C. C. Claiborne ardently advocated the creation of an effective school system. In April 1805, the Legislative Council of the Territory of Orleans responded with an act creating a system of public primary and secondary schools to be capped by The College of Orleans. It was, however, an institution on paper only until 1811 when the legislature was persuaded to appropriate $20,000 so that it could open its doors. For fifteen years it eked out a precarious existence until 1826 when all appropriations were withdrawn and the college of Orleans died. It did leave a legacy, however. It left a few notable alumni, among them the historian Charles Gayarré. It had also established the precedent of a state-supported system of education.

But there was another bequest of a negative nature. The failure of the state to support the College of Orleans was due in a large measure to the growing antagonism between Creole New Orleans and the upcountry. This, of course, was not peculiar to Louisiana, for it existed to a degree in almost all the states of the Old South bordering on salt water. There was, for example, Savannah versus the upcountry, and Charleston versus the upcountry, but in Louisiana it was a particularly virulent form of sectionalism, and nothing seemed to provoke a rash of it more than the location of institutions of higher learning. In the case of the College of Orleans, members of the legislature from the upcountry succeeded in establishing

18

two other state schools—one near Alexandria and one at Natchitoches —which competed with the New Orleans institution for appropriations and in the end produced an anemia which made it unable to withstand the Lackanal incident. In 1823 Joseph Lackanal, one of the regicides of the French Revolution, was elected president. Using his alleged deism and radicalism as a pretext, plus the fact that he was an apostate priest, the legislature cut off all appropriations; and, unfortunately, this was not the last example of intrastate sectional feeling. More would show up in the development of the University of Louisiana.

In 1834, a much less ambitious but in the history of Tulane University a much more significant educational venture was launched. In that year seven young physicians in New Orleans resolved to found a medical college. The motivation for such a venture seemed to have been simply the consciousness on the part of these young doctors of the need for more trained physicians in a city where cholera and yellow fever were both endemic and epidemic. New Orleans had earned for itself the unenviable appellation of "the necropolis of the South"; and not only this, but from reliable evidence one gathers that the practice of medicine was so lacking in standards and in the training of many "doctors" as to be almost on the witch doctor level. So these seven young doctors—Thomas Hunt, Charles A. Luzenberg, John H. Harrison, Thomas R. Ingalls, Augustus H. Cenas, J. Monroe Mackie, and Edwin B. Smith—set out to raise standards and to provide facilities whereby competent physicians could be trained.

As one looks back at the efforts of these young doctors who had migrated to New Orleans but recently (Augustus H. Cenas was the sole native in the group) he is almost astounded at what they were able to accomplish with very limited funds. The ingenuity they displayed is remarkable. From the night of January 5, 1835, when the school opened with exercises at the Congregational Church, until the institution was firmly established, theirs is the story of making brick without straw.[1] In the beginning they had no building, little equipment except their personal instruments, no money, and no clinical facilities. Moreover, they encountered stiff opposition from many local "doctors" with little or no professional training.

Step by faltering step they overcame the odds against them. Through the efforts of State Senator Albert Hôa, the Medical College of Louisiana was incorporated by an act of the legislature on April 2, 1835. But even before the institution was fairly launched Thomas Hunt, the first dean, encountered the first of a series of faculty turnovers for reasons of health, pressure

---

[1] This was the church of the controversial Dr. Theodore Clapp. Although his church was officially named First Congregational it was commonly referred to as Unitarian. In 1853 it was called the First Unitarian Church and in 1870 was legally incorporated under that name.

of practice, or internal dissension. Edwin B. Smith resigned before the college opened and was replaced by Edward H. Barton, a courageous experimental scientist and compiler of statistics on health, climate, and disease. Shortly thereafter Harrison resigned for reasons of health and was replaced by Warren Stone, a native of Vermont and the first doctor in New Orleans to use ether as an anesthetic. Soon Stone and Luzenberg, the Austrian, were quarreling violently over professional ethics and over faculty decisions concerning their duties. In the middle of the 1836–1837 session Stone resigned in great bitterness. But Dean Hunt did not have to handle this quarrel, for he himself had resigned late in 1835. In his place a system of rotating deanships was established.

In spite of faculty dissension, however, the college pushed ahead. New appointments strengthened the faculty. Above all there seemed to pervade in these early years an indomitable will to succeed, come what would. The faculty had no buildings, no equipment nor library, and little income. But these deficiencies they themselves supplied. In 1836 the faculty offered its services to the state without compensation in the Charity Hospital and in addition agreed to educate one indigent boy from each parish in return for a building, equipment, and a library. When the legislature took no immediate action the faculty decided to provide its own building. In March of 1843 it leased from the state a plot of land on Common Street between Baronne and Philippa (now University Place), payment for the lease being made in professional services to the patients of Charity Hospital. The faculty then borrowed money and constructed a building, the first building in Tulane's history. In this same year the donation of Dr. Isadore Labatut's library of several hundred volumes greatly augmented the college's facilities, but for scientific journals the faculty members again had to dig into their own pockets.

Of major importance, of course, was the fact that the college was training doctors. Eleven candidates were awarded degrees at the first commencement, held on April 5, 1836. By 1848 the number of graduates had more than doubled. Moreover the college was beginning to take on the attributes of a regional, even national or international, medical training center. By the late 1830s a majority of the students were from states other than Louisiana, with now and then a foreign student enrolled.

Clinical facilities at Charity Hospital offered excellent opportunities for the student, but instruction when measured in terms of practices today was sketchy and students rarely handled patients or completed case histories and clinical reports. They learned by following the doctor on ward rounds and taking notes on his discussion of cases. The basic pattern for medical education was a blending of the old apprenticeship system with the emerging idea of college training. Thus in order to graduate, a student was required to spend one year of study under a practicing physician and two

sessions at the medical school. Otherwise requirements were not very rigid. Almost any young man of good moral character who could read and write and who had the $150 annual tuition fee could matriculate.

The need for trained pharmacists led to the opening in 1838 of a school of pharmacy. A diploma or certificate was to be awarded to those attending a full course of lectures in chemistry, materia medica, and pharmacy, and who also worked four years in a dispensing pharmacy, or who completed two courses of lectures plus two years of practical experience. The school opened in the basement of the Methodist Church at the corner of Carondelet and Poydras Streets just seventeen years after the first school of its kind was established in the United States and fourteen years before the formation of the American Pharmaceutical Association. The institution did not flourish, but its existence added to the concept of a regional medical center at New Orleans, a center which the first issue of the *New Orleans Medical Journal* envisioned as serving the Mississippi Valley, the Southwest, and Latin America.

Actually the Medical College of Louisiana was the matrix of the University of Louisiana. Its persistent though precarious urge to live helped to keep alive in the minds of many leaders the ideal of Governor Claiborne for a state-supported system of education capped by a college or university in New Orleans. The meeting of a new state constitutional convention in 1844 gave friends of higher education in New Orleans their chance to implement their thinking. Four remarkable citizens of New Orleans— George Eustis, Chief Justice of Louisiana; Christian Roselius, foremost scholar of civil and Germanic law; Pierre Soulé, a fiery political leader; and Judah P. Benjamin, later known as the brains of the Confederacy—prepared and presented to the convention a plan for the establishment of a Univeristy of Louisiana in New Orleans. Such an institution would consist of four faculties—medicine, law, letters, and natural science. The medical faculty, it was pointed out, was already in existence.

The presentation of such a plan fanned into flame once again the antagonism of the upcountry toward New Orleans, and a bitter controversy ensued.[2] The fight centered around a none too subtle resolution introduced by the country delegates to the effect that the constitution should carry an article prohibiting future legislatures from appropriating funds for a university. On this Eustis, Roselius, Soulé, and Benjamin concentrated all the power of their formidable influence, and for days the convention resounded to the clash of verbal weapons. In the end the four New Orleanians won, but it was only a partial victory. On May 14, 1845, the convention adopted the new constitution with an enabling article which authorized the

---

[2] This convention provided for the removal of the capitol of the state from New Orleans after 1848. Numerous towns and cities put in bids, but Baton Rouge was finally selected.

legislature to make provision for a University of Louisiana, but at the same time explicitly relieving future legislatures from the obligation to support such an institution financially.

For months the first legislature following the constitutional convention took no action. Finally in February 1846, a bill prepared by Speaker of the House Preston W. Farrar and Dean Thomas Hunt, now back in the medical school, was introduced. It finally passed, and on February 16, 1847, Governor Isaac Johnson signed it. The legislature had carried out the first part of the constitutional mandate: It had established the University of Louisiana. Then it faithfully carried out the second part of the mandate: It and subsequent legislatures felt no obligation to support the institution financially. Sporadic appropriations were made, but the university never knew from year to year what it could depend upon, especially in the matter of money for faculty salaries. Actually the convention in 1845 had no intention of creating a strong institution in New Orleans, for at the same time that authorization was given for the New Orleans institution, establishment of the Louisiana State Seminary of Learning and Military Academy in Rapides Parish near Alexandria was authorized with the provision that it was to be the official state university.[3] It was generally recognized that the seminary would be favored by the country legislators in the matter of appropriations.

Legislative appropriations were not entirely withheld from the University of Louisiana, however. In 1847 the university was granted the use of half of State Square facing Common Street, and an appropriation of $25,000 was made to enable the University Medical School to construct another building. In 1850 another appropriation of $25,000 was made so that the medical school could buy equipment. In all a total of $117,000 was received from the state between 1847 and 1861, an average of approximately $8,300 per year, the greater portion of which went to the medical school. Some idea of the financial difficulties under which the university operated may be gained from the fact that in 1850 after an appeal had been made to the citizens of New Orleans for donations its total cash assets amounted to only $1,602.

By virtue of its achievements and the independent course which the faculty truculently insisted upon following, the medical school became almost autonomous. Legislation chartering the university had provided for a Board of Administrators, but when it attempted to exercise authority over the medical school it ran into a veritable forest of snags. There was, for example, an instance of the Medical School refusing to turn over to the board the university seal. They had paid for it, the faculty members main-

---

[3] Due to the tardiness of legislative appropriations and the time needed for the construction of buildings, the seminary did not open until 1860. This was the parent institution of Louisiana State University.

tained, and they didn't propose to surrender it. In the face of this intransigence the board had no course except to buy a new seal. But the board put the medical faculty in its place by resolving that no diploma would be legal without the new seal. In the case of the $25,000 appropriation for equipment, referred to above, the board was startled and annoyed to find that the medical school had got hold of the money and had a representative in Europe purchasing the equipment before the board had even had a look at the appropriation, much less a chance to authorize the purchases. Although there eventually came to be a President of the University he did not bring about centralization. Each faculty scrounged for what it could get in the way of money and equipment, and the medical school did the best job of foraging.

It was also doing an excellent job of building itself into a first-rate medical school. The period between 1847 and 1860 was the most productive one in its history prior to its becoming a part of Tulane University. It improved the curriculum, increased co-ordination of lectures, made notable advances in clinical teaching, and even took under consideration the feasibility of requiring a program of premedical training for prospective students. Research became an important part of its functions. Professor John L. Riddell, who headed the School of Pharmacy, among other duties, brought international fame to the university in 1852 with the invention of a practical binocular microscope. In 1853 Edward H. Barton became chairman of perhaps the first sanitary commission in the country to investigate the origin of epidemic diseases. A monthly medical publication was established, the size of the library was greatly increased, and enrollment grew steadily. By 1858 there were 258 students largely from the surrounding states, but with a liberal sprinkling of foreign students.

The law school was the second to develop of the quadripartite plan of medicine, law, letters, and natural sciences. As with the medical school its beginnings were humble. It had no building, no library, no equipment; but like the medical school it had a picturesque faculty of individualists who quarreled and made up, who resigned and were reinstated. Perhaps it was just as well that faculties of the departments did not meet as a faculty of the whole. The fireworks would indeed have been magnificent when Professor Riddell, the stormy petrel of the medical school, tangled with fiery Randell Hunt of the law school over finances or entrance requirements, or ethics, or a dozen other subjects over which these early faculty members wrangled.

At the first meeting of the Board of Administrators of the newly created University of Louisiana in 1847 a committee was appointed to consider the organization of a law faculty. Within two weeks it was ready with its report. Four professors from the rather brilliant array of talent which composed the New Orleans bar were recommended and approved; and a more interesting faculty would be difficult to imagine. Henry Adams Bullard was an associate justice of the Louisiana Supreme Court, a native of Massachusetts, a Harvard alumnus, and a man of the most catholic interests ranging from ancient history to African colonization. Federal Judge Theodore H. McCaleb was a South Carolinian who had studied law at Yale and in the office of Rufus Choate in Salem, Massachusetts, and who counted among his friends Thackeray, Chateaubriand, and de Tocqueville. Richard Henry Wilde was a native of Dublin, Ireland. A morose and brooding poet, he was cut down by yellow fever before he could occupy his professional chair. Randell Hunt, another South Carolinian, was the fourth member of the faculty. An aggressive extrovert, he forcefully preached a bright future for the university.

On the evening of December 6, 1847, Judge Bullard, the first dean, formally opened the law department in the federal courtroom of the Customs House. His address stressed the significance of the event, particularly the fact that the University of Louisiana was the first institution in the Southwest to teach civil law; and indeed this was significant, as the years were to prove. Prior to 1803 Louisiana (which at that time was largely New Orleans) had a legal system based on French and Spanish law which in turn was based on Roman law. After the purchase of Louisiana, English common law was introduced into the territory, but it did not meet with the approval of the Creoles. By congressional enactment in 1805 the civil law was approved in so far as it did not conflict with the Constitution or statutes of the United States. As a result a dual system of civil and common law developed, a fact which is reflected in the partially dual curriculum of the Tulane School of Law today.

On the evening following the opening exercises Professors McCaleb and Hunt gave the first lectures, and the law department was launched. The curriculum consisted of civil law, commercial law, criminal law, law of evidence, public and international law, common law, admiralty and maritime jurisprudence, and constitutional law. When the process of shaking down was over a faculty rather remarkable for its stability of tenure and its qualities of legal scholarship emerged. After an initial turnover of seven professors the faculty of 1850 consisted of McCaleb in the chair of admiralty and international law: Randell Hunt as professor of commercial and criminal law: Alfred Hennen, a noted legal scholar in New Orleans who occupied the chair of common and constitutional law; and Christian Roselius, who had labored so earnestly to bring the university into being, who taught civil law.

Despite a rather comprehensive curriculum and a faculty of competent, even brilliant, men the law school did not flourish; and again the old, familiar lament must be recorded—no money, no building, no library, and consequently precious few students. Enrollment varied from twenty-three students in 1847–1848 to a high of fifty-one in 1860–1861. Entrance requirements were substantially those of the medical school; any literate young man who could pay the tuition of $100 per year could be admitted. Perhaps the fact that students did not enroll in the Law School in as great numbers as in the medical may be due in part to the fact that New Orleans at this time was short on doctors and long on lawyers. The law school also lacked the foreign students who swelled class rolls at the medical school. At any rate the law school did not quickly become a regional center of education as did the medical school.

At the time the law school was being organized, the Board of Administrators were looking about for a President of the University. It was obvious that a man possessing all the necessary qualifications would be hard to find. Men of broad achievement and administrative ability were not particularly scarce, but when the third qualification of an independent income was added, the field was narrowed considerably. Such a man, however, the board found right at home in the person of the Reverend Dr. Francis Lister Hawks, Rector of Christ Episcopal Church in New Orleans. On paper he was an ideal man for the position. He was a native of New Bern, North Carolina, and a graduate of the University of North Carolina and of Yale. After practicing law for a decade he entered the Episcopal ministry, serving in New Haven and at St. Stephen's and St. Thomas's in New York. For a brief period he taught at Washington (later Trinity) College in Hartford and for a slightly longer period he unsuccessfully ran an academy at Flushing, New York. In 1843 he moved from New York to Mississippi, where he was offered a bishopric. A quarrel with the national convention caused him to reject the offer, however, and instead he came to the rectorship of Christ Church. On July 21, 1847, he was named president of the University of Louisiana.

Perhaps the choice of Dr. Hawks was not the most fortunate one the board could have made, yet it is difficult to see how any man could have done a really first-rate job under the circumstances. A penurious and adamant legislature refused essential financial assistance in a manner which today suggests a conspiracy to weaken the New Orleans institution. Now and then it grudgingly made small appropriations for buildings and equipment, but it withheld any money for operating expenses or salaries.[4] At the same time the citizens of New Orleans did little better. Despite several appeals during the first three years of operation only three gifts of any significance were made by New Orleanians. In 1848 Judah Touro gave $500 to encourage the study of Hebrew and eventually to help endow a

---

[4] Many of the true friends of higher education felt that the legislative proscription against state appropriations for faculty salaries was a wise one. If the state should pay salaries, it was feared, it might also control the thinking and teaching of the professors.

chair of ancient history; Glendy Burke gave a similar amount for the encouragement of elocution; and Maunsel White donated several city lots which because of defective titles were lost to the university. These gifts, however, came after Dr. Hawks had tired of asking for bread and receiving a stone. On March 28, 1848, he submitted his resignation. The board persuaded him to remain temporarily, but after a year he returned to New York without the formality of another resignation.[5]

One of the most disappointing aspects of his efforts was his inability to organize the academic department. This department, it will be recalled, was to consist of a faculty of letters and a faculty of natural sciences. But putting down such and idea on paper and the implementation of it were two different matters entirely. In 1848 President Hawks set aside $1,000 to buy equipment for the academic department, but the failure of the legislature to make an appropriation nullified his effort, much to his chagrin. The matter was not dropped here, but before an academic department finally became a reality a preparatory school was established. This, it was hoped, would serve as a feeder for the academic department. On November 23, 1847, the board authorized President Hawks to organize the preparatory department without delay. This he did promptly, for it opened for students on December 1 in the East Wing with 40 pupils enrolled and a faculty of a principal and five teachers.[6]

Meantime efforts to activate the academic department were being continued, but it was a tortuous and often frustrating process. Early in 1848 a plan to purchase the equipment of the defunct Jefferson College in St. James Parish had to be abandoned. In that same year Maunsel White proposed to activate the collegiate department by endowing a chair of commerce and statistics with his gift of city lots, but the lots proved almost worthless. Then J. D. B. DeBow, peripatetic editor of the *Review,* came into the picture. He had for more than a year been preaching a crusade for a commercial department in the university. Now under White's gift he was named the first professor of political economy. He outlined a curriculum for a department of commerce, appealed to the merchants of the city for funds, and delivered some lectures.[7] But even so gifted a man as he was unable to stimulate enough interest to get the academic department into

---

[5] President Hawks was succeeded by Theodore Howard McCaleb who served 1850–1862. Other presidents were: Thomas Hunt, 1865–1867; Randell Hunt, 1867–1883. The university was closed from 1862–1865.

[6] At this time the physical plant of the university consisted of three buildings— a Grecian-type "Central Building" housing the medical department, and matching East and West wings. These were built on Common Street between Dryades (now University Place) and Baronne Streets. In 1880 the University Board bought the Mechanics Institute Building on Dryades Street. The center of this building was approximately where the University Place entrance to the Roosevelt Hotel is now.

[7] One may see in DeBow's efforts the first faint beginnings of a school of commerce and business administration.

operation. He carried on lectures almost without an audience until early in 1850 when he was forced to admit that the problem was beyond him.

Meanwhile in late December 1849, George Anthon, principal of the preparatory department, reported to the board that there were graduates of his department ready for college; and once again, as it had so many times in the past, the board resolved that a collegiate department should be inaugurated. Now, however, definite steps were taken to accomplish it. Public schools in the state had an enrollment of 23,000 pupils in 1849–1850, and it was felt that many of these would enter college. Too, New Orleans had recovered from the depression and hard times of 1837–1842 and was again prosperous. The times, the board felt, were propitious. By the fall of 1850, a faculty of seven men had been appointed with Claudius Wistar Sears, now elevated from the preparatory department to professor of mathematics and natural philosophy in the collegiate department, in an executive position comparable to a deanship.[8] Announcements were published, giving the curricula, entrance requirements, tuition fees, and the advantages of going to college in New Orleans.[9] Everything was in readiness that fall, and at last it seemed the long anticipated academic department would become a reality. When the time came to register students, however, optimism melted away. Not enough students were present to warrant opening the college. In the fall of 1851 the college's offerings met with a slightly better reception, however, and it opened with a student body of twelve freshmen and two sophomores. For two years it limped along, and then in the summer of 1853 it received an almost fatal blow in the form of a disastrous yellow fever epidemic which struck the city. Between June and October of that year thousands of persons died, and although the college survived, it clung to life by a thin thread. The Board of Administrators, tiring of their role of the mythological Sisyphus condemned forever to rolling a huge boulder to the top of a hill only to have it roll down again, virtually ceased to function. Only because of the tireless efforts of Dean Sears did any semblance of an academic department remain alive.

The board was reorganized by governor Paul D. Hebert in the spring of 1855 and again in 1856. A third reorganization in 1860 brought to the presidency of the board Theodore G. Hunt, brother of Thomas Hunt, dean

[8] The other members of what may be considered the first faculty of today's College of Arts and Sciences were: John Lawrence Smith, chemistry and mineralogy; Richard H. Chilton, geology; Marc Roux, French language and literature; Herman Kohlmeyer, Hebrew and Oriental languages; William M. Duncan, classical languages and literature; and J. D. B. DeBow, head of the commerce department.

[9] A civil engineering course was advertised which required that the student complete the classical curriculum except for Latin and Greek and then "strength of building material, masonry, stone cutting, limes, cements, mortars, foundation and concrete work, framing, bridges, roads, railways, canals, aqueducts, viaducts, rivers, sea coast improvements, architecture, topographical engineering, topographical and linear drawing." This ambitious curriculum never went into effect.

of the medical school, and of Randell Hunt, dean of the law school. The university was thus dominated by three men, none of whose interests were acutely concerned with the academic department. Every year seemed to be the last for it despite frantic appeals to Southern fathers and mothers that they send their sons to an institution uncorrupted by abolitionist propaganda. "The academic department or college proper can hardly be said to exist at present," the board recorded in its minutes of 1856. "The dean . . . and the several professors support themselves by the pupils of the grammar school attached."

In its extremity the board listened with favor to a proposition submitted by the ubiquitous Professor Riddell and Louis Dufau, president of the struggling Louisiana College at Convent. The plan contemplated the establishment of a combined preparatory-collegiate department operated by Dufau and Riddell for private profit, control, however, to be in the hands of the board. The collegiate department actually operated under this plan for a period of three years, but general discontent and friction spoiled whatever chances the scheme might have had of succeeding.[10] The one bright spot in the entire history of the academic department came on July 25, 1857, when a class actually graduated. Joseph Arsenne Breaux, who became one of the distinguished judges of Louisiana and who later bequeathed a large scholarship fund for students of Tulane University, received the university's first Bachelor of Arts degree. To the other two members of the class, Charles Gaudin and William Valloft, went the degree of Bachelor of Science.

When the lowering clouds of sectional strife burst into the devastating storm of the Civil War the University of Louisiana, thus, was the shadow of a university but hardly the substance. The medical school was soundly established and was attracting widespread attention to itself. The law school, in spite of a comprehensive curriculum and a faculty of brilliant teachers, showed little tendency toward growth into a really significant regional center for the study of law. The academic department was precariously suspended between life and death, with death the final victor. Parsimonious legislatures and lethargic citizens of New Orleans had failed to kill the university, but the war now administered the *coup de grâce*.

For almost four years the buildings were silent and deserted. A few students conferred now and then with some of the older faculty members left behind, but the windows looking out on Common Street were brown with rainstreaked dust, and the empty classrooms and halls amplified the sound of scampering rats in the attic. Alumni, students, and faculty members were fighting and dying on a hundred battlefields scattered over the

[10] Dissatisfaction over the fact that Riddell and Dufau had rented university classrooms "to ice cream vendors and clubs" appears to have been the culminating item in a series of discordant episodes which led the board to terminate the arrangement.

vast stretches of the South between the Red River and a creek called Bull Run. Soon the casualty lists began to come in, and the wells of learning all over the South became brackish with the salt of human tears. This was the inevitable price of war. New Orleans itself saw little of actual fighting, however, for in April 1862 the forts below the city surrendered to a federal naval force and on May 1 of that year General Benjamin F. Butler and his army entered the city and inaugurated a six-month period of occupation which was so obnoxious to the local citizenry that reverberations of it still have not ceased among older people of the city. Butler was relieved by General Nathaniel P. Banks in December 1862, and the tensions and resentments eased, but nothing could relieve the horror of the casualty lists of Louisiana troops as they fell at Antietem, Gettysburg, Chickamauga, Atlanta, and finally at Franklin and Nashville where John Bell Hood's Army of Tennessee was destroyed and the Confederacy was primed for the knockout blow which Grant delivered at Petersburg at Easter time, 1865. Now there was a great calm, and the casualty lists ceased, and there was peace. Now the Southern colleges and universities could reopen, among them the University of Louisiana.

The history of this institution from 1865 to 1884 is a strange mixture of success and failure, of gaining ground only to lose it again, of heartbreak and half-fulfilled dreams. Strangely enough, the University of Louisiana fared better under the Reconstruction regime that it had under the antebellum government of native Southern whites. In the new constitution of 1864 the institution's maintenance and support were written into the organic law of the state. Article 143 of this constitution stipulated that "a university shall be established in the City of New Orleans. . . . *The Legislature shall provide by law for its organization and maintenance.*" This was in contrast to the original act establishing the university in which it was made optional whether the legislature should provide funds or not. Moreover, the principle of legislative responsibility established in the Constitution of 1864 was reaffirmed by the Radicals in the Constitution of 1868, the document which inaugurated the carpetbagger regime. In addition, the Constitution of 1868 gave the university a source of revenue in permitting it to share in poll tax revenue.

Thus, under what appeared to be a rather firm legislative and financial foundation, the university reopened its doors. On November 14, 1865, the medical department resumed instruction in the Central Building. A week later, on November 20, the law department began its first postwar session and shortly thereafter acquired a home in the West Wing.[11] The academic department did not reopen. Upon the three major administrative officers

[11] The first organization of the medical faculty in 1834 was called "The Medical College of Louisiana." With the organization of the University of Louisiana in 1847 it became "The Medical Department" of the university. Similarly at this time the law school was officially "The Law Department."

—President Thomas Hunt, Dean Tobias Richardson of the medical department, and Dean Christian Roselius of the law department—fell the initial impact of the task of reconstructing the university. But reconstruction was not a matter to be achieved in a few months or even a few years. Consequently, there were major changes in administrative and faculty personnel before the process even approached completion. President Thomas Hunt died in 1867 and was succeeded by his brother, Professor Randell Hunt of the law department. Roselius was succeeded by Carleton Hunt as dean of the law department in 1872. But though personnel might change, the problems did not, while old prewar faces were showing up on the faculties, old prewar vexations and afflictions returned to sit in the classrooms with them and plague them like extremely unpleasant ghosts which would not be exorcised. Equipment, salaries, the repair of buildings, student enrollment, the rebuilding of faculties—these were the devils with which faculty and administration had to wrestle; and it was often not clear who would win.

The financial structure for which foundations had been laid in 1864 and 1868 appeared by 1875 to be a delusion. Authorization for the university to participate in poll tax revenues was one thing. Getting the money was entirely another. Warrants on the state treasurer were issued. After state officials, public schools, and other favored groups had received cash for theirs, the university was free to present its warrants, and they would be paid *if there were still funds in the Treasury*. Under the carpetbag regime the Treasury was often empty, however, or if not empty it lacked sufficient funds to pay the face value of the warrants. The result was that the administrators had to accept whatever might be available at the Treasury or dispose of the warrants to speculators at heavy discounts. Under such a system it was impossible to construct any sort of realistic budget. Actually little or no revenue was received from this poll tax percentage plan. In 1879 the new state constitution authorized a flat appropriation of $10,000 a year, but since the basis of this was also state warrants the situation was little better than it had been before the enactment. The board was thus forced to fall back upon calling for donations, upon student fees, and upon borrowing from year to year. Since the citizens of New Orleans showed no inclination to give money, and student fees were sadly inadequate, deficit financing became the rule. It was 1883 before the university received $10,000 in cash for $10,000 in warrants. The only bright spot in postwar finances was the fact that modest sums were made available for renovation of the buildings. The total amount allocated for this purpose between 1866 and 1880 was $34,425.[12]

---

[12] Not included in this amount is $18,500 paid for the Mechanics Institute Building, the university's fourth building, in 1880. In this purchase the board paid $3,500 cash and gave a five-year mortgage for the balance. Paul Tulane paid off this balance plus accrued interest.

To many faculty members, however, financial exigencies were not new. They had walked away from their unstable lecterns and donned gray uniforms. Now they returned, dislodged the Freedmens' Bureau Negro school from the West Wing and the New Orleans Academy of Science from the East Wing, and once again stood behind unstable lecterns. In the medical department, tall, scholarly Dean Thomas Hunt, who had served during the war as a Confederate army surgeon, resumed his post as professor of physiology and pathology. The first dean of the medical department at 26, he now at 57 was ill and prematurely old. Soon death removed him. John Leonard Riddell, the faculty gadfly and long-time professor of chemistry, served during the war as postmaster of New Orleans where, with his habit of independent thinking and his penchant for ferocious disputation, he spent a great deal of his time feuding with loyal Confederates in the city who were incensed at his alleged unionist sympathies.[13] The war over, he died near the end of 1865, leaving to posterity a twenty-eight-volume disputatious diary. From the standpoint of the future growth of the revived medical department it would be difficult to determine who was the more important of two returning faculty members, Tobias Gibson Richardson or Stanford Emerson Chaillé. Richardson, professor of anatomy and surgery, had been chief surgeon of the Army of Tennessee and upon the death of Dean Hunt in 1867 was elevated to the deanship, a position he was to hold for two decades. It was he who supervised the transition of the medical department of the University of Louisiana to the medical department of the Tulane University of Louisiana. A kindly, infinitely patient, dignified man with deep-set eyes and a beard of patriarchal proportions, he developed the medical department to a point where it achieved national recognition. Chaillé, an alumnus of the class of 1853, was appointed to the minor position of demonstrator in anatomy in 1858. In 1860 he went to Paris to study under the eminent physiologist Claude Bernard. At the outbreak of the Civil War he returned to New Orleans before enlisting in the Confederate Army where he rapidly rose in rank to medical inspector on the staff of General Braxton Bragg, commander of the Army of Tennessee. After another period of postwar study in Europe during 1866 he became professor of physiology and pathological anatomy. But it was not in this capacity that this volatile, hard-driving little man who seemed to be everywhere at once made his reputation, but rather in the field of preventive medicine and public health. In 1885 he succeeded Richardson as dean, thus becoming the first medical dean of the newly named Tulane University.

Familiar faces also were again in evidence in the law department, even though their numbers were few. With the exception of Sidney L. Johnson, who died in a federal prison in Elmira, New York, and Judge McCaleb,

---

[13] He was appointed in 1860 by President James Buchanan. Although two other appointments were made by Confederate authorities, neither of the appointees was able to dislodge him.

who died peacefully in bed, the prewar faculty members resumed their posts. The deanship went to Christian Roselius, the erstwhile penniless German immigrant boy who rose to be attorney-general of Louisiana. Now as a man of 62 he was a ripe scholar in the field of civil law, even though he still had trouble with his *v*'s and *w*'s. Persuasive, eloquent Randell Hunt began to teach again, and in 1867 succeeded to the presidency of the university. Present again for duty was the aging Alfred Hennen. There were new faces, too. In 1865 Alfred Phillips accepted the chair of admiralty and international law, and in 1879 Thomas A. Clarke succeeded Alfred Hennen, who died that year at the age of 83. In 1872 Carleton Hunt, son of Dean Thomas Hunt, took over the deanship, thus continuing the tradition of the Hunts in Tulane's history.

But it was in the department of medicine that changes were so significant. This significance is due to the fact that many of the new faculty members were not merely replacements but new men to occupy new chairs in a rapidly expanding School of Medicine. It is impossible to comment on all the changes, but a few must be mentioned in order to show the growth of this department. In October 1865, John W. Mallet, formerly a professor at the Mobile Medical College, was appointed professor of chemistry in place of the deceased Riddell. Mallet had been one of the foremost military chemists of the Confederacy, organizing a system of fertilizer and gunpowder plants. Between 1863 and 1865 his wooden tank wagons had become common sights as they moved over the South collecting urine for his chemical processes. In January 1867, Dr. Bolling A. Pope was appointed chief of the clinic and lecturer on diseases of the eye and ear. In June 1868, clinical instruction was systematized by the appointment of four faculty members as clinical professors whose duty it was to supervise rotating squads of students in the Charity Hospital. In May 1875, the department of anatomy was strengthened by the addition of two demonstrators of anatomy—Edmond Souchon, who became famed for his prosections, and Albert B. Miles, who became an outstanding surgeon. In 1877 John B. Elliott, Sr., late of the University of the South, became professor of materia medica and therapeutics. Around him Chaillé built a series of courses in public health and hygiene in which he himself was so interested. Meantime Chaillé's lean figure and drooping mustache became familiar sights on lecture platforms all over the country as he advocated the teaching of hygiene in the public schools. If he was not the father of health education in the United States, he narrowly missed the honor of this paternity. Train children, he urged, and later generations of women would "eschew those corn manufactories, high heeled shoes, those lungcrampers, tight corsets, and those skin befoulers, poisonous lotions, powders, and paints."

Graduation exercises in the spring of 1870 were symbolic of the trend of the university. In that year the first joint ceremony of the law and medical departments was held with President Randell Hunt conferring degrees on seventy-four medical seniors, seven law seniors, and one pharmacy graduate. It was symbolic for at least two reasons. The complete absence of any graduates in liberal arts meant that the institution was not a real university but a fragment. The great preponderance of medical seniors revealed that the prewar drift toward an institution dominated by the medical school was being accentuated in the postwar period. It was not that the law school was doing a poor job. On the contrary, with its permanent quarters in the West Wing, its newly acquired library donated by the state, and a faculty of brilliant teachers it undoubtedly was doing the best work in its history up to this time. The complete absence of a liberal arts department and the inability of the law school to flourish suggest that there may have been something in the times which made such a situation almost inescapable.

Beginning as early as the 1870s a body of thought was congealing in the minds of leaders both north and south to the effect that what the South needed in the way of education was a system which would contribute first to her physical rehabilitation. The South was plagued by malaria, typhoid, yellow fever, and hookworm. Therefore doctors were needed. The collapse of the old plantation system had left in its wake the necessity for combating erosion, for more scientific farming methods, and for finding a solution to a one-crop system. Therefore, schools of agriculture were needed. The South needed buildings and railroads and factories. Engineers, skilled workers, and technicians must be supplied. In none of these endeavors could many Southern leaders see any urgent need for lawyers or for liberally educated young men who could read Greek and Latin poetry in the original.[14] In a more leisurely Old South the sons of planters could go to college and argue endlessly on constitutional points or read poetry on wide, pillared verandas. But this was not the old South. It had been riven by war, and now men must look about them not only for ways and means of building a new social system but to a new economic order as well. The South's body must be fed and healed, leaders reasoned, before anyone could treat the pathology of her spirit. Give the Southern people healthy bodies, rebuild their cities, factories, and railroads, teach them new ways to make the soil yield abundant crops—this was the credo, at least on the surface. Economic exploitation, of course, was at times a concomitant phase.

It is not surprising, therefore, that New Orleans should have had an agricultural and mechanical college before the University of Louisiana could revive its academic department. In spite of the fact that Louisiana still had a carpetbag government in 1874 the legislature, under the land grant provisions of the Morrill Act of 1862, founded a Louisiana Agricul-

[14] Compare with the views of Paul Tulane and many members of the first Tulane board as explained in Chapters 1 and 3.

tural and Mechanical College in New Orleans and instructed the administrators of the university to provide rooms for it in the East Wing.[15] At the same time an appropriation was made to purchase a demonstration farm at Chalmette in St. Bernard Parish below the city. But the institution had a short life in New Orleans. To the medical professors occupying the East Wing the new college was an unwelcome intruder. In 1876 a plan was developed to move part of the school to the Chalmette farm, but at the same time to maintain in the East Wing the mechanics portion. But the medical department was still unfriendly and unhappy. In 1877 the whole matter was resolved by moving the school to Baton Rouge and consolidating it with Louisiana State University. Thus, the upriver institution received its full name, "The Louisiana State University and Agricultural and Mechanical College."

Apparently there was no widespread alarm in New Orleans over the fact that the A.&M. college was moved, but even as plans were maturing for the transfer, a much more important consolidation movement was being generated—a plan to move the entire University of Louisiana to Baton Rouge and there to unite it with Louisiana State University. It was a project dear to the heart of David F. Boyd, president of the latter institution. In 1876 he had made friendly overtures to the trustees and the faculty of the University of Louisiana, suggesting that a union of the two institutions would be mutually advantageous. The next year a legislative resolution authorized the appointment of a committee "to examine the charters of the University of Louisiana and the Louisiana State University, with a view to effect a union between the two." Pursuing his objective with increasing zeal, President Boyd in his annual report in the spring of 1878 dealt extensively with the proposal, presenting logical and cogent reasons in support of unification. The Board of Trustees of the University of Louisiana, tired from its unrewarding labors and despairing of the future, acquiesced in Boyd's dream and actually sponsored a resolution favoring partial amalgamation, the issue to be voted upon by the people as a constitutional amendment.

Before the proposal was submitted to the people, however, a roar of protest went up in New Orleans. The citizens had never given appreciable financial support to the university, but now, when it appeared that it might be shifted to Baton Rouge, a mighty howl of indignation resounded from the newspapers, from articulate civic groups, and even from individual

---

[15] During the period 1872–1890 agricultural and mechanical colleges for Negroes were established in all but one of the former Confederate states. The major A.&M. colleges established for whites were: Georgia Institute of Technology, 1885; Mississippi State, 1878; North Carolina State, 1891; Clemson, 1889; Texas A.&M., 1876; Virginia Polytechnic, 1872. Alabama Polytechnic Institute (Auburn) was established in 1859, but it was not functioning effectively until the period of the 1870s.

citizens who had hitherto displayed no interest in education. The idea that New Orleans youth might have to go to Baton Rouge for an education was too big a pill to swallow. So great was the pressure that the Board of Trustees was forced to reconsider its position. In doing so its course of action was to establish an academic department, so that at least there existed on paper a full-fledged university, and then go to the people and ask them to defeat the unification amendment.

President Boyd tore his hair in anger and exasperation at what he considered the board's duplicity. Between May 1878 and the November election both sides appealed to the electorate in speeches, broadsides, and newspaper articles. Perhaps no educational issue in the history of the state, up to that time, had engendered more heat. When the votes were counted, however, the unification proposal was defeated and Dr. Boyd was left bitterly resentful.

Thus it was out of such turmoil that the academic department of the University of Louisiana was reborn. In the fall of 1878, following closely upon one of the city's worst yellow fever epidemics, the department began to function with a faculty of three men, one in Latin, Greek, and English, and to serve as dean; a second to teach mathematics and natural sciences; and a third for the chair of French language and literature. To fill these positions the board appointed able men. Richard Henry Jesse, an alumnus of the University of Virginia and an excellent combination of scholar-administrator became dean and professor of Greek, Latin, and English. James Lucius Cross filled the chair in mathematics and natural science, and M. P. Julian, that of French language and literature. A part-time instructor, R. B. Montgomery, taught "penmanship and commercial course."

In spite of financial hardships the academic department made rather good progress, considering the difficulties and delay encountered in its renaissance. In November 1879, a year after the reopening, two new faculty members were added. Edward Coles Harding was appointed professor of English literature and Greek, and John Hanno Deiler, a rotund German immigrant who had formerly taught at the University of Munich, became professor of German. In 1880, Alcée Fortier, foremost exponent of Creole culture and one of the university's most productive scholars, was transferred from the preparatory department to succeed Julian as professor of French. In that same year Brown Ayres, a twenty-four-year-old engineer-physicist, was named to the chair of physics and natural philosophy. And to round out the faculty Robert Sharp, the only Ph.D. on the faculty, was appointed professor of English and Greek to succeed Harding.

It was a time in the history of higher education generally when the personality of the teacher was as important, or even more important, than libraries and laboratories. Courses, and thus professors, were likely to be more catholic in their interests and more broadly oriented than modern specialized courses and professors. One hears less and less today (perhaps unfortunately) among college alumni about the colorful antics of the professors under whom they studied. But in 1880 in the University of Louisiana there was no dearth of scholarly eccentricity and color. The tales are legion about Professor Fortier, for example, who strode up and down in front of his classes, his whiskers quivering as he berated in a harsh and strident voice the dullards who could not master a perfect French pronunciation. Likewise, students remembered the fragile, scholarly Dr. Sharp, who could recite a whole Shakespearean play and make the reading a profound emotional experience for himself and his class. The youthful Ayres they remembered because of his almost uncanny ability to improvise gadgets for his physics laboratory. Dean Jesse they feared and respected. He was harsh, exacting, and at times disagreeable, but no one ever questioned his fairness or his ability to teach Latin and Greek. His administrative ability was such that in 1891 he was called to the presidency of the University of Missouri.

Broad scholarship, emphasis on teaching, and color had to a great extent to compensate for the lack of an adequate library and even for a wel-rounded curriculum, for both of these left much to be desired. In 1882 the Fisk Library, an endowed semipublic library, was placed at the disposal of the university, but funds for adequate additions were lacking, and many of the books were unsuited to university purposes. Between 1882 and 1884, for example, only $1,000 was expended for books. The curriculum at the opening of the academic department in 1878 was extremely flexible. In fact, there were no degree requirements. Students took the courses that parents and faculty members agreed they should take. This plan was abandoned after two years, however, and four-year curricula leading to bachelors' degrees in arts and sciences were established. Concurrent with the new curricula was a plan of admission of students by examination in fundamental subjects.

The university was a mosaic of bright and lusterless titles. Small gifts stood out here and there to add a bit of color. Through careful management the principal of the Touro and Burke gifts had almost doubled in size. In 1881 Charles T. Howard gave $1,000 for the physics and chemistry department. In 1882 Louis Bush gave $324 to endow a French medal. In that same year Philip Sims gave what was probably the first unrestricted endowment gift in the history of the university, 2,437 acres of land. But as had proved the case with the earlier Maunsel White gift, title was found to be defective and thus the value was nullified.

Among the discouragingly somber spots were student enrollment and the lack of income from student fees. In no year was enrollment in excess of ninety students in the college. At the maximum tuition rate of $50 per year, income from this source was pitifully inadequate. Even from this small income must be subtracted the amounts represented by scholarships; and the university was adopting a scholarship policy which carried on in Tulane through the years. In January 1879, the board formed a standing committee on scholarships to interview ministers' sons who were qualified but financially unable to attend college. Scholarships were also offered to the sons of faculty members. Then in 1881 five city scholarships to be filled by nomination of the mayor were created in return for the city's waiver of back taxes of the Mechanics Institute building purchased that year. In 1883 this was expanded to ten scholarships. And one must add to the dull tiles what apparently was a matter of great concern to the academic faculty. Discipline among the pupils in the preparatory department was extremely loose. These adolescents wrestled in the halls, poured out on Common Street shouting and shoving, and wandered to Canal Street where, merchants complained, they interrupted business. No formal recreational program or organized sports existed for either preparatory or college students. Thus it is small wonder that in the lusty, brawling New Orleans of the 1880s students should be a disciplinary problem.

As the historian looks back on the record of the old university he is made conscious of the fact that it was a microcosm, an epitome of the South. Discerning minds even in the 1880s knew that the period of the Civil War and Reconstruction had wrought profound changes of an almost revolutionary nature in Southern life. In the spring of 1884 the University of Louisiana graduated its last class. In that year both the university and the larger world of the South stood astride a great divide. Behind them were the turbulent years after 1860. Ahead was the future veiled in a fog of obscurity. Like the South, the university was poor, and until its poverty was alleviated it suffered the diseases associated not only with physical infirmities but with cultural malnutrition. Fortunately, however, these infirmities were not malignant. They could be cured by transfusions. In Princeton an old man had supplied the first whole blood for the university. It was symbolic of what was to take place in the life of the whole South as Northern capitalists and philanthropists poured new wealth into the veins of an emaciated region. What emerged was not simply a rejuvenated Old Order but a New South with a new personality.

CHAPTER 3

The Tulane University of Louisiana

THIS, THEN, WAS THE University of Louisiana which by a vote of nine to seven the administrators of the Tulane Educational Fund had decided to foster and develop. The decision, it was clearly stated in the resolution which the board adopted, was subject to the approval of Paul Tulane; and when the decision was presented to him he disapproved of it. He virtually vetoed the plan by voicing in a rather positive manner his objections to the use of his money to foster the academic department of the university. He also expressed a preference for an entirely new institution which would basically be technological in nature.[1] As evidence of his interest in such an institution he offered the board a check for $125,000 to secure a site and construct a building. In view of this the administrators had little choice except to reverse themselves and begin to lay plans for a new school; that is, they had little choice if they expected the old gentleman at Princeton to continue his gifts. (Gibson was at this time talking to the administrators in terms of $3 million he thought Tulane would finally give.) Consequently on the ninth of January, 1883, the administrators voted to establish "The Tulane University of New Orleans" and a few days later chose William Preston Johnston, then president of the Louisiana State University, as the new president of the nonexistent university. Not only was it nonexistent, but even its essential nature was still to be determined. Yet this fact obviously was in no way a deterrent to Colonel Johnston's acceptance. He was unhappy at Louisiana State University, and the political trend indicated his days as president probably were numbered. Apparently, he did not debate with himself at any great length as to whether or not he ought to accept the invitation to the new job extended on behalf of the administrators by his friend, kinsman, and former college mate, Randall Lee Gibson. He was elected by the board on January 16, 1883, and three weeks later he assumed his duties.

In many ways he was a fortunate choice for a university in Louisiana. The Johnston name was not a strange one in the state. Two of his uncles

[1] One of the most exasperating phases of the board's relations with Paul Tulane was that he never would say precisely what sort of institution he favored.

and three of his half-uncles had migrated from Kentucky to Rapides Parish in the early 1800s. Here they and their sons were fruitful and populated the countryside. Another tie was the fact that shortly after his graduation from Yale in 1852 he had married Rosa Duncan, daughter of Judge and Mrs. John Nicholson Duncan of New Orleans. Also there was around him the roseate aura of the Confederacy and of his father, General Albert Sidney Johnston, who had died at Shiloh. He himself had served in the Civil War, first as an infantry officer and then as a colonel on the staff of President Jefferson Davis. He had been at Davis's side when the President was captured at the close of the war and, along with General Joseph Wheeler and Colonel F. R. Lubbock, had been confined for a period of some three months in solitary at Fort Delaware. Moreover, he was a scholar and an urbane gentleman. In November 1866, he was appointed professor of history and English literature at Washington College, where for approximately thirteen years he served under the presidency of Robert E. Lee and his successor, Custis Lee. During this time he was also working on the biography of his father, a well-written but highly controversial book. As a professor at Lexington he was noted for his urbanity, poise, and his gentility—graces which he would sorely need at Baton Rouge and New Orleans.

As time went on it became clear that his ideas about education stemmed from several sources which may be reduced to two basic ones—"Christian" and "Southern." He was a devoutly religious man; and intimately related to this was a marked poetic quality in his thought and action. Associated with this poetic and religious nature were certain qualities which have in the post-Civil War South been lumped together under the term "Southern chivalry." In this pattern he was idealistic, romantic, and to some degree mystic. He was, in addition, moralistic and somewhat Puritanical in his general outlook. He was a Kentuckian of good birth (born January 5, 1831, in Louisville), a son of a religious and romantic soldier, and had all the sentimental appeal of a man who had fought bravely for a great cause and lost.

The influences inherent in his environment and background might have served seriously to limit him. It is a measure of his stature, however, that though these qualities were basic in his makeup, they did not seriously limit him as they unfortunately did so many others of his kind who were forced to make the transition from the Old to the New South. "My heart was buried with the Confederacy," he once wrote. "On it will be found engraved at the day of doom, 'C.S.A.'" But this was the poet speaking of a thing of sentiment. Instead of becoming the professional "Southern gentleman" who looked back with nostalgia to the good old days, he spent little time weeping for lost causes. Thus he never permitted the tragedies of the South to serve as a substitute for thought and action. There was in him a streak of hard practical sense, and he saw clearly two things—that much work had to be done to rebuild the South, and that educational institutions would have much to do with the rebuilding. He also possessed a remarkable sense of public responsibility, even of private institutions, and exhibited impatience with the "ivory tower" concept of education. Time after time he spoke out boldly for "the dignity of labor."

As president of Louisiana State University in 1879, President David F. Boyd was at war with factions of his faculty, with the state legislature, with the governor, and with the state superintendent of education. Perhaps the bitter fight generated over his efforts to unite the two universities was at least partly at the root of the difficulties. Be that as it may, the facts are that Dr. Boyd's enemies gained control of the Board of Supervisors of the university and in September 1880, under the guise of "reorganization," he was dismissed. The position was offered first to Colonel Samuel H. Lockett, who declined it, whereupon the invitation went to Professor Johnston at Washington and Lee. He accepted and on October 4, 1880, was officially elected.

If the new president thought he could unite the warring factions at Louisiana State University he was never more wrong. Bitterness had burned itself deeply into the souls of many faculty members. Politicians fished in the troubled waters. Ex-President Boyd kept the fight alive through an appeal to the courts and to the alumni. Virtually every known device was used by Boyd's partisans to embarrass and discredit the new President. He stood it for two and a half years until the welcome invitation came from the administrators of the Tulane Educational Fund.[2]

When he reported in New Orleans for duty early in 1883 the administrators were deeply involved in the matter of what sort of institution they could and should build. At his first meeting with the board in February 1883, he was asked to give it the benefit of his opinion. This he did; and his views are almost strangely prophetic of the type of institution Tulane University eventually came to be. It was his dream, he said, "to erect a great Southern university, the rival and peer of older institutions in the

---

[2] In the latter years of his life, Thomas Duckett Boyd, brother of David F. Boyd, is quoted as relating to the late Marcus M. Wilkerson of Louisiana State University that the reason Tulane University was founded was to make a job for Colonel Johnston. Wilkerson uncritically reported this as a fact in his *Thomas Duckett Boyd* (Louisiana State University Press, 1935), p. 75. Mr. Wilkerson's statement is as follows: "Johnston resigned in 1883 to become President of the Tulane University of Louisiana which had been organized to give him the position of president. It came about this way. Senator Randall Lee Gibson and Colonel Johnston were intimate friends, the two having served together in the War between the States, the former under the latter's father. When Senator Gibson saw that Colonel Johnston could no longer remain at the head of the University because of political difficulties, he visited the wealthy Paul Tulane, a retired merchant of New Orleans, then living in New Jersey, and persuaded this philanthropist to endow in the city of New Orleans a college to be named for himself."

Just how far astray Mr. Wilkerson was led by Dr. Boyd's faulty memory is obvious.

North and East." To accomplish this, he continued, a threefold program was essential:

1. Teaching youth and teaching them well, as he expressed it, "the higher education of our youth would be carried out by a harmonious development in each province of the realm of human knowledge."

2. A community-oriented program of adult education—"the instruction of the masses by lectures, public libraries, museums, and other modes of reaching them."

3. The development of human knowledge through research—"the increase of knowledge and its application by original, scientific investigation and research, and by furnishing the means for this in laboratories and otherwise."

Such a program, he felt, could not be fully realized immediately for "we must cut our coat according to our cloth," but it should be attacked boldly. "Boldness is the better part of prudence," he thought.

On the matter of a separate institution versus absorption of the University of Louisiana he had very decided views. The board should, he felt, take over the existing university. It had buildings, a student body, a faculty, and a history. To build a new institution which would have to acquire all these, he thought, would be unwise. Political control could be eliminated, he stated, and tax exemption secured. At the same time the University of Louisiana would not lose its identity completely. "The University of Louisiana would be absorbed as the waters of the Ohio might mingle, but are not lost, in the great Father of Waters."

A few weeks later he made his first visit to Paul Tulane at Princeton. Here they talked of the two proposals for the new school and exchanged views on their respective educational philosophies. The two men were not far apart in their views on the need for technological education in the South, but their basic rationale was poles apart. To Tulane a technical education was for immediate, practical purposes—get a technical education and then become productive as quickly as possible. To Johnston the matter went deeper than that. A technical education was but one phase of educating the whole man, inseparable from the development of his other parts. In later years he reduced his thoughts to words. The first questions he had to seek an answer to, he wrote, were: What is higher education? What are the best agencies and methods a university can employ for advancing it in Louisiana?

To these he had an answer and in his answer is found at least a part of the guiding philosophy of the institution he helped create.

The question was, "education of what?" Of man. And what is man? Body, mind, soul; but not body *and* mind *and* soul, as is so often erroneously stated. The whole man is one, and these pervading substances are not parts of him, but constitute his organism. He is not, as the Buddhist says, a vase containing an ethereal perfume, or more transcendentally stated, including a part of the space which we call the soul. This is a false analogy; for vase, perfume and space are one, integral, individual, personal—man. We cannot separate spirit and matter in our thinking of man. . . . Our object is not mechanically to make a mere cog for the great wheel of society, but to round out a human being to the possibilities of his nature . . . a rounded academic education [is] one that both informs and trains.

Paul Tulane was firm in some things—that a new institution should be built, for example—but he was absolutely adamant on one principle, the *sine qua non* of tax exemption. Obviously there was only one way in which this could be determined and that was through a court decision. With Tulane insistently urging it on, the administrators filed a test suit on March 18, 1883, in the Civil District Court of New Orleans. On April 10 this court held that the proposed new institution would be tax-exempt. The state appealed, however, and on May 7, the State Supreme Court reversed the lower court, holding that a tax-exempt status could not be accorded the proposed new school.

Thus Paul Tulane was faced with the prospect of seeing the administrators of his gift pay taxes on the institution it would create and on its investments. Rather than submit to this, Tulane was willing to take over the University of Louisiana, academic department and all. That is, he was willing with certain reservations. Apparently he was not discouraged over the outlook, however, for he continued his gifts. In January 1883, the check for $125,000 came through. In December of that same year he turned over to the administrators $269,000 in stocks and bonds.[3]

Tulane's chief fear in absorbing the University of Louisiana was that the new institution would be subject to political control. That plus his reluctance to sponsor education of an "impractical" nature appear to have been his major reservations. The latter, of course, could be overcome by introducing into the curriculum subjects of a "practical" nature, and this was done. Removal of political control, on the other hand, took some doing.

Apparently it was clear to the lawyer members of the Board of Administrators that legislation was necessary to accomplish the desired ends, and thus a bill was introduced in the Louisiana Senate seeking a contract between the administrators and the state. The bill easily passed both houses and on June 5, 1884, was signed by Governor S. O. McEnery. The

---

[3] In addition to the original gift of real estate, Tulane's gifts were as follows: January 1883, $125,000 in cash; December 1883, $269,000 in stocks and bonds; February 1884, $19,026 in cash; July 1884, $7,000 in cash; December 1884, $50,000 in cash; December 1885, $40,000 in cash; in June 1887, $50,000 in cash. To this, of course, must be added the $20,000 which he gave the Mechanics Institute building for the University of Louisiana. Depending on how one values the original gift of real estate, the total of his donations would be from $1,049,000 to approximately $1,150,000.

board of the old university had long since expressed its approval of the merger. Now the legislature removed the last barrier, and included tax exemption.

Act No. 43 of the General Assembly, Session of 1884, is an interesting document well worth reading in its entirety (see Appendix II). Here couched in legal language is the culmination of forty years of effort on the part of a relatively few men of vision who in spite of almost overwhelming odds against them persevered in their efforts to build and maintain a university. It is a montage of young Dr. Thomas Hunt opening the medical college; of Randall Hunt and Christian Roselius; of Dr. Tobias Richardson; of Dean Jesse and Judge Kennard; of Randall Lee Gibson and Judge Fenner; and over it all is the image of the dour old merchant of Princeton. If the university and the South stood astride a great divide in the 1880s and looked ahead into the impenetrable future, some of the fog clouds for the university at least were dispelled by Act No. 43. The administrators, the new president, the faculty, and the citizens of New Orleans rejoiced that new foundations had been laid. Somewhat flamboyantly a New Orleans newspaper predicted:

We have but to open the door of opportunity to our aspiring youth and show profitable returns for applied thought or creative genius to induce the bright, quick-minded sons and daughters of this section to ascend with royal tread the proud eminence of success, coping even with the proud savants of France, the philosophers of thoughtful Germany, and measuring mechanical and commercial skill with proud England.

President Johnston was less florid but equally optimistic. In his mind the new university would

. . . cover the whole wide area of human knowledge, rising through regular gradations, higher and higher, to the utmost attainments of the human mind. . . . It will have the ability, and therefore will have the right, and should feel the duty of assuming the *leadership in public education in the State*.[4]

Certain significant portions of the act will convey the essence of its full meaning and importance. The major provisions were:

1. That the Board of Administrators of the University of Louisiana should be wholly replaced by the Administrators of the Tulane Educational Fund and that they should have power to fill all vacancies which might exist. The only qualifying reservation was that the governor of the state, the state superintendent of education, and the mayor of New Orleans should become ex-officio members of the new board.

2. The new board of administrators was given complete title to and

---

[4] Italics mine. It is significant, however, that President Johnston had the concept of a privately endowed university assuming the role of leadership in *public* education in Louisiana.

control of "all the property belonging to the State of Louisiana, and now dedicated to or used by the University of Louisiana. . . ." This included equipment, books, papers, and archives. The qualifying reservation in this case was that the property could never be sold without legislative sanction.

3. The name of the university was officially changed from "The University of Louisiana" to "The Tulane University of Louisiana" in honor of Paul Tulane and in recognition of his beneficent gifts. . . ."

4. The Tulane board was to have "irrevocably upon the adoption of . . . [a] constitutional amendment" complete control of the new university.

5. The new institution was given a tax-exempt status as long as its funds were used for the purpose specified in the act.

6. The board waived all legal claim upon the state of Louisiana for any appropriation from the state Treasury.

7. The Tulane board agreed "to give continuously, in the academic department, free tuition to one student from each Senatorial and from each Representative district or parish to be nominated by its members in the General Assembly. . . . The free tuition herein provided for shall continue until each student has graduated from the academic department, unless his scholarship has ceased from other causes."

8. It was provided that the entire matter be submitted to the people as a Constitutional amendment.

Following passage of this act by the General Assembly, events moved rather rapidly. To the Administrators of the Tulane Educational Fund the old board immediately turned over buildings and equipment valued at $157,728; $14,575 in cash; and $5,000 in state warrants. With what one may well imagine was a sigh of relief, Judge Kennard handed over the official seal, and the transfer was made.

Two other legal matters yet remained, however. Act 43 had to be voted upon by the people of the state, and the tax-exempt provision had to be passed upon by the courts. In December, 1885, the administrators instituted another test suit on tax exemption, and this time the State Supreme Court held for the administrators. Two years later this decision was cemented in the organic law of the state by a vote of the people.

To William Preston Johnston the new university had personal significance. Not only did its development present a challenge of the highest order, but for the first time in his life he had a position with a salary ($5,000) which would enable him at last to live comfortably. The years at Washington and Lee had been barren so far as money was concerned. Often, literally, the Johnston family had not known from where the next week's food would come. At Louisiana State University he had done better for himself financially, but even here he only drew $2,500 annually. Now, at age 52, he could look forward to a tenure unthreatened by political factions or abject poverty. To a man of his sensitivity and insight, however, the thing uppermost in his mind was the challenge of the job he had accepted. He undoubtedly was aware that a powerful personality in the presidency of an institution can mold it to the pattern of his mind or to the pattern of his prejudices. He apparently knew that the dominant idea, the guiding thought, the essential meaning of a college or university is not infrequently interwoven so closely with the mind and spirt of the president that the man and the institution are almost inseparable. The evidence indicates that it was more good than bad that such was the case with Colonel Johnston and the formative years of the newly created Tulane University.

To the Board of Administrators the creation of the new university was the culmination of three years of work and worry. Theirs had not been an easy job. Negotiations with Paul Tulane had at times been difficult. They were not professional educators and at times the problem of what sort of institution they should create made them sleep restlessly and miss meals. They had spent hundreds of hours meeting and discussing every detail of the new organization. Now from their labor had emerged what showed every promise of being a first-rate institution. It had the largest income of any educational institution in the state, and Paul Tulane obviously had led them to believe his gifts would grow larger as time went on. With a competent president in charge, the administrators felt they could ease out from under some of the burdensome administrative minutiae they had carried so long. This to a large extent they did, but with an occasional exception. The membership of the board was composed almost entirely of New Orleanians living in the shadow of the university. They were aware of the day-by-day happenings on the campus, and it was natural that now and then they would irritatingly interest themselves in small matters which might best have been left to the judgment of the president. On the whole, however, the relationship was worked out by trial and error with President Johnston standing up rather well with the passage of time. It was a relationship based on common consent rather than on any body of written agreements. The president became the chief executive officer of the university, acting for it in its relations with faculty and students, often the public, and in all academic matters. On the other hand the board held a tight rein on fiscal and other major policy matters. There were, and still are no sharp lines of demarcation marking the point where the board's powers and functions end and those of the president begin. Actually, of course, the president's powers were and are only those delegated by the administrators, but the precedent of allowing President Johnston rather wide discretion within broad policy areas has been fairly consistently followed since that time. Certainly the office of president of Tulane University carried with it much more power and authority than had the same office in the University of Louisiana. President Johnston made an effort toward more coordination of semi-autonomous departments, an effort, it might be added, which was a most difficult one and one which was not successfully carried out until much later.

Over and above all this, however, Act No. 43 had a much greater significance. It meant the establishment, in the heart of a good trading and merchandising center serving the enormous Mississippi Valley, of a privately endowed university uncontrolled by any political or religious interests, and thus a free university—free to set its own standards for admission and achievement, free to determine its own programs and policies, free to do unrestricted research in whatever fields it might choose, free to make the classroom a forum rather than a place for indoctrination. There was no other similar university within five hundred miles in any direction from New Orleans, a fact which meant that Tulane University had within itself the potential of a great regional institution. That it did not, except for medicine, realize that potential for many years is part of the story to come in later chapters. The South in 1884 was on the threshold of an era of growth undreamed of in the days of the sugar and cotton kingdoms. Except for the city of New Orleans itself, however, Tulane can claim little credit for giving substantial direction to much of this trend, because for many years after it was founded its outlook was parochial. Actually it was not until the 1930s, wishful thinking to the contrary notwithstanding, that Tulane University actually became a truly regional institution—and again one must except the School of Medicine, which was regional almost from the start.

It would have been difficult, or even impossible, for any one present at the opening exercises of the new university on October 4, 1884, to have conceptualized the physical growth in the years ahead, for there were registered on this date 73 students in "Tulane College";[5] 136 in the high school department; 223 in the medical department; and 17 in the law department.

[5] The academic department was renamed Tulane College.

CHAPTER 4

The Formative Years (1883-1888)

WILLIAM PRESTON JOHNSTON WAS president of The Tulane University of Louisiana for approximately sixteen years (1883–1899), if the period before the university actually opened in 1884 is counted. If one looks for a single theme which ran through and characterized these years it undoubtedly would be expressed in the word "expansion." During his term of office Tulane University grew rapidly, at times too rapidly to suit the conservative nature of Paul Tulane, for he saw the income from his gifts being spent almost to the last penny every year and that did not please him, for he wanted a large reserve fund set aside against the barren years which he felt would inevitably come. Nevertheless, the president and the administrators carried out their plans for a first-rate university, and that took increasing amounts of money. Between 1884 and 1900 the faculty more than doubled in size, and likewise the budget. The student body increased by about the same proportions, the curricula were multiplied and diversified; and, above all, there was a complete change in the physical plant. The old buildings on Common Street were abandoned and a new campus was established. During this same period the H. Sophie Newcomb Memorial College was founded.

It is too much to expect that all this could be carried out in an atmosphere of complete harmony, calm, and singleness of mind. It was, therefore, a trying and difficult period for everyone—faculty, president, and administrators. Periods of very rapid growth and change in a university are likely to be vexing, for there arise so many problems of a nonacademic nature that the mind of the academic man is often troubled and distracted. It is not surprising, therefore, that President Johnston encountered now and then uneasiness and unrest among his faculty. Too, fluctuating property values made budget-making a frustrating experience at times. The critical attitude of many citizens of New Orleans toward the new university often taxed the patience of president and administrators alike. Jealousy and hostility between upstate and downstate were revived over attempts made by the Tulane administrators to get financial aid from the state treasury. Efforts were made by upstate politicians to wipe out the university's tax-exempt status. Poor public relations resulted in a rather general public misunderstanding of the role of the university. Even the great gift of Mrs. Josephine Louise Newcomb for the foundation of a women's college almost turned to ashes in the mouths of the president and the administrators because of unforeseen fears generated in the mind of the donor. Student enrollment was often below expectations. And added to all this were the deaths of two of the founding fathers. Paul Tulane died in March 1887; and Randall Lee Gibson, in December 1892. In each death, something of great value financially and spiritually went out of the university. Paul Tulane left no will, and thus the university received no further gifts from him or his estate. Randall Lee Gibson had furnished enlightened leadership on the Board of Administrators from the time the university was but an idea in the mind of Paul Tulane.

These formative years of expansion, therefore, were not placid years. Growth there was, but painful growth. Even the life of the president was sorely troubled by personal problems. Year by year he suffered more and more from the chronic bronchitis which had plagued him since his early army days. At times he barely was able to speak above a whisper, and his summers were spent commuting between seashore and mountains seeking a cure, or at least surcease. In October, 1885, almost exactly a year after the university opened, his wife died, and a few weeks later his twenty-four-year-old son, Albert Sidney III, passed away.[1]

None of these things, however, prevented the president and the administrators from attacking their problems boldly, Seen from their point of view, the most pressing and immediate of these problems were faculty and budget—especially faculty and budget for Tulane College. It was, and always had been regardless of its name, the least secure and stable of the three major departments of the university; and yet it was clear that if Johnston's vision of developing the whole man was to be realized, this college had to be strengthened and expanded. It is not strange, therefore, that the liberal arts and sciences should receive a major portion of attention.

The 1884–1885 school year saw few changes in personnel, structure, or educational theory. President Johnston and the administrators simply took the old university as it was set up, with the program which had already been announced for the year, and operated it without much tinkering. By the next year, however, changes were becoming obvious on all sides. In line with Johnston's theories the institution was organized on a unified plan which, except for nomenclature, was not radically different from the plan of the university today. Beginning with the high school, which would not be

---

[1] On April 25, 1888, President Johnston remarried. His second wife was Margaret Henshaw Avery, a young woman prominent in civic affairs in the state. They lived at what is now 2423 Prytania.

a part of the modern university, there was progression through the Bachelor of Arts degree program to the "university" department, a rather unusual name for the graduate school. Here degrees were awarded at the master's and doctorate level.[2] The professional schools of law and medicine were not considered part of the university department but were placed on the same level as Tulane College. The high school was divided into three classes called preparatory, intermediate, and sub-freshman. Every student in the preparatory class took a standard prescribed course of English, mathematics, geography, natural science, physiology and hygiene, drawing, penmanship, gymnastics, and manual training. Above that, in the college, students were permitted to elect a course, but the requirements in the course were fixed. Curricula were classical, literary, natural science, mathematical, commercial, and mechanical, all leading to the B.A. degree. The elective system was also abandoned in Tulane College. The old elective system, President Johnston thought, "is as rational as to throw open an apothecary shop to a sick boy. Diagnosis ought to be the first step; and the next, prescription. The doctor should be able to use even a limited pharmacopoeia more intelligently than his patient." Also the classes in Tulane College were now divided into the familiar freshman, sophomore, junior, and senior classifications, and the undergraduate degree program was set at four years.

Other changes in the organization included some shifts of personnel and the alteration and addition of professorships. Randell Hunt, president of the old university, was retired as emeritus rector of the law school. Under a resolution of the administrators the deanship of Tulane College was abolished and its duties were assumed by President Johnston. Dean Jesse was made vice-chairman of the faculty and professor of Latin. Otherwise the very excellent faculty of the University of Louisiana was taken over *in toto*; Richard H. Jesse in Latin, Alcée Fortier in French, Robert Sharp in English and Greek, John R. Ficklen in English, Brown Ayres in physics, J. H. Deiler in German, J. L. Cross in mathematics, and all the others who had made real contributions to the development of the old university now were given an opportunity to enlarge the scope of their influence and scholarly contributions.[3] Ashley David Hurt was brought from the presidency of the Florida Agricultural College to be headmaster of the high school. At the same time John Morse Orway came from the Massachusetts Institute of Technology where he was chairman of

[2] The graduate degrees, however, were hardly research degrees. Rather they consisted largely of a continuation of studies in a given field. Two years were required for the M.A. degree. The Ph.D. degree was conferred "for further and eminent attainments."

[3] Three of these became presidents of important universities: Jesse, of the University of Missouri in 1891; Ayres, of the University of Tennessee in 1904; Sharp, of Tulane University in 1912.

the faculty. His special field was industrial chemistry, but he also had an enormous interest in mechanical and manual training which he had acquired in Sweden. It was largely for the purpose of developing the high school manual training department that he came to Tulane. To complement Ordway's work, William Woodward was appointed professor of drawing. Other instructorships and lectureships brought the faculty of Tulane College to twenty-five for the year 1885–1886. In the Law Department there were still five faculty members. In Medicine, seventeen teachers were able to carry the largest student load in the university.

It is obvious that President Johnston's three-fold program of good undergraduate teaching, adult education, and research was a carefully thought out one. It is also equally obvious that he was very much in earnest about seeing that education should contribute to the development of the whole man. To accomplish this he felt that young men should be acquainted with manual skills—not necessarily for vocational purposes, but because the student ought to realize that civilization had advanced not only through intellectual pursuits but through the use of tools. He would like to see a young man study Greek and pipefitting; literature and carpentry; philosophy and the principles of the electric motor—believing he would be a better citizen for his knowledge of the practical and the classical. Moreover, he strongly felt that the New South not only had need for technological leadership itself but for a frame of mind on the part of its young people generally which would appreciate the dignity of labor and the worth to society of the laborer. If the university could bring all these things into a harmonious whole, he felt, it would "have the lifting power of a hydraulic machine" on the culture and prosperity of the area it served.

It is not remarkable, therefore, to find the university, through its high school, requiring its students to learn to use their hands in the manual training department. The year 1884 was an especially appropriate, perhaps almost symbolic, time to launch an educational project of a technological nature, for in this year New Orleans itself made a dramatic effort to lift herself out of the economic doldrums which had characterized a great deal of her life since 1865. The first step had been the construction of the jetties at the mouth of the river, from 1874 to 1879, in which project Congressman Randall Lee Gibson had been especially useful in Washington. Now, in December 1884, New Orleans opened the great World's Industrial and Cotton Centennial Exposition calculated to impress the world with the fact that the city was on its way back economically. It was the largest exposition the world had ever seen, the exhibit halls covering eighty-one acres, halls which dwarfed the Crystal Palace Exposition in London and the Philadelphia Centennial Exposition. At the city's edge at Audubon Park more than $3 million was spent for buildings in which were displayed the wares of the world. And not the least of the exhibits was the work of the manual training department of Tulane University.

In 1884 the administrators had purchased for the manual training program under Professor Ordway the building known as Turner's Hall at the corner of Lafayette and Dryades Streets. For it they had paid $11,500, and then had spent another $24,000 for repairs and equipment. In this building were conducted the manual training classes not only for the high school boys but for adults as well. As a matter of fact, Turner's Hall became a sort of community center for adult education. During the 1885–1886 session the university had created a mild sensation by announcing free evening instruction in drawing and mechanics for teachers and workers—and women were included, to the consternation of many old-timers in the community. Applicants by the hundreds hastened to apply for courses. So great was the response that many disappointed latecomers had to be turned away. The university was having its first rewarding experience in adapting a part of its program to the immediate needs of the adult population of its local community. And it did not stop with this work in drawing and mechanics. Soon a more comprehensive program of adult education was inaugurated, a program in keeping with the spirit of the extension education movement which by 1885 was being proclaimed nationally as a movement to take education to the people if they could not come to the universities. Even the medical faculty members participated at Tulane. In the winter of 1884–1885 Drs. Chaillé and Elliott lectured every Friday afternoon in the amphitheatre of the Medical Department on physiology, hygiene, and public health to between four and five hundred teachers and other lay people. The following year free Saturday morning classes for teachers were added in shorthand, school methods, and English. In 1886–1887 the program was still further expanded to cover two courses totaling thirty-seven classes in a wide variety of subjects ranging from French literature under Alcée Fortier to electricity and magnetism under the indefatigable Brown Ayres.

Nor was the third phase of Johnston's program being overlooked, for efforts were made to build the university's library and laboratories so that research and investigation could go forward. In his first budget, Johnston included $30,000, nearly 40 per cent of the budget of Tulane College, for laboratories and the library. In 1886 the resources of the library were listed as follows: The State Library of 26,000 volumes in the custody of the Law Department; the Fisk Library of about 8,000 volumes, the endowment of which was sufficient to add about 500 volumes per year; the Tulane Library of some 7,500 volumes, of which the medical section comprised some 3,400 volumes and the scientific some 1,200; some 5,000 volumes donated by the Southern Art Union. The staff of 1884 consisted of William O. Rogers, secretary of the Board of Administrators, as librarian, with two assistants, an arrangement which continued for several years. Laboratories were developed slowly, and the university was free to admit that they were only adequate for teaching purposes, not for research.

Another project dear to the heart of President Johnston was the museum established in July 1885 and housed in Tulane Hall. Through a gift from Paul Tulane the university was able to buy as a nucleus the Ward collection of minerals and paleontological and zoological specimens. In addition, the New Orleans Academy of Science gave its entire collection. To those were added odds and ends left over from the exposition, some of value, some worthless. Soon, however, the museum took on the aspect of a curiosity shop. Donors to museums often have an exaggerated opinion of the value of their relics, but college presidents dare not refuse such gifts for fear they may be entertaining an angel unawares. Thus the university found it desirable to print in its annual catalog a list of donors who gave such things as a butterfly, a scorpion in alcohol, the tooth of a whale, two emu eggs, and a doll from Sweden.

The narrative of the development of the university for men founded by Paul Tulane must be abruptly broken off at this point, for there occurred with dramatic swiftness in 1886 an event which changed its nature and the entire course of its history. The event was heralded by a letter written from New York on October 11, 1886, and addressed to the administrators. The letter read:

Gentlemen:
In pursuance of a long cherished design to establish an appropriate memorial of my beloved daughter, H. Sophie Newcomb, deceased, I have determined, at the instance of my friend, Col. William Preston Johnston, to intrust to your Board the execution of my design.

Feeling a deep personal sympathy with the people of New Orleans and a strong desire to advance the cause of female education in Louisiana, and believing also that I shall find in the board selected by the benevolent Paul Tulane the wisest and safest custodian of the fund I propose to give, I hereby donate to your Board the sum of $100,000, to be used in establishing the H. Sophie Newcomb Memorial College, in the Tulane University of Louisiana, for the higher education of white girls and young women.

I request that you will see that the tendency of the institution shall be in harmony with the fundamental principles of the Christian religion, and to that end you will have a chapel or assembly room in which Christian worship may be observed daily for the benefit of the students. But I desire that worship and instruction shall not be of a sectarian or denominational character. I further request that the education given shall look to the practical side of life as well as to literary excellence. But I do not mean in this my act of donation to impose upon you restrictions which will allow the intervention of any person or persons to control, regulate, or interfere with your disposition of this fund, which is committed fully and solely to your care and discretion, with entire confidence in your fidelity and wisdom.

Invoking the favor of Divine Providence for your guidance in the administration of the fund, and for your personal welfare.

I am, very respectfully, your obedient servant,

JOSEPHINE LOUISE NEWCOMB

Revealed in this letter is the story of a precocious and sickly child and of the pathetic, overprotective attachment of the mother for that child. It is the story of a wispy, lonely little woman who combined in one mind and personality the astute business sense of a Hetty Green and the sentimental, ethereal qualities of an Elizabeth Barrett Browning. An orphan herself and estranged from her dead husband's kin by a bitter fight over his will, she had decided to lavish upon the memory of her greatest joy in life her entire fortune. But over and above the personal element, looking between the lines of this letter, as one might peer through the louvers of a jalousie, the observer can see in the foreground Newcomb College, the country's first degree granting coordinate college for women established within the framework of a major university for men. In the background, their forms as yet indistinct on the horizon, one can see Radcliffe at Harvard, Barnard at Columbia, and the Woman's College of Western Reserve. The coeducational college was not an entirely new thing in 1886 and neither was the independent college for women; but the coordinate college was.[4]

Josephine Louise Newcomb was born Le Monnier on October 31, 1816, in Baltimore, the granddaughter of Philip Waters, an English sea captain, and the daughter of Alexander Le Monnier, a prominent Baltimore businessman. Upon the death of her mother in 1831 she moved to New Orleans to live with her only sister, Eleanore Ann, who had married William Henderson of that city. Although not wealthy, the Hendersons and young Miss Le Monnier were able to follow the custom of the better New Orleans families of that day of leaving the city during the summer months and going to fever-free places to the north. The Hendersons had selected Louisville as their summering place and on one of their visits they met Warren Newcomb, a prominent and successful young businessman of the city.[5]

Young Newcomb, however, was not a native of Louisville. He had been born on a farm at Bernardston, Massachusetts, on October 15, 1814, one of the twelve children of Dalton Newcomb and his wife Harriott. Most of the children became farmers, farmers' wives, or tradesmen in New England, but Warren and his older brothers, Horatio and Hezekiah, went west to the Kentucky country. Hezekiah became captain of a river steamboat and Warren became a clerk aboard her. Horatio set up a wholesale grocery

---

[4] Radcliffe was founded in 1879 but was not chartered and empowered to grant degrees until 1894. Barnard and the Woman's College of Western Reserve were established in 1888. Their founders had studied the Newcomb plan.

[5] On one of these visits Miss Le Monnier also met and became acquainted with William Preston Johnston.

business in Louisville. It was an ideal combination—Horatio was the manager, Warren the buyer in New Orleans, and Hezekiah looked after the transport end.

Warren spent the greater part of each winter in New Orleans buying rice, sugar, and molasses—often the whole crops of planters. Hezekiah took the cargoes up the river to Louisville along with coffee and other imported foods and beverages. The three brothers made money handily. Dapper and courteous, with a sparkling sense of humor, Warren was popular in the best social circles. It was natural that he should call frequently upon his friends the Hendersons and that he should see Miss Le Monnier at their home. Apparently rather slowly and over a considerable period of time a romance developed between the bold and enterprising young merchant and the fragile and demure Josephine Le Monnier. On December 15, 1845, at fashionable Christ Church (Episcopal) they were married. The officiating priest was the Reverend Francis Lister Hawks, destined nineteen months later to become the first president of the University of Louisiana.

Following their marriage Mr. and Mrs. Newcomb spent the remainder of the winter of 1845–1846 in New Orleans, and then moved to Louisville. Each winter for several years, however, they returned to New Orleans where Mr. Newcomb carried on his buying for the firm. Soon the two of them developed into great travelers together, spending considerable time in the East. While they were on a visit to New York a daughter was born to them (their first child, a boy, had died in infancy) on July 29, 1855. They christened the child Harriott after Mr. Newcomb's mother and Sophie after Mrs. Newcomb's mother.

In 1863 Warren Newcomb, now a man of wealth, withdrew from the Louisville firm and retired with his wife and daughter to New York. After an extensive tour of Europe, however, he tired of inactivity and in 1865 opened a New York branch of the Newcomb wholesale grocery business. But Warren Newcomb and Company did not have a lengthy career, for its founder died on August 28, 1866. The surviving mother and child now drew closer together than ever before if that was possible. Sophie was a precocious and delicate child who, at least the mother believed, required her constant attention and supervision. Until she was ten she was educated by tutors. For a year prior to her father's death she attended a private school in New York, but the mother accompanied the child to and from classes. In October 1867, Mrs. Newcomb took her daughter to Baltimore where for a few months she was enrolled in another private school. The evidence clearly shows, however, that from Mr. Newcomb's death in 1866 to the young girl's death in December 1870, mother and daughter were not separated for as much as a single day.

Following the brief period of schooling in Baltimore, Mrs. Newcomb returned with her daughter to New York and more private schooling. The summer of 1870 the two of them spent at Clifton House, the Newcomb summer home at Niagara Falls. And then in the early winter after their return to New York disaster struck. Never very strong, the young girl fell ill with diphtheria on the ninth of December 1870. Day by day her mother nursed her, but by the sixteenth her condition was extremely critical. On the afternoon of this day she murmured weakly, "Mama, take me on your lap—Mama, how dark it is." And with a gasp Harriott Sophie Newcomb passed away—age 15 years, 4 months, 17 days.

As Mrs. Newcomb stood dry-eyed and motionless near the grave of her infant son and that of her late husband and watched the remains of her beloved daughter interred, there began in her life the years of emptiness and mourning which ended only when she herself was buried with them. For months after the funeral her friends feared for her sanity, and when the shock had given away to the dull prolonged pain of remembrance she went into virtual seclusion. Undoubtedly strained relations with her husband's kin also had much to do with her sorrow. When her husband died he left an estate valued at from $500,000 to $850,000. Mrs. Newcomb was left a life income of $10,000 a year, and $200,000 was put in trust for the daughter. In the event the daughter died childless the bequest was to go to Mrs. Newcomb. A few months after his death his relatives entered suit to break the will. They were unsuccessful, but the litigation left in its wake intense bitterness on both sides.

Slowly the tiny, black-clad woman emerged from her seclusion. She traveled widely in Europe, but soon the pleasure of new places and faces faded. Two passions then seem to have possessed her life—to make money, lots of money, and to find a suitable memorial to her daughter.

In the former she was unusually resourceful. Through shrewd investments she amplified her inheritance to the point where at her death she had earned more than $4 million. The accumulation of wealth, however, only spurred her on in the really great quest of her life, a monument to Harriott Sophie Newcomb. In her search she tried various plans before she hit upon the one which seemed to satisfy her. Before his death, Warren Newcomb had in 1866 given a Harriott Sophie Newcomb scholarship fund of $10,000 to General Lee at Washington College. (It will be recalled that William Preston Johnston was just beginning his career as a teacher there in 1866.)

In 1882 Mrs. Newcomb added $20,000 to this for a library building. She then founded a school for poor girls in Charleston, South Carolina, and about the same time gave $20,000 to the Confederate Orphan Home in the same city. Always searching for the satisfying memorial she continued her gifts. To the school for the deaf in New York went $10,000. A bed in the Eye, Ear, Nose and Throat Hospital in the same city was endowed in memory of Sophie. But always there was something lacking, something less than the perfect monument.

It was Mrs. Tobias G. Richardson of New Orleans, wife of Dr. Richardson who had served the medical school so long, who came up with a suggestion which caused Mrs. Newcomb to make up her mind once and for all.[6] On Mrs. Newcomb's visits to New Orleans the two women had become close friends. Together they had discussed their charities, and in between visits had written each other about them. At first they had discussed the establishment of an orphan's home to be known as "St. Sophie's Home." Then Mrs. Newcomb offered financial assistance to Mrs. Richardson's favorite charity, St. Anna's Asylum. A large bequest in the will of a prominent New Orleans doctor, however, made further gifts to this cause unnecessary.

It was then apparently that the idea came to Mrs. Richardson. She had absorbed some of her husband's devotion to Tulane and she was a good friend of William Preston Johnston and knew of his desire to have a part of the university devoted to the education of women. Why not, she reasoned, help Tulane University and at the same time help Mrs. Newcomb in her search for an appropriate memorial? She discussed the matter with President Johnston who, in turn, wrote Mrs. Newcomb and then made a trip to see her. Apparently the influence of Johnston and Mrs. Richardson was potent for there seems to have been little hesitation on Mrs. Newcomb's part in reaching a decision. Then she wrote the letter quoted earlier in this chapter.

There was, of course, much scurrying about among the administrators and other officials of the university, for the establishment of a new college for women in the university was no small matter. A physical plant had to be erected, a faculty and administration developed, policies laid down. And these matters were not made easier by the fact that there were no precedents anywhere in the country upon which they could draw. This coordinate college at Tulane was a pioneering venture.

Two of the first questions which confronted the administration were these: What sort of college shall this be? What will be its relation to the rest of the university?

Mrs. Newcomb herself had partially supplied in a general way the answers to both questions. It was to be, she specified, a college for women "in the Tulane University of Louisiana." This college was to be founded and maintained "in harmony with the fundamental principles of the Christian religion" but nonsectarian; and it was stipulated that daily chapel of a religious but nonsectarian character be conducted and that the education to be given "shall look to the practical side of life as well as to literary excellence." As in Paul Tulane's letter of donation the administrators, at least in theory, were given wide discretionary authority. Not much time had

---

[6] Dr. Richardson's first wife, Sara Short Richardson, and their three children were all killed in a steamboat explosion in 1860. He later married Ida Ann Slocomb, a woman of considerable wealth. It was she who was so influential with Mrs. Newcomb.

passed, however, before it became rather clear what the relationship of the coordinate college was to the rest of the university. Although established within the framework of the university and thus under the supervision of the Board of Administrators, Newcomb College prepared its own curricula, maintained the endownment as a separate fund from the rest of the university, and determined its own academic policies. The fact that the first head of the college was designated as a "president" gives a good idea of the almost autonomous position of the college. It was a part of and yet separate from Tulane University. The fact that it had an entirely separate campus for many years also contributed to its feeling of autonomy.

As far as the president and administrators were concerned the most immediate problems, however, were those of a physical plant, an administrative head, curricula, and a faculty.

To house the new college the administrators purchased a two-story brownstone house on the corner of Camp and Delord (now Howard) Streets. This became the main classroom and administration building. A short while later a small brick house fronting on nearby Tivoli (now Lee) Circle was bought and converted to use as a laboratory building. It was not a pretentious beginning. There were no dormitories, and the rooms and furnishings were severely simple. The most ornate room undoubtedly was the first floor assembly hall with its huge gilded floor-to-ceiling mirrors, glistening crystal chandeliers, mahogany altar, and brass candelabra. This room doubled as assembly hall and chapel. Above were classrooms furnished only with long wooden tables and chairs. The library was conspicuous by its absence, although each classroom did contain some books.

The president and administrators made an early selection of the first "president" and then had a rather difficult time persuading him to accept. The man was Brandt V. B. Dixon, principal of Central High School of St. Louis.

Early in 1887, the Reverend Robert A. Holland, Rector of St. George's Church in St. Louis, and a friend of President Johnston, urged that Dixon be considered on the basis of his fine work in St. Louis. In the spring of the same year Johnston, after conferring with the administrators, invited him to New Orleans to look over the situation. Dixon came, but he was not impressed. The endowment was too small, he stated, and there were no "feeder" secondary schools for girls upon which the new college could draw. Thus he rejected the offer. But the administration of the university had decided he was the man and the declination was not taken as final. Terms of Dixon's own choosing eventually were met, and in June 1887 he accepted the appointment, an event of paramount importance to the new college, for Dixon was an able scholar and administrator.

A spirit of educational pioneering undoubtedly was largely influential in causing him to accept the new position. The opportunity was, as he himself expressed it, "an appeal that aroused the desire to create one's own world." President Johnston was highly pleased over the turn of events. Dixon's decision he saw as "a guaranty of the success of this undertaking which is the inauguration of real higher education for women in the Southwest, if not the entire South." And well might Johnston have been pleased, for it soon developed that the plump, bushy browed, and ruggedly handsome Dixon was a captivating speaker, a man of broad culture, and an indefatigable planner and worker. Perhaps it is safe to say that it was he more than any other single person who charted the future course of the H. Sophie Newcomb Memorial College.

Several months before the appointment of Dixon, President Johnston had drawn up tentative curricula for the college. There were to be three degree programs: classical, industrial, and scientific, each covering five years, the first of which was preparatory. When Dixon arrived he expanded the offerings somewhat by adding a fourth degree curriculum, the literary.[7] He also made provision for part-time and special students in the fields of "industrial and free-hand drawing, decorative design, modeling, wood-carving, water and oil painting, and drawing from the antique and from life." A certificate was awarded those completing prescribed special courses. The classical and literary programs differed from each other largely in the language requirement. The classical required Latin and Greek; the literary permitted the student to take a modern language. In essence both these curricula were basic liberal arts programs. The scientific and the industrial likewise were closely related. They, too, were fundamentally liberal arts with a sparse sprinkling of vocational or semivocational subjects such as bookkeeping, industrial drawing, decorative art, and painting. Actually all the curricula were, when viewed in the light of modern vocational courses in many colleges for women, strongly fundamentalist in nature. One looks in vain for courses in home economics or a major in physical education. It was in the words of the university catalog, "liberal and thorough."

President Johnston likewise had named a core faculty before Dixon assumed his duties. Several members of existing faculties were assigned teaching duties in the new college. From Tulane College, Florian Cajöri taught mathematics; John M. Ordway, biology; William and Ellsworth Woodward, drawing. From the faculty of the medical school, Dr. Chaillé taught physiology and hygiene. Others of this first faculty were: Brandt V. B. Dixon, professor of history and mental science; Mrs. J. C. Nixon, professor of English and rhetoric; George Gessner, professor of Greek and

---

[7] The preparatory year of the regular programs was classified as the "academic" year. The freshman year was called "collegiate." Then followed the sophomore, junior, and senior years.

Latin; Mrs. E. W. Ordway, professor of chemistry and physics; Auguste T. L. Kisian, professor of French and German; Mrs. S. J. Gomez, professor of Spanish; Victor Leovy, instructor in stenography; J. R. Buchanan, part-time instructor in bookkeeping; and Florian Shaffter, director of vocal music.

Applicants for admission to the academic (senior year of preparatory department) year were required to be at least fourteen years of age and to pass an examination in the basic fields of English, history, geography, and arithmetic.[8] The school year was divided into four quarters of nine weeks each, and the tuition for a full academic load was $25 per quarter. When the first opening exercises were held, on October 13, 1887, fifty-nine regular and ninety-one special students were in attendance. That same year seventy-nine men were enrolled as full-time students in Tulane College and seven as special students.[9]

Thus the new College of Tulane University was launched. At the end of its first year President Johnston reported:

It is the aim of this college to offer to the young women of Louisiana and the adjoining states a liberal education, similar to that which is now given to young men by Tulane University, and to young women also by other institutions of the first rank in distant parts of the United States.

The last few years have witnessed an extraordinary impulse to the cause of female education elsewhere; colleges similar to this have sprung up in various localities, and have been filled to overflowing whilst in our own community the increasing desire for similar advantages has arisen to an imperative demand.

To meet these educational needs a system of instruction was devised a year ago, which is believed to be liberal, thorough, and specially adapted to the prevailing conditions. The success which has attended the opening of the college and the gratifying results of the first session's work encourage the belief that the effort which is here being made to establish in Louisiana a female college of the first rank has been appreciated, and that the college will continue to receive the support necessary to its future usefulness and prosperity. By the generous liberality of its founder the endowment fund has been recently increased, and the Administrators are thereby enabled to offer for the coming season increased facilities for thorough instruction.

At a time when a fresh stream of money was flowing into the university from one source, however, the springs which fed the original stream suddenly dried up. On the evening of March 27, 1887, near the end of his eighty-sixth year, Paul Tulane died at his home in Princeton of pulmonary complications resulting from a cold.

His death was not a complete surprise, for the precarious state of his

[8] Actually, few young women in New Orleans were prepared to enter as full college freshmen. Entrance requirements, therefore, during the early years of the college were expressed in terms of the preparatory department rather than the college.

[9] The adult free courses had 838 students, however.

health had been known for months and, after all, men past eighty might ordinarily not be expected to survive for many years. Nevertheless there was a certain amount of shock and of genuine sorrow at his passing. In New Orleans many business houses were closed, classes at the university were suspended, and Tulane Hall was draped in black. Immediately a group of New Orleanians, including President Johnston and the Messrs. McConnell, Strong, Richardson, and Stauffer of the administrators, left by train to attend the funeral.[10]

The sorrow of his death quickly had added to it the elements of incredulity and consternation. No will was found, and thus the university named for him was cut off without a penny. Those who knew, or thought they knew, Paul Tulane well were utterly incredulous. Here was a man wise in the ways of business, frugal in his personal expenditures, generous in his gifts, and without any relatives closer than nieces and nephews for whom he had no particularly warm attachments. He had given a university his name and had led its administrators to believe it would be treated handsomely. He had left no will, or at least none was found. Why? Why? was the almost angry cry which ran through the halls of the university and spilled into the city.

Did Paul Tulane never make a will? Did someone destroy the will during the three days between his death and search for the will? Or did Paul Tulane himself destroy his will shortly before his death?

It is known that during the closing months of his life he had an obsession that the administrators were spending his money recklessly and for purposes which he did not approve. In August 1886, approximately seven months before Tulane's death, Gibson visited him at Princeton and reported that he found him "sick and almost bitter on the subject of the extravagance of the Board and the President of the faculty." "Had I known how much money was being wasted on trifles," Gibson reports him as saying, "I would not have given the last $50,000. I count on you [Mr. Gibson] to stop all their extravagance. You must go down there and put your foot down. There is no reserve fund, no guarantee fund against loss. If there were a $10,000 or $15,000 reserve that would show that they are safe and understand business." Did Tulane, in view of this obsession, tear up his will so that his estate would go to his relatives?

These are questions which the historian cannot answer with certainty in the light of existing evidence. There are, however, two interesting statements on the matter—one by James McConnell, Tulane's attorney in New

---

[10] For years Tulane's grave in Princeton was neglected except for being kept clean of grass. No flowers were planted, nor was it decorated on anniversary dates of his death. When in 1937 John S. Kendall visited Princeton and reported this, President Rufus Carrollton Harris inaugurated annual memorial services at the grave. These ceremonies began on the fifty-first anniversary of Tulane's death.

Orleans and a member of the Board of Administrators, and one by George O. Vanderbilt, Tulane's attorney in Princeton.

McConnell had a special reason to be shocked at the failure to discover a will. Four years prior to Tulane's death he had prepared at his request a codicil leaving his entire estate to the university. Whether Tulane ever signed and executed this codicil is not known, but McConnell had every reason to think he did. Now, after the funeral, he expected to find the document he had prepared. But he didn't find it, and his pain and disappointment are clearly reflected in his report to Gibson in New Orleans. The letter was written from New York on April 2, 1887, three days after the funeral. It reads in part:

The search for the will of Mr. Tulane has so far proved to be a vain and fruitless one—and I feel so sad and pained at the result, that it is only from a sense of duty to the Board, that I write at all at this time. I do so however because I deem it proper and important that you and the Board should be informed of the investigation so far as it has progressed.

On arriving at the residence of Mr. Tulane, we found that the "relatives" were residing there and had been for several days. Mr. Vanderbuilt [sic] was very courteous but had assumed control of all papers, etc acting as he stated under the sanction of the Probate Judge of the County. After the funeral, we assembled in the parlor of the residence, and after some explanations of a perfectly agreeable character,—it was decided that search for the will should be made first in the dwelling house, and if none were found there—then to proceed to New York —Accordingly a thorough over-hauling was made of all the private papers, found in the bedroom, its armoirs, secretaries, drawers, desks, books, &c, &c. I devoted myself specially to this work, assisted by Mr. Strong, the heirs, or relatives, being present, and Mr. Vanderbuilt, conducting the proceeding. Several hours were thus consumed—the work indeed being continued so late that Mr. Strong and I had to remain in Princeton last night. This morning we came to New York. We, that is Mr. Vanderbuilt, three of the "relatives," a Chosen Citizen of Princeton Mr. Elijah Leigh (who by the way was a very fair and friendly man) with Strong and myself, proceeded at once to the Safe Deposit Company where we found a bank box belonging to Mr. Tulane—The Offices opened the box, examined and replaced the Contents merely to see— if a will was to be found. The box was opened, upon a table when we were all around, and had fair opportunity to see every paper in it. There was no will found in that box. It however contained a large quantity of bonds and certificates of stocks. We next visited a second large Safe Deposit Co where Mr. Strong said Mr. Tulane had formerly kept a box—but were informed by its officers that Mr. T. had no box, nor property of any kind there. Next we went to the Manhattan Company [Bank] in which Mr. Tulane has been a depositor for many years and were informed by its cashier Mr. Baldwin, an intimate friend of Mr. Tulane, that he had no box there—Learning that probably Mr. Peck of the firm of Henry Talmage and Company, an old friend also of Mr. Tulane might possess some knowledge on the subject, we all proceeded to the office of that firm—Mr.

Peck was not there, but in its polite principal Mr. Henry Talmage, we recognized a friend of long standing of our deceased friend, who had shown his friendship by going to Princeton to attend the funeral. Mr. Talmage told us, that he was satisfied Mr. Peck knew no more than he did, which was nothing of a positive character, but that both he and Mr. Peck were convinced that Mr. Tulane had made a will in favor of our institution. He said however that this conviction resulted simply from what they had heard generally—not from any thing told them by Mr. Tulane.

Having no further places to visit, where we were justified even in supposing that Mr. Tulane had a bank box—the party making the search, composed as above described—disbanded—Before doing so however I had them assembled and in the name of the Board thanked them for the courteous manner in which they had all assisted in the search, and informed them, that although no will had so far been found, I was satisfied still, from all the information that came to my knowledge, that Mr. Tulane must have made a will, and that we should continue to search for it—Thus we parted, Mr. Vanderbuilt promising me to write you the result of the investigation.

Mr. Vanderbuilt showed me a letter from Mr. Elmer C. Green, the Atty of Mr. Tulane in Trenton, from which the inference is quite plain that he has no knowledge of a will, but I have thought it prudent to write him and will know from his answer to me whether he does or not. Words cannot express the disappointment I have realized in this *failure.*

A few weeks later Mr. Vanderbilt gave a story to the press on the mystery. His statement is as follows:

I am often asked why it was that Mr. Tulane made no will. That is a mystery that will never be solved. He never mentioned anything to me about making a will, never even talked on the subject, and I never said anything to him about it. I always supposed, of course, that he had made a will before I became his attorney. I took that for granted. Judge Caleb S. Green, his former attorney, whom I succeeded, recently told me that he never said a word to him about making his will. I have heard that years ago, when he would go south, he would make a will, leaving it with Gov. Olden, and on his return would destroy it. About 1873 he had Mr. John F. Hagerman, Sr., draw some heads or items for a will, but never got farther than that with it. He seemed to have abandoned it. Hon James McConnell, his lawyer in New Orleans, and a warm and close friend of Mr. Tulane, told me that about four years ago while attending as a delegate an Episcopal convention in Philadelphia, Mr. Tulane came there and desired him to draw a codicil to his will for the benefit of the Tulane University, and that he spent part of two evenings with Mr. Tulane at the Continental Hotel in talking it over and drawing a codicil; that he finally drew it and gave it to him. This is all I have been able to ascertain concerning a will. Whether he intended to make one and put it off to a more convenient season or whether it was his intention not to make one I cannot say. He was nearly eighty-six years of age and one would suppose that if he could have expected to live some years (which I think he did), and thought he had time enough in which to do it.

All this is forever locked in the grave. Any theory is mere speculation. He was a very reticent man and disclosed but little of his business to his most intimate friends. A diligent and thorough search has been made in every possible place for a will, but none has been found, and I am convinced there is none. If there had been one the person who wrote it and the witnesses who signed it would have come forward by this time."

Mr. Vanderbilt was entirely correct in one respect: the mystery was never solved, and no will was ever found. The court appointed him and Paul M. Tulane, a nephew, co-administrators of the estate, which was composed largely of stocks, bonds, and mortgages with a book value of approximately a million dollars. The entire estate went to Paul M. Tulane and several grandnieces and grandnephews.

CHAPTER 5

Toward the Turn
of the Century (1888-1900)

IF ONE LISTENS WITH a trained ear to the overture of an opera he may at times detect in it rather distinct suggestions of scenes and arias which will develop as the full production unfolds. In a very real sense the second phase of the formative years of Tulane University, roughly from 1888 to 1900, may be considered as the overture of the drama which began to have a meaningful plot by the turn of the century. One may discover in these years many suggestions of what the university was to become in a more mature period. These included intimations of a liberal arts college with a strong faculty placing emphasis on first-rate instruction at the undergraduate level; professional schools of medicine, law, and engineering with a minor note now and then of a school of commerce; an almost unique coordinate college for women; a rather notable early program of adult education; and some scanty research and investigation facilities presaging a future graduate school in the modern sense. One may also see in these years foreshadowings of the problems which Tulane as a privately endowed university would come to know. There is the suggestion of a capable faculty and inadequate financial resources; of an unusually generous plan of scholarships for impecunious students with good minds; of the attempts to build an adequate physical plant; of the need for libraries and laboratories; and, above all, of the necessity for educating the public to a better understanding of the role of a university in the development of a region's cultural as well as physical resources.

In the final analysis, perhaps this latter was the most important task of all, for if the public came to accept the university as the generator or resuscitator of its culture, then in the long run the necessary finances would be provided by that public. It was to this cultural ideal that the academic departments of Tulane University early came to be devoted, but by the very nature of its size and facilities it had to reject the idea of mass education for Everyman and concentrate its energies on developing potential leaders with general enlightenment for the professions and for citizenship. "We take nobody into the college intentionally who is not well qualified to keep up with his studies and advance with ease," President Johnston wrote in 1892. "The consequence of this is that you see fewer students and fewer graduates than if we throw our doors open to a mob who would study what and as much or as little as they pleased. But our students are regulars, not militia and when they come to fight the battle of life you will discover that they can hold the fort." Unfortunately, however, this scholarly sentiment was not at the time well understood and accepted by the public.

The university did not overlook, of course, the vocational aspects of law, medicine, and engineering, nor did it often permit its philosophy of selective education to interfere with the adult education program, but, as will be pointed out, there came to be more and more emphasis placed upon general or liberal education as a prerequisite for the highest type of professional and cultural leadership. But this was not easy to "sell" to the public. It should be repeated that the South (and perhaps most of the nation) in the 1880s and 1890s saw as its pressing need the practically trained man who could "do things." It was, therefore, difficult for a university to hold to the ideal of developing the whole man. "It is astonishing," President Johnston wrote, "to find how well the program is understood and appreciated in other parts of the country but not at home in New Orleans." Apparently he was not willing to admit that part of the fault might lie with the university, or perhaps he was only dimly aware of the importance of good public relations in a privately endowed institution.

For the administrators themselves there were strong intimations that the death of Paul Tulane meant the emergence of a new concept of their role in the affairs of the university. During the life of Tulane the administrators had played for the most part a somewhat passive role. That is, they had administered a fund, but the situation did not demand that they be active in seeking out new sources of revenue. Also their initiative was somewhat restricted by the constant thought that their actions might displease the founder. While this fear was removed by his death, there soon came the realization that with revenue from the original source shut off, the administrators would necessarily have to become more active in raising money if the university was to grow and expand. This obviously was a revealing and frustrating experience to many members of the first board, for few of them were fully aware of the financial considerations involved in building and maintaining a first-rate institution of higher learning.

Unconsciously, perhaps the administrators were also determining another aspect of the university's immediate future: The early administrators, by and large, did not conceive of Tulane, except possibly for the Department of Medicine, as a large regional university. Rather they thought in highly restricted local terms—a frame of reference not difficult to understand in view of the circumstances during the formative years. Paul Tulane had specified that his money was to be used for the education of white young persons "in the City of New Orleans." The membership of the board was limited by the charter bylaws to citizens of Louisiana, which generally meant that members would come from New Orleans. These two factors alone would have produced a strong feeling of insularity; but the geographic factor must be included as well. New Orleans was the one even faintly bright spot in an otherwise somber and unattractive Gulf regional backdrop.

An approximate definition of the Gulf Region may be made by beginning at Corpus Christi, Texas, and drawing a line on the map three hundred miles northward to the Red River. Turning at right angles the line may be continued six hundred miles east to Columbus, Georgia; thence in a southeasterly direction to Gainesville, Florida, and beyond. In this area of some two hundred thousand square miles the resources to support a good university appeared in the 1890s to be singularly limited. East Texas was in a semifrontier stage of development. Southwest Louisiana was marshy bayou country inhabited largely by Cajun trappers and fishermen. North Louisiana was almost wholly a rural, small-farmer area identified with a cotton economy. South Mississippi, south Alabama (with the exception of the Black Belt and Mobile), and west Florida made up the pine barrens, a sandy soil region with little to commend it economically. The industrial awakening of the upper South had in 1890 hardly touched this Gulf region. Moreover, there was in the region a conspicuous lack of cultural resources. There barely existed in the entire area a single first-rate high school, college, library, or laboratory. Public elementary schools were poor, high schools almost nonexistent. Health conditions were bad. Per capita wealth was even lower than the $376 average for the South as a whole, and this figure was about one-third the average for states outside the South.[1]

It is small wonder, therefore, that the administrators thought largely in terms of New Orleans. But it is more important to note that the economic development of the region and the expansion of Tulane University went forward together, each reinforcing the other. As might be expected, Tulane emerged as a strong regional institution at about the same time that the region achieved through the utilization of its resources a high level of production and wealth. The story of this development can probably best be told by writing brief accounts of the individual colleges. These episodes when taken as a whole in the perspective of time reveal the struggles of a Southern university to achieve in the period between the Old and New South a place for itself in the widening area of higher education.

Perhaps a three-sentence summary may be expanded somewhat to tell

---

[1] Secondary education in the South before 1900 was at a very low level. In 1890, for example, New Orleans was the only place in Louisiana where one would find a public high school. President Johnston labored unceasingly for the establishment of a good system of secondary schools, particularly in Louisiana.

the story of the professional schools at Tulane prior to 1900: (1) The law school remained small and provincial and was almost constantly in search of a permanent home for itself. (2) Medicine increased its prestige, expanded its facilities, and came to occupy an even more dominant position in the university, in New Orleans, in the region, and even in the nation. (3) The immediate foundations of a school of engineering were laid in the creation of the College of Technology.

The law department made the transition from the old university to the new with relative ease. There were, however, a few coincidental faculty changes between 1883 and 1890. In March of 1883, Dean Carleton Hunt had resigned to accept a seat in the United States House of Representatives, and William Francis Mellen had become dean. Mellen was an alumnus of the University of Mississippi, a Confederate veteran, and a successful lawyer in Natchez and St. Louis. In spite of failing health he served as dean until 1888, when he was succeeded by Henry G. Miller, professor of admiralty and international law. Dean Miller steered the department through most of the Johnston administration, resigning in 1897 and being replaced by Henry H. Hall, professor of criminal law and the law of evidence. During the school year 1888–1889 three new faculty members were added: Thomas J. Semmes, Harvard Law graduate and former president of the American Bar Association, became professor of constitutional law, common law, and equity; Frank A. Monroe became professor of commercial law and the law of corporations; and Henry H. Hall succeeded to the deanship in 1897.

The change which most profoundly affected the law department, however, was the retirement in 1888 of the almost venerable Randell Hunt, who had been connected with the university old and new for forty-one years—twenty-four years as a law professor and seventeen years as president. In addition to his teaching and administrative duties this portly, bearded, eloquent man had conducted a law practice which brought him nationwide attention to the extent that Lincoln in 1861 had considered him, because of his ability and his staunch Unionism, for a cabinet appointment. Undoubtedly his most important case was as attorney for the plantiffs in the famous Slaughter House case in 1873, one of the earliest cases in which a new interpretation of the Fourteenth Amendment was sought. The years brought him fame but not fortune. In 1884, when he was replaced as president by William Preston Johnston and made rector emeritus of the law department, the salary which the administrators voted him for this office and his professorship was quite important in providing a comfortable living for him. Often he was too ill to meet his classes, but he clung to his lecturing as only a man who loved his job could. Finally in 1888 his physical condition forced his retirement, and four years later he died.

Through the years the law department had periodically resembled an autonomous band of medieval scholars and fellows searching out places in the city where it might hold its lectures and disputations. It will be recalled that the law department of the old University of Louisiana began its lectures in 1847 in a federal courtroom. Then it moved into a wing of the university buildings on Common Street. When in 1893 Tulane University moved to its present location on St. Charles Avenue the law department moved into Tulane Hall on the old campus. Then Tulane Hall was sold in 1903, and the faculty secured classrooms in the new Richardson Medical Building on Canal Street. From here the department moved to the new Gibson Hall on the uptown campus. It was fairly easy for it to move, however, for outside of its modest library it had little equipment. Enrollment, too, was rather small—17 students in 1884–1885; 49 by 1892.

These facts, of course, are in no sense a disparagement of the law department. As a matter of fact during these years it had an excellent and at times brilliant array of legal talent on its faculty. Rather, enrollment figures cited above are a commentary on the state of economic development in the South (and the nation, for that matter) prior to 1900. During the 1890s the young lawyer set up an active court practice or he entered politics. The vast complex of our present economic system which demands more and more lawyers for positions in which legal training is merely an auxiliary skill had not clearly emerged. Too, there was no "big government" with its demands for a score of lawyers in every bureau. Consequently most of the American law schools were small during this period. When big business and big government did develop in the twentieth century, enrollment in the nation's law schools, including Tulane, went up. Enrollment at Tulane rose when it finally was understood in other states that common law as well as civil law was taught. Louisiana had to live with her sister states with the common law.

On the whole the 1890s were stable, even tranquil, years for the law department. Changes were few. Lectures, oral examinations, and class schedules went on in the time-honored fashion. In fact, lectures came to be so standardized that a student could buy a copy of last year's lectures from John Westly and thus avoid the necessity of attending this year's class sessions. (Westly was the Negro janitor of the law department, but he was much more than that. He is described as being a "sort of registrar, clerk, keeper of rolls, truant officer, and assistant to the professors." One university official laughingly referred to him as "Executive Dean.") No notable changes were made in the extremely flexible entrance requirements. To gain admission the student had to be literate and be known to a professor. When he finished his course his grade was the gesture of the professor's head which nodded in approval or shook in disapproval. A student attended two years, or one year plus a year of experience in a law office, and took his examinations; if he passed and was twenty-one years of age he received the degree of Bachelor of Laws. If he was not twenty-one he waited for his degree until he reached his majority. The curriculum, too, followed old familiar patterns. In the main it consisted of common law, equity, the law of corporations, admiralty and international law, evidence, pleading, land laws, and civil law.

There were innovations, to be sure, some of them of major importance. As early as December 1873, the law alumni formally organized an association; and in the fall of 1886 students and alumni formed the Law Students' Club to "promote the pleasure and advancement of members by mutual intercourse and the formation of a moot court." On January 10, 1899, the first student-organized moot court session was held. Another innovation of considerable significance was the admission of the first woman student to the law department. Under an act of the state legislature in 1894 colleges were permitted "to confer diplomas upon women in the practice of law." In October 1897, Miss Bettie Runnels of New Orleans was admitted, and in 1898 she received her degree, the first ever conferred by the law department on a woman.

In striking contrast to the Law Department, the Medical Department during the late 1880s and the 1890s was characterized by rapid change and expansion.[2] The researcher who delves into the source material of those years gets a feeling of urgency on the part of these medical scientists, of a passion for trying out new techniques, of an unquenchable thirst for medical knowledge and a willingness, even eagerness, to experiment. The result was a period of scholarly ferment. New admission and graduation standards were developed; the curriculum was expanded; what came to be a graduate division for advanced study was instituted; a new and, for its day, modern building was erected; new equipment was added; new professors joined the faculty; new programs of research were started; and the library was expanded.

The leading figure in all this was Dean Stanford E. Chaillé, a compulsive, tobacco-chewing martinet with fierce piercing eyes, walrus mustaches and a little unruly tuft of beard on his lower lip. Since 1858 he had been a member of the faculty, dean from 1885. Despite his eccentricities and his peremptory manner he commanded the respect, even admiration, of his faculty, and his qualities of leadership were unquestioned. Even in his old age when he made a practice of resigning as dean every year to, as he expressed it, protect the university "from the infirmities of senility" his

---

[2] Both law and medicine were still officially designated as "departments" at this time. The nomenclature was changed in 1913 to "College of Medicine," which embraced the School of Pharmacy, the Graduate School of Medicine, and the School of Dentistry. "Law Department" was changed to "The College of Law" in the same year. In 1932 "College" was changed to "School" for Medicine. In 1952 the same change was made for Law.

faculty annually gave renewed expression of its confidence in him by requesting him to remain.

Perhaps the most important of his achievements was in selecting and directing a new and changing type of faculty. When he became dean in 1885 he had a faculty of nineteen. By the turn of the century this number had grown to forty-nine. By the time of his retirement in 1908 there had been an almost complete turnover. But the quantitative growth of the faculty was not the factor which was of such importance during this period. Chaillé believed that good doctors were trained as much in the laboratories as in the clinics. As a result he put more and more emphasis upon basic courses in medical science—on bacteriology, chemistry, physiology, pathological and microscopical anatomy or histology, toxicology, and many related fields. To teach these basic laboratory courses a new type of faculty member was needed. This new teacher had to be a combination of clinician and specialist in a given field. He had to be a man who could assist the student in the laboratory to discover that the modern doctor is first and foremost a scientist who relies upon the results of research to determine the cause of disease and thus to prevent it rather than a practitioner who prescribes medicine in an attempt to cure an ill, the basic pathology of which he does not understand. In a very real sense the Chaillé period was the beginning of scientific preventive medicine at Tulane. It also gave impetus to medical research, for the student was required to equip himself with a basic scientific knowledge upon which his growth in future years might well depend.

All the faculty members of the Chaillé period cannot be treated in this general history of the university. There is a great temptation to write fully about Dr. Edmond Souchon, professor of anatomy and clinical surgery, Dean Chaillé's unofficial assistant dean; or of Dr. Ernest S. Lewis, professor of general and clinical obstetrics; or Dr. Louis F. Reynaud, professor of materia medica and clinical medicine; or of Dr. John B. Elliott, professor of the theory and practice of medicine; or of the renowned Civil War surgeon, prolific writer on medical subjects, and president of the Louisiana State Board of Health, Dr. Joseph Jones, professor of chemistry and clinical medicine. These and others who could be named were foundation stones upon which the medical department rested during the 1890s. In a history of the medical school itself their work would receive full recognition; but in this volume it appears that attention should be directed largely to certain figures who typify the new emphasis in the medical department.

Twenty-three-year-old Abraham Louis Metz of New York was appointed as instructor in the School of Pharmacy in 1887.[3] He drove him-

[3] The department of pharmacy had a struggle for existence during the 1890s. Enrollment was small and finances were uncertain. In May 1899, the faculty sought permission to abolish the department, and the administrators consented. However, it was not closed until 1933.

self as hard as he did his students and as a result took the Master of Pharmacy degree in 1889 and the Doctor of Medicine degree in 1893. Upon completion of his medical degree he was made instructor in chemistry in the medical department and given an assistant. A disputatious and cantankerous man, he nevertheless made his way upward in the faculty, often putting his own funds into laboratory equipment. When Dr. Joseph Jones died in 1896, Metz was chosen to succeed him. Now he was given two assistants, and with that chemistry was well on its way as a basic scientific study required of all students. Methodically and relentlessly Dean Chaillé pursued his goal of training his young doctors to find in the test tube and in the lenses of the microscope the key to hygiene and preventive medicine. "Never before in man's history," he declared, "have there been such assuring promises of the triumph of medical science in preventing disease." In 1889 his annual report stressed the necessity of creating new laboratories where "normal and morbid" anatomy might be studied microscopically. Within two months the faculty had approved a new position of "demonstrator of microscopical anatomy and bacteriology." P. E. Archinard, a pupil of Pasteur and Koch, was selected to fill the new position. At first the course was optional, but at the beginning of the 1893 school year it was required of all students.

Chaillé was not a mere ivory tower scientist. As early as 1877 he had actively interested himself in public health affairs by heading a United States commission to study yellow fever in Cuba. He took with him as interpreter and assistant a promising seventeen-year-old medical student, Rudolph Matas by name, who spoke fluent Spanish, French, and English. Together these two sought to find through Professor Riddell's microscope the cause of the plague which year after year took its huge toll of New Orleans as well as Cuban citizens. Together they made the first large-scale photomicrographs of the blood of yellow fever patients, and although they did not find what they were searching for, both man and boy remained unchanged in their opinion that they or someone else would discover in the blood stream the organism which they felt caused the disease. And their views were reinforced by the theories of Dr. Carlos Finley of Havana whom they met and with whom they worked. Dr. Finley believed, and committed his beliefs to paper in an article on the subject, that the mosquito carried the dread Bronze John. It was the erstwhile young medical student, now Dr. Matas, who in 1882 translated this paper into English and thus brought it to the attention of American doctors.

But if young Dr. Matas did not himself discover how to control yellow fever he at least was physician to the man who did learn how to conquer it. In the same year (1882) that he translated Dr. Finley's paper he was called to Brownsville, Texas, to help fight a yellow fever epidemic there. His personal immunity to the disease plus his experiences in New Orleans and Cuba made him an invaluable doctor in the outbreak. One of his patients was a young captain, William Crawford Gorgas by name, only three years out of medical school. A few years later this young doctor was promoted to surgeon-general of the Army, and through his mosquito control methods the completion of the Panama Canal was made possible.

The recurrence of the name of Matas in the preceding paragraphs is indicative of the importance he came to have in the medical department as one of the world's great surgeons and teachers of surgery. Born in 1860 of well-educated Spanish parents (his father was a physician who did postgraduate work in Paris) at Bonnet Carré in the sugar country near New Orleans, he entered the University of Louisiana as a medical student in 1877. He took his degree in 1880, set up his practice, and shortly thereafter was appointed demonstrator of anatomy in the medical department. For the next forty years as full professor and practitioner of surgery he built a reputation hardly excelled in the annals of American medicine. His brain and hands possessed a genius which exhibited itself best in thoracic and vascular surgery. This short, dumpy young doctor with his pudgy cheeks, dark, deep-set, searching eyes, and well-trimmed beard had a catholicity of interests. He liked to write, and was a close friend of a then unknown young New Orleans newspaper reporter named Lafcadio Hearn. He was interested in local anesthesia and was among the first, if not actually the first, American doctor successfully to use spinal anesthesia.

But he was above all a great teacher, not only to his medical students but to his fellow doctors as well. His lectures and demonstrations at the medical school on Thursdays were significant events for the medical students, but his other days in the operating rooms at Touro Infirmary and Charity Hospital were equally anticipated by his peers. Often performing as many as fifteen to twenty operations a day, he seemed never to tire nor to lose his almost feminine deftness of touch which, together with his minute knowledge of anatomy, enabled him to find his way with a minimum of shock and loss of blood into the tangle of vital organs, blood vessels, muscles, and nerves which make up the human body. Always around the table with him was a group of doctors learning from the master surgeon and teacher who so seldom made a mistake.

A contemporary of Dr. Matas was another young doctor destined to achieve fame in a different area of medicine, Galveston-born, Yale-educated Isadore Dyer, an alumnus of the medical department class of 1889. Dr. Dyer was appointed lecturer and clinical instructor in dermatology in 1892. Later he became a full professor and in 1908 dean of the department of medicine, succeeding Dr. Chaillé. The fact that he did become dean undoubtedly has somewhat obscured his earlier achievements in the field of dermatology. At first his interests in the field were general, but eventually he came to have almost a passionate obsession for research and therapy in the ancient and most horrible of all scourges, leprosy. Undoubtedly his interest in the disease was partly kindled by Dr. Joseph Jones, parish health officer as well as professor of the university, who wrote and lectured on the subject. But it is likely that the most powerful stimulus to work in the field was the presence in New Orleans of numerous cases of the disease.[4] Seven of those cases were patients in the isolation ward at Charity Hospital. For these he introduced the remedy which had been used in India for centuries, oil of chaulmoogra, an internal medication which continued to be used almost exclusively until the discovery of sulphone therapy in the early 1940s.

Dr. Dyer's interest in leprosy was humanitarian as well as scientific. Always a kindly and sympathetic man, his heart went out to these unfortunate people either unattended or confined to the incredibly filthy pest house maintained by the city. The need as he saw it was for a hospital where these lepers could be isolated, studied, treated, and, above all, given the humane treatment accorded other sick people. Just at the time when his feelings were becoming almost uncontainable, a young reporter, John S. Kendall, wrote a series of articles for the *Picayune* on the horrors of the disease in the city and the almost unbelievably callous treatment which the sufferers received. Public indignation was fired by the newspaper's revelations, and Dr. Dyer took advantage of it. Ably seconded by Allen Jumel, a member of the state legislature, he presented the matter in a series of resolutions to a receptive Orleans Parish Medical Society on June 9, 1894.

Approval of the society was unanimous. It went on record as demanding that the legislature take immediate action to provide an isolation hospital open to all races which would be based "upon the highest humanitarian motives" and would be "an asylum of refuge rather than one of horror and reproach." Quickly the two men, Dyer and Jumel, took the matter to the legislature, and the response on its part was equally swift. In August 1894, it appropriated $5,000 for a building and $10,000 annually for the care of the patients. All that remained, then, was to select a site. Dr. Dyer was chosen president of the board which was to administer the act.

Locating the hospital, however, proved difficult, for the public fear of leprosy amounted almost to hysteria. New Orleans, although it had had lepers walking the streets for years and had maintained a leper's pest house within the city limits, refused a location for the new institution. Surrounding areas fought the location in their midst, even to the extent of physical violence. Finally, under the guise of establishing an ostrich farm, the board secured an abandoned plantation house with contiguous slave quarters in

---

[4] In 1916 Dr. Dyer in testimony before the U.S. Senate Committee on Public Health and Quarantine reported there were 37 known cases of leprosy in New Orleans and that for every known case there were at least 3 undiscovered cases. Using this formula one arrives at a figure of over 100 cases in 1892.

Iberville Parish, 85 miles up the river from New Orleans. This deplorably run down and decayed place was called Indian Camp Plantation. On the night of November 30, 1894, seven patients, five men and two women, began the journey upriver by barge.[5] Both the railroads and steamship lines had refused them passage, but Dr. Dyer had secured a barge and a tow from a tug. As the barge eased up the river with the patients aboard, a spectator observed that this was like a sorrow-laden vessel gliding up the Nile to the cities of the dead. But it was a voyage into hope, as subsequent events were to prove, for Dr. Dyer lived to see the day when Indian Camp became the United States Public Health Service Hospital for lepers at Carville, Louisiana—the world's hope for the eradication of leprosy.

It was, then, such young men as Metz, Archinard, Matas, and Dyer who were setting a new pace for the medical department. But there were advances in areas other than research and instruction. Entrance requirements were tightened; the time required for a degree was lengthened. Cooperation was extended to the newly established Polyclinic, the library was expanded, new equipment was added, and, above all, the department moved into a new and modern building.

It has been pointed out that admission requirements for both law and medicine in the immediate post-Civil War years were, when measured against today's standards, very lax. The absence of any system of accredited high schools made it impossible to use high school graduation as a criterion for admission; so the medical faculty turned to the one standard which seemed to possess some semblance of validity and uniformity. The student, it was decided in 1893, must meet the standards of a second-grade teacher's certificate.[6] Along with this tightening of entrance requirements went an extension of the time required for a degree. In 1892 the time required for a degree was raised to three years, and for all students entering after January 1, 1901, the full four-year program was required. The extension of the time period for required study and the addition of new courses, as would be expected, resulted in an increase in tuition, for the very life of the medical department depended upon student fees. Under the two-year program, total tuition and fees for a year were approximately $175. Under the three-year program, tuition and fees were raised to $225 for the year.

This matter of student fees, of course, raises the whole question of how

[5] The next year four Daughters of Charity of the Order of St. Vincent de Paul assumed the nursing duties. Sisters of this order have continued to carry out these duties to this day.

[6] Second-grade teacher certificate requirements in Louisiana were the passage of examinations in arithmetic, geography, English grammar and composition, U.S. history, natural philosophy, and physiology. For the first-grade certificate the subjects were spelling, grammar, algebra, rhetoric, literature, history, botany, philosophy, arithmetic, geography, and geometry.

the medical department was financed during the 1890s. In answering it, some fundamental considerations must be kept in mind. The first is that the medical department had no endowment of its own nor did it participate in the general endowment funds of the university.[7] Except for an occasional small donation by the administrators for equipment, the medical department had to support itself. A second consideration is the fact that most of the faculty members were doctors with an established practice in New Orleans and thus were not dependent upon their professorial compensation for a living. If there was something left at the end of the year they divided it among themselves. If there was nothing to divide, then that was that. Usually, however, there was something. The year 1889 may be taken as an example. There was an income for this year of approximately $70,000. At the end of the year the faculty members voted to give themselves a salary of $4,500 each and to divide the balance into equal parts for equipment, each professor receiving a share for his department and the dean receiving a share for general purposes.

On any basis other than this the department could not have survived, to say nothing of providing improvements and expansion. And the greatest expansion in its history up to that time came upon it almost out of the blue.

For several years it had been apparent that the old medical building facing Common Street had become entirely inadequate for a growing faculty and a student body which averaged nearly four hundred a year. The faculty had discussed the matter frequently, but the prospect of building a new physical plant was discouraging. The administrators could offer little encouragement because they were faced with the fact that all the buildings on the Common Street campus were inadequate, and thus there loomed the prospect that an entirely new plant might be required for Tulane College and the Law Department.

The problem for the Medical Department was solved quite dramatically by a letter from Dr. Tobias G. Richardson to Dean Chaillé on March 2, 1891. His wife, Ida Ann, he advised, wished to donate $50,000 for a building to house laboratories and anatomy rooms, provided the Board of Administrators would allocate space for it on the campus. Dean Chaillé urged an immediate acceptance of the offer, but the administrators had a better plan. Instead of locating the new building on the already inadequate old campus they purchased most of the square of ground on Canal Street bounded by Robertson, Customhouse (now Iberville), and Villere Streets. Encouraged by this cooperative spirit on the part of the administrators, Mrs. Richardson doubled her donation, thereby making possible the erection of an entirely new building to house the entire Medical Department.

Dr. Edmond Souchon and architect Thomas Sully were chosen for an

[7] The department of law was similarly financed.

inspection trip to various medical schools over the United States to discover new features which might be incorporated into what was expected to be the most modern medical building in the country. While they were away Mrs. Richardson gave an additional $46,000 for equipment and furnishings. When the two men returned, their ideas were thrown into the pool with the others and the result was a somewhat ornate, gingerbready, multichimneyed four-story building. What it lacked in outward beauty, however, was more than compensated for by the utility of its interior. Here at last professors could have ample space for lecture rooms and laboratories. Even Dean Chaillé could have room for his cuspidors whenever he desired them.[8] Above all there was a sky-lighted amphitheatre seating 535 students and doctors should that many at one time wish to hear a lecture or witness a demonstration. The location, too, had many advantages. The new building was only a long block from Charity Hospital, on Tulane Avenue, and the Polyclinic.[9] These three institutions—Charity Hospital, the Polyclinic, and the Tulane medical department—were during the 1890s forging ahead to make of New Orleans a great medical center.

Classes were held in the new building for the first time in October 1893, but Dr. Richardson had not survived to see this memorial to himself put to use. He died in 1892, and his death seemed to inspire the widow even more than during his lifetime to see the building symbolize his years of service to the medical department. She personally supervised the landscaping of the grounds, often having trees and shrubs from her home in the Garden District transplanted to the yard of the medical building.[10] She was a frequent and interested visitor, almost reverently planting and decorating, for this was the monument to her husband. Significantly, she stands out as the first major donor after the original gifts of Mr. Tulane and Mrs. Newcomb— and it should be recalled that she was a major influence in Mrs. Newcomb's decision to found a college at Tulane.

It is difficult to convey in a few pages a really comprehensive appraisal of the growth and usefulness of the Medical Department during the 1890s. It not only concerned itself with training more and better doctors but with standards and the professional aspects of medicine as well. Its successful

[8] The dean refused to use spittoons because he said, they splashed. Instead he had square sand boxes made and scattered at strategic points where he could find one in any direction he might turn.

[9] The Polyclinic was a voluntary association of New Orleans doctors, many of them Tulane alumni, organized in the 1880s for the purpose of furthering their postgraduate studies in medicine. Although not an integral part of the Tulane medical department, cooperation between the two was such that they had the appearance of being one and the same. Actually, the Tulane medical department was such an important factor in the Polyclinic that it might well be said that the latter was the foundation of the graduate school of medicine at Tulane.

[10] In her landscaping activities Mrs. Richardson had planted just outside the dean's office a fine orange tree. A cutting from this tree was transplanted to the uptown campus but cold weather eventually destroyed it.

efforts to raise its own entrance and graduation requirements have already been related. But it went outside its own classrooms to help raise medical standards generally. During the 1890s it took a leading part in the movement to force substandard medical schools either to improve their instruction or go out of business. This it accomplished by supporting the passage of a law in Louisiana (Act No. 49, 1894) which deprived diplomas from any medical school of their status as automatic licenses to practice. Exclusive power to admit physicians and surgeons to practice was vested in a state medical examining board. The "diploma mill" medical school, as far as Louisiana was concerned, was out of business unless its graduates possessed sufficient knowledge to pass the examinations. (Between 1897 and 1900 only six Tulane graduates failed to pass their board examinations.)

One thing, however, the medical department failed to get around to in the 1890s. It did not admit women as medical students. Although they were legally entitled to admission, Dean Chaillé and several members of his faculty were unalterably opposed to women doctors. In view of this the best the medical department could do in the way of a concession to women applicants was to admit three to the pharmacy department.

As the medical department was flourishing in its new building on Canal Street, the College of Technology (the third and youngest in the professional schools) was taking root in new soil on the recently acquired uptown campus. This College of Technology was simply another name for a school of engineering.

Actually the university had been considering a department of engineering from the time it became Tulane University. As early as 1884 random efforts were made to organize a technical curriculum, but the course offerings had few takers and most of them thus did not materialize. In the high school department, as has been related, the mechanical and manual arts program flourished, but for several years the faculty was unable to go in its thinking beyond a sort of ambivalent trade school–semiprofessional concept which was called the mechanical course. Undoubtedly the fact that the program was administered within the framework of the academic department accounted at least partly for the cavalier manner in which it was treated. But there was one man, Brown Ayres, the versatile physicist, who never rested from his efforts to create a real school of engineering. He was not, of course, alone in his efforts, but to him perhaps more than to any other man should go the credit for the establishment of an engineering department which ultimately was separated from the Academic Department. By 1888 his efforts were bearing fruit, for in that year the "mechanical course" was changed to the "engineering course," and a separate faculty listed for it. Upon examination, however, it is revealed that with one exception the faculty was composed of members of the Academic Department. The exception was one new man, William H. P. Creighton, stern and impeccably formal Navy officer who had taught at Purdue and was brought to Tulane as professor of mechanical engineering.

It was not until 1894 that the engineering department achieved a separate status for itself. In that year the academic department moved from its campus on Common Street to the present uptown location. With the move the department was divided into a College of Technology and a College of Arts and Sciences. The College of Technology thus for the first time had an identity, its own building and laboratories, its own faculty, and a program devoted exclusively to engineering. Logically Brown Ayres was named dean as well as professor of physics and electrical engineering. Associated with him was the first faculty (some old, some new), composed of John M. Ordway, professor of industrial chemistry and civil engineering; W. H. P. Creighton, identified above; John W. Caldwell, professor of chemistry and geology; William Woodward, professor of drawing and architecture; Douglas S. Anderson, assistant professor of physics and electrical engineering; William J. Cooper, assistant professor of experimental mechanics and shopwork; William P. Brown, instructor in workshop; and Tudor T. Hall, mechanician in the physics laboratory.[11]

The engineering program outlined for 1894–1895 sounds remarkably modern. It was a four-year program leading to the Bachelor of Engineering degree. A student could pursue one of four curricula: mechanical and electrical; chemical (first in the South); civil; or architecture. In 1897 a fifth curriculum, sugar chemistry, was added, but was later abandoned. Admission requirements were similar to those of the College of Arts and Sciences except for the slightly higher requirements in mathematics for prospective engineers. Graduates of approved secondary schools were admitted on certificate of graduation; all others had to take entrance examinations in English, mathematics, history, and a classical or mordern language.

Actually the College of Technology, after it was given a separate status, developed more rapidly than any other department of the university save Medicine. During the first year seventy-five undergraduate and twelve graduate students were enrolled, and within five years undergraduate enrollment had materially increased. Having taken numerous technological courses prior to the formal organization of the College of Technology, seven young men received their engineering degrees at the end of the first year. Year after year thereafter the college poured into the stream of Southern life an increasingly important ingredient of technically trained young men with a practical orientation to the South's problems.

Faculty and students alike made their contributions. Albert Baldwin

[11] The name of the "College of Technology" was changed in 1920 to the "College of Engineering." In 1953 this was changed to the "School of Engineering." The College of Technology was housed in the present Stanley Thomas Hall, originally built as a two-story structure.

Wood, who received his degree in 1899, designed the pumping system which now drains the city of New Orleans. Young Professor William B. Gregory, fresh from the Cornell University School of Engineering, cooperated closely with Chaillé, Matas, and other medical professors in improving health conditions in New Orleans. The School of Medicine educated people on the need and desirability of a safe water supply, proper drainage, and modern sanitary precautions. The faculty of the College of Technology through advice, supervision, and experimentation aided city authorities in providing the physical systems that protected public health or insured public convenience. It would be difficult to imagine a more community-oriented educational institution than the College of Technology during the nineties. The faculty served as consultants on buildings and construction. Its members encouraged a trend toward modern concepts of architecture, better foundations, and more effective use of common building materials. Their influence was felt in the selection of paving for the streets and in the design and construction of bridges. In a city rapidly sloughing off the somnolent past and looking ahead to modernity these engineers were invaluable. New-fangled electric street cars were beginning to replace the old mule cars, and the telephone was becoming an indispensable means of communication. Such progress required research and testing, and above all, it required trained technicians. It is small wonder, then, that the faculty took such pride in the engineers it turned out. They had a sense of mission and, moreover, they could see results which could be measured. This ability to see perceptible and immediate results from educational training gave engineering and medicine a great advantage over the general education program of the College of Arts and Sciences.

It is, of course, always easier to measure the tangible than the intangible; and a materialistic society is likely to place a premium on the physical rather than on the intellectual and spiritual aspects of life. The liberal arts, therefore, are at a disadvantage in such a society. This condition was clearly discernible in Tulane's College of Arts and Sciences during the 1890s. There was growth; but it was slow and at times discouraging. The important factor in the life of this college during the period, then, was not sheer growth but a preparation for future growth. This preparation was firmly infixed in the decision of the administrators to dispose of the old campus on Common Street and to move to a more commodious setting.

By 1888 it had become obvious to administrators and faculty alike that the narrowly restricted area of the old campus provided no chance for growth and expansion of the physical plant. Moreover, it was situated in the heart of the city's rapidly growing business area, a fact which year by year made it more and more unfit for educational purposes. During the years 1888–1890 there was hardly a meeting of the administrators in which the matter was not discussed. Finally in 1890 a legislative act (Act 94) was sought and obtained, authorizing the administrators to lease or sell the Common Street property provided the proceeds from such a sale should be reinvested in immovable property within the City of New Orleans to be bought and used for university purposes.

Act 94, however, was a preliminary step. Two major problems remained: selecting a site for the new campus and profitably disposing of the old buildings and grounds.

The question of the new location was the subject of numerous conferences among the administrators and between them and the faculty. Apparently it was the logical arguments of Brown Ayres which were partly or even perhaps largely responsible for the final decision. Utilizing maps upon which he plotted population trends and city growth, he convinced himself, and apparently the administrators, that the Foucher Tract across St. Charles Avenue from Audubon Park and the old Exposition grounds was the best location for the new campus. Whatever Ayers' part may have been, the facts are that on April 27, 1891, for a purchase price of $37,500, the administrators bought from the estate of Mrs. William Henry a portion of the Foucher Tract. It had a frontage of 407.8 feet on St. Charles Avenue and extended back 12,181 feet in converging lines to a point near the New Basic Canal.[12] Although it had once been a low and swampy area, the coming of the Exposition had led to a general improvement of the entire vicinity. The land had been drained by canals and when purchased by Tulane was sufficiently dry to be used for truck farming except for the wooded area adjacent to the Claiborne Canal.

The following spring (1892) Senator Gibson made what proved to be his last report to the administrators, urging certain changes in the organization of the university and insisting that more land be purchased. He dwelt upon the necessity of obtaining "ample space for all our buildings . . . for the accommodation of our faculties and students, with homes and grounds for recreation and physical training, which has become an indispensable part of education."

The administrators adopted his recommendations almost in toto. On April 10, 1893, four months after Senator Gibson's death, they effected a sweeping schedule of reorganization of Tulane College. The outstanding features of the plan were the abolition of the high school, the division of Tulane College into a College of Technology and a College of Arts and Sciences, and the purchase of more property on St. Charles Avenue.[13]

[12] In later years Ayres was quoted as expressing great disappointment and dissatisfaction over the fact that the administrators did not purchase a larger tract. He is reported to have stated that the property now occupied by Loyola University might have been bought in 1891 at a price only slightly in excess of the $37,500 paid for the portion purchased, but this hardly holds up since Loyola University bought its property in 1889, thus antedating Tulane's purchase by two years.

[13] It will be noted that the name "Tulane College" was changed to "College of Arts and Sciences." Rumors current at the time that this was done because Mr. Tulane had failed to provide for the university at his death seem to have no basis in fact.

In May of 1893 the administrators purchased for $30,000 an additional 175 feet joining the original tract. This gave Tulane a frontage of 582.8 feet on St. Charles Avenue. At the time, the board had an option on 400 feet more which would have extended the university's property through the present Audubon Place to the present Newcomb Boulevard, but the option was not exercised. Apparently the administrators felt that the 58 acres they had purchased were enough. Near the front of the tract the administrators decided to erect at a cost of approximately a quarter of a million dollars three buildings—an all-purpose administrative-classroom-library building facing St. Charles and behind it a physics and a chemistry building. Before construction was begun a fourth building to house the new College of Technology (the present Civil Engineering building) was included in the plans.

On the afternoon of January 27, 1894, the cornerstone of the Arts and Sciences building (now Gibson Hall) was laid with appropriate ceremonies. Present were the faculty, the administrators, students, alumni and townspeople, and other guests including Governor Murphy J. Foster, New Orleans' Mayor John Fitzpatrick, and A. D. Lafarge, state superintendent of education. President Johnston presided. There was an invocation by the Reverend B. M. Palmer and then the Glee Club sang. At the conclusion of their song a group of students gave a college yell, presumably to add the proper collegiate touch. A dedicatory poem was read by Professor Dillard and the main oration delivered by the Reverend Beverley Warner, rector of Trinity Church. Then Judge Charles E. Fenner declared the cornerstone well and truly laid. A band played "Hail Columbia," the collegians gave another yell, the benediction was pronounced by the Right Reverend Davis Sessums, Bishop of Louisiana, and the crowd broke up into little groups to talk about the exercises and to wonder what Tulane would do with such a big building as this one promised to be.

It was something of a gala occasion, but there must have been at least one person in the audience who reflected on what faith and imagination it took to build a university. Such reflections were scarcely unavoidable for the comtemplative man present at the exercises, for there was little save courage and vision to commend this new site. The basement was complete and the walls a few feet high here and there so that one could see pretty clearly what the size of the complete building would be; but the total picture was rather drab and unlovely. A few door and window frames had been set in place, but they only emphasized the nakedness of the whole environs. St. Charles Avenue was paved on the Audubon Park side, but the strip running in front of the new building was muddy in winter and dusty in summer. There were a few scrub water oaks on the front part of the raw campus, but they did little to relieve the severity of the scene. As one stood amidst builder's rubble, piles of lumber, and stacks of gray Bedford stone blocks and looked toward Claiborne Canal he saw little but a monotonous stretch of barren crawfishy land broken intermittently by live oak trees, a vegetable patch grown up in winter dead weeds, or occasional pools of stagnant water defying one and all to drain them.

There was, however, a distinct note of sadness for many who participated in this otherwise happy occasion. Tulane's great and good friend Randall Lee Gibson had passed away on December 15, 1892. As Judge Fenner guided the cornerstone into position, he must have felt that there were other hands than his on the trowel and that mixed in the mortar which bound together every stone in the building was the spirit of this man who had done so much for Tulane, New Orleans, and Louisiana as a whole. His educational efforts were not confined to Tulane alone. In the spring of 1886 he had worked untiringly and successfully as U.S. Senator to secure for the Louisiana State University the federal barracks in Baton Rouge and their grounds for use as the university's first real campus. Being a modest man he undoubtedly would have been embarrassed to read the encomiums heaped upon his memory. Perhaps a simple statement in one paper would have pleased him most. "He was," the statement ran, "a constructive statesman, serving his state, section and nation well."

Meantime, the administrators were making every effort to turn the old Common Street buildings and grounds into cash, but without any immediate success. On May 26, 1893, they adopted a resolution to sell the property, but it was two years before any offer was made to purchase it and this for only $125,000 on a deferred payment plan. This offer was refused; nothing less than $150,000 would be acceptable. In May 1896, a New Orleans real estate firm undertook to sell or lease the property, but it, too, was unsuccessful. The firm did report that a client had under consideration an offer of $200,000, and about the same time Dr. Edward Kells, Jr., requested a thirty-day option for purchase at a price of $150,000. The administrators took no action on either proposition, however, for a better offer was made by Thomas Nicholson, builder of the St. Charles Hotel. His offer was a 99-year lease at an annual rental of $10,000 payable in advance. This was the equivalent of a net revenue for 99 years on the basis of 4 per cent on a valuation of $260,000. Moreover, at the expiration of the period of the lease, the property would revert to the administrators. It was, they felt, a good offer, and it was accepted. Governor Foster approved, and the lease was signed on March 25, 1897. But if the administrators thought they had heard the last of this matter of a lease they were mistaken. Subsequently it rose up to plague them.

All the while, of course, classes were held on regular schedule in Tulane Hall (old Mechanics Institute building) until October 1894, and thereafter in the new building on the uptown campus. With the transfer to the new campus, James Hardy Dillard became dean of the College of Arts and Sciences. For nine years President Johnston had been his own dean, but now failing health and frequent speaking engagements away from the campus made it necessary that he shift part of his administrative load to other and stronger shoulders.

Thirty-eight-year-old Dean Dillard had been appointed to the faculty in 1891 as professor of Latin. He was an attractive man personally with his wavy red hair, neatly trimmed little beard, smooth voice, and jutting, determined jaw. Moreover, he was a scholar of catholic tastes equally at ease in mathematics, literature, and Latin. He had been a student at Washington and Lee University when President Johnston taught there, and Johnston had followed his career as a teacher ever since. In 1891, when he came to Tulane, he was principal of Mary Institute, the women's division of Washington University, St. Louis. It was at Tulane, however, that Dean Dillard achieved what his biographer has called "the fullness of his powers."[14]

The faculty over which he presided was composed largely of old-timers, several of whom had come over from the University of Louisiana when it was absorbed in 1884. Ashley D. Hurt was still professor of Greek; Robert Sharp, professor of English; J. Hanno Deiler, professor of German; Alcée Fortier, professor of French: John R. Ficklen, professor of history and political science; William B. Smith, professor of mathematics and philosophy; Brown Ayres, professor of physics and astronomy; John W. Caldwell, professor of chemistry and geology; Henry B. Orr, professor of biology; and William Woodward, professor of drawing. Younger members were Charles G. Gill, assistant professor of Greek; J. W. Pearce, assistant professor of English and mathematics; Douglas S. Anderson, assistant professor of physics; and William P. Brown, instructor in Latin and English.[15]

The curriculum of the College of Arts and Sciences is of special interest in that it reflected a compromise between two extremes of educational thought and practice current in the 1890s.

When Charley W. Eliot was inaugurated as president of Harvard University in 1869, he said in part: "The young man of nineteen or twenty ought to know what he likes best and is most fitted for. . . . When the revelation of his own peculiar taste and capacity comes to a young man, let him reverently give it welcome, thank God, and take courage. Thereafter, he knows his way to happy, enthusiastic work, and God willing, to usefulness and success."

In 1894 the catalog of Tulane University said about the College of Arts and Sciences: "Not trusting in the ability of immature students, or even of parents who have seldom duly considered the subject, the College of Arts

---

[14] Dean Dillard had long been an advocate of higher education for the Negro. In 1904 he was made president of the Jeanes Foundation and in 1910 president of the Slater Fund. In 1917 he became a member of the General Education Board and vice-president of the Phelps-Stokes Fund. It was for him that Dillard University, established in New Orleans in 1929, was named.

[15] All these were also listed on the faculty of the College of Technology.

and Sciences now offers four courses of study with *prescribed* branches, each leading to a baccalaureate degree."

The contrast between the philosophies embodied in these two statements is a striking illustration of the two theories of university education that were being widely debated and practiced in this country during the last quarter of the nineteenth century and the first decade of the twentieth. Simply stated it was a conflict between the elective system and the prescribed system. But the matter went much deeper than that, for it was a clash of social philosophies, a major difference of opinion of the kind of mind and personality that higher education was expected to produce. The fundamental issue was one of values. Each point of view, of course, had its merits. The elective system tended to give better training for specialized careers, and its rationale seemed consistent with the ideas of a secular society. It added, so the arguments ran, to the total efficiency of society by conforming to the principle of division of intellectual labor. It recognized individual differences in backgrounds, tastes, and aptitudes of students. It was democratic in the sense that it candidly accepted the decline of a gentleman's education and emphasized the need of educating people of all origins. On the other hand, it was said, the elective system threatened higher education with a loss of seriousness and spiritual tone in its entire fabric. The orthodox, prescribed, classical curriculum had been formed upon the assumption that knowledge was not a mere tool, that it was somehow a part of the innermost character of man. It gave to the educated portion of the public some common core of knowledge that made of it a community, small though it was.

Until after the turn of the century, at least, Tulane's College of Arts and Sciences had on the surface rather rigidly prescribed curricula with a stated purpose "to prepare and and discipline the students for the professions or for leadership in the manifold and ever widening spheres of active life." Beyond this it contemplated "a harmonious evolution of intellect and character" rather than efficiency or a vocational orientation. To accomplish those objectives four curricula were offered, each leading to the degree of Bachelor of Arts.

The classical curriculum. In this program Latin and Greek were offered through the four years. This afforded to the student "willing to submit to the invaluable and unsurpassed mental discipline of these studies the opportunity to obtain a solid classical education." This curriculum also provided work in English, history, mathematics, and some work in science.

The literary curriculum. This program differed from the classical in the omission of Greek and the substitution of more work in French, German, American history, and civics. In the senior year additional work in political economy could be substituted for Latin. Mathematics and English closely paralleled the classical program.

The Latin-scientific curriculum. This program provided for the study of Latin through the sophomore year, and for the same amount of French as the Literary course through the freshman and half of the sophomore year. German was the same as for the Classical course. In the junior and senior years, instead of more advanced work in the languages, courses in chemistry, physics, mathematics, and biology were required.

The scientific curriculum. This course differed from the Latin-scientific curriculum chiefly in the substitution of shopwork and drawing for Latin.

In analyzing the curricula two points are rather obvious: (1) The emphasis on scientific studies was growing, and (2) Tulane had by 1895 reached a compromise between the prescribed and the elective system earlier than many universities. In spite of the fact that the catalog proclaimed that the College of Arts and Sciences would have no part of the elective system, in actual practice the four curricula provided a way for the student to have some choice of subjects. Anticipating the modern B.A. and B.S. curricula, those during the 1890s required certain basic subjects for all— English, mathematics, a science, a foreign language, history—yet were sufficiently flexible as to allow the student some judgment of his own in filling out degree requirements.

Closely allied with the College of Arts and Sciences as far as faculty and administration were concerned was the University Department of Philosophy and Science, which functioned as the graduate school. This department was inherited from the University of Louisiana but had become a permanent feature of Tulane. Although it did award graduate degrees (the first master's degree in 1885, the first doctorate in 1887) it did not until modern times become a strong feature of Tulane. It had no separate administration, no dean, and no adequate research facilities in the university library and laboratories.[16] Graduate work was offered in Latin, Greek, English, German, romance languages, history and economics, mathematics, physics, chemistry, biology, and engineering. Requirements for graduate degrees included a thesis, but otherwise were rather flexible, provided a year above the baccalaureate level was spent in study for the M.A. degree and two years above this for the doctorate.

The university catalog of 1895–1896 carried the announcement of a new department related to both the College of Arts and Sciences and the grad-

---

[16] When the university moved to its new uptown campus the city refused to permit the Fisk Library of some 14,000 volumes to be moved. This library, founded in 1845 by a donation of Alvarez and Abijah Fisk to the city of New Orleans, was located in the Mechanics Institute building when it was acquired by Tulane. Thereafter until 1894 it was considered an integral part of the university library. The library on the uptown campus without the Fisk collection was only about 15,000 volumes including government documents. Dr. Charles G. Gill was the librarian. Miss Minnie Bell was his assistant. Laboratories, especially for physics and chemistry, were more adequate than the library.

uate school, although not actually a part of either. This was the University Department for Teachers, an interesting experiment in teacher training above the normal-school level.

Several features of the new department attracted interest. It was offered by the university as a public service without cost to the teacher. No degree was offered in the field, but teachers might earn a certificate or diploma upon the completion of a prescribed number of regular college courses. Although it was stated that eventually the university would offer courses in "the philosophy and science of education" the first few years of the program were devoted exclusively to subject matter areas in which the secondary school teacher might acquire greater proficiency. Normally about sixty teachers per year availed themselves of the opportunity for advanced study, but by and large the great mass of teachers was content with normal-school training. Eventually the time did come, however, when courses in "education" were offered in the late afternoon, evenings, and on Saturdays—a fact of great importance in later years when University College, the evening and adult education division of the university, was formed.

In the field of public service adult education the university provided two other types of programs: free lectures in its "extension" division and Professor Woodward's free drawing classes.

The word "extension" to describe a rapidly developing innovation in American education came into use in Tulane's publications in the early 1890s at about the same time that Johns Hopkins and the University of Chicago were becoming exponents of the English-born idea that the university should extend its offerings to adults who might not be able to come to the campus. But long before the idea had a name, Tulane was offering this type of work through its free lecture series. As early as 1885, rather ambitious lecture courses covering literature, geography, philosophy, applied science, and many other fields were offered to any citizen of the community who might care to join with a group for serious listening and discussion. But the most popular of Tulane's adult courses were the free drawing classes. During the nine years of its existence this feature attracted a total of 4,702 registrants from all walks of New Orleans life, an average of over 500 per year. When the change was made to the uptown campus, this program was dropped, but not without howls of indignation from certain segments of the population.

As a matter of fact, protests against Tulane came fast and furiously during the late 1890s and extended over into the new century. The university's troubles came not singly but by battalions! The administrators and the city administration of Mayor John Fitzpatrick were feuding. There were widespread protests over the university's methods of awarding scholarships. The selective system of admitting students came under attack. Tulane, they said, was a rich man's school and the poor boy stood slight chance of being admitted. Other groups protested against Tulane's tax-exempt status and passed around greatly exaggerated gossip about the amount of real estate the university was acquiring and transferring to a tax-free status. The discontinuance of the high school at the end of the 1894–1895 session brought forth a fresh series of attacks. A resolution was introduced in the state legislature which would have required the attorney-general to enter suit to annul Tulane's charter. The university encountered severe financial strains. The mayor of New Orleans formally called upon the administrators to pay city taxes on its property, and another fight threatened, only to be dropped by the city. And as if all this were not enough, a yellow fever epidemic in 1899 prevented the opening of the university until late November.

President Johnston felt that one of the chief causes of the "idle rumors" and "malignant stories" was the fact that the university under its policy of selective admission had to reject many applications; and, of those admitted, failures were numerous. "The student who does his part faithfully and receives our diploma," the President wrote, "is almost sure of immediate, honorable, and remunerative employment. . . ." But, he added, "we do not profess to take worthless, idle or untrained lads, and convert them into saints and scholars by some sort of hocus-pocus. The student must do his part. We surround him with the best moral influences, extend to him extraordinary facilities for improvement, and give him the help of an able, learned and enthusiastic faculty. The rest he must do himself. . . . It is in the interest of the public that the standards of the University be kept high in every way."

Perhaps gossip and rumor might have remained in just that category had it not been for the fact that Tulane's admission requirements, academic standards, and scholastic policies become involved in local politics of the Fitzpatrick administration.

John Fitzpatrick was mayor of New Orleans from 1892 to 1896. He was a man of humble origin, a sportsman and prize fight referee, and an official of reputed integrity, but there were those who felt that he overreached himself at times in his zeal for and attachment to the welfare of "the common man." Taking account of the current bad feeling in certain quarters against Tulane, he apparently determined to humble what some people called a proud, rich institution which catered only to sons of the better families. The focus of his attack was the university's scholarship policy. The story begins back in 1880, during the time of the University of Louisiana.

The University of Louisiana in 1880 had sought to buy the Mechanics Institute building but was deterred by a claim against the building for city taxes. To quiet the title the city remitted its claim, provided the university would bind itself to give free education to five boys of indigent parents, these to be appointed by the mayor. When Tulane absorbed the University of Louisiana the administrators, of course, acquired its obligations, including this agreement to grant five scholarships. In 1883, however, a mild dispute arose between the administrators and Mayor Behan. Did this agreement mean that five boys were to be appointed each year or that five boys were to be appointed and only the vacancies, if any, filled each year? Mayor Behan was of the opinion that five would be appointed each year, which meant that there would be in residence each year twenty scholarship students from this source alone. The administrators contended that only the vacancies should be filled and thus there would be only five scholarships students from this source in residence each year.

It was not a very heated controversy, and a compromise was worked out whereby the administrators agreed to admit ten mayoralty scholarship students each year but only the vacancies would be filled. This compromise lasted through the administrations of Mayors Guillot and Shakespeare, but when Mr. Fitzpatrick came to office he refused to honor it. When advised by the administrators that his protests should properly be referred to the courts he did precisely that, with the result that he won. The State Supreme Court held that the compromise was not binding on the mayor and that he had the right to appoint five indigent students annually. But in the hour of his triumph the mayor spotted a windmill on the horizon and launched an attack against it.

Just at the time this court decision came the university was in the process of moving to the new uptown campus. Among other changes which were announced was the discontinuance of the Tulane High School. It had served its purpose of preparing young men for college in a period when secondary schools were poor or nonexistent. Now, in the opinion of the university, it was no longer needed. But the mayor failed to understand what was being discontinued (or there was semantic confusion over the term "academic") and promptly jumped to the conclusion that the university was discontinuing *its academic department* in order to circumvent the court decision in his favor. Accordingly on May 29, 1894, Bernard J. O'Neill, editor of a small weekly newspaper in New Orleans and representative in the lower house of the state legislature, played the role of Sancho Panza to the mayor by introducing a resolution in the lower house which would require the attorney-general to enter suit for the forfeiture of Tulane's charter. But Mr. O'Neill went the Mayor one better. He charged that Tulane was discontinuing its academic department in order to avoid the contractual necessity of giving a scholarship to one student from each senatorial and representative district.

The resolution, in spite of its obvious absurdity, passed the House only to be killed in the Senate. If anyone had cared to investigate the matter he would have found the administrators at almost every one of their meetings were discussing ways and means of increasing scholarships. He would have found that for the school year 1893–1894 a total of 139 scholarships were awarded in the high school, College of Arts and Sciences, College of Technology, and graduate department with a total enrollment of 242 students. In short, approximately 57 per cent of the students were on scholarships. A year before Mr. O'Neill's bill was introduced the administrators had voluntarily added 25 scholarships in addition to those granted senators and representatives, the mayor, and to public and private high school honor students.

The affair did leave its imprint, however. For years people were repeating the old canards, and with no public relations department the university was hard put to refute them. As a matter of fact, one of the important deficiencies of the total university administration at this time was its failure in its Olympian complacency to conceptualize the need for interpreting the university to the community. The most alarming aspect of the fight, however, was the concern it caused Mrs. Newcomb. She was spending a great deal of her time in New Orleans and was well acquainted with the political attacks on Tulane; and her reaction was a perfectly normal one. She became frightened for fear the university would come under political domination. She had been assured when she made her original gift that Tulane was free from political pressures, and this assurance had weighed heavily in her decision to found Newcomb College. Now, in view of the attitude of certain political factions she wavered in indecision as to what she should do. At one point she seriously debated attempting to recover her endowment and to move the college to another state, or, failing in that to insist upon a complete divorcement of Newcomb College from Tulane University. While her fears were temporarily allayed, there were other anxious moments in the spring of 1898 while a new constitutional convention was in session at Baton Rouge. Fearing that an attempt would be made to alter the university's charter, the administrators appointed a law committee to safeguard Tulane's interests. This committee made several recommendations to the convention for strengthening the university's status. It must have come as something of a surprise to the members to find that their recommendations were adopted without much opposition. Tulane thus emerged in a much stronger legal position, but troubles with politicians were not at an end.

The canard that Tulane was a rich institution must have been a sort of grim joke to the administrators, who knew what was happening to university finances near the turn of the century. The new university had started off in excellent financial condition. Mr. Tulane's original gift had yielded an income of $38,000 per year. By 1887 his other gifts had increased this to approximately $73,000 annually. During this time expenditures were low, and thus reinvestments of income were possible. By 1886 income had climbed to about $82,000, but expenditures had likewise climbed—to approximately $68,000. By 1887 President Johnston was warning that the situation would bear watching, but the prosperous period in New Orleans from 1890 to 1893 enabled the administrators, through investments, to build the endowment back to $981,000, not far from the total amount Mr. Tulane had given. There was an illusion of well-being.

This temporary prosperity, however, did not last. Two factors destroyed it: (1) a heavy investment of endowment funds in the new uptown campus and buildings; (2) the depression which swept the country in 1893.

The new physical plant consumed fully a third of the total endowment funds of the university.[17] Had flush times remained this could have been replaced from income; but income plummeted during the depression years. In 1894 there was a deficit of $6,500; in 1895 the deficit had climbed to $11,571.59. Total income, which had stood at close to $92,000 in 1890, had fallen to $69,000 in five years.

Tuition fees of $105 a year brought in little revenue—seldom more than $7,000 a year. Even had the University been permitted to share in it, the Newcomb endowment was hardly sufficient even to support that college. The climate of local opinion was such that a local drive for funds seemed hopeless and was not resorted to. This left the administrators with the options of reducing faculty salaries and other expenses, or, in spite of the limiting clauses of Act 43, appealing to the state for money. President Johnston was unalterably opposed to the reduction of faculty salaries, and this was abandoned.[18] Overtures were made to the legislature for assistance, but feelers along this line were dismissed rather unceremoniously by that body. Thus the administrators were forced to raise tuition and to adopt a policy of rather severe retrenchment. It was a time when a matter of fifty dollars for trees and shrubs for the campus was important, a time when the administrators felt they had to turn down an offer of the new telephone company to install even one telephone. Finally the telephone company made the installation gratis.

[17] It should be borne in mind that endowments for Newcomb and Tulane were entirely separate funds, although both were administered by the administrators of the Tulane Educational Fund.

[18] There was no fixed salary schedule during the 1890s, but these salaries were actually paid and represent the nearest approach to a schedule:

President of the university	$6,000
Deans of Engineering and Arts & Sciences	$3,000–$4,000
Full professors	$2,500–$3,000
Associate professors	$2,000–$2,400
Assistant professors	$1,000–$1,500
Instructors	$ 500–$ 800

CHAPTER 6

Newcomb in the Nineties

Newcomb College, too, was faced with the problem of finances during the nineties, not because of serious deficits but because of the uncertainty of further donations from Mrs. Newcomb. The original gift for endowment purposes, it will be recalled, was $100,000. This amount, it was hoped, would be substantially increased by subsequent gifts from the donor; but as time went on she proved to be, by turns, reluctant and willing. She could be velvety, placid, and generous and then suddenly shift to an exacting and fretful attitude, especially in petty matters. Thus it soon became clear that the future of the college would depend largely upon her whims and moods, and this caused gnawing anxiety. That President Dixon realized this and was able to placate and tactfully guide her were in no small sense responsible for the success of the college during the formative years.

The original building, as has been pointed out, was a two-story brownstone house on the uptown lake corner of Howard and Camp. Subsequently a lot facing Tivoli (Lee) Circle was purchased, and the two small brick houses on it were converted for use as laboratories. A small annex adjacent to the main building was secured for the high school. There were no dormitories, but a few young women were accommodated at the Christian Women's Exchange on Lafayette Square or quartered in private homes judged to be "protective to virtue and good morals."

However, it soon became obvious that almost everything about the physical plant was unsatisfactory and inadequate. Traffic noise and dust made it unpleasant. There was no room for expansion. Above all there was little privacy for the students. Men loitered on the banquettes, watching the girls in their ankle length skirts take their genteel exercises in the yard. Even the mule cars sometimes stopped as they passed so that the male passengers could have a good look at the Newcomb girls doing their dancelike calisthenics.

Dixon had not been satisfied with the location from the first day it was occupied. For three years he, along with others, urged Mrs. Newcomb to finance a change, and finally she consented. On May 27, 1890, the administrators agreed to sell to her for $45,000 the almost palatial Burnside Place which previously had been purchased for the Tulane High School. Situated in the lovely wooded setting of the Garden District on a square bounded by Washington Avenue, Sixth, Chestnut, and Camp Streets, this basement and one-story, plastered brick "Italian villa" had long been a New Orleans show place. James Robb, who originally built the place for himself, had spent a fortune on the house, the lush gardens, and the priceless art objects. Overtaken by bankruptcy, he had been forced to give it up, and then by successive sales it had become the property of Miss Sallie B. Miles, a granddaughter of Robb's business partner. It was from her that the administrators had acquired the place.

The house and gardens were somewhat run down when Mrs. Newcomb purchased it, but she gave her check for the additional $11,000 (subsequently increased to $25,000) to place it in good condition and to add a story. Almost immediately the place was alive with painters, carpenters, and masons. In the gardens the German landscape gardener, Francis Buhler, cut out the underbrush, revived the fountain, planted new shrubs and formal flower beds, tended the grass, and brought the place back to its former beauty. Called College Hall, the Robb House became the heart of "old Newcomb" and to many of the older alumnae the only true Newcomb. And it was a spot to stir nostalgic memories. The property embraced a three-acre square in which giant live oaks spread their low branches to create the soft cool gloom which only this tree can give. Interspersed with the oaks were tall magnolias, towering camphors, laurels, and flagpole palms with their feathery tufts. One entered the house from an ample, tiled terrace broken by massive stone urns and japonicas. Inside the front a great hall ran the length of the house and opened on the formal gardens in the rear, primly neat with their geometrically designed flower beds. For the contemplative person it was a retreat; cool and verdant for this dutiful weighing of evil with good, of truth with error.

It is small wonder that faculty and students alike were anxious to move from the bare and cheerless environs of Camp and Howard. It was expected that the carpenters, masons, and decorators would finish in time for the fall 1890 session to open on the new campus. In this atmosphere of anticipation the first commencement exercises were held on the morning of June 17, 1890, in the chapel of the red building. The Reverend Benjamin Palmer, ubiquitous at Tulane ceremonies, spoke, and President Johnston awarded degrees to eight graduates and certificates to two others. These, the President said, were "the firstlings of our flock . . . rare primroses in the springtime of Newcomb's existence . . . the first flowers of its morning." All went away confident that they had seen the last of the old building. The next day carts began moving furniture and equipment, and a few days later the old building was leased as a boarding house.

As June gave way to July and July to August, however, the remodeling, especially the building of the second story, went on behind schedule. Chairs, tables, and piles of books were pushed into corners or gathered moist dust in the basement. By late August it was obvious the building would not be ready by September, and a sort of panic seized Dixon. The old building was rented, the new one was not ready. He searched the city but found no temporary facilities available, and it looked as though there would be no opening of Newcomb in the fall of 1890. But at this critical moment the vestry of Trinity Episcopal Church came forward with an offer. The vestry had decided, the spokesman informed Dixon, to offer Newcomb the use of the church's large basement Sunday school room. It was a case of any port in a storm, and the entire university was grateful. Conditions, however, were far from satisfactory, as might well be imagined. The appearance was that of a one room country schoolhouse with the confusion of many voices and many classes going on simultaneously without the benefit of partitions. Had it not been so serious, Dixon observed later, it would have been ludicrous.

In January of 1891, however, the fifteen faculty members and 174 students were able to occupy the new building, and everyone sighed with relief. While only 63 of the young women were full-time college students (the rest were high school and special students) this move seemed to presage stability and growth. "With the new location we acquired an added sense of security, a feeling of permanence, a sort of guarantee for the future success of the College," Dixon wrote. "Fresh courage and a larger ambition were the natural results."

This "larger ambition" soon manifested itself in numerous ways. So many things were needed. There were no dormitories; the curriculum had to be expanded and new faculty members added if Newcomb was to carry out its stated plans of offering young women an education on the same level and of the same type as that afforded young men at Tulane; the endowment had to be increased; the college must be made into a college and the high school reduced in importance; books and equipment were needed; a reputation had to be built. To the accomplishment of these objectives President Dixon gave the rest of his life and Mrs. Newcomb gave about $3,600,000.

In providing the money for the expansion of the college Mrs. Newcomb displayed magnificent generosity, highly seasoned with caprice and piquant uncertainty. Dixon learned well as time went on that when Mrs. Newcomb asked "what will it cost?" she meant exactly that and not approximately what the cost would be. If he miscalculated, he knew, he would receive a tongue-lashing. By leaps and bounds she assumed a proprietary interest in administrative matters and tried at times to dictate the policies of the faculty. Often she was rebuffed, but she seems never to have lost her confidence in Dixon and appeared to respect him for his courage in opposing some of her ideas.

As long as she remained in New York the problems were less acute because they were handled by mail. In 1892, however, she and her friend, F. Walter Callender, came to New Orleans.[1] Characteristically they arrived almost unheralded during Mardi Gras week when hotels were full to overflowing. University officials had known in advance that the visit was in the offing, but they had hardly expected them to come when they did. Consequently there was much scurrying around to locate accommodations, a problem which was settled by finding rooms for them in the boarding house at Camp and Howard which two years before had been the first Newcomb building. On the afternoon of February 22 Mrs. Newcomb attended a reception at Newcomb Hall and for the first time she saw the college which was her daughter's memorial. Although frail and nervous (76 years of age) she stood in the receiving line with Mrs. Ida Richardson and Mrs. William Preston Johnston to meet the students, faculty, and many townspeople. When it was over she was obviously tired but pleased.

The amenities disposed of, she, Callender, and Dixon got down to the matter of the college, its needs, and its future. As a matter of fact she brought up the matter as Dixon drove her in his carriage back to the boarding house after the reception. "What," she asked bluntly, "are your plans for the future of the H. Sophie Newcomb Memorial College?"

Dixon, a little taken aback by the suddenness of the attack, asked that he be allowed at least an overnight period to consider his answer. And in the morning he made it: The library was a great need. A high school building was imperative. The endowment must be increased.

Then came the inevitable question: "How much will the building cost?"

Dixon was not prepared to answer in such detail but he ventured to estimate. "Forty-five thousand dollars," he replied.

Mrs. Newcomb said nothing, but before she left in May to return to New York she gave $5,000 for the library, a pledge of $45,000 for the building, and another pledge of $100,000 to increase the permanent endowment.

This visit in the spring of 1892 was the first of her annual visits which lasted until 1895 when she became a permanent resident of New Orleans— that is, permanent during the winter months. From 1892 until her death on

---

[1] Callender was a native of Boston, but a resident of New York City. He was often referred to as Mrs. Newcomb's secretary, but this was not the case. Rather he was a close friend and counselor. At this time he was in his fifties, a widely traveled man of considerable culture, pleasing personality, and possessing modest wealth (at his death in 1910 he left $65,000 to Newcomb College). Just how the friendship between him and Mrs. Newcomb began is not known, but there can be no doubt that he exercised great influence on her. During the latter years of her life he was with her almost constantly and often it was difficult to tell whose purposes, hers or his, were being carried out at Newcomb College.

April 7, 1901, Newcomb College became the great passion of her life. At times she argued, had fits of pique, was imperious, exacting, and obstinate —but in the end she not only built the physical plant of a college, but left the imprint of her ideas on curricula and faculty as well.

Dixon spent a great deal of the summer of 1892 drawing plans for the new high school building. Actual construction was begun in September, and the building was complete and ready for use in October 1893. There was, thus, a pause of something like a year when activities were confined to discussion and planning; a period when the Newcomb faculty could take time to consider the curricula of the college in terms of its educational objectives.

In presenting this phase of Newcomb's development it seems desirable to refer again to the wording of the first bulletin, issued in 1887. "It is the aim of this college," the announcement stated, "to offer to the young women of Louisiana and the adjoining states a liberal education, similar to that which is now given to young men by the Tulane University, and to young women also by other institutions of the first rank in distant parts of the United States." Thus liberal education for women on a level equal to that available for men became Newcomb's avowed purpose.

Today such a statement of educational policy hardly causes the lifting of an eyebrow even by the most conservative, but in the eighties the question of what a woman ought to study was, to say the least, moot. Before 1860 the American public, by and large, had refused to pay its dollars for the thorough education of women, and this sentiment carried over strongly into the post-Civil War seventies and eighties. Socially ambitious mothers and many of the masculine lords of creation insisted that what a girl needed was education in poetry, music, art, the social graces, and homemaking; or if spinsterhood threatened, training for teaching. On this rationale was based the "seminary" for young ladies which taught, sometimes superficially, the things which it was felt would enable women to fulfill their roles as wives and mothers together with sufficient "culture" to make them guardians of the arts and of standards of taste. Whether a young woman could or should learn mathematics, science, and economics was debatable. That is, it was debatable until the founding of such colleges as Newcomb, Vassar, Wellesley, Smith, Barnard, Bryn Mawr, Radcliffe, and others in the period 1870–1890. Thereafter many people had either to revise their opinions about the education of women or to end their days with a doleful shaking of heads.

As it emerged, higher education for women took three forms: coeducation; colleges for women only; or the coordinate college such as Newcomb, Radcliffe, and Barnard. Partisans of each of these forms could advance valid and convincing arguments to support their points of view. Particularly is this true of these who supported the idea of the coordinate college which, of course, is a compromise between the other two types. All the advantages of both the coeducational and the strictly woman's colleges were claimed for coordinate colleges. Except for the almost fortuitous circumstances under which Newcomb was established, Tulane might well have become coeducational. Even before Newcomb was founded, President Johnson had been an ardent advocate of higher education for women. But he was not doctrinaire and thus was willing to embrace the idea of a coordinate college as a means by which a thorough education for women might be made possible.

In carrying out its avowed aims Newcomb offered during the nineties three curricula leading to degrees, a program of special courses for college women, and a complete high school curriculum.

Having satisfied the entrance requirements by graduation from the Newcomb high school or another accredited high school or by taking an examination, the Newcomb freshman had before her the choice of three degree programs. She might take either the classical or modern language course leading to the degree of Bachelor of Arts, or the scientific course for a Bachelor of Science degree. Her tuition charges for the year were $100 exclusive of fees for special music and art instruction. And the programs were thorough. Before the freshman could receive her degree as a senior she had to complete, regardless of the curriculum being followed, forty hours of basic work in mathematics, English, history, physics, chemistry, astronomy, geology, and psychology. If she took the classical course she virtually took a major in Latin and Greek; in the modern language course it was French and German; in the scientific course she took more mathematics and more science. There were, of course, limited electives in each course.

Among the electives, art became the most popular. Undoubtedly this popularity was due to the enthusiasm and fine teaching of the Woodward brothers, Ellsworth and William. The latter had developed an enormous interest in art, not only at Tulane but in the community and at Newcomb where he taught for a brief period. Ellsworth, however, was largely responsible for the growth of interest at Newcomb and for the national recognition which the college rapidly acquired in the field. He traveled widely in Europe and in this country, sketching, lecturing, and studying to improve his own techniques. In New Orleans his annual December shows were events keenly studied and enjoyed by citizens as well as students. He was a modest though opinionated man who managed to convey to many in his classes his own burning passion for constant study to the end that teacher and students might grow together. His life was an incessant and urgent continuum of conscious striving toward perfectibility in his own painting and toward encouraging others. The new art building constructed in 1894 was, of course, a dream come true for him and was shortly followed by the organization of a four-year curriculum in the field.

Integrated with the Art School was the Ceramics Department. The New Orleans expositions of 1885 and 1886 had demonstrated the value of pottery clays in the South and had revealed the potentials of a pottery industry. William Woodward at Tulane, while offering his free drawing courses, had at the same time started a movement to encourage young women in the community to experiment in clay modeling. The Tulane Decorative Art League which he had formed as a community project also interested itself in pottery, and when Newcomb College was founded Mr. Woodward urged President Dixon to add pottery work to the art program. From these modest beginnings there resulted a ceramics program which in a few years attracted world attention.

Dr. Dixon called from her home in Covington, Kentucky, Miss Mary Given Sheerer, formerly associated with the Rockwood Pottery in Cincinnati to head the program. Soon she, Ellsworth Woodward, and Joseph Fortune Meyer, a local potter, were experimenting with new clays, glazes, and colors. Their most spectacular results were obtained from a combination of St. Tammany Parish clay with loam filtered from the muddy waters of the Mississippi River. They gave to their product a new glaze and new tints, characteristics which were first given recognition at the Paris Exposition of 1900. In this year a few odd pieces had been sent to the show in Paris without much expectation that they would be honored, but to the amazement and gratification of everyone the small exhibit received the bronze medal. "Newcomb pottery" was thereafter a well-known name among collectors and connoisseurs.

The college also was interesting itself in the field of physical education for women, a subject of considerable controversy among the general public all over the country during the nineties. "There is a growing recognition in this as well as in foreign countries," the college catalog stated, "of the need of combining physical training with mental work. Only where these are properly united can the best educational results be secured." . . . . "On this account physical training has been added to the work required of all students, except such as are excused by written request of parent or guardian."

To develop the program, President Dixon brought Miss Clara Baer from the Possa Normal School of Gymnastics, a school which specialized in the Swedish method of gymnastics. But gymnastics in shirt waists and long flowing skirts was, to say the least, rather cumbersome. It was not until 1894 that the way was paved for a more diversified physical education program. In that year Newcomb girls made the daring and almost spectacular transition from long skirts to bloomers. The change, of course, was hedged about with restrictions. Bloomers could be worn only in the gymnasium. Black cotton stockings were a necessary part of the decor and they could not be rolled so that any portion of the leg was exposed. And the bloomers had to be baggy and long enough to reach downward almost to the ankles. But even with those precautions the girls were sometimes embarrassed in their new freedom. On one occasion when President Dixon was escorting a group of visitors over the campus the group entered the gymnasium occupied by a class of bloomer-clad girls. When they spotted the visitors every girl promptly fell to her knees, sat back on the calves of her legs, and with downcast eyes awaited with becoming modesty the departure of the intruders.

The vigorous and well-muscled Miss Baer developed a rather flourishing program for its day. A watered-down version of men's basketball called "basquette" was invented and soon spread to other colleges for women. A normal-school program of training physical education teachers was instituted. But over the years Newcomb came to put less and less emphasis on high seriousness in bloomers (except for recreational sports) and more on art, music, and the liberal arts. Music was a casual and almost sometime thing during the early years of the college, but, as will be related later, it eventually came to be a vital part of the college's educational plan to place emphasis on the liberal arts.

From the very beginning it was the liberal arts faculty which set the tone of the college; and throughout the nineties it grew in quantity and to a degree in quality.

When the college opened in 1887 it had eight faculty members. Before the year was over it had fourteen. By 1891, eighteen persons were listed for staff and faculty combined. By 1900 the increase was to thirty.

This doubling of the faculty and staff within a period of less than fifteen years is, of course, indicative of progress. But there are negative factors which somewhat becloud the picture. These were: inadequate formal preparation of many of the faculty; a large faculty turnover; and the slow growth of the collegiate student body.

During the first year of 1887–1888, exactly half the faculty held no degrees of any sort. For the session 1893–1894, there were only six persons out of a faculty of nineteen with any sort of degree. As late as 1900 only 47 per cent of the faculty held degrees. Dixon had, however, added one Ph.D. in 1893 (Frederick Wespy, professor of Greek and German); and another, Mary Leal Harkness, professor of Latin, had earned her doctorate by 1900. To a marked degree the college was depending upon young instructors without degrees for much of its teaching. This situation was rather rapidly improved after 1900, but during the nineties it was a distinct impediment to academic progress.

It seems certain that the presence on the faculty of a large number of relatively untrained instructors contributed to the rather heavy faculty turnover. Dixon undoubtedly spent many a restless night cudgeling his brain for ways and means of stabilizing his faculty, but still they came and went. It seems likely, too, that Newcomb's low salary scale was a direct factor in this flux. Full professors at Newcomb, for example, were paid only approximately two-thirds the salary earned by full professors in the College of Arts and Sciences. Other ranks were scaled down accordingly, which meant that not a few instructors earned no more than $50 a month.

There were, of course, those who were outstanding on the faculty because of tenure, characteristics, or scholarly contributions. In addition to Ellsworth Woodward in painting, Clara Baer in physical education, and Mary Given Sheerer in ceramics one could hardly overlook the services of Mrs. Evelyn Walton Ordway, professor of chemistry and physics, and one of the few women of her day who could be classified unmistakably as a scientist; or mild and gentle Swiss born Florian Cajori, alumnus of Wisconsin and Johns Hopkins, who married a faculty colleague, Miss L. G. Edwards, an instructor in Latin, and moved on to the University of California where he became a renowned figure in the field of pure mathematics; or John M. Ordway, professor of biology; or the greatly respected Emma Rossner, principal of the high school; or of Alice Bowman, first "lady-in-charge" of the first dormitory.

These and others like them were laying academic foundations upon which the future of the college depended. In passing, however, one must single out one early faculty member for special comment. She was Mrs. Jennie C. Nixon, professor of English and rhetoric, and the first member of the faculty appointed in the new college. In many ways she exemplified the emancipated and educated woman Newcomb hoped to develop. In 1870 she had been left a widow with two children. At a time when a widow was expected to wear her weeds and sit demurely watching the passing parade she struck out on her own to support herself and her children. Obtaining a position as society editor of the *Times-Democrat* she used her spare time to read and study to the end that she might become a liberally educated woman. Abandoning the role of newspaper editor she took up that of teacher in the public schools. In addition to her teaching she spent a great deal of time in community service. During the Cotton Centennial Exposition she was a commissioner for the state of Louisiana in charge of women's work. At Newcomb she was noted for her hustle and mild eccentricities. Few students who took English under her ever forgot the vibrant woman who popped into class with her hat askew, bubbling with enthusiasm for her subject, her community service, and for the role of the educated woman in contemporary society.

The problem of the almost imperceptible growth of the collegiate student body sorely troubled Dixon and some of his faculty. Between 1887 and 1900 the total enrollment climbed from 150 to 304, but during this same period the number of full-time collegiate students increased only from 59 to 66 with one year (1892–1893) in between when the enrollment reached 70. High school diplomas and special certificates were awarded in abundance, but in the ten-year period from 1890 until 1900 an average of only 12 students per year received degrees.

The reasons for this state of affairs are obvious. Few young women in New Orleans who were not graduates of the Newcomb High School could meet the college's entrance requirements. Few girls from distant parts were enrolling, either because Newcomb was new and not widely known or because of the nationwide belief that New Orleans was a very unhealthful city, expecially because of yellow fever.[2] There is also the fact that the departments of art and physical education almost overshadowed the liberal arts, and special students flocked to courses in these fields. Indeed they were encouraged to do so. They were rewarded by certificates, and many went out to become teachers of these subjects.

But Mrs. Newcomb was not among those who were troubled over the shortage of college students. She saw the total enrollment climbing, and that was enough for her. Thus she busied herself with building and helping run the college, or, more accurately stated, she and Callender busied themselves with building and helping run the college. Between 1892 and 1895 she made annual visits to the college, checking on its progress and providing the money for buildings and endowment. As has been pointed out, in 1892, upon the occasion of her first visit she gave money for the library and a $100,000 gift for the endowment, and provided for the new high school building. In 1893 she bought two residential properties near the campus because she considered the owners objectionable. At the same time she laid before Dixon her plans to build a chapel, a project close to her heart. Dixon protested that a dormitory and an art building were more vitally needed.

"How much would all three cost?" she threw at him.

And this time he was ready. "One hundred and twenty-five thousand dollars," he replied.

The next day she wrote a check for this amount, and within a few weeks the foundations were laid for the chapel, the art building, and for the dormitory, which was named "Josephine Louise House." The buildings were completed by the fall of 1894.

During 1894 Mrs. Newcomb watched the progress of the buildings but gave no additional funds except $2,500 for an iron fence and a sidewalk around the campus. But Dixon had underestimated the cost. The fence was put up, but the money ran out before the walk could be finished. Rather than bring down on himself Mrs. Newcomb's well-known ire, the job was

---

[2] There was hardly a Newcomb catalog issued during these years which did not carry a statement about New Orleans' favorable climate and the fact that "medical records disclose the fact that the health of New Orleans is not surpassed by any other large city in the United States; it has had but two epidemics of yellow fever in the past thirty-five years."

left incomplete. So far the records show it was never finished. Perhaps Dixon purposely left the uncomplete walk as a reminder of the donor's exactitude.

In 1895, after the completion of Josephine Louise House, Mrs. Newcomb made Room Number 1 her New Orleans home during her ever-lengthening visits. During these visits the girls were warned time and time again to be quiet, but they could never be quiet enough so that she could enjoy her customary hours of sleep. Finally tiring of dormitory life, she purchased in 1897 a house at 1225 Fourth Street and became a New Orleanian again after a half century of living in the East.[3] There were trips back to the North during the summer months, but she now considered New Orleans her home.

It was only a few blocks from her home to the college, and almost daily she was on the campus checking on something. The chapel particularly was an object of her affection, for it seemed to symbolize her almost religious veneration of her dead daughter. She ordered from Tiffany's three large stained glass windows picturing the Resurrection, and one could hardly fail to note that one of the angel figures bore a strong resemblance to Harriott Sophie Newcomb. The specially built organ she had bought for Newcomb Hall was moved into the new chapel, and a bronze memorial tablet to Harriott, bearing an inscription composed by President Dixon, was installed. Truly the chapel was her shrine.

Both she and Callender came more and more to think of Newcomb in a possessive manner. They delighted in buying furnishings, statuary, paintings, and equipment as though the college were their personal estate. In 1897 Callender donated white marble busts of the Newcomb family—Mrs. Newcomb, Warren, and Harriott Sophie. In 1896 Mrs. Newcomb built a pottery and an arcade connecting the high school building with College Hall. Three years later another dormitory, "The Gables," was acquired. The physical plant was growing, and so was Mrs. Newcomb's petulance. From time to time she and Callender attempted to advise Dixon on faculty appointments and other administrative matters. Upon one occasion she sulked for weeks in her house because she was sure one of the students had set the fire which broke out in the attic of Josephine Louise House. She revived her visits only when it was discovered that the fire was set by a rocket carelessly fired during a parade.

Her moods, however, came to have more important dimensions, and for a period of time it seemed that the college's very existence hung in the balance.

It seems impossible today to ferret out all the reasons for her discontent. It is much better to say that between 1894 and 1900 the relations between

---

[3] This fact had enormous significance later when her will was contested by relatives.

her and the administrators became at times strained and unhappy. There are, however, certain reasons which the evidence shows rather clearly: (1) She was disturbed over the political attacks on Tulane and the attempt made by politicians to take away the charter. At the same time she was alarmed over the attempts of the president and the administrators to secure state financial aid by *having Tulane declared a state institution.* One of the assurances given her when she founded the college was that Tulane was free from political control. In view of the developments she was not now at all sure this was true. (2) Knowing of the financial plight of the university during the 1890s she feared, despite assurances given her to the contrary by a resolution of the administrators in 1887, that attempts would be made to divert Newcomb funds to the general use of the university. (3) In 1900 the administrators turned down her demand that Newcomb funds be turned over to her broker for investment. (4) In the same year the administrators refused her demand that Dixon be made president of the university, succeeding William Preston Johnston who had recently died.

Apparently urged on by Callender she made a series of moves calculated to ease her fears. With the insight of an accountant she regularly examined Newcomb's ledgers. By 1899 she was convinced that the endowment fund must be increased, but instead of turning over additional funds to the administrators she called in Dixon and advised him that she proposed to set up a secret $300,000 fund in a New York bank for which he would act as sole trustee. When Dixon explained to her what an awkward position this placed him in vis-à-vis the administrators she relented to the extent of permitting him to name two co-trustees, Joseph C. Morris, president of the Canal Bank and a member of the board, and Joseph A. Hincks, secretary and treasurer of the board. These three men, Dixon, Morris, and Hincks, thus became privy to one of the strangest financial arrangements in American educational history.

At about the same time these arrangements were being made, Mrs. Newcomb discussed with Dixon and Callender the desirability of demanding that the administrators turn over to her all of the college's endowment funds entrusted to them. Apparently Dixon was able to stall her off until 1900, but in this year the fight came out into the open. Through her attorney she made a formal demand that the endowment funds be returned to her. With equal legal formality the board declined on the grounds that the money had passed into the realm of a public trust. Angered by this and by the board's failure to appoint Dixon to the presidency, she apparently determined to begin building a new college in Thomasville, Georgia. According to Dixon's own account she said in substance, "Very well then. You have the $300,000 I gave you. We will let the Tulane administrators keep what I have given, and you and I will build a new institution at Thomasville. There we will be appreciated."

At the time Mrs. Newcomb was at her summer home in Richfield

Springs, New York, and Dixon was her guest. His account of the affair relates that he dissuaded her from going through with the schism, but that about two months after his return from New York he received a deed of transfer of her entire estate made to him personally, she reserving only enough income to support herself. This Dixon refused to accept. But by now the little old lady in black was too old and too ill to keep a fight going. She had planned to return to her New Orleans home in the fall (1900) and, indeed, did start the journey, but by the time she had reached New York City she was too ill to travel further. Through the winter she grew weaker and finally, on April 7, 1901, she died at the home of her old friend Mrs. John Chamberlain at 587 West 145 Street.

Dixon had gone back to New York as soon as it was determined that her illness was serious. Undoubtedly he felt a strong personal obligation to the lonely old woman, but there was another reason why his presence might be necessary. In 1898 Mrs. Newcomb had made a will leaving her estate to Newcomb College and naming Dixon and Hincks as co-executors. In view of the fact that Mrs. Newcomb's collateral relatives had let it be known before her last illness that they proposed to enter suit to break the will if she left her money to Newcomb College, Dixon had other than sentimental reasons for being at her side.

He arrived a few days before her death, and, seeing her condition, advised Morris and Hincks, co-trustees with him of the fund which she had refused to entrust to the administrators, that the money ought to be turned over to the board immediately. A hasty meeting of the admininstrators held in New Orleans officially transferred the amount to them. In his telegram to Hincks about this matter, Dixon also urged that as co-executor with him of Mrs. Newcomb's will he ought to come to New York. Hincks went, but he arrived the day after her death. Her will was probated in New Orleans that same day, and by court order the two men were officially made executors. Immediately after the funeral they conferred with Mrs. Newcomb's New York business agents, Pomeroy Brothers, as to what they could best do to protect the estate's securities against attachment in case of a suit. They were advised to remove the securities from the jurisdiction of the New York courts. Accordingly, Hincks, Dixon, and A. J. Pomeroy packed into suitcases over $2 million in securities and slipped across the Hudson into New Jersey. Not feeling completely safe there, they proceeded to Philadelphia, where the securities were placed in a bank vault.

On July 1, 1901, the expected suit to break the will was filed in Surrogate's Court in New York on behalf of William H. Henderson, son of Mrs. Newcomb's sister in whose New Orleans home the young Josephine Louise Le Monnier had lived as an orphan before she married Warren Newcomb. Although Mrs. Newcomb had given $150,000 to her sister's family in 1871 this had not improved strained relations between her and them. Now, during the trial which lasted off and on for eight years, all the family skeletons were dragged out and put on parade, in testimony and briefs which were printed and made up to twelve fat volumes. All Mrs. Newcomb's eccentricities were portrayed as the actions of a woman of unsound mind. In addition, it was contended, undue pressure had been brought on her by Dixon, Callender, and others. And added to this was the contention that the will was illegal because Mrs. Newcomb was not legally a resident of New Orleans.

The charge of mental aberration hardly stands up, however, for she had foreseen all the charges and had taken steps to protect herself. She had in 1897, a year before the will was made, had herself officially declared a resident of New Orleans. She had surrounded herself with the best legal aid procurable (James McConnell was her New Orleans attorney), and her will was a model of simplicity. After a few personal bequests she simply left the residue of her estate to the administrators of the Tulane Educational Fund for the use of Newcomb College. She had quarreled with the administrators from time to time, but her love for the institution she had founded and her determination that the Hendersons were to have none of her money gave her no choice except the one she made.

And the will stood up. In 1909 the Supreme Court of New York upheld the decision of the lower court that the will was valid, and thus the entire estate in the amount of $2,668,307 went to Newcomb College. This brought the total she had invested in the college to $3,626,551.

But there were at Newcomb by the turn of the century other developments besides those concerned with buildings, endowments, faculty, curricula, and Mrs. Newcomb. It was certainly true that much physical growth had been made—seven buildings, a growing faculty, a modestly adequate library and laboratories, a nest egg endowment fund—but over and above these physical aspects there was developing an intangible thing of the spirit, a feeling for Newcomb on the part of the students and faculty. It is a difficult thing to describe or define, for it was not one thing but an aggregate of many intangibles; but one has only to talk with an alumna of old Newcomb to realize it existed, and that it grew with the new campus. Perhaps the quiet beauty of the campus had something to do with it. Certainly people living, working, and playing together tend to develop common interests and loyalties. But this feeling for Newcomb appears to have transcended these and to have been composed of an almost mystical sense of mission or destiny, coupled with a feeling of fierce pride in the pioneering achievements of the college. But it did not extend to the university as a whole, for Newcomb was both physically and spiritually separated from Tulane University. Newcomb was a college within the framework of the university, but that was all. Neither faculty nor students felt themselves to be a part of the whole. They were Newcomb people.

CHAPTER 7

Into a New Century (1900-1904)

THE TURN OF THE century was important in Tulane's history not merely because an old century passed and a new one dawned, but because in close proximity to 1900 death intervened to make changes. Paul Tulane and Randall Lee Gibson had been the first of Tulane's founders to go. Now, on July 16, 1899, William Preston Johnston died in Lexington, Kentucky. In 1900 a new president came to Tulane, the second in its history as the Tulane University of Louisiana.

For two or three years before his death the condition of President Johnston's chronically poor health had perceptibly worsened. At the university's commencement exercises in June 1899, it was obvious that he presided with the greatest difficulty; in fact, many of his friends had wondered for several years how he carried on his duties at all. But he refused to give up, insisting that a trip North to visit his daughters would help relieve the racking paroxysms of coughing and the choking asthmatic wheezing which he had endured since his Civil War years when he suffered almost simultaneous attacks of pneumonia and typhoid fever. But the trip failed to help him. After a few days' visit to one daughter in Pennsylvania he went on to Lexington, Kentucky, to the home of another, Mrs. Henry St. George Tucker. Here he died in the bed in which he had been born sixty-eight years earlier.

Mrs. Newcomb's legacy had been a large sum of money. Johnston was a poor man, but he, too, left a legacy—a record of dedicated and almost always wise leadership in the early days when the university was young and unknown. He was a scholar, and the emphasis of his years was on scholarship, at times to the neglect of other important aspects of university life. He was austere, and sometimes unable to forget his rank of colonel. Consequently, discipline at Tulane was often severe to match the bare classrooms and the equally barren grounds. But to him a university was a place for a young man to get an education, not to enjoy leisure. He might have forgotten at times to take into consideration the effect of the university's policies on the popular mind, but he never overlooked the importance of the relationship between student and professor.

Interestingly enough the new president of Tulane University attended the last commencement exercises over which Johnston presided in May 1899, received from the ailing president the degree of Doctor of Laws, and addressed the graduates of the medical school. Although young Edwin Anderson Alderman, president of the University of North Carolina, had, at the time, no idea he would be offered the presidency of Tulane (and neither did the administrators, for that matter) he made such a favorable impression that the administrators after Johnston's death made no further serious search. Almost by unanimous consent they concentrated on Alderman, and the following April he accepted.[1]

The impression which Alderman made on the board apparently was due largely to his powerful and persuasive oratory, his genial manner, his dignity, and his impeccable correctness in clothes. Moreover, they were impressed by his zeal for the uplift of the South through education and for his Jeffersonian concept of the relation of education to democracy. Perhaps what the administrators saw most clearly was that here was a man likely to be skilled in dealing with the public, in the ability to meet people and win friends for the university—in short, a counterbalance for the austerity of the Johnston regime during which public relations at times were strained.

There were members of the faculty who thought (and said so openly) that this handsome, swarthy man with the solid appearance of a Roman senator was a demagogue, and perhaps there was something of this in him; but he came to Tulane with a record of solid achievement behind him. A native of North Carolina, he had taken his bachelor's degree from the state university in 1882 in the firm conviction that he ought to be a teacher. Shortly thereafter he began work with the then nascent State Department of Education. For six years he and the renowned Charles D. McIver traveled throughout the rural sections of the state, holding teachers' institutes and exhorting the rural people to take a greater interest in public education. In 1889 he was made assistant state superintendent of education, a post he held until 1892. He was then called to Chapel Hill as professor of pedagogy, and on August 1, 1896, at the age of thirty-five, became president of his Alma Mater.

He had achieved a statewide reputation in North Carolina as a powerful and convincing speaker, but there was more to the man than oratory. He courageously advocated equal educational opportunities for Negroes. He worked unceasingly to bring about a close articulation of the secondary schools with the colleges through the use of the Carnegie unit as a measure of high school achievement. Above all he worked with J. L. M. Curry, A.

---

[1] William O. Rogers, secretary (registrar) of the university, served as acting president until Alderman took over. Alderman was a bachelor at the time of his acceptance. Shortly afterward, however, he married Bessie Green Hearn of New Orleans.

S. Frissell, Charles W. Dabney, and the New York financier, Robert Curtis Ogden, to interest Northern philanthropists in the educational needs of the South, a venture which caused him to play a prominent part in the Southern Conference for Education and in the Southern Education Board, both agencies which did important work in correlating and coordinating the activities of several educational foundations in their relations with Southern institutions.

What the full impact of Alderman's leadership on Tulane's future would have been is conjectural, for he held the presidency only four years. There is a basis for believing, however, that quite possibly he was what the university needed at that particular time. He was a prototype of what many modern university presidents, either by choice or expediency, are: propagandists for education rather than scholars; public relations men who can build enrollment and placate the alumni personalities calculated to impress the world of business and thus to attract money. These qualities Alderman possessed to a remarkable degree. Had there been a Rotary Club in New Orleans at that time the chances are that he would have been president of it and would have preached to his fellow members the gospel of higher education at Tulane and the businessman's stake in it. And this would not have been hypocrisy, for he believed in the university. To Walter Hines Page he wrote: "Tulane is a strategic point here. It alone stands for higher training in this region." In a similar vein he wrote the president of his own administrators: "Tulane is destined to be the source of educational power in the Southwestern portion of our nation."

His work begun (October 1900), he turned his attention to matters which he felt contributed to building a new spirit at Tulane.[2] He interested himself in student and alumni activities; he injected a note of academic formality into university exercises; he established Founder's Day in order that the memory of Paul Tulane could be perpetuated; he proposed a program of major expansion in building and other facilities and worked untiringly with business groups to raise money to supplement the university's inadequate income; he attempted administrative reorganization. His was no mean program.

To the students his encouragement of campus activities and school spirit was welcome, and they responded with applause to his Wednesday assembly speeches on school spirit and athletics. Athletics properly safeguarded, he believed, would "subserve the strength of mind and body." "I should rather see a boy of mine on the rush line fighting for his team, than on the sideline smoking a cigarette," he stated. College was to a great extent, he thought, "a joining of fellowship among the students." But this fellowship should have its dignified aspect, he felt, and thus he instituted the practice of wearing caps and gowns at formal university occasions. To this, too, the

[2] His formal inauguration did not take place until March, 1901.

students responded. In fact it appears he was by far the most popular figure on the campus. "The creations of his progressive spirit are everywhere around us," the *Tulane University Magazine* editorialized, "binding us into closer bonds of college fellowship. . . . In our studies, in our pleasures, in our athletics, he is with us heart and soul. We feel him, we are attracted by his personality as iron filings to a magnet."

Even the Board of Visitors felt compelled to praise his work.[3] "Many factors," it reported, "have united in bringing new life into, and brighter hopes for, the future of Tulane, but chief among them, and the inspiration of many of them, we cannot fail to note is the tact, the ability, the eloquence, and the buoyant ardor of the President."

To the business interests of New Orleans he preached a gospel of industrial development and profits. Experience was teaching him daily that the future of the university depended upon the growth of wealth in the community. Thus he admonished the business leaders: "There is but little money made in producing raw material. Let this city be what it is destined to become, one of the world's greatest manufacturing cities, and then it will shelter within its walls millions of the most intelligent, industrious and prosperous people on the globe."

But in this same speech there was an observation which undoubtedly caused some puzzlement among conservative businessmen. Profits were legitimate and necessary for business, he said; but not so for a university. "A university that spends less than its income is as remiss in its duty as a bank is that spends more, for there is a polar difference between working for dividends of gold and dividends to society." He hastily threw up an oratorical smoke screen under cover of which he escaped to another topic, but he had given expression to a truth which has been hard for many people to grasp. Why is it, some ask, that higher education requires more and more money as the years come and go? Why can these universitites not live within their incomes? These questions Dr. Alderman answered over a half century ago: As the needs of society for educated men and women become greater the university which curtails its services or fails to improve its services is cheating its students, its faculty, and above all the society it serves.

This problem of university income in relation to university services was with Alderman a condition and not a theory. He had inherited a pattern of budgetary deficits extending back into the late 1880s. As the administrators had expanded library facilities, laboratory equipment, buildings, and other educational accouterment they had been forced to dig into capital

---

[3] The Board of Visitors referred to here had little resemblance to the existing Board of Visitors. In 1901 the administrators created a Board of Visitors composed of three administrators and two alumni to "visit and examine the affairs of the institution and report their conclusions to the Board."

endowment funds or income. Unless these funds were replaced income would be progressively reduced. And this replacement was difficult. Student fees could be counted on for an almost negligible portion of the total budget. The New Orleans community simply did not have the wealth which would provide anything like adequate relief. State aid was not forthcoming. Year after year budget deficits were from $6,500 to $16,000 in spite of stringent economies.

In the face of this, however, Alderman recommended an expansion program, but the administrators did not go along very far in his direction. Apparently Alderman felt he could raise substantial sums in the city and, although he deprecated what he called "begging," he went to the businessmen of New Orleans for relief. During this first year they gave $15,000. The next year he could obtain but $7,000.[4] When at the end of the year 1903 a deficit of $14,000 loomed, he approached the foundations for money. The General Education Board gave $2,000, and 210 citizens of New Orleans gave $13,263. Alderman was meeting deficits but little more. Like the Red Queen in *Through the Looking Glass* he was running very hard to stay where he was. But his plans contemplated much more than this stationary running. He called for an increase of $50,000 per year from permanent endowment, construction of a combined auditorium and gymnasium to cost $125,000, establishment of schools of education and commerce, and $20,000 for books, equipment, and campus beautification. "It [the university] cannot stand still and mark time," he almost shouted from the roof tops. "It is like a wave. If it does not advance, it breaks."

But the administrators did not concur in Alderman's plan, a fact which probably influenced him in his decision to leave when an attractive offer came from the University of Virginia. But the administrators did carry out a plan of expansion. In fact there was a spate of buying, selling, and building. In 1901 the first dormitory, a three-story brick building (now the home of the School of Social Work) was built. In this same year the refectory (now the biophysics laboratory) was authorized. At approximately the same time a new library building was under construction as the result of gifts in 1900 and in 1906 totaling $77,500 by Mrs. Frederick W. Tilton who wished to perpetuate the memory of her deceased husband, a wealthy and cultured New Orleans iron merchant. This building today is occupied by the School of Law which in it found a permanent home at last.

On the Newcomb Campus the new pottery building was erected in 1901–1902, and a year later three nearby residences were acquired for dormitory purposes. In addition, Newcomb was considering moving its entire campus further uptown. In 1904 Dixon was authorized to negotiate

[4] Two citizen groups were formed to raise money: The Citizens Endowment Fund and the Citizens Auxiliary Association.

an option on thirty acres of land on the west side of Napoleon Avenue immediately south of Broad Street. In 1905 the property was purchased for $100,000—but Newcomb did not move. Later the property was sold at an excellent profit.

The administrators were following a plan of investing in New Orleans real estate, a plan which through the years has yielded an excellent return in university income. In 1904 they purchased a large portion of the square bounded by Canal, South Claiborne, Cleveland, and South Derbigny Streets. In 1903 the Mechanics Institute building (Tulane Hall) was sold for $75,000 to Theodore Grunewald, who wanted the property for his expanding hotel. On the campus, too, improvements were being made. Low spots were filled in, a few trees and flowers were planted, walks were constructed, and the semicircular drive in front of Gibson Hall was laid out. And not to be overlooked was the installation of seventeen telephones, one at the medical school and the others at Newcomb and on main campus.

Late in 1903, Tulane and the Jesuits, who had purchased the strip of land next door and upon which Loyola University would be built in 1912, agreed to donate connecting strips of land for a road to reach from St. Charles to Claiborne. The road was never built, but when the Jesuits offered for sale that part of their holdings extending from Freret Street to Claiborne Avenue, Tulane purchased it.[5] It was a strip of approximately 367 feet frontage on Freret. The purchase price was $150,000. Perhaps this sale evened the score on regrets. In 1893 Tulane could have purchased a great deal more land fronting on St. Charles. But the administrators felt they had bought enough. They had not, and thus their regret within a few years. The Jesuits now sold a considerable portion of the land they had acquired, and this, in the years ahead, they came to regret.

Undoubtedly the most spectacular single incident in the Alderman period was the legacy of $750,000 left to the administrators for the use of the medical department in the will of Alexander Charles Hutchinson, a man, like Paul Tulane, born in the East but who had, like Tulane, made his fortune in New Orleans. Hutchinson, a native of Brooklyn, had moved to New Orleans while still a young man and had in his more mature years become a successful railroad and steamship executive. After the death of his wife in 1895 his own health began to fail, and in 1897 he sought the professional services of Dr. Rudolph Matas.

Acting on Matas' advice he began to consider philanthropy as a satisfying way of disposing of his modest fortune. His first gift, and the only significant one before his death, was $50,000 in 1897 for a nurses' home and training school at Charity Hospital. Shortly before his death in 1902 he made his will. When it was read after the funeral it was disclosed that he

---

[5] The final consummation of the purchase was delayed until November 1908. It was thought that this tract would be ideal for the new Newcomb campus.

had, after a few minor bequests to relatives and friends, left the greater part of his estate to educational and charitable institutions. The Eye, Ear, Nose, and Throat Hospital received $20,000; a like amount went to St. Anna's Asylum, an Episcopal home for aged women, and to the House of Good Shepherd, a Roman Catholic house for wayward girls. The remainder of his estate, amounting to approximately $750,000, was left to Tulane "for the sole and exclusive benefit of its Medical Department." He set forth as his objectives the improvement and greater effectiveness of the medical school and the maintenance of clinics and laboratories to serve the poor.

As in the case of Mrs. Newcomb's bequest, considerable litigation followed. Mr. and Mrs. Hutchinson had no direct heirs, but in late 1902 Andrew J. Thomas, a brother of Mrs. Hutchinson, and other collateral relatives filed suit to set aside the will. It was a rather complicated case involving alleged irregularities in the succession of Mrs. Hutchinson which, it was contended, made it unlawful for him to dispose of the estate. The case was first heard in Civil District Court in New Orleans which found for the executors and thus for the university. The case was appealed, and on December 14, 1903, Judge Fenner reported with great satisfaction to the administrators that the Louisiana Supreme Court had upheld the decision of the lower court. In 1903 another suit was filed, this one by Mr. Hutchinson's brother, Edward. The contention in this case was that Tulane University did not have the corporate right by virtue of its charter to receive property on behalf of the medical school. In April 1904 this case went against the plaintiff, and Tulane was assured of full control of the money coming from the bequest. Twenty-five years later, however, when it had been determined that the Hutchinson bequest would be used largely to construct a new medical building on Tulane Avenue, Margaret Hutchinson, a sister, and other relatives brought another suit on the grounds that the university had failed to use the money in the manner specified in the will; that is, for free clinics and hospitalization for the poor. Again the Civil District Court found for the university, and again there was an appeal in which the State Supreme Court upheld the decision of the lower court, the ruling coming in 1930 just at the time the new Hutchinson Memorial building was being dedicated.

For the first time in its history the medical department had sufficient funds to use for expansion. It had received small summer shower gifts before, and one not so small in the case of Mrs. Hutchinson, but never such a thirst-slaking downpour as this one. Almost immediately after court decisions had made the money available, the faculty and dean began to busy themselves with new plans and new ideas for "the improvement and greater effectiveness" of their department. The aging but still vigorous Dean Chaillé could now pursue more vigorously than ever his threefold program of raising standards, of emphasis upon preventive medicine, and of insisting more and more upon a program of basic science as a foundation for medicine.

Freed from the necessity of depending wholly on student tuition fees for its income the medical department was able to raise its entrance requirements, lengthen its terms, require higher standards of achievement, and raise the standards for graduation. High school graduation or entrance examinations were required of all entering students. The passing grade was raised from 65 to 70. The school year was lengthened from 24 to 28 weeks with only four holidays. Regulations were tightened to prevent cheating. But enrollment did not decline as expected in the face of stiffer requirements. Three hundred and eighty-five students registered in 1902, and 445 in 1904.

Although prospective medical students were urged to study physics, chemistry, anatomy, and physiology during their high school days, few did so. Often the entering freshmen were deficient in English and mathematics as well. The result was serious attrition. But one fact stands out about the medical department: It had by 1904 become a truly regional institution. In that year every state in the Deep South was represented by at least one student. In addition, three students were from foreign countries, and three were from north of the Mason Dixon line.

Faculty changes, too, were in the offing as younger men were brought in and departments were enlarged. Seven professors were the foundation stones upon which the medical department of Tulane University was built when the transition from the University of Louisiana was made. These were, in the order of their appointment, Drs. T. G. Richardson, Samuel M. Bemiss, Stanford E. Chaillé, Joseph Jones, Samuel Logan, Ernest S. Lewis, and John B. Elliott. Now in 1904, some twenty years later, only three of these, Drs. Chaillé, Lewis, and Elliott, were still alive and active, and they were not far away from retirement. An intermediate group of teachers had come on the scene, each filling his place in the program—Matas in surgery, Metz in chemistry, Louis Favrot Reynaud in the clinic, and Edmond Souchon, the inimitable Souchon, professor of anatomy, who amused his students with his free and uninhibited speech. As founder of the anatomical museum he relentlessly pursued his goal of finding a preservative in which specimens would not fade. If he could not find enough specimens from a human cadaver he would use substitutes. Many a medical student received a mild shock to discover intermittently along the long lines of large glass jars an occasional one in which a thick steak was suspended in the preservative. But the steak always retained the natural color of muscle. He had found the chemical which would not only preserve the specimen from decay but also make natural color permanent.

But the burden of the new emphasis in medical education was now falling on younger men either newly appointed or serving in a minor capacity and meriting ultimate promotion. In this latter group were men such as Isadore Dyer, promoted in 1904 to the newly created rank of associate professor of diseases of the skin, a man who in 1908 would become dean of the medical faculty. John B. Elliott, Jr., was likewise promoted to associate professor in his field of clinical medicine. Erasmus D. Fenner, son of Judge Charles E. Fenner, became associate professor of the diseases of children, although it is William W. Butterworth, lecturer and clinical instructor in the practice of medicine, who is usually referred to as the founder of the department of pediatrics. John T. Halsey, one of the great teachers in the modern history of the medical school and the man who made a science of pharmacology, succeeded Dr. Reynaud. At about the same time P. E. Archinard, who had done so much to build the microscopical laboratory, was promoted to associate professor of diseases of the nervous system. And among the younger members of the faculty were those who in their time would also make their contributions. Hamilton Polk Jones, son of Dr. Joseph Jones and grandson of Bishop-General Leonidas Polk, had been named an assistant demonstrator in the clinical laboratory in 1896, the very year of his father's death. Later Charles L. Eshleman and Samuel Logan began their careers as assistant demonstrators, the former in physical diagnosis and the latter in operative surgery. In this same year of 1904, George S. Brown, a Tulane alumnus, was appointed lecturer and demonstrator in the pharmaceutical laboratory. Before his career was finished he would become known as the man who put pharmacy on its feet.[6]

However, the Hutchinson legacy had one unforeseen result. It was responsible for the medical department being deprived of a part of its autonomy, for late in 1904 the administrators required its budget to be submitted to them for approval. This, of course, was, to use a gross understatement, very unpopular with the medical faculty.

Since the time of its founding the dean and faculty had run their own organization. The dean had collected the fees, and he and the faculty had decided how the few dollars would be spent. Now that there were more dollars to be spent, the faculty squirmed and protested the decision—but it was stuck. The first step in a more centralized system of fiscal administration had been made in 1893 when the Law Department began to receive an annual subsidy of $5,000 from the administrators. The Newcomb endowment, of course, had from the beginning been under their control. By 1910 the law school's budget had come completely under the supervision of the administrators. This may be said to be the year when a system of budgetary control closely resembling that of today came into being, where strict ac-

---

[6] The department of pharmacy was continuing on a rather uncertain basis. In 1904 there were only 12 students enrolled in the program.

count is kept of the income of each endowed school or college but all income is managed by the administrators.

Elsewhere in the university:

The College of Arts and Sciences and the College of Technology underwent considerable transformation during the Alderman period. As a matter of fact they were, at least on paper, transformed out of their identity, for one of the first administrative changes made by Alderman was to consolidate the two colleges and to abolish the deanships of both. There resulted a case of button, button, who's got the button? In 1899 Brown Ayres bore the official title of "Dean and Professor of Physics and Electrical Engineering" in the College of Technology. In the same year James Hardy Dillard was "Professor of Latin and Dean of the College of Arts and Sciences." The next year Ayres appears as "Vice-Chairman of the Faculty and Professor of Physics and Astronomy" in the College of Arts and Sciences and as "Vice-Chairman of the Faculty and Professor of Physics and Electrical Engineering" in the College of Technology. Dillard is now listed merely as "Professor of Latin." That was it. Alderman had become his own dean as had William Preston Johnston in the early days. The next year, however, Ayres was again listed as a dean, but this time of both colleges. The next year (1903) Ayres had both titles, "Vice-Chairman of the Faculty" and "Dean of the Academic Colleges and Professor of Physics and Astronomy." Dillard was still Professor of Latin. Actually it was an intolerable situation against which Ayres protested heatedly and Dillard maintained a smoldering silence—but the plan was carried out to its conclusion in 1911.[7] To Alderman's credit, however, must be recorded the fact that he advocated the establishment of a university council to supervise the academic affairs of the university. This, of course, was the forerunner of the present University Senate, and although the first meeting of the council was not held until February 1906, it may well be said that the idea was Alderman's.[8]

But this does not end the story of administrative change. In the early summer of 1904 Alderman left to accept the presidency of the University of Virginia, whereupon Ayres was made acting president of Tulane. He held this position for a month and then, in what appears to have been a state approaching dudgeon, resigned to accept the presidency of the University of Tennessee. Then everything fell upon Dillard. He became for a brief period acting president, dean of the College of Arts and Sciences, dean of the College of Technology, acting dean of the graduate school, and

---

[7] The two colleges were separated again in 1911, with Professor William H. Creighton as dean of the College of Technology and Professor Walter Miller as dean of the College of Arts and Sciences.

[8] It was not until 1915 that the powers of the University Council were outlined by the administrators. In May 1940, the present University Senate replaced the University Council.

in charge of teacher training. But he left in 1908 to become president of the Jeanes Fund.[9] Thus it would appear that Dr. Alderman's attempt to secure administrative efficiency through centralization had, charitably expressed, made slight progress.

There were, however, achievements in the two colleges despite administrative distractions.

Although the enrollment was small (95 students in 1901, 86 in 1902, 97 in 1903, 75 in 1904), what before President Alderman's administrative reform was called the College of Arts and Sciences did not experience complete stagnation. Actually three rather important innovations made their appearance: (1) Curriculum revision broke the hammerlock of the prescribed course of study and made provision for a rather generous system of electives in the degree program; (2) a new department of economics and sociology was set up in 1901, and Morton A. Aldrich, assistant professor of economics at Stanford University was appointed to head it; (c) a new chair of pedagogy was established.

The revised curricula did not provide for a system of completely free electives. Rather it required the student to select his electives from specified groups. The first two years of all curricula (the Latin-scientific program was eliminated, leaving the classical, literary, and scientific) were carefully prescribed. In the junior and senior years, however, the student could elect all his courses provided he followed the pattern of limited electives laid down for him. What the new plan really said was that the classical or literary student must elect some courses in mathematics and science and the scientific student must elect some courses in the social studies and humanities. As at the present time, 60 year hours (or 120 semester hours) were required for graduation.

Along with this modest liberalization of the liberal arts program came the appearance of two new names in departments. Professor Aldrich was named professor of economics and sociology. Economics had first come into the curriculum in 1893 in connection with history, but sociology was new. It is difficult to find how much sociology in the modern sense was in any of Professor Aldrich's courses, for he was an economist and the founder of the College of Business Administration. Nevertheless, inclusion of the term in his title did indicate a recognition of the expanding field of the social studies.[10]

To fill the new chair of pedagogy and philosophy Alderman selected Ernest Edward Scheib, a native of Baltimore with his doctorate from the

---

[9] After his resignation he was elected a member of the Board of Administrators. Thus he served the university in every possible capacity except that of porter, and there are those who say he did at times sweep out his office.

[10] History and political science made up a combined department from the beginning of the university.

University of Leipzig. He was considered a very capable man in the philosophy of education, and but for his untimely death in March 1903, the University Department for Teachers, established in 1897, undoubtedly would have developed more rapidly. Alderman and Scheib were planning in 1903 the establishment of a summer school for teachers, but this was delayed. Actually, with the establishment of this chair, supported by a president brought up in the teacher-training tradition, it appeared that Tulane was ready to bring together all its miscellaneous courses for teachers into a unified and purposeful program—but the death of Professor Scheib and the resignation of Alderman postponed further action until a later date.

In Newcomb, the degrees of Bachelor of Science and Bachelor of Arts were given until 1903. After that date, for a period of time, only the Bachelor of Arts was awarded. Here, too, there was a system of electives, one actually more liberal than that in the College of Arts and Sciences. Following two years of prescribed study the Newcomb student was permitted to take 24 out of her last 30 hours in free electives. The special and normal art classes were still a thriving part of the college's work, but physical education was receiving less emphasis than in previous years. Miss Baer was still on the faculty in 1904, but it is quite clear that the emphasis at Newcomb was rapidly being focused on basic liberal studies and on art. A mere glance at the faculty roster in 1904 demonstrates this. Whereas a few years earlier fully half the faculty had no degrees, recruitment of new faculty members rapidly changed this. By 1904 all the new faculty members had degrees; most of them had graduate degrees including a liberal sprinkling of Ph.D.'s. The faculty, too, had become more stable. Men like James Adair Lyon in physics, Pierce Butler in history, and women such as Mary Leal Harkness in Latin, Imogen Stone in English, and Ann Hero in chemistry meant stability and a high type of teaching.

Perhaps Newcomb's record in supplying the graduate school with students is an indication of what was going on at the undergraduate level. In 1900, in a far-from-flourishing graduate department, there was 33 students. Twenty-two of these were from Newcomb and 3 from Tulane. In 1901, Newcomb was represented by 17 out of 35, with 4 from Tulane. In 1902 it was 14 out of 39, with 5 from Tulane. In 1903 exactly half the 36 graduate students were from Newcomb, with only 2 from Tulane. It appeared that without Newcomb there would not have been much of a graduate school, a fact apparently recognized by the administrators in 1901, when they required a payment of $100 from Newcomb for each graduate student and in addition, in 1902, a payment of $2,500 per year to the support of the graduate program and $2,000 per year to apply toward the salary of the president of the university. Dixon protested, and his protests were seconded by much headshaking and tongue-clicking among Newcomb faculty members and alumnae. Some of them pointed out quite openly that Mrs. Newcomb's fears that the administrators would, if given an opportunity, divert Newcomb money to Tulane now were being realized.[11] "Tulane only married Newcomb for her money," the more cynical whispered from ear to ear. Regardless of the legality of the matter it is not difficult to imagine that this incident widened the spiritual gap already existing between the two parts of the same university.

In 1904 the medical department led in enrollment with 433. Newcomb was second with 184. Third was 152 students in the College of Technology. Although it was administratively bracketed with the College of Arts and Science, its offerings in the annual catalog were listed separately, as was its faculty, with the exception of the dean. Actually Brown Ayres was dean until 1904 regardless of his different title. Titles might change but in actuality Ayres and Dillard never really thought of themselves as anything but what they were before the paper consolidation took place.

During the early years of the twentieth century the College of Technology did not blossom effulgently, but it did show distinct signs that it might do so at a later time. With a full-time professional faculty of six, together with seven from the College of Arts and Sciences who taught mathematics and other basic subjects, four degree programs were offered—mechanical (including electrical), chemical, sugar, and civil. Admission requirements for that day were high with the result that a considerable number of probationary or special students were admitted.[12] High admission requirements plus the rigorous curriculum meant few graduates (seldom more than 11) each year, but Ayres, Creighton, Gregory, and others responsible for the teaching had the satisfaction of seeing the graduates make an almost 100 per cent record of success in their profession.

The law department greeted the new century with characteristic composure and lack of feverish ambition to build an empire for itself within the university. Undoubtedly part of the somewhat lackadaisical attitude was due to the fact that the law department had no permanent home for itself. Its four part-time professors presided over by a part-time dean, Harry Hinckley Hall, had to find new quarters again in 1903. It will be recalled that when the old campus was disposed of, the law department moved into nearby Tulane Hall. This building was sold in 1903, however, so Law found refuge in the new Richardson medical building on Canal Street, a domicile it knew was temporary; but where next? There seems little doubt but that its trauma was due largely to insecurity.

Law's student body remained small (57 in 1903), its entrance require-

---

[11] Newcomb's endowment was at this time considerably larger than the general university endowment.

[12] One student admitted in this category was James M. Robert who later became dean of the College of Engineering.

ments were the lowest of any department in the university, and its requirements for graduation were likewise low. The faculty did try to bring about
some tighter academic standards in 1901 by voting to require written
examinations of all students. It even went so far as to appoint quiz masters
to grade papers, but the students protested so vigorously against the new
procedure that the faculty reversed itself in 1903 and went back to the
practice of giving oral examinations.

The saving quality in the situation was that the dean and faculty were
quite aware of the need for higher standards and were willing to work
toward that end. However, they knew that merely raising the standards at
Tulane was not the whole answer to the problem. In January 1902, a
committee composed of three administrators, three law professors, and
President Alderman was appointed to consider the matter of legal education at Tulane. But over and above this was the fact that graduation from
law school carried with it automatic license to practice. Dean Hall and his
associates knew quite well that, as had previously been the case with
medicine, many poorly prepared graduates were thus being licensed. Hall's
remedy for law was the same as Chaillé's for medicine—a state examining
and licensing body. But in the law school this did not come about until
years after Hall had retired as dean.

CHAPTER 8

Expansion and Conflict (1905-1912)

PRESIDENT ALDERMAN RESIGNED ON July 7, 1904, and shortly thereafter moved to Charlottesville. But none of Tulane's problems traveled with him. They remained behind, squatting and grimacing like gargoyles on the eaves of Gibson Hall. Financial insecurity, poor administrative organization, faculty discontent, intercollege jealousies, inadequate libraries and equipment, a weak graduate school, insufficient physical plant—these were some of the monsters with which a new president would have to contend.

Of immediate concern, of course, when Alderman's resignation was accepted, was the matter of his successor.[1] The administrators passed over both Ayres and Dillard, either of whom would have made a president highly acceptable to the faculty, in favor of an outsider. Numerous names were discussed by the special committee in the course of its deliberations. These included Chancellor Fulton of the University of Mississippi; Dr. Jesse, president of the University of Missouri and former Tulane dean: and Dr. W. M. Dudley, professor of chemistry and dean of the Medical School at Vanderbilt University. However, Edwin Boone Craighead was the choice after the matter had narrowed down to him and Dudley. The recommendation was made, the committee stated, in full recognition that "the

[1] There were numerous changes in the composition of the Board of Administrators between 1899 and 1904. The members who had selected Alderman were: President, Charles Erasmus Fenner, lawyer; James McConnell, lawyer; Robert Miller Walmsley, banker; Edgar H. Farrar, lawyer; Rev. Benjamin M. Palmer, Presbyterian minister; Walter R. Stauffer, merchant; Joseph C. Morris, banker; George Q. Whitney, banker; John B. Levert, merchant; Ashton Phelps, newspaper publisher; Charles Janvier, insurance executive; Walker B. Spencer, lawyer; Rev. Beverly Warner, rector of Trinity Church; Walter F. Denegre, lawyer; Governor Murphy J. Foster, ex-officio; Mayor Walter C. Flower, ex-officio; State Superintendent of Education Joseph V. Calhoun. (Flower was an active as well as ex-officio member.) Flower died October 11, 1900, and Eustis on December 2 of that year. Dr. Palmer died May 22, 1902, and Joseph C. Morris on June 3, 1902. In 1904 Dr. Warner resigned because of leaving the city, but resumed his duties upon his return in 1905. George Q. Whitney resigned in 1903. To fill vacancies the following were elected: John Dymond, Jr., 1901; Judge Daniel C. Scarborough, 1903; John W. Castles, 1903; Gustaf R. Westfeldt, 1903; Ernest B. Kruttschnitt, 1904; Charles Rosen, 1904. Rosen, an alumnus, was only twenty-six years of age at the time, the youngest administrator ever elected.

choice was a lottery." On September 26, 1904, after a visit to the campus, Craighead accepted the position at a salary of $6,000 per year, the same as Alderman's.

At the time of his election the new president was 43 years of age with a wife and three children. He was a man well above average height with dark hair combed over his temples, a perpetual stray lock drooping down toward bushy eyebrows which shaded deceptively mild eyes like an awning. His field of scholarship was Greek, but he was hardly the timid, wizened, tweedy caricature of such a professor. Rather he was vigorous, forthright, and often blunt and tactless in his compulsion to get a job done. The impression he made on the selection committee, headed by Dr. Warner, was that he was "a man of great power" and "a cultivated scholar, of great executive ability, a fine speaker."

His undergraduate work was at Central College, Missouri, with graduate work in Greek at Vanderbilt followed by two years' study at the universities of Leipzig and Paris. Upon his return from the latter institution, he became professor of Greek at Wofford College, and then in 1893 became the first president of Clemson Agricultural College. Four years later he went to Central College, his Alma Mater, as president. From this position he transferred to Warrensburg, Missouri, in 1901, as president of the State Normal School.

Perhaps the unfortunate aspects of his personality were responsible for the fact that his tenure at each place was of relatively short duration. The qualities of truculence and impatience came out most obviously when he was drinking; not that he was a chronic alcoholic, for the evidence is against that. Rather he appears to have been a man who should have practiced total abstinence, for apparently he did not "hold" his drinks well, even in moderate quantities. Alcohol always seemed to bring out the worst in him, and on occasions his conduct appears to have been rather undignified. Apparently it was this condition, greatly magnified in the course of faculty quarrels, which has left with posterity the erroneous legend that he was under the influence of alcohol most of the time. In a city where drinking was hardly frowned upon, his sin seems to have been a positive genius for drinking at the wrong time.

His formal inaugural was a brilliant social and academic affair heightened by the fact that it was the first event of a two-day Founder's Day celebration. In ceremonies that took place at the Tulane Theatre on March 16, 1905, honorary degrees were conferred upon Dr. Warner and upon Brown Ayres, then in his first year as president of the University of Tennessee. Then came Craighead's inaugural speech. Contemporary accounts indicate it was more aggressive than rhetorical and characterize it as "hard-hitting and bold." The new president had come to Tulane with his fighting clothes on.

"Shall the President spend his time tramping the streets of New Orleans begging the mere maintenance of an all-important state institution?" he demanded. And then he answered his own question. "No," he thundered, "Tulane is a public institution, entitled to state aid." And what was more, he proposed to see to it that this was recognized by the state legislature. "The State herself [must] add the strength of her own strong arm to the noble efforts of undividuals."

There were suggestions of other reforms he wished to see brought about, but state aid was the primary objective. This was the subject William Preston Johnston had timorously presented to the legislature and on which he had been rebuffed. Alderman had contemplated such a move, but never got around to it. Now Craighead decided to force the issue, and in the words of a contemporary "provoked the damndest dog fight over education Louisiana had ever seen." "The Battle of the Colleges" it was called. Hardly had he become accustomed to his office in Gibson Hall before he and Judge Fenner were in the midst of the fight. And it was a bare knuckle, knock down and drag out fight with eye gouging in the clinches and no holds barred. Leading the Tulane forces were Craighead, Judge Fenner, and Edgar H. Farrar. The Louisiana State University group was under the direction of Colonel Thomas Duckett Boyd, president of that school. The battleground was the chamber of the state legislature. The time: spring and early summer, 1906.

The position of the two opposing groups was fundamentally rather simple. Tulane maintained it was a state institution, Act 43 of 1884 to the contrary notwithstanding. Colonel Boyd, fearful of inroads upon state funds which might otherwise go to his institution, bitterly denounced the idea and fought it with every resource at his disposal. Both sides brought an array of brilliant legal talent into the battle to argue fine points of law before the confused legislators.

As pointed out by President Boyd early in the struggle, it was up to Tulane to prove its claims upon the state treasury to be justified. This Craighead, Judge Fenner, and Farrar attempted to do. It is not possible here to relate all the legal arguments, but two quotations from a pamphlet distributed widely throughout the state of Louisiana by Tulane indicate the major hypothesis. "No one can read the Constitution of the State, the Legislative Acts and the judicial decisions bearing on the subject," the pamphlet reads, "without perceiving that the Tulane University of Louisiana is nothing more nor less than the University of Louisiana established by the State in 1847, continued under a slight change of name and under control of Administrators appointed in a different way from that formerly pursued, but deriving their authority directly from the State." Furthermore:

. . . it enjoys the use of valuable property of the State, dedicated to it by the State; that all property, the revenues of which are devoted to the support of the University, is declared to be exempt from taxation on the express ground that all such property is dedicated "to the service of the State in maintaining and developing the University of Louisiana, an institution, recognized in the Constitution, etc."; that it is under the obligation of giving free tuition to a large number of students selected by the State through its Legislative representatives; and finally, that it is expressly recognized in the existing Constitution of the State, as a constituent part of its Public Educational system.

The administrators did not claim, however, that there was a constitutional mandate compelling the legislature to make appropriations to Tulane. "We prefer," they wrote, "that any appropriation which the Legislature may now, or at any future time, see fit to make in aid of the University, should rest, not upon any mere forced performance of a constitutional obligation, but upon a free determination by the legislative department, in the exercise of its discretion, that such appropriations are proper and requisite in the highest interest of the people of the State."

President Boyd, recognizing the possible threat to the state university's appropriations, was alert, with his legal counsel, to make his position clear and to make known to one and all that he was willing to fight to the bitter end to see it triumphant. His was a direct denial and refutation of all Tulane claims. Tulane, he maintained, was a private institution, and this was recognized in Act 43 of 1884 when the administrators of the Tulane Educational Fund agreed to relinquish all claims upon the state for appropriations. Moreover, he said, the state really had no control over Tulane. Would the people of Louisiana allow an institution that they could not control to destroy one that belonged to them and that they could control? he demanded. There was no need for two state universities, he insisted. One or the other would die, for there were not enough white young men in the state to support both. Furthermore, Tulane's status should be a matter of judicial rather than legislative determination.

Both sides recognized, however, that the issue would not be decided on legal technicalities but upon the emotional reactions of the legislators and upon the amount of pressure put on them by their constituents. Consequently both Craighead and Boyd resorted to a widespread campaign of propaganda designed to arouse the people. The presidents of the two alumni associations worked diligently to make clear what they considered the issues at stake and to stir up sentiment on behalf of their respective universities. Craighead sent out a form letter to the women of the state urging them to bring pressure on the legislature because of the advantages which would accrue to the young women of the state through Newcomb College if the state aid were granted. A group of ten women in New Orleans (including Mrs. Tilton, Mrs. Richardson, and Miss Sophie B. Wright) issued a similar appeal.

In the midst of the jockeying, Governor Newton C. Blanchard took a stand in favor of Tulane's position, and this was soon followed by a favorable report from the appropriations committee, carrying an item of $25,000 for Tulane. That is, presumably it was so designed, but a hitch occurred. While the bill was under consideration by the committee both sides were working feverishly. "Tension between the warring camps was so strong that violence was talked of if not actually contemplated for practice," the New Orleans *Times-Democrat* reported. When the committee's report reached the House floor in printed form on June 16, someone had inserted with a pencil a provision which obviously was not a part of the original. This surreptitious insertion (the blame for it was never determined, or at least the guilty person's name was never made public) made the stipulation that the $25,000 appropriation would be conditioned upon Tulane's giving free tuition to all Louisiana students in its academic departments, including Newcomb.

Instantly the House was in an uproar with denials, charges, and counter charges flying thick and fast. As a result the whole matter was recommitted and, as the *Times-Democrat* phrased it, "the war of the colleges was begun anew." The legislature was again "deluged with telegrams, telephone messages, personal calls, threats and everything else supposed to have weight with a susceptible politician." But the second report of the committee contained no mention of an appropriation for Tulane. The Tulane forces, therefore, had only one other way open to them. They could try to get the committee report amended from the floor. This they tried, but in the midst of the move Judge T. J. Kernan, a representative of East Baton Rouge Parish, dropped a bomb into the Tulane camp in the form of a telegram from Supreme Court Justice Edward Douglass White, former Tulane administrator. In response to a telegram sent him by Judge John Randolph Thornton, a legal counselor for the L.S.U. group, Mr. Justice White expressed his opinion very clearly and forcibly to the effect that Tulane was a private institution and should neither ask for nor receive financial assistance from the state on the basis that it was a state institution.

Shortly after the message was read an overwhelming negative vote killed Tulane's chances in the lower house. An effort was made to obtain favorable Senate action, but this, too, failed. The president and administrators of the Tulane University of Louisiana would have to look elsewhere for money.

While this fight was roaring toward a climax in Baton Rouge, the university was plunged into another unfortunate and unhappy situation. This was the affair of Judge Fenner who resigned as president of the administrators in August 1906 in order to relieve the administration of possible embarrassment over charges by his political enemies that he was guilty of malfeasance in office. In order to understand the uncomfortable position in which the president of the administrators found himself, it is necessary to refer again to the lease of the old campus in downtown New Orleans.

It will be recalled that it was only under the greatest of difficulties that the property was finally leased to Thomas Nicholson for $10,000 per year for 99 years. At a special meeting of the administrators called on December 18, 1896, to approve the lease, Judge Fenner advised his fellow administrators that his son, Charles Payne Fenner, and his law partner and relative, Sam Henderson, Jr., were interested parties, and for this reason he felt he should withdraw from the meeting. He was persuaded to stay, however, while the lease was approved by his colleagues, who felt they were making an advantageous deal for the university. The lease was approved by Governor Murphy J. Foster on March 25, 1897. Immediately thereafter Nicholson formed a corporation known as the Tulane Improvement Company, and the lease was transferred to this corporation whose stockholders were Nicholson, Henderson, Charles Payne Fenner, John S. Rainey, and C. M. Seria.

The last few years of the nineteenth century were barren ones for business. The effects of the panic of 1893 still hovered over the nation, and the Tulane Improvement Company found the going to be very heavy. It was paying $10,000 a year to Tulane, but was unable to sublease to any business on any terms. The stockholders sought to bring in new capital, but failed. The company was threatened with bankruptcy.

In this extremity, Henderson and Charles Payne Fenner appealed to Judge Fenner to save them. This he did by using his wife's funds to buy stock in the company. At the same time Mrs. Fenner purchased one-third of Nicholson's stock. When Rainey and Seria got nervous about their holdings they were purchased by Walter C. Flower, another administrator (and mayor of New Orleans). Then when the rejuvenated Tulane Improvement Company issued bonds they were purchased by Flower and Judge Fenner. Thus, there developed a situation pregnant with ugly possibilities. The president of the administrators, his son, his wife, his law partner, and a fellow administrator controlled a company which in turn owned a lease on university property.

Apparently no one who really understood how these things had come about had any question of Judge Fenner's integrity, but, in view of what developed, there were those who came to question his good judgment. And the worst did happen. The Tulane Improvement Company negotiated, what rumor said was a profitable lease, with the Klaw and Erlanger Theater interests for a portion of the property.[2] Then a torrent of vilifications generated by his political enemies descended upon the judge's head, an attack he felt did much to defeat Tulane's case in the legislature. On every side, according to certain opposition newspapers, there were angry mutterings that the judge was profiting from his position in an immoral and illegal manner, and his political enemies made capital of the rumors; charges of

---

[2] Actually the lease brought the company only $6,000 a year, but the stockholders hoped to erect business houses on the rest of the property and thus realize a profit.

nepotism were also brought up when it was pointed out that Charles Payne Fenner had been retained by the administrators as legal counsel in the Hutchinson cases and that Erasmus Darwin Fenner, another son, was a member of the faculty of the medical department.

The administrators' defense of their president was swift and vigorous. First, they made their own investigation and having found him guiltless they then employed an investigating committee composed of three impartial lawyers from out of the state. These men after a thorough investigation concurred in the administrators' findings, but this apparently was more than the New Orleans *Daily-States* could stomach. "Whitewash," it cried. "The Administrators have set up their own court to try their own wrongdoings." "The trouble with Judge Fenner and his board," the paper editorialized, "is that they live and move in an artificial atmosphere created by their own absurd assumption that men of their kind can do no wrong; that the code of morals was made for men of meaner clay, and that their exalted reputations give them license to fracture the Ten Commandments, or any other of the canons defining the obligations imposed by good morals."

This, in turn, was a little more than the administrators could tolerate, so they slapped a libel suit on the *Daily-States,* asking for $10,000 in punitive damages. The lower court found for the defendant, but in the State Supreme Court this finding was reversed, and the administrators were awarded damages in the amount of $50. In awarding this small sum of money the court stated that what the administrators were seeking was vindication and not money. In this the court was eminently correct (although the $10,000 probably would have been welcome), and the administrators would undoubtedly have let the matter drop with their victory had it not been for another suit. In 1909 the legislature, by resolution, instructed the attorney general to enter suit to annul the lease on grounds of fraud, but on January 17, 1910, the Supreme Court again reversed a decision of the lower court and held that there had been neither fraud nor bad faith in the lease and that it should stand as written.

Meantime, Judge Fenner had done what he could to relieve the university of any further embarrassment. He resigned in August, and in October he, Mrs. Fenner, and Charles Payne offered to sell to the administrators, at cost, their holdings in the Tulane Improvement Company. This offer the administrators accepted, paying $22,603 for the stock; and thus the matter was closed except for a few diehards who kept muttering in their beards.[3]

The fight in the legislature and the Fenner case, while distracting, had

---

[3] In 1920 the administrators bought the Henderson and Flower interests, and in 1936 the Klaw-Erlanger sublease. Inadvertently they thus cleared the way for a lease in 1949 to the company which built the Roosevelt Hotel annex and the Shell Oil building.

not prevented President Craighead from hammering away at his program for the university. His first point, financial aid from the state, no longer had any meaning; but administrative reform and the raising of academic standards could be pursued.

Administrative reform in the form of more centralization of authority in the hands of the president and the administrators, it must be understood, was not unilateral with Craighead, for the administrators strongly favored his plans, even, in several instances, initiating some of them. There seemed to be a feeling that the university had developed to a point where it was unwise and inefficient for each college to go its own way without due regard for the effects of the separate policies and actions on the entire university. But academic tradition is strong, and some of the colleges, notably Medicine, Law, and Newcomb, were not easily convinced that centralization of authority was best for them. Each faculty felt an almost fierce pride in its own achievements and was extremely reluctant to surrender what it considered its traditional autonomy. Anyone who tampered with this feeling was in for trouble, as the president was soon to discover.

Craighead's first step in attempting to secure greater unity was to implement the University Council which had been authorized during his predecessor's short tenure in office. By bringing together representatives of the various faculties for the consideration of university-wide problems it was hoped that nothing resembling coercion would ever be necessary. But results from this plan were, to say the least, not encouraging. The council's powers were not clearly outlined by the administrators for several years, and an examination of the minutes of the body clearly reveal that the most fundamental problems of the university were not being resolved, or even discussed by it. The council did discuss such matters as a uniform diploma for all colleges, the holding of one commencement for the awarding of all degrees, whether or not caps and gowns should be worn, (this, the minutes state, was discussed in a jocular vein), and whether or not Founder's Day should be a holiday. (Dean Chaillé was opposed to the holiday because he said it only afforded his medical students an opportunity to visit Storyville, New Orleans' notorious red light district.)

For a period the council met frequently, and then gradually it almost fell into desuetude, months intervening at times between meetings. Its minutes when read today reveal as nothing else does the extent to which the faculties were devoted to their own colleges and to their own colleges alone. Perhaps Craighead should have learned from the council that the matter of unification was one which would require great patience and tact on his part if strife was to be avoided. But it was difficult for him to spar successfully. He ordinarily came out of his corner slugging. However, the administrators themselves showed little more patience with what they considered the picayunish foibles of faculty members. Perhaps before the issue had run its course, all—faculty, board, and president—had learned something.

Hardly had the medical faculty finished giving vent to its feelings over having its financial affairs controlled by the administrators when another ruling came from the board. In December 1907, the president of the university was made responsible to the board rather than to the faculties, and all matters of communication with the board had to be transmitted through the president. When the professors and deans showed little inclination to accept this, the board strongly reiterated its stand to the extent of rapping President Dixon over the knuckles by returning a letter to him with instructions to submit it through the president. Dixon fumed, but he submitted the letter through channels. Hardly had this new rule gone into effect when the board again intervened in what the faculties considered their personal liberty. In February 1908, permission for outside employment for faculty members was made subject to board approval. Perhaps the Board of Visitors, however, stirred up the loudest protest. This group made periodic inspections of the university, talking to deans, professors, even alumni. Its reports to the board were confidential and thus incurred suspicion and distrust from already disturbed faculty members. The Board of Visitors was, in the minds of many teachers, downright inquisitorial and was thus a threat to their freedom and security. And the best target for their attack was Craighead, whether he was responsible or not. One hardly wonders that he took refuge now and then in the bottle. Rightly or wrongly, he was charged with the activation of new and unpopular policies; and every time new charges were brought, faculty morale declined. There were those who disliked Craighead as a person, and who were convinced that his social life was not in keeping with the dignity of his position. Others blamed him for the loss of autonomy suffered by their departments. Another group accused him of trying to eliminate their jobs. Rumors, charges, countercharges, and factional strife reached proportions indicating a breakdown in executive authority and control.

Vignettes of the bad feeling might be sketched almost to infinity, but a few, some trivial, some serious, will show to what lengths the bad feelings had gone.

In 1910, Professor Douglas Anderson of Technology and the president were exchanging angry notes. Anderson was defending the engineering faculty against the implications that it was philistine and uncultured. Rumor had it that the president had said that the engineers were opposed to literary societies.

In the same year the president directed Professor Walter Miller, dean of the academic colleges, to petition the administrators on behalf of the Graduate School for a grant of $20,000 a year to be drawn from Newcomb funds. Dixon knew nothing of this at first, and when he found out about it he well nigh had apoplexy, and the administrators felt constrained to pass another resolution declaring the Newcomb money inviolate. But this did not pacify irate Newcomb faculty members and alumnae. They could, they felt, protect the Newcomb endowment from pilferage only by being constantly vigilant and well armed. A few months later Professor Pierce Butler of the Newcomb English department (formerly professor of history) defied the recently established protocol and wrote a wrathful letter directly to the administrators, fiercely protesting Craighead's appeal to the faculties for donations to the gymnasium fund.

Butler's letter was tabled, but two months later came one they could not ignore. This one was from Dean Miller and was considered of sufficient importance that he was permitted personally to appear before the board and read it. It was a candid letter that minced no words. He stated there was among the faculties neither peace nor confidence in the future; that the unpublished confidential reports of the Board of Visitors had disrupted faculty morale, and that the conditions necessary for sound, creative scholarship were not present. No one, he said, was any longer certain of his tenure, and there were rumors that a number of people would not be retained. The matter of academic tenure, then, was of primary importance in faculty unrest, according to Dean Miller. Only after pointing out that most of the faculty members were so discouraged they were ready to leave did he get around to "the factional strife, tale-bearing, and informers" that had wrecked the peace of the faculties.

It is perfectly clear that outside the faculty, which must accept some of the blame, there were two factors in the unhealthy situation; the administrators and the president. The president was sometimes imprudent and given to hasty and ill-advised decisions. But there is also the fact that the Board of Administrators assumed an Olympian attitude which kept it from understanding the academic man and his reactions to two sorts of threats: exposure to the risk of being deprived of academic freedom and tenure, and the danger he sees in the scarifying of well-trodden paths of the *status quo*. Undoubtedly the fact that no faculty member had tenure was basic. No man was sure he would not be fired merely because someone in the administrative echelon did not like him. Nor did the administrators approve a written code of tenure. They did abolish the Board of Visitors, and when the alumni demanded it they investigated Craighead's conduct of affairs (and exonerated him); but there is no evidence to indicate that the administrators ever realized they could not deal with a university faculty in the same way in which the board of directors of a business might deal with employees. Nor did it appear that communication between faculty and administrators showed any immediate signs of improvement.

The paradoxical part of this period of strife, however, is the fact that almost unparalleled progress in the growth of the university is so evident. A great deal was happening besides coffee and pistols at dawn under the campus live oaks.

Not all the moves toward reform in administration, for example, brought waves of faculty indignation. Few were accomplished without any protests at all, but, on the whole, there were many changes which caused no real upheaval. Ellsworth Woodward designed a uniform diploma which was adopted by all the colleges in 1907. The next year, at the French Opera House the first unified commencement exercises were held. In 1911 the clerical workers of the university were placed under the control of a newly created central office of Registrar, an office which replaced the registrars of the various colleges (except Newcomb) and included the office of bursar as well.[4] In 1912 largely through the efforts of William R. Irby, successful New Orleans businessman and member of the Board of Administrators, a system of purchasing at wholesale through a central university agent was instituted. D. F. Layman became the first purchasing agent of the university. Contemporaneous with these moves toward a more centralized and efficient operation came other reforms. The university's bookkeeping system was given a thorough study. In fact, almost every phase of the university's operations was given careful scrutiny, even the work loads of stenographers and number of students in each professor's class.

Finances, of course, were a major area of probing, and once again it was a case of "this is where we came in." From 1893 to 1910, the study showed, there were only three years without operating losses. Net deficits of $92,000 had been accumulated during these eighteen years. Nor was there relief in sight. The failure to obtain funds from the state has been related. Likewise, public contributions did little to relieve the gnawing pains of the institution's hunger. The Citizens' Auxiliary raised $20,000 in 1905 and again in 1906, $10,000 during the next three years, and then in 1910 gave up the ghost with a total of $308 raised. An appeal to the alumni brought negligible results. Likewise a proposal to Andrew Carnegie produced no results. Things were so bad that not even the president had a travel and expense account. And things kept happening to increase rather than decrease expenditures. By 1910 New Orleans was modernizing itself. With the development of a modern city sewerage and water system, the university had to set aside considerable sums for pipe, equipment, and labor to bring these necessities to the campus. (As late as 1912 there were still outmoded cesspools on the campus which overflowed after heavy rains.) Paving of major streets also increased university expenses. A bill for nearly $5,000 had to be paid for street paving in front of the Medical School on Canal Street. A similar amount was necessary for the university's share of St. Charles Avenue paving costs in front of Gibson Hall.

It would be wholly unreasonable to expect much expansion and progress in a university so beset by financial, administrative, public relations, and faculty morale problems. Yet, as has been previously suggested, this period of confusion and insecurity was also characterized by enormous growth— not only of the physical plant but in an expansion of the university's

---

[4] In 1913 the office was split into registrar and bursar. Richard K. Bruff became the first registrar of the University and Benjamin Crump the first bursar.

usefulness and in its academic offerings. That it was able to experience this growth was due in no small part to the management of the university's meager finances by the administrators. This body often failed to fathom the minds of the faculties, it sometimes created false impressions by failing to let the public know what it was doing, but when it came to stretching a dollar its actions seem today almost like legerdemain. It borrowed from capital funds, it bought and sold real estate, it reinvested capital funds at higher returns, it saw that strict economy was practiced, it shifted money from one pocket to another, it cut strips off the top and sewed them on the bottom, thereby miraculously making the whole fabric longer. It did about everything except organize a lottery, and it might well have resorted to this. The Louisiana Lottery was in its heyday, and even churches were copying its operations to build their houses of worship. But the administrators would never resort to a lottery, if for no other reason than the fact that a great deal of the aggressive and intelligent leadership in the antilottery fight was coming from some of its members. Although the entire board partici- pated in the financing operations, no small amount of the credit must go to the president, New Orleans banker Robert M. Walmsley (who succeeded Judge Fenner); to merchant and bank director Gustaf R. Westfeldt, chair- man of the finance committee; and to insurance executive Charles Janvier, chairman of the real estate committee.

Although the physical plant is certainly not the most important part of a university, nevertheless it is a major factor. Certainly for Tulane between 1904 and 1912 the expansion of its physical plant enabled it to widen the university's influence and usefulness. During these years four new buildings were added, others enlarged, and an athletic field with a small stadium was constructed.

Mention has already been made of the fact that the Tilton Memorial Library building was expanded in 1906 through an additional gift by Mrs. Tilton. Likewise the gifts of Mrs. Richardson and Mr. Hutchinson were manipulated so that it was possible to build a new dormitory, a new medical classroom building, and to expand the chemistry building, all on the uptown campus. The manner in which this was done illustrates the legerdemain previously mentioned above. The decision had been made to move the first two years of medicine to the uptown campus, but funds were not available for buildings unless the administrators dug into the restricted Hutchinson fund. In order to do this they sold the Canal Street medical building to the Hutchinson fund and renamed the building Hutchinson Memorial. With the proceeds of this transaction there was built on the main campus a large, high-ceilinged, four-story-and-basement medical building which was named Richardson Memorial.[5] In addition a new dor-

---

[5] When the new building was dedicated, on May 19, 1908, a few roots of ivy from the Canal Street medical building were transplanted during the exercises. Thus originated "Ivy Day" which is still observed.

mitory for young medical students (now Alcée Fortier Hall) was constructed and likewise bore the appellation Richardson Memorial, as did the renovated chemistry building.

New money for unrestricted purposes came to the university in 1910. In that year Stanley O. Thomas, Civil War veteran and New Orleans cotton factor, died, leaving to Tulane the sum of $60,000. Since it was an unrestricted gift for which there were so many needs, heated discussion was aroused over the question of where it was most needed. But the aggressive and fast-developing school of technology won out, and in late 1910 work was begun on Stanley Thomas Hall, a new engineering building. The building was completed a year later and dedicated in February 1912.

Mention has already been made of the acquisition from the Jesuits of a sixty-acre tract extending from Freret to Claiborne and of the purchase of a large block of property on Napoleon Avenue as the site of a new campus for Newcomb College. A portion of the Jesuit tract was utilized as an athletic field in 1910. In 1909 a wooden grandstand seating 10,000 people had been erected in the quadrangle adjacent to Gibson Hall to accommodate the crowd which came to listen to an address by President Taft. This grandstand was removed to the new athletic field and Tulane had its first stadium. Shortly thereafter, in 1912, a new gymnasium (now the ROTC building) was built on Freret Street adjacent to the playing field.

The matter of a new campus for Newcomb was, however, difficult and complicated. President Dixon, his faculty, the alumni, and amost everyone else, seemed to be aware of the fact that Newcomb was outgrowing its restricted campus on Washington Avenue. But the matter of where and when it would move was a matter of deliberation and debate. In this there was more than a mere decision of whether Newcomb would move or not. The matter of *where* the new campus would be was of the utmost importance, for bound up in this decision was the question of whether Newcomb would draw closer to the rest of the university or whether it would continue its physical as well as spiritual apartness. The decision in 1908 to sell the Napoleon Avenue property and to seek a new home for Newcomb nearer the main campus was one of the really important long-range decisions made during the Craighead era. Newcomb did not move anywhere immediately, but the important basic decision was made, whether there was a conscious recognition of this fact at the time or not. The purchase of the present Newcomb site in 1908 cemented the decision.

The academic expansion of Tulane, and thus the enormous increase in its ability better to serve the needs of the region, was so vast that the historian is puzzled as to how he can best relate it. A Teachers' College and a Summer School were established; a new school of architecture was founded; four new schools of major importance were created in the Medical Department; three new departments were created at Newcomb; and general entrance requirements were drastically revised upward.

The history of a formal teacher training program at Tulane goes back to the early months of 1892 when afternoon and evening classes known as University Extension were inaugurated. These courses were well attended, and in 1897 the program was expanded and renamed University Department for Teachers. Under this plan teachers or those preparing for teaching were given free tuition, and several hundred teachers availed themselves of the opportunities it offered. With the arrival of Dr. Edward Scheib in 1901 the department was renamed department of pedagogy and under the new professor made excellent progress. After Scheib's untimely death in 1903 the old title of department for teachers was restored, and in 1905 reverted to "extension courses." For two years it carried this title. In 1907 Joseph Marr Gwinn of the Missouri State Normal School was selected by Craighead as professor of education, his appointment being in Newcomb. In that same year the president also received board approval for a "Teachers' College" which, it was asserted, would "take academic rank with the professional colleges of Law and Medicine."

The new college got off to an excellent start. A two-year course of study was formulated and soon had expanded into a four-year degree program. The training school of the Free Kindergarten Association of New Orleans became a department of the college in 1908, and at the same time practice teaching facilities were secured in the public schools and in the Isidore Newman Manual Training School. The teacher-training program was going well, but then it received another setback. In 1910 Professor Gwinn resigned to accept the position of superintendent of the Orleans Parish public school system. His departure, plus a lack of funds and of someone in authority in the university with a background in pedagogy, led to a greatly diminished interest in the field. Dean Albert B. Dinwiddie of the College of Arts and Sciences reorganized the program as a department in the college and brought in David Spence Hill as professor of psychology and education to direct the department. Hill resigned after one year, and his duties were assumed by James Adair Lyon, professor of physcis at Newcomb, who headed a university committee on teacher training. Professor Lyon held this position for many years and tried faithfully to keep alive a good program. It is now clear, however, that teacher training could not thrive in a negative or hostile environment such as that in the College of Arts and Sciences at the time. Too many professors had no concept of what a teacher-training program ought to be and were thus either unconcerned or antagonistic. As will be pointed out, Newcomb had a more thorough teacher-training program than the College of Arts and Sciences; but it was the Summer School which seemed to hold most promise in the field of pedagogy.

Tulane's first summer school, held in the summer of 1908, was under the joint auspices of the university and the State Board of Education, with 860 teachers in attendance. Nicholas Bauer, an alumnus and assistant superintendent of Orleans Parish public schools, was in charge, and all reports indicate the success of the new venture. In 1909 the summer session was directed by Professor Gwinn and in 1910 by Dean Dinwiddie assisted by Edward A. Bechtel, professor of classical languages. Under all its directors the department grew. Enrollment in 1909 was 789. In 1910 it was 938, and by 1912 had grown in enrollment to 1,072. Everyone apparently was greatly encouraged over the results and within a comparatively brief period of time it seemed generally accepted that the summer school would be a permanent part of the university's services.

Meantime the engineering faculty, assisted by the New Orleans Chapter of the American Institute of Architecture, was laying plans for the development of a school of architecture or at least a department of architecture within the School of Technology.[6] In 1907 the planning bore fruit when the department was firmly established, one of the two pioneering efforts in the field in the entire South. (Alabama Polytechnic Institute at Auburn established a similar department in the same year.)

Plans for the program were modest, calling for an insignificant outlay for equipment and for a staff of only four part-time teachers. There was apparently no grandiose dream of a great regional school of architecture, but rather efforts seemed to center around immediate local needs. Samuel Stanhope Labouisse, a prominent young New Orleans architect, and William Woodward, of the drawing department, were the faculty mainstays at first. In 1912, however, one full-time professor of architecture, Nathaniel Cortland Curtis of Auburn, was added to the faculty to help develop the degree program authorized by the administrators in 1911. (Actually two degree programs were authorized that year, one in architecture and one in architectural engineering.)

The quality of instruction was very high, if one may judge it from the records made by the alumni in professional life or as students in other schools. No better example of this can be found than in the 1912 examinations for entrance into the Paris *Ecole des Beaux Arts*. In this year, 185 non-Frenchmen took the examinations, and only eight passed. Two of the three Americans in the successful group had been students in the new architecture program at Tulane. In spite of the quality of the work, however, it was touch and go for several years as to whether the department would survive or not. Enrollment was small, student fees were insignificant, and the budget of the College of Technology was inadequate to absorb the deficits. For a period of time, consideration was given to abolishing the department completely, but local groups interested in seeing it continue came to the rescue financially. By the time President Craighead left in

[6] A course in architecture was included in the College of Technology in 1894–1895, but was soon dropped.

1912 the department was on a solid footing. With the completion of Stanley Thomas Hall it was given a permanent home on the third floor with some room for expansion.

Within the framework of the medical department four new schools of major significance were created during the Craighead era. These new schools were Post-Graduate Medicine, Pharmacy (from a mere department), Denistry, and Tropical Medicine.

Graduate medical instruction did not, in contrast to most of the other departments, evolve slowly from small beginnings. Rather it was full grown from the very day it was born, for it was created by the absorption of an established institution, the New Orleans Polyclinic. Previous reference has been made to this organization, which was founded in 1887 by Rudolph Matas, Charles Chassaignac, John Harrison Bemis, and other New Orleans doctors who felt the need for advanced study. Within a decade it had developed into a highly regarded and widely known center of graduate medical training. Before its amalgamation with Tulane in 1906–1907 the Polyclinic had acquired a building of its own near Charity Hospital. Here its members studied and worked out their theories in the clinics of Charity Hospital. Many of the members were Tulane alumni, so there appears to have been no friction when amalgamation occurred. The post-graduate medical department began its first session in 1906 with Dr. Chassaignac as dean. There were 29 doctors that first session, but within a few years this had tripled.

The graduate medical school had been in operation two years when another department was established, or, more accurately, given what appeared to be an independent status. In June 1908, the medical faculty approved Metz's resolution calling for an independent School of Pharmacy with its own faculty. The Board of Administrators approved the change, and in the fall of 1908, at least on paper, there was a separate school established. The separation, however, was far from complete. The budget remained a part of that of the medical school and its deficits were absorbed by Medicine. Administration continued to be exercised by the dean of the undergraduate medical school, and the pharmacy faculty did not meet as a separate unit until 1912. It was 1920 before Pharmacy issued a separate bulletin, and 1931 before a separate dean was appointed, and by this time the pharmacy program was on its last legs. It had never been a success. Increased costs of operation and a dwindling student body caused heavy pressures on the medical school budget. And there seemed to be no relief. There was a steady decline in students after the 1908 session. In 1909 there were eight students, and in 1913 there were seven. No one in Medicine was ever very happy about Pharmacy.

The School of Dentistry was another new division which came into being full grown. It was created by the incorporation of the independent New Orleans College of Dentistry into the Medical Department in October 1909.

Prior to the establishment of the new school in Tulane there had been several years of negotiation looking toward eventual amalgamation. The New Orleans College of Dentistry had been founded in 1899, and within three years was cooperating with the Tulane medical school in exchange of students, facilities, and faculty members. In 1908 its building burned, and the faculty sought refuge in the Hutchinson Memorial building. When in 1909 the Louisiana State Dental College was organized, the older college sought a permanent affiliation with Tulane. This was accomplished, and Tulane had a new school with Dr. Andrew G. Friedrichs as dean.

Classes in the new school were held along with those of medicine on the uptown campus and in Hutchinson Memorial. Women were admitted on equal terms with men, but only one woman, Marie Blanche Fassy, had graduated during this early period. The new school also opened a dental clinic and in time treated hundreds of patients. But, like Pharmacy, Dentistry was doomed to founder on the rocks of financial insecurity. A bequest of $28,000 from Dr. Watson Woodward in 1913 provided some scholarship relief, but the burden carried by the medical school budget became serious enough to precipitate a strong sentiment, even in the early days, for the discontinuance of the project.

On the graduate level the Polyclinic had for several years been giving instruction in tropical medicine. Undergraduates were also given some information on symptoms, diagnosis, modes of transmission, and therapy of a few of the better-known tropical diseases, but only as part of a general medical education. Since 1901, for example, students had been taught that the stegomyia mosquito transmitted yellow fever, but the general topic of yellow fever was largely academic until 1905 when New Orleans suffered one of the worst epidemics in its history. On every side men and women dropped like flies, and the entire resources of the medical school were marshaled to combat the dread disease. Undoubtedly this did much to convince everyone that Tulane ought to do more in such tropical scourges than merely teach about them in a general way. In 1907 there was organized a national association of doctors, hygienists, and business interests called the American Society of Tropical Medicine, and in May 1911, this group met in New Orleans. Almost every speech, especially that of President W. W. Thayer of Baltimore, urged that Tulane undertake the establishment of a school of tropical medicine. It was the principal medical center of the South, it was pointed out. Moreover, New Orleans' commerce with the tropics was extensive, and from the surrounding countryside came many cases of malaria and other diseases common to the tropics. In short, New Orleans, being the connecting link between Panama, Cuba, Central America, and South America, could hardly escape its destiny. A few weeks later Colonel William C. Gorgas spoke in the city and added his appeal to that of the tropical medicine society.

This does not mean that the Tulane authorities were dragging their feet on the matter. Actually it was a question of finances which deterred them. In July 1911, however, Samuel Zemurray, a New Orleanian who became president of the United Fruit Company, gave $25,000 toward the new venture, and other gifts brought the total to $32,500. With this modest financial support the administrators approved, in October 1911, a department of hygiene and tropical medicine in undergraduate medicine. But it was not intended solely for medical students. Students were admitted to portions of the program for purposes of research and study in fields other than pure medicine. Engineers interested in sanitation were among these nonmedical students. Likewise teachers of hygiene were admitted.

The program was put under the direction of Dr. Creighton Wellman who, in spite of a pronounced tendency toward emotional instability which led to a very brief tenure, directed national attention to the new department and especially to the research of Dr. Charles C. Bass in parasitology. The entire city and university were disappointed that Colonel Gorgas declined the directorship, but this did not interfere with the department's growth. By 1913 the department's laboratories comprised the Chaillé Memorial Laboratory of Public Health and Preventive Medicine, the graduate and research laboratory of tropical medicine, and the junior and senior laboratories of tropical medicine. From every direction Tulane was being hailed as the coming center of a worldwide study of tropical diseases.

There were other events during this period in the medical department which, though they must be classified as miscellaneous, were important.

Late in the summer of 1907, the Era Club of New Orleans, an organization of progressive women, broadcast an appeal to all Southern women who wished to enter the medical profession to communicate with the club's headquarters. The reason back of the appeal was that President Craighead had promised that if ten properly qualified women applied for entrance to the Tulane Medical Department he would ask that they be received. But the club's efforts came to naught. Eight women applied, and thus Craighead's promise was not tested. The matter of women in the medical school had, of course, been debated for years, but this is the closest it had come to facing the issue squarely. Actually the incident frightened some medical faculty members and administrators alike. Like death and taxes the admission of women was inevitable, but they chose to put it off as long as possible. Faculty barriers were lowered, however, and two women received appointments on the faculty. Dr. Edith Loeber Ballard was appointed as assistant in the department of clinical obstetrics and Dr. Mary Elizabeth Bass in the department of pathology.

As it inevitably must, time took its toll of the medical faculty during these years. In June 1907, Dr. Souchon was retired as emeritus professor of anatomy and appointed curator of his beloved anatomical museum. At the same time the administrators decided to retire Drs. Chaillé, Lewis, and

Elliott. In anticipation of Dean Chaillé's retirement, Dr. Isadore Dyer was made associate dean in 1907 and in 1908 made the new dean of the medical department.

But these are more than mere routine facts recorded in the annals of the university, for with the passing of them from the scene an element of greatness passed with them. At the farewell dinner given Dean Chaillé he revealed that in his half-century's connection with the medical school he had taught all but 690 of the 4,115 medical students who had graduated since the department was established in 1834. Dr. Ernest S. Lewis, who had served for 39 years, was the founder and pioneer of surgical gynecology and abdominal surgery in the Deep South. He received many honors from national surgical organizations, but perhaps no tribute stands out above that of Dr. Matas. "Dr. Lewis," he said, "was my gratefully acknowledged master." Nor can Dr. John Barnwell Elliott, who retired three years later, be overlooked. The only doctor on the faculty with both the M.D. and the Ph.D. degrees, he was noted for his research and teaching in the field of clinical medicine. He had served a total of 37 years. With men like these on the faculty one does not wonder that Tulane was consistently ranked among the top medical schools in the country by virtually every medical organization and accrediting group.

All these things—expansion of physical plant, addition of departments, administrative reform—probably would have come about under any man who happened to be president at the time, for they were inexorable processes in institutional growth. In one area, however, Craighead exhibited strong qualities of leadership in a matter which would have been easy to put off until a more convenient season. This was a bold and sweeping plan to raise entrance requirements and academic standards throughout the university. His motives appear to have been twofold: to obtain for retiring professors the benefits of the new Carnegie pension plan and to bring the university to the point where "people . . . will speak of Tulane as the Harvard of the South."

In implementing his ideas Craighead went straight to the source. In November 1905, he conferred personally with Andrew Carnegie. So impressed was Carnegie with Craighead's earnestness that he requested his appointment as one of two Southern educators to the board of the Carnegie Foundation. With this appointment he was able to speak with more authority, especially to the faculties of his own institution. He pushed the matter of tighter entrance requirements. On May 7, 1906, he spoke to the medical faculty about the matter and it, in turn, followed his suggestions by adopting a resolution requiring a high school education or its equivalent of all entering freshmen beginning with the entering class of 1907. (Three years later this was expanded upward to one year of college.) A week later the president addressed a joint meeting of the Newcomb, Arts and Sciences, and Technology faculties on the same subject, and these faculties likewise approved. On and after October 1907, all students entering these colleges would be required to present fifteen Carnegie units from an approved high school. This left outside the new plan only the law department.

Today such a decision hardly seems dramatic, but at the turn of the century this was indeed a bold step in the South, for few secondary schools were up to Carnegie standards. This meant that Tulane faculty members had to scatter over the state for conferences with and assistance to public school administrators as they tried to bring their schools into conformity. By 1910, however, great progress had been made both at Tulane and among the secondary schools in working under the new plan. As a matter of fact Tulane extended the requirements to the law school in that year, thus becoming the only Southern university to have all its colleges or departments on the Carnegie list. In the rankings made by the foundation that year the medical department was ranked among the first three in the nation, and the law school was ranked eighteenth in a list of two hundred.

That the law department should have suddenly achieved such a ranking was due to a series of far-reaching reforms carried out in an amazingly short period of time.

In 1906 the law department moved from the Richardson medical building on Canal Street to Gibson Hall on the uptown campus. This was a sharp break with the past, with the more than fifty years of Common Street memories. With the new and permanent home, changes came swiftly.

The most basic factor in the reform movement was a reorganization of the faculty. In 1906, Eugene Davis Saunders, professor of constitutional law, common law, and equity, succeeded Professor Harry Hinckley Hall, dean since 1897. Coincidental with this change, two young New Orleanians returned from Eastern universities, where they had taken their law degrees, and joined the Tulane law faculty. The new dean and these two young assistant professors with the support of President Craighead changed things in rapid order.

In 1902, Monte M. Lemann and Ralph J. Schwartz received the Bachelor of Arts degree at Tulane. That fall both of them went East for their law degrees, Lemann to Harvard and Schwartz to Columbia. When they returned home to New Orleans in 1906 they were added to the faculty—Lemann as assistant professor of admiralty, torts, and conflict of laws; Schwartz as assistant professor of constitutional law and equity. Hardly had they received their appointments before they were in conference with Dean Saunders over an agenda containing a list of reforms which the two young men felt would bring the law department up to the level of Eastern law schools. Craighead and the administrators supported virtually every recommendation of Dean Saunders with the result that it is possible here to enumerate a comprehensive list of changes for the better.

The law faculty was virtually reconstituted under Saunders when the law department moved to the uptown campus. Dean Hall did not make the transition; neither did Henry Denis, professor of civil law, nor Thomas C. Ellis, professor of admiralty, international law, and constitutional law. Nor did the three quizmasters survive the change. Sole survivors of the downtown campus era were Saunders and Judge Frank Adair Monroe, professor of commercial law and the law of corporations. To replace the casualties, appointments were given to Lemann, Schwartz, Robert Hardin Marr; and from outside the city, Garvin Dugas Shands, one-time lieutenant-governor of Mississippi, was appointed professor of common law. Doctor (LL.D.) Shands became the first full-time professor in the law department's history.

Profound and far-reaching renovation came in the wake of the faculty shakeup. Discarding the antiquated lecture method, the faculty instituted the more practical and effective case system of instruction whereby problems taken from the actual record were related to theory to better ground the student in subject matter. Whereas previously any youth "of good moral character" who was properly introduced to the professors could attend their courses, no matter how poorly qualified he might be, he now had to be a graduate of a standard four-year high school or possess the equivalent. Abandoned was the custom of conducting classes only in the late afternoons and early evenings. Almost all formal instruction now came in the forenoon hours.

But these were not all the changes.

Through 1906 the law course had consisted of ten lectures a week for twenty weeks during each of two years of study. In October 1907, this was changed the three years of continuous instruction of twenty-seven hours a week for thirty weeks each year. Moreover, it was required of all graduates expecting to practice in Louisiana to demonstrate a reading knowledge of the French language.[7] As a result courses in the academic department were opened without charge to law students.

Professor Shands taught common law and common law pleading and practice. The course was set up as one of new importance at Tulane, the faculty having a two-fold purpose in mind. First, it thought that by separating the civil law from the common law subjects and emphasizing their distinctions, more students from common law states could be attracted to its classes. Secondly, the professors realized the unusual opportunity in New Orleans for the development of instruction in comparative jurisprudence. This modest beginning of one new course led in 1909 to two independent curricula, one in the common law and one in Louisiana law, including civil law. The combination course leading to the B.A. and the LL.B. degrees was instituted the same year.

The law department was on its way with the "new look" of the Saunders

<hr>

[7] In Louisiana, French was an official language along with English until 1921. Publication of all official matters was in both languages.

period. It had a library of its own in Gibson Hall, the money for it having been subscribed by citizens of New Orleans. It had a spacious study room and adequate classrooms. Moot court was re-established and conducted under the supervision of the professors. The Law Debating Club found new life. Plans were under way for the establishment of the *Tulane Law Review*. Professor Bechtel of the College of Arts and Sciences began his affiliation with the department in 1908, teaching Roman law. In that same year Dudley Odell McGovney, a Columbia University law graduate, was brought from the University of Missouri as the second full-time professor of law. The department was receiving a larger subsidy out of general funds of the university. With justifiable pride Dean Saunders, Professors Lemann and Schwartz, and Edgar H. Farrar, who had given so much support as a member of the Board of Administrators, could point to the fact that Tulane was one of two Southern law schools on the Carnegie approved list (Trinity College, now Duke University, was the other) and that in 1911 the school became a member of the Association of American Law Schools. Enrollment, which had dropped precipitately with the institution of higher standards, was making a comeback. With more adequate financial support the law department by the end of Craighead's administration was ready to be a first-rate college.

The College of Arts and Sciences experienced no changes comparable with those in the medical and law departments, but there were developments which should be mentioned. The establishment of a department for teachers has already been discussed. Expansion and improvement in the scientific work of the college was made possible through an enlargement of the museum under the direction of George Eugene Beyer, assistant professor of biology. Beyer gave his own collection of birds to the museum, which already included the Gustave Kohn group of Louisiana fauna, the George Soulé collection of mammal skeletons, and the Joseph Jones collection of reptiles. The whole collection now numbered approximately 170,000 items. To match this improved opportunity for the study of animal life a chair of botany was endowed in 1909. Again Mrs. Ida Richardson had come to the aid of the university she and Dr. Richardson loved so much. Her gift for endowment of the chair consisted of $55,000 worth of real estate situated in the business district of New Orleans. The first incumbent was her good friend Reginald Somers Cocks, an Englishman who was a product of Eton, Trinity College of Cambridge, and the University of London, where he had studied under Thomas Huxley. He had come to New Orleans in 1891 while on a tour of the United States. He liked the city and decided to stay, but the only job open to him at the time was that of a high school teacher of Latin. He took it and then moved on to the Latin Department at Tulane as an assistant to Professor Walter Miller in 1908. The next year, on Mrs. Richardson's request, he was named the first Ida A. Richardson professor of botany. Before he died in 1926 he had discovered 30 new varieties of trees in the United States, 14 of which were Louisiana natives and were named for him by Charles Sprague Sargent of Harvard.

The period also saw the separation of the unnatural and unpopular combination of the College of Arts and Sciences and the College of Technology into a grouping known as "The Academic Colleges." Brown Ayres was at home in either liberal arts or technology, but neither James Hardy Dillard nor Walter Miller, a classical philologist, was fitted to be a dean of a technical school. Miller (1907–1911) was the last of the double-duty deans. In 1911 the College of Technology selected one of its own staff, the rigid disciplinarian and professor of mechanical engineering, William Henry Creighton. Albert Bledsoe Dinwiddie, professor of mathematics, was named Dean of the College of Arts and Sciences, replacing Dean Miller.

Other personnel changes, as in the medical department, reflected the transition which goes on as an institution matures. In 1907 Professor John Hanno Deiler, likable and long-time (1880–1907) professor of German, retired to devote his remaining years to research in the history of the early Germans in Louisiana. In the same year John Rose Ficklen, professor of English, history, and political science since 1884, was killed in an accident. He, too, had devoted his research to local history. Dean Dillard, as has been previously noted, resigned in 1907 to head the Jeanes Fund. But others of competence were beginning their work. Edward Ambrose Bechtel joined the faculty in 1907 as assistant professor of Latin and Greek. Within four years he was a full professor and heading toward an important role in the university. In 1907, Ulrich Bonnell Phillips accepted the position of professor of history and political science, succeeding Ficklen. However, he remained at Tulane only three years before transferring to the University of Michigan where he developed his reputation as one of the great scholars in the field of Southern history.

Between 1904 and 1912 things at Newcomb were buzzing almost as much as at the medical department. Perhaps the climax of the period for Newcomb was the court decision in 1909 which brought the college the $2,668,000 residue of Mrs. Newcomb's estate. For years it had looked forward to this money, and for years afterward looked back to it. Another gift, too, augmented the larger one. In 1910, Frank Walter Callender, Mrs. Newcomb's good friend, died, leaving $65,000 to the college.

There were many things which could be done with the money, but nothing stood out as a greater need than a new campus. Since 1904 it had become obvious to Dixon, his faculty, and the administrators that the Washington Avenue campus could not much longer be expanded to meet the growing needs of the college. President Dixon thought he had found the ideal location on Napoleon Avenue, and the property was purchased in 1905, but the delay in settling the Newcomb will litigation prevented moving the campus to the new site. Before the Newcomb legacy was made available by the courts, however, another site closer to the main campus became available. The Napoleon Avenue property was sold for a good profit, and in November 1908, the present Newcomb campus was bought for $435,672. The entire second block of Audubon Place and two squares bounded by Zimple, Broadway, Plum, and Audubon Streets, were chosen because this property adjoined the main Tulane campus, and it was the intent of the administrators to unite Newcomb more closely with the university of which it was a part. The physical isolation would be ended. Perhaps a spiritual unity might come in time.

Dixon himself favored the move because if "promised greater economy in the way of libraries and laboratories, permitted the employment of professors for both colleges where the classes in either alone would not justify it." But mention of the word "unity" alarmed the alumnae. They feared that once again a trap was set; that the administrators were trying to destroy Newcomb's independence. So they began to bombard the board with memorials and resolutions demanding that all care be exercised to see that their college on a new campus did not lose its autonomy and individuality, even to the extent of urging that a distinctive type of architecture be used for the proposed new buildings. But their fears were a bit premature. Newcomb did not move to the new campus for a decade.

It was on the old campus, therefore, that in 1909 the new schools of Music, Education, and Household Economy were established, and the art department was converted into the School of Art with no changes except for the name. (It simply was given the recognition of a "school" in its own right, with a definite course, rounded out by electives from the regular academic subjects, all leading toward a degree.)

The School of Household Economy offered courses in domestic science, domestic art, biology, and education to teachers and managers of hospitals and other institutions and to housekeepers and homemakers. Household economy was a major in the B.A. curriculum, but the great majority of the large numbers who entered the program did so as special students rather than degree students.

The School of Education, which began to function in 1909, was the least well populated of any of the new departments. Only 13 students registered for the program during its first year, but this was hardly indicative of Newcomb's program for the professional training of teachers. That is to say, by no means all the students at Newcomb who planned to teach were enrolled in the new department. Many prospective teachers were pursuing straight subject matter courses and not majoring in professional courses in pedagogy. Closely allied with the teacher's program was the Callender

Psychological Laboratory. About $15,000 of Mr. Callender's bequest went into scholarships, the balance going into this laboratory for the study of child psychology, particularly of the exceptional child.

It was music, however, which became the bellwether for all the new programs at Newcomb. Before 1909, music instruction at the college had been haphazard and almost entirely by private teachers who instructed special students on the campus. But the school which was created in 1909 was a far cry from this; in fact, it was something startlingly new to most New Orleans music teachers. The new program aimed to provide not only a variety of practical musical instruction to university students, but to couple these technical studies with certain academic requirements and electives in a four-year course directed toward the degree of bachelor of music.

Over the opposition of New Orleans musicians, who regarded the new enterprise as ruinous competition, the school was opened. Many predicted its early failure. What music student, they asked, would tolerate such unnecessary subjects as chemistry, biology, and algebra? But in spite of dire forebodings the school flourished. A broad cultural training, Newcomb maintained, was as necessary as adjunct of the art of music as of any other art form. Practical and theoretical instruction was offered for three main classifications of students: those intending to follow music as a profession, either as composers, performers, teachers, or critics; special students who wished to study the subject for general cultural purposes; and regular students of the college who were interested in music history, appreciation, or composition as electives in their degree programs.

The distinguished Chevalier Giuseppe Ferrata, pupil of Franz Liszt, was the first appointee to the music faculty in 1909, an appointment which was to last until 1928. Born in Rome, he had begun to study piano at the age of six, winning at fourteen a scholarship to the Royal Academy in Rome. As pianist and composer he continued to win acclaim, including knighthood from the kings of Italy and Portugal. After coming to New York in 1904 he won a name for himself in this country, not the least of his accomplishments being the doctor's degree in music from the Grand Conservatory of the City of New York. Composing and teaching were Dr. Ferrata's great passions. In 1908 he took first prize in all four classes of composition— string quartet, piano, piano and violin, and choral—in the Pittsburgh Art Society competition. In all he composed about three hundred pieces, including two operas. Between times he liked to teach, and there are scores of Newcomb alumnae of his day who remember the swarthy and volatile bushy-haired Italian pacing the floor, hands clasped behind his back, murmuring and nodding his head in encouragement or exploding with gesticulations and mock imprecations in a thick Italian accent at the dullards.

Leon Ryder Maxwell also joined the faculty of the school of music in

1909 as professor of voice and composition, and in 1910 was made director of the school. A tall, well-built man of quiet dignity and considerable charm, he quickly made a place for himself as a personality, a musician, and a teacher. His background and training were excellent for the sort of job he was to do at Newcomb for the next forty-odd years. He had graduated from Tufts College with the B.A. and M.A. degrees, and for three years was supervisor of music in the public schools of Reading, Stoneham, Lexington, and Belmont, Massachusetts. He appeared in vocal concerts in Boston as soloist and as conductor of choral groups for the Boston Symphony Orchestra. He continued his study of music, receiving a diploma in the theory and practice of teaching public school music from the American Institute of Normal Methods. At the same time he was continuing the study of voice at the New England Conservatory. Following his training at the conservatory he studied abroad in the fields of composition, orchestration, and diction.

He thus acquired a well-rounded musical education. He was an artist in his own right, a thoroughly trained teacher of music, and a composer of choral works, organ preludes, fugues, and small orchestral works. But above all this was his philosophy of music in the college. He did not wish to establish a conservatory at Newcomb. Rather, he felt that music was an integral part of a larger program which would help give balance and harmony to a student's life. Music, to him, was not nearly so much perfection in a small field as it was an understanding and appreciation of the world of music in the vast planetary system which is life. His concept of musical training could not be separated from a well-rounded academic education and from life.

The coming of Ferrata and Maxwell greatly strengthened the Newcomb faculty, and there were retirements which indicated that Newcomb, too, was maturing and changing. The ebullient Jane Caldwell Nixon retired in 1907. Preceding her retirement was that of John Morse Ordway, professor of biology, in 1904, and Evelyn Walton Ordway, professor of chemistry, in 1905. Since the earlier days of rapid faculty turnover, however, Newcomb had by 1910 achieved a high degree of faculty stability, to say nothing of an appreciable increase in quality.

The graduate school during the Craighead period can be mentioned almost as a postscript. There was a Graduate Department. There were graduate courses leading to the M.A. and Ph.D. degrees. There was a faculty and a dean (James H. Dillard from 1904 to 1908 and Robert Sharp from 1908 to 1912). There were a few students. And having said this, one has about told the story of the graduate school. Just about everything which goes into a good graduate school, except a good faculty, was lacking; but the faculty was so heavily engaged in undergraduate teaching it really had little time for graduate courses. But, above all, the library was weak. The enlargement of the Tilton Library building had only made available row after row of empty shelves. The best reference library in the city was the privately endowed Howard Memorial on Howard Avenue near Lee Circle, opened in 1889.[8] Including fiction, government bulletins and reports, and obsolete books the Tilton Library had approximately 37,000 volumes by 1912. The Howard Library had more than twice that number in reference books alone. It is small wonder, therefore, that enrollment in the graduate department was small (never more than 60 in any year, with the average being closer to 45), and that few degrees were conferred (only one doctorate from 1905 to 1912).[9]

No pounding of the reader is necessary here to impress upon him that the Craighead administration was a period of almost spectacular growth, a growth perhaps not equaled until the Harris administration which began in 1937. There was expansion in almost every department of the university except the graduate school. Enrollment reached a new high of 2,358 in 1908, and remained well above 2,000 for the next few years. It is also equally obvious that Tulane was making a somewhat painful transition to modernity. Forces were set in motion during this period which continued to be felt, at times with uncomfortable intensity, down to the present.

The tragedy of the period was a personal one—it was Edwin Boone Craighead. By 1912 it was obvious, even to him, that the wounds opened during his tenure of office would never be healed. In that year an offer of the presidency came from the University of Montana, and he accepted it. Just before his departure the post-graduate medical faculty adopted a resolution asking him to remain "in order to continue with the progressive policies the initiation of which has been due mainly to his energy." If this reflected the real sentiments of this faculty, it probably was the only one that felt that way. No one realized better than Craighead that his days of usefulness were over at Tulane.

[8] This library was built and endowed by Mrs. Annie Howard Parrott in memory of her father, Charles T. Howard, who had made a fortune as one of the owners of the Louisiana Lottery. There is a persistent legend (probably true) that the money which went into the Howard Library might have gone to Tulane had it not been for the fact that several members of the Board of Administrators, notably Dr. Palmer, were leading opponents of the lottery.

[9] During this period 16 honorary doctoral degrees were conferred.

CHAPTER 9

University Life (1884-1914)

WHAT WERE THE CHARACTERISTICS of university life at Tulane from the time of the transition from the University of Louisiana in 1884 until the early part of the twentieth century? What was the general tone, the flavor?

There is, of course, an answer, but it is not easily put into words. Recreating the atmosphere, the feel, of a place or an institution is a difficult task for a writer, as difficult as for the painter to capture the nuances which make a human personality assume character on the canvas. This we know, however: A university reflects something of its milieu, and, thus, perhaps this account should begin with a suggestion of what New Orleans was like during the period. Added to this ought to be something of the faculty, the campus, and student activities.

Between 1884 and 1914, New Orleans was a sprawling, carelessly put together city of approximately a quarter of a million people. Like "all Gaul" it was divided into three parts: the Vieux Carré below Canal Street, the Garden District above Canal Street, and a newly developing area in the general direction of Carrollton known as "Uptown."

Having thus laid out the city by geographic areas one has stated about all the facts upon which there probably would be general agreement among its older citizens. From this elementary statement of geography one may proceed in many directions without possibly ever discovering the true New Orleans. As a matter of fact there was no one New Orleans, no "true" New Orleans. The city was a potpourri of people, sights, sounds, odors, and customs. It was a poorly lighted, poorly drained, poorly paved city. On Congo Square in 1890 could still be heard the throb of voodoo drums and the stomping of black feet. Flashily dressed madames who presided over the elegant parlors of their houses in Storyville openly advertised the arrival of every bevy of new girls. From the dives on Basin Street came the sound of music with a new strong beat. Happy music, it was called, or jazz. Members of the Mafia murdered a policeman on the dark streets. Almost everywhere men guzzled whiskey, straight or in Sazerac cocktails. On a prominent street corner was the building housing the lottery, an octopus which sucked into its ravenous body the dimes and quarters of the poor;

that is, those which did not disappear in craps or poker games in the gambling houses which with the aid of political connivance ran almost openly. In the dim gaslight riverfront saloons, seamen roistered with their slatternly women and knives swished at the slightest provocation. Every few years, almost in rhythmic cycles, yellow fever struck the city, and thousands died with the dread black vomit.

This was the lusty, brawling New Orleans which had always been sinful and corrupt. Always the river washed the city's feet, but never its body. But there were other facets of the city. Only a few blocks from Basin Street was the French Opera House, and from its stage the great voices of the world sang to cultured and sophisticated audiences. Almost within a stone's throw were three legitimate theaters where the country's best actors trod the boards. Further uptown was the Howard Memorial Library at Tivoli (Lee) Circle, opened in 1889, containing a splendid collection of books and objects of art. There were in 1890 seventy-one public, private, and parochial schools and a somewhat larger number of churches of all denominations. Each year at carnival time hundreds of the cream of New Orleans society put on costumes and masks and danced to sprightly waltzes at scores of colorful balls—danced and presented their daughters at the court of make-believe. These were all other faces of New Orleans representing culture and gentility.

But above everything loomed a stark and ugly fact—New Orleans was poor. Her poverty was reflected in almost every part of the city's life—in the budget for schools and public improvements, in her support of charitable and educational institutions, even in the carnival balls, for it was not uncommon for a father to go into debt in order that he might be a king or his daughter a queen. There were, of course, those who could afford to live well, but the wealthy families could be counted on the fingers of one hand, and taxable wealth existed in limited quantities.

For thirty-five years and more after the Civil War, the Vieux Carré, the French Quarter, old New Orleans, was a frowzy *grande dame* sitting on the sagging gallery of her house and looking nostalgically over the levee of the river. She sat and looked backward in time, remembering old things—gay parties; beautiful ladies in Parisian gowns escorted to the opera by gallant gentlemen who could make love or fight a duel to the death with equal prowess; elegant dinners served with finesse by candlelight from china which gave out with the resonant ring of genuineness and gentility; good wine and absinthe frappés; a *femme de coleur* in her *tignon* dressing a young girl's hair before her first ball; polite conversation in soft liquid French over brandy and coffee in cool patios; the clopping of horses' feet and the ring of carriage wheels on the paving stones: the well-dressed ladies and gentlemen filing down the gangplank of a packet boat just arrived from Natchez.

These were things from a romantic past when New Orleans was truly the "Queen City by the River." Now she was poor, giving the appearance of decadence. The iron grillwork around her gallery was rusty, and below the patio the flapping of clothes drying on a line was a mockery of the once pleasant gurgling of the now dead fountain. In her kitchen she cooked red beans and rice instead of dining on *filet de truite amandine* or *poulet Chanteclair* at Antoine's. Her way of life had been mortally wounded by war and the devastating swiftness of change in its wake. Old things existed now only in her memories. Creole culture was rapidly losing its importance as a group culture, leaving only a legacy of its name and its cuisine.

Two miles up the river was the Garden District, the American section of the city, its stately pillared white mansions set in the lush greenness of well-tended gardens. But in this postwar period, its paint was also peeling, and many of the gardens were growing up in weeds. It, too, was poor, for the people here depended for a living on trade, on shipment of cotton abroad, on imports from the marts of the world destined for the Mississippi Valley. But the mouth of the river had filled with silt after the war, trade withered, and many of these people, like the Creoles in the Vieux Carré, sat and remembered things long lost.

Beyond the Garden District toward Carrollton a new section of the city was growing up along St. Charles Avenue and its satellite streets. This new part of the city was largely American, and the Creole sometimes shook his head in dismay at what had happened. Not much French was spoken uptown, and one had only to count the new Baptist, Methodist, and Presbyterian churches to see how things were straying from old patterns. There were in this new area as late as 1900 large stretches of wasteland, the remnants of sugar plantations, and on one of these barren areas there was developing a new campus for Tulane University, a secular university dominated largely by Americans.

This is not to say that New Orleans was no longer a cosmopolitan city and that she was doing nothing about her plight. She was still, in some ways, the polyglot city of the golden days. French, Italian, Spanish, German, English (not to mention the pure Brooklynese of the Irish Channel) were the languages her people spoke. She had not lost her taste for good food, wine, and black coffee, nor her avidity for gambling and wenching. And she was trying to pull herself up out of the mire of her streets and the devastation of her poverty. In 1884 she had opened the great World's Exposition and Cotton Centennial to notify the world that the mouth of the river was open to ships of all sizes and tonnage, and that New Orleans was again in the world's commercial picture, anxious to grow and regain her greatness. Too, the city was becoming electrified. Streets were being paved, drainage and sewerage systems were being installed. A good supply of pure water was in the process of development. And above all, after 1905 Bronze

Paul Tulane and Randall Lee Gibson.

Mrs. Josephine Louise Newcomb.

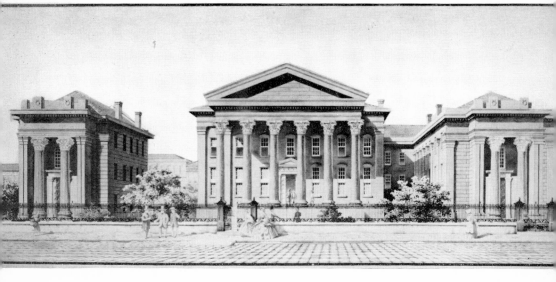

The old campus facing Common Street, 1847–1894.

Newcomb College, *circa* 1940.

First home of Newcomb College, Camp and Howard Streets, 1887–1890.

Newcomb in the Garden District, 1891–1918.

Tulane University on uptown campus, 1895.

Tulane campus, 1927.

The *Jambalaya* staff of 1900 holds an informal session.

And these are Newcomb girls.

GROUP OF FACULTY, 1899

Bottom row seated, left to right: JOHN R. FICKLEN, History and Political Science; ROBERT SHARP, English; JAMES HARDY DILLARD, Latin; WILLIAM O. ROGERS, Secretary of the University; BROWN AYRES, Physics and Engineering; B. V. B. DIXON, President of Newcomb College; WILLIAM BENJAMIN SMITH, Mathematics. *Second row standing, single:* ALCEÉ FORTIER, French. *Top row standing, left to right:* THOMAS CARTER, Greek; WILLIAM P. BROWN, English and Latin; GEORGE E. BEYER, Natural History; LEVI W. WILKINSON, Sugar Chemistry; H. F. RUGAN, Engineering; BENJAMIN PALMER CALDWELL, Chemistry; W. H. P. CREIGHTON, Mechanical Engineering; DOUGLAS SMITH ANDERSON, Electrical Engineering; WILLIAM WOODWARD, Art (NEWCOMB); JOHN E. LOMBARD, Mathematics; J. HANNO DEILER, German; RICHARD K. BRUFF, Assistant Secretary of the University; JOHN W. CALDWELL, Chemistry and Geology; WILLIAM B. GREGORY, Engineering; HENRY B. ORR, Biology.

Alceé Fortier teaches a class in French, *circa* 1905.

The first University Center, basement Gibson Hall, 1904.

The present University Center.

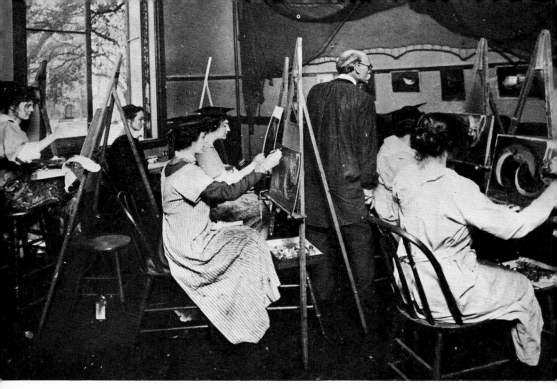

Ellsworth Woodward conducts an art class at Newcomb, *circa* 1914.

Richardson Medical Building, Canal Street, 1893–1930.

Older portion of the campus and the new.

TULANE ROSE BOWL TEAM, 1932.
University of Southern California–21, Tulane–12. *Front Row, left to right:* Coach Bierman, Lodrigues, Payne, Zimmerman, Dawson, Haynes. *Back Row, left to right:* Scafide, Dalrymple, Upton, McCormick, Felt, De Coligny.

Alternate halfback "Wop" Glover makes a shambles of Southern California's ends. (Rose Bowl Game, 1932)

MEMBERS OF THE FACULTIES OF THE COLLEGE OF ARTS AND SCIENCES AND ENGINEERING, NOVEMBER 1926

Bottom row, left to right: George E. Simmons, Claiborne G. Latimer, William P. Brown, Donald Derickson, Reginald Somers-Cocks, Edward A. Bechtel, Douglas S. Anderson, William B. Gregory. *Second row:* John M. McBryde, Samuel A. Mahood, Robert L. Menuet, Charles B. Dicks, Jr., Charles S. Williamson, Jr., Hal W. Moseley, Archibald L. Dunlap, Daniel S. Elliott. *Third row:* Ernest H. Riedel, William F. Smith, Robert Seward, Richard R. Kirk, Garrett P. Wyckoff, Reinhard A. Steinmayer, Edward S. Hathaway, Herman F. Hustedt. *Top row:* John S. Kendall, Albert B. Dinwiddie, Robert G. Polack, Richard K. Bruff, John H. Thomson, Frederick H. Fox, Irving E. Gray, James M. Robert.

Claude "Big Monk" Simons. Trainer, coach, professor of physical education, and friend of Tulane athletes, 1920–1943.

Randall Lee Gibson
1882–1892

Ashton Phelps
June 1903–November 1903

Charles Erasmus Fenner
February 1893 to June 1903
November 1903 to July 1904
November 1904 to August 1906

Henry Ginder
July 1904–August 1904

Robert Miller Walmsley
1906–1919

William Ratcliffe Irby
1920–1926

Esmond Phelps
1926–1950

Joseph Merrick Jones
1950–1963

Darwin Schriever Fenner
1963–
(Title of President
changed to Chairman,
February 18, 1965)

ADMINISTRATORS AND OTHER OFFICIALS OF THE UNIVERSITY—1965

Front row seated, left to right: Edmund McIlhenny, Board Attorney; Fred R. Cagle, Vice-President for Development; Clarence Scheps, Vice-President and Comptroller; Herbert Eugene Longenecker, President; M. E. Lapham, M.D., Provost; Charles C. Sprague, M.D., Dean of the Medical School; A. P. Generes, Secretary-Treasurer. *Second row standing:* Administrators: Edgar B. Stern, Jr.; Harry B. Kelleher; Sam Israel, Jr.; Lester J. Lautenschlaeger; Darwin S. Fenner, Chairman; Jacob S. Landry; Gerald L. Andrus; Joseph McCloskey. Administrators, *top row:* Mrs. George M. Snellings, Jr.; George A. Wilson; Leon Irwin, Jr.; Richard W. Freeman; Isidore Newman, II; George W. Montgomery; Ashton Phelps; Arthur L. Jung, Jr.; Clifford F. Favrot.

PRESIDENTS OF TULANE UNIVERSITY (PRESIDENTS OF THE UNIVERSITY OF LOUISIANA AND ACTING PRESIDENTS OF TULANE NOT INCLUDED.)

William Preston Johnston
1884–1899

Edwin Anderson Alderman
1900–1904

Edwin Boone Craighead
1904–1912

Robert Sharp
1912–1918

Albert Bledsoe Dinwiddie
1918–1935

Rufus Carrollton Harris
1937–1960

Herbert Eugene Longenecker
1960–

John was conquered. In the very year of the great Cotton Exposition the General Assembly of the State of Louisiana had passed Act 43 which created The Tulane University of Louisiana, a coincidence fraught with almost incalculable significance for the future. This new New Orleans would have higher education as well as electricity, sewerage, and paved streets.

In a limited sense the university reflected something of the larger community. On its faculty were names such as Edouard Michel Dupaguier, Charles Louis Chassaignac, Alcée Fortier, Sidney Philip Delaup, Nina Marie Preot, Pierre Leonce Thibaut, and Louis Favrot Reynaud. Too, there were names such as Giuseppe Ferrata and Pietro Ghiloni. The names of J. Hanno Deiler and Herman Bertram Gessner bespeak the German element. And since in New Orleans an Irishman was likely to pop up most anywhere, names such as Marion Herbert McGuire must be included. On the Tulane Board of Administrators one finds the same blending of Creole and American. There were on the board from time to time men with the names of John Baptist Levert, Gustaf Reinhold Westfeldt, Charles Janvier, and Walter Denis Denegre to offset the American names of Joseph Morris, Daniel Culpepper Scarborough, Ashton Phelps, and Beverley Ellison Warner. Here as in the faculty the American element was dominant but here also was the blending of the old and the new, Creole and American. One has only to look at residence street addresses to realize how the ancient apartness of the two groups was without ill will or conscious prejudice being perpetuated. Almost without exception the Creole faculty members lived in the French Quarter—on Esplanade, Rampart, Royal, St. Peter, Burgundy, or Dauphine Streets. For the American faculty members, again almost without exception, residences were in the Garden District—or further uptown on St. Charles, State, Napoleon, Soniat, Calhoun, or Palmer.

But the university was much more than a mere montage of creeds and tongues. It joined, and led, the forces working toward a more modern and different city. The medical school turned out doctors every year who worked earnestly for better sanitary conditions and, thus, for a healthier people. These doctors had learned preventive medicine under Dean Chaillé and his colleagues. In the College of Technology, faculty members and students worked with motors, dynamos, and pumps to electrify and drain the city. At Newcomb, local clays were turned into objects of art. In the College of Arts and Sciences, men were being trained for the professions and for citizenship. Both the new city and the university shared a common poverty, a common opportunity, and a common task. This is given added emphasis when it is recalled how much of a local institution Tulane was in the 1880s and 1890s. For example, in 1888 not more than 15 per cent of the student body (except for Medicine) was from outside New Orleans, and this figure could be used for many years to come. The result was that although early Tulane was cosmopolitan, it was a sort of parochial cosmopolitanism which at least to a significant extent rejected much of the Creole culture.

The old campus facing Common Street in many ways symbolized the city itself. The three buildings had imposing facades but behind them were great bleak rooms with creaking floors and stairs leading to attics where rats nested and gamboled. There were few facilities for students. There was no gymnasium, no space for playing fields, no dormitories, no indoor plumbing, virtually no library. Behind these buildings was Mechanics' Hall, converted to the use of the academic department, but it was like the rest with its dreary high-ceilinged rooms. It, however, lacked even a redeeming classical facade. It was Victorian gingerbread with variations plus a touch of Grecian.

The central position of the medical building was not purely a matter of location. It was symbolic of the department's prestige and importance in the university. It was the oldest of the departments; it had on its faculty many of the city's leading doctors; and, perhaps above all, it was engaged in training young men for the very practical purpose of saving human lives. Moreover, its graduates became leading citizens almost immediately in the communities where they practiced. Then one must add to all this the fact that a certain element of the esoteric is a part of medical school tradition. Whatever the reasons may be, it is true that for many years after 1884 Tulane was known largely for its medical school.

After its rebirth in 1878 the academic department was the only division of the university with a full-time faculty until Newcomb College was founded. Medicine and law both depended almost wholly on practitioners of the community who devoted an hour or so every day to teaching. These part-time professors always were outstanding members of their professions; yet their compensation was small or even nonexistent. They taught for the love of teaching and for the personal prestige which came to them by virtue of the fact that they were members of a university faculty. These men in the academic department, however, taught for a living. They were professional teachers and as such merit more than a word of description. What was the early Tulane professor in the liberal arts department like?

He was, first of all, a teacher and not a man skilled in or even primarily interested in research. In 1884 only one member of the faculty, Robert Sharp, held the earned doctor's degree. Two years later Brown Ayres received his Ph.D. In 1887 an assistant professor with the doctorate was added to the faculty. By 1895, when the university was secure in its new buildings on the uptown campus, only five out of seventeen full professors held the earned doctorate. At the same time two of its most distinguished professors, Fortiér and Deiler, held no degrees at all. Professor Dillard held only the M.A. degree, and Professor Ficklen only the bachelor's degree. This faculty was, by and large, composed of men of catholic tastes, widely read, and, on the whole, stimulating teachers; but research was a secondary matter with them. When they did do any research and writing it quite commonly was in some field other than their field of teaching. Thus Fortier wrote about Louisiana history, Deiler in the same field, and Dillard in literature, philosophy, and mathematics. It was a period before the passion for Ph.D.'s took over the American college campus, a time before the professor had to publish or perish, a time when he dared get out of his own narrow field and write something within some other discipline. It was a leisurely and noncompulsive sort of life, which, for example, allowed Deiler and Fortier endless time to argue the relative merits of French and German culture ("The Franco-Prussian War" the students called it).

The professor was also a man of dignity and substance who had strict discipline in his classes. There was a distance between professor and student. There was hardly such a thing as a professor sitting down with his class and conducting a seminar or a "socialized" recitation. He was the master. He stood at the head of the class and lectured, and when class was over there was little fraternization between professor and student. Professor Deiler, of course, enjoyed getting student groups together to sing German folk songs but everyone agreed that the Herr Professor was a bit eccentric. "He is a German, you know," explained everything.

The professor was, finally, a man who zealously guarded the sanctity of the liberal arts. He was a missionary for culture in a philistine society, a guardian of true learning, a watchman on the ramparts of civilization. These things he felt deeply, so deeply that at times he was pedantic, intolerant, and stuffy—but his values were real, almost sacred to him. He was a conservative man who talked of the past and devoted little time to contemporary matters such as Henry George, or Populism, or the growing power of the great monopolies. By and large the classical curriculum turned minds back to antiquity. Contemporary social and economic problems were lightly touched upon. In philosophy he was a transcendentalist, and pragmatism got short shrift. Because he was by training and experience a conservative man "radicalism" was abhorrent to him, and thus it was not until 1915 that the university had a serious case involving a professor accused of corrupting the mind of youth by writing unorthodox books.

Intellectually the period between 1885 and World War I in the United States was paradoxical in the extreme. It was at once a period of complacency and a period of unrest and upheaval. Forces and philosophies were being generated which eventually shook fundamental social concepts to their very foundations. This controversial dichotomy in American intellectual life, however, hardly touched the Tulane campus in these years. In the College of Arts and Sciences and at Newcomb the same general atmosphere prevailed. Perhaps smugness is too strong a word to describe it; adherence to the litany of the *status quo* may be a kinder term. On the whole, professors lived rather comfortably on their $2,500 to $3,000 a year salary, probably more comfortably than their successors today, considering the purchasing power of the dollar then and now. It was a well-ordered life with time for wide reading. In his reading, however, the Tulane professor was more apt to read Plato than William James, and his predilections made him choose Herbert Spencer over Lester Ward.

The tremors produced by the shifting substratum of American life, however, were causing the old-fashioned college professor to walk on unsteady legs. Indeed, he was rapidly becoming an anachronism; and, in addition, the faculties, almost universally, were losing control of the universities and colleges. Not that anyone willed it thus. No junta decided to undermine the old professor and remove him from control. Rather the change resulted from the mute, irresistible, and all-comprehensive forces which were moving America in new directions. A suggestion of some of these forces will be given below, but it should be said here that there were at least four factors in the general disintegration of the old way of university faculty life: the loss of faculty autonomy in administrative matters; the growth of the free elective system; the emergence of a high degree of specialization in teaching and research; and the increased tempo of student life and activities, especially in intercollegiate athletics.

The loss of faculty autonomy and control followed the rapidly developing plan of centralized corporate control in business around the turn of the century. Presidents and boards of the new form of business organization called the corporation exercised almost complete control of the firm's policy-making functions, long-range planning, and fiscal affairs. How Tulane followed this pattern may be seen by merely referring again to the period of centralization of the Craighead era. Faculties which had long been virtually autonomous found their power slipping away into the hands of a central administrative authority—the president and the administrators. That this was an inevitable development did not make it any more palatable to them. They opposed the new trend and lost. There were qualifications, of course; Newcomb College yielded more slowly than the other colleges. Too, not all prerogatives were shorn from the faculties. In academic matters they were still potent, but in fiscal and policy matters they became largely advisory. As time went on various presidents pursued policies of cracking down on or softening the use of the power they and the administrators had gained. But it never was returned to the faculties. The Administrators of the Tulane Educational Fund were not absentee trustees. They lived in New Orleans, and they were not inclined to be figureheads.

In many universities the free elective system weakened the power of the faculty in the education of the student because the student was permitted to pick and choose courses almost at will. Consequently, the faculty member became less important in dictating academic standards and policies. But, it must hastily be said, such a condition never prevailed at Tulane, and thus this topic can be dismissed.

The growing specialization within disciplines, however, cannot be so readily disposed of. The Ph.D. was conspicuous because of his absence from the faculty roster of 1894 both at Newcomb and on the uptown campus. In the roster of 1914 the Ph.D. was conspicuous by his presence. This change was indicative of a trend which was further revealed in the listing of courses he taught. The professor of literature was coming to teach and do reading and research in a specialized field of literature. The same could be said for history, philosophy, political science, the physical sciences, and in other disciplines. The catholic scholar who read widely, taught, and wrote in more than one field was being displaced by the scholar who had narrowed his interests to a segment of one field. This segment, for better or worse, he pursued relentlessly. It is profitless to argue whether this passing of the old generalist and the appearance of the scholarly specialist and the addition of what one alumnus called the "numerology" of Carnegie units and semester hours took more out of university life than was added. Certainly the romanticist can justify a part of his thesis that the heart of liberal education was seriously damaged when the well seasoned, all-round scholar ceased to teach undergraduates. On the other hand, the academic specialist at Tulane, as well as at the other American universities, made possible the development of research programs in the graduate school; and university research has made an incalculable contribution to American life. It is the realization that both have much to offer which is leading the modern university to look for and develop that rare individual, the scholar-teacher or the widely read specialist.

The matter of student activities will require more telling, not necessarily because they came to dominate university life, but because of the interest they hold for the alumni or old friends of the university. As a matter of fact, student activities at Tulane were not nearly so dominant as in many other comparable universities of the same period. Because of the preponderance of local students and because of the fact that most of the out-of-town students lived in small groups in boarding houses rather than in dormitories, student life was somewhat less phrenetic than that of institutions where the reverse was true. However, by 1890 a pattern of student folkways had crystallized in the American college, and its configurations were observable on the Tulane campus. Songs, dress, clubs and fraternities, publications, and organized sports came to play an increasingly important part in the student's college life. It did the same at Tulane.

What was the Tulane and Newcomb student like in 1890? (Or, for that matter, what were they like in 1910? The pattern of college mores was fairly uniform from 1885 to World War I with only minor variations.)

The average Tulane student was, by and large, much more naïve and immature than the student of today; and the same can be said for the Newcomb girl. Both, the evidence indicates, studied less and took college much less seriously than their successors do at present. Reports of deans and department heads throughout these years give emphasis to this. "Scholarship in the college is not satisfactory," Dean Ayres reported in 1903. "I think the average student of the College of Arts and Sciences has too little to do. We ought to increase the hourly load from 15 hours to 18 or 20," he added. And from the faculty members came reports of preponderately immature freshmen with inadequate high school training. The Tulane male student more often than not wore a mustache, his hair parted in the middle and combed down toward his ears. His suit was tight-fitting, complete with vest, high starched collar, derby hat, and high laced shoes. The Newcomb girl was a creation by Charles Dana Gibson with her tiny wasplike waist, puffed sleeve shirtwaists, and long flowing skirts which all but covered her pointed, high-buttoned shoes. Her coiffure was upswept in front and on both sides with a knot in the back. Her hat for most occasions was a pert straw sailor complete with a veil to help the long hatpin hold it firmly against the breezes. These were the collegians and for them college, more often than not, was something of a hazy interlude to be enjoyed before life became serious.

School "spirit" in most colleges meant shirt-tail parades, bonfires, pep rallies, tears shed at the loss of a game, and dying for dear old Siwash. But at Tulane this spirit was less fanatical; and this fact worried the journalists who felt called upon to beat the drums until the students were in a frenzy. Again one can see the effects of a largely local, off-campus student body. There were parades (a professor even led one through downtown New Orleans), rah-rah yells, cane rushing, and some hazing. But this did not satisfy the Tulane college editors who were constantly exhorting the students to be more like Sewanee or Vanderbilt. (And the editors there were urging their students to have more spirit like Tulane.)

These students of the carefree days before war destroyed their world lived according to the pattern and tempo of their times. The male sang his sentimental songs accompanied by a tinkling mandolin. He sang about unrequited love, good girls gone wrong, broken hearts, "Just a Song at Twilight," "After the Ball is Over," and "Ta-ra-ra-boom-de-a." Tiring of these he began to take a lively interest in the new music with a strong beat which he probably first heard on Basin Street. But one song native to the campus perhaps best expressed the spirit of the day. It was called "The Newcomb Girl." With a lilting tune it went:

Skip along,
Dance and song,
Clear the way,
Life is gay:
And so is the Newcomb girl.

Laughing eyes,
Dainty feet,
Summer skies,
Life is sweet:
And so is the Newcomb girl.

To music's sound,
Banjo and fiddle,
Away we bound.
Life is a riddle:
And so is the Newcomb girl.

The male student had, at least in theory, his own code of morals. There were "good" girls and "fast" girls and his code taught him how to conduct himself with each. Newcomb girls generally were "good" girls in his book, and Newcomb officials took pains to see that they remained in this category. There were teas, receptions, and dances attended by students from all the colleges, but if a boy wanted to do a little private courting he encountered nothing but frustration. First of all, it was a good three miles by poor transportation from the main campus to Newcomb; and secondly, when and if he got there for a date he found the place patrolled by formidable lady chaperones. Few ever tried to date Newcomb girls at the college, for the rules were clearly calculated to thwart the course of young love. They required "quiet, lady-like behavior at all times"; a student must not go walking alone but always in company with a teacher or another student; whenever she desired to leave her dormitory, except to attend classes, special permission had to be obtained. No student was permitted to go out in the evening except in company of a suitable chaperone. Permission to go out and to receive callers was only given for Friday evenings, or for such other evenings as immediately preceded a school holiday; all others had to be devoted to "study and rest." All students were required to be at home on Sunday evenings for more rest. Undoubtedly the Newcomb girls were in the pink of health, for in addition to all these safeguards, all lights were turned out at 10:15.

It is small wonder that to ease his frustration, many a lonely male student frequented the "shop" of Mr. Edward Del Corral on Prytania Street just across Audubon Park from the campus. Mr. Del Corral advertised in *The College Spirit* that he sold milk, sandwiches, cakes, and "soda water." But it was a "soda water" of which President Johnston definitely did not approve. Being of an austere nature, the President had encouraged the Women's Christian Temperance Union in 1896 to set up a canteen in the basement of Gibson Hall called "The Varsity"; and a specialty of the house was lemonade. "But, sir," one student commented, "I am told that the W.C.T.U.'s lemonade is to the other as the faint glimmering of the lightning bug's tail is to the glorious effulgence of the noon-day sun. I am told that the former is a weak, dyspeptic mixture, a seedy concoction, the same from day to day, fixed and constant as the North Star. But the lemonade of Del Corral!" In general, it was of a light, amber hue, served in glass mugs of ample hold, and of such good measure that a foam always rose on the top and had to be blown off before the nectar could be reached. But a word to the bartender—waiter, I mean—and the whole strength and virtue of this wonderful lemonade could be condensed into a minature bell-shaped glass, sparkling with melted topaz, or better still, into two inches of reddish brown fluid, with seltzer at the side, which was called by the old-timers a straight lemonade, and deemed a drink "fit for the gods."

That President Johnston should have encouraged the W.C.T.U. in the New Orleans of that day was an anomaly of the first order. But he went further than this. The smoking of cigarettes on the Tulane campus was for a period banned. Fraternities were tolerated, but no houses were located on the campus, and partying was discouraged. He was always fearful of hazing, student pranks, and dormitory life. The craze for football gave him acute discomfort. His earliest recorded reaction to the game is more than faintly reminiscent of what many college presidents have said since that time: "We must control it or get rid of it." Then, again like some modern presidents, he later modified his point of view. While still deploring "The morbid craving for excitement," he admitted that "so great and strong is the tide of public feeling, in which parents as well as students are swept away. . . . I am convinced that no attempt by us to abolish it would be successful."

Order, moral austerity, discipline—these were the words which President Johnston emblazoned on his shield against the forces of unrighteousness. They are strongly suggestive of the Calvinist ethic; and it is in this regard that Tulane made its sharpest break with the ancient New Orleans culture pattern. Tulane was a secular institution and as such was singularly free from prejudice against any religious group. Jew, Protestant, and Catholic were all of the same footing; and yet there is no denying that the control of the university and its codes of conduct for students while on the campus were in the Calvinist tradition. This was symbolic of what had been happening in New Orleans since the time shortly after 1803 when the American Protestants began to arrive in ever increasing numbers, making their inroads upon the Creole, Catholic culture. By 1900 it was becoming evident that this American group was having a profound effect upon the city and its way of life, perhaps even playing the dominant role.

As far as student life was concerned, campus austerity merely changed the incidence of what President Johnston called "profligate student pastimes" from the campus to the city. Particularly was this true with the local student. He might respect all the Puritanical rules of the university while he was on the campus, but once he was away from it he was likely to indulge in the traditional pleasures which old New Orleans had passed on to him. There was less of the Puritan in President Alderman, and student life received something of a reprieve through his encouragement. President Craighead was too busy with other things to do much one way or another about student life. With Presidents Sharp and Dinwiddie, however, there was a revival of much of the Johnston outlook. Or, if the student did not change the locale he often merely ignored the university rule. This was particularly true of smoking. Cigarettes were *entirely* banned on the campus. Then the rule was relaxed to permit smoking on the grounds but not in the buildings or on the steps. But even this proved unenforceable. "I beg to call attention," Dean Ayres wrote President Alderman in 1903, "to the academic rule restricting smoking on the grounds and forbidding it in the buildings and on the steps. The rule is disregarded by the faculty and students alike."

University life insofar as it concerned student activities during the period may be considered under these heads: publications; clubs and fraternities; student discipline and government; social and recreational life; organized sports; and alumni activities. Publications were among the earliest student activities. No fewer than eleven different school papers were published between 1890 and the founding of *The Hullabaloo,* present campus newspaper, in 1920; and this does not include alumni publications or those of the law and the graduate schools, or *Jambalaya,* the yearbook founded in 1896.

First of the student publications were *The Rat* and the *Gazette* (changed to *Topics* after the first issue). Both appeared in November 1890 as nothing more than single typewritten sheets tacked to bulletin boards on the old campus. Apparently the major achievement of either of them was that President Johnston suppressed one issue of *The Rat.* This was almost enough to guarantee its popularity and its perpetuity, but not quite. Within a few months it joined the *Topics* in limbo, leaving several aspiring young journalists unemployed.

In December 1891 appeared the *Tulane Collegian,* a bimonthly newspaper under the editorship of Charles Rosen. It took on the surviving members of *The Rat* staff and for three years showed signs of developing into a paper of considerable merit. Newcomb students contributed to it as well as to their own *College Student.* Mrs. Newcomb read it with great pleasure, but it apparently received little faculty support. In 1894 a rival in the form of a weekly paper, *College Spirit,* came into being and in 1896 the *Collegian* decided to convert itself into a monthly. It continued in this form until 1900 when it merged with still another journalistic venture, the *Tulane Magazine.* After the merger the new publication was called the *Tulane*

University Magazine, a journal devoted to the interests of the entire university and virtually out of the category of a student newspaper. The university thus had a monthly and a weekly publication. In 1896, however, a rival weekly paper, *Olive and Blue,* under the management of Ernest Lee Jahncke, later Assistant Secretary of the Navy, sprang up. Soon it was evident that two weekly papers could not survive, so the well-worn plan of consolidation was adopted. In January 1897, the *Olive and Blue* and *College Spirit* merged into the *Daily College Spirit.* In February 1897, the first issue appeared, and for three months Tulane had the only daily in any Southern institution of higher learning. But the student body was not large enough to sustain it, and after a brief span of life, it gave up the ghost. Facetiously, the *Jambalaya* stated that the reason for the demise was that "it was everywhere apparent that the daily papers of New Orleans were being ruined by the competition."

But this did not end the recurring cycle of birth and early death of student papers. After the demise of *College Spirit,* the *Olive and Blue* was revived in December 1897, only to succumb in 1905. Out of an almost amazing fecundity, however, still another was born, the *Tulane Weekly,* in November 1905. This proved to be the most persistent of them all, lasting until it was renamed the *Hullabaloo* in 1920. Newcomb, as would be expected, had its try at a newspaper. The college had representation on the staff of the *Weekly,* but this did not satisfy the Newcomb students, who felt little empathy with the rest of the university. Moreover, they felt Newcomb news did not receive proper attention from the regular college paper and thus that they should have a publication which would reflect the Newcomb personality. The result was the *Arcade,* a quarterly, which first appeared in 1909. But it had a perilous existence, full of troubles and woes for the editors. Somehow it failed to hit the proper note for the Newcomb girl. Student interest was low, and the faculty was critical of "typography, proof reading, grammar, and contents."

Throughout the university similar criticisms and problems were almost constantly being discussed by faculty and the administration about all student publications. Since a campus newspaper was likely to be interpreted by the public as an official organ of the university, the problem came to be largely one of the extent of faculty supervision. What should be done about an irresponsible editor who put sensationalism above propriety, even truth, in the news? Should there be a faculty censorship? Was there a real issue involved when the student editors, threatened with faculty supervision, yelped about freedom of the press? What was the real function of a college newspaper? Did it have a responsibility of properly interpreting the university to the students and the public? These questions were being asked in 1900, 1910, in 1920, in 1940, and still today.

Among the publications of a nature different from the newspaper must be mentioned the *Jambalaya,* the student yearbook. After a precarious beginning in 1896, it gradually grew in popularity until in 1902 it was firmly established as a first-rate record of student life. Alumni activities also produced another sort of publication. In 1907 the *Tulane Alumni Journal* made its appearance and three years later was replaced by the *Tulane Graduates' Magazine.*

In these (and those mentioned are not all) journalistic activities the fraternities took a leading part. In fact, the fraternities took the leading part in most campus activities—clubs, student government, athletics, social life, and all the rest. Fraternity men were in the minority, but they were articulate and organized while the larger group of independent students was not. Thus with a minimum of conflict the fraternity men exercised control in most student matters. President Johnston had been a fraternity man himself in his college days and contended that this exonerated him from all suspicion of being opposed to fraternities. Yet he was frightened at the specter of loose discipline which might exist in the unsupervised houses. Thus he kept a wary eye on the fraternities and sororities which came to the campus during his administration.

Newcomb's contributions to the Greek letter circles prior to 1914 were Pi Beta Phi in 1891, Alpha Omicron Pi in 1898, Chi Omega in 1900, Kappa Kappa Gamma in 1904, Alpha Delta Pi and Phi Mu in 1906, and Kappa Alpha Theta in 1914.[1] The oldest fraternity at Tulane was Phi Kappa Sigma, dating from 1858, but with the coming of the Civil War the chapter was discontinued until 1893. Other chapters of social fraternities were: Pi Kappa Alpha, 1878; Kappa Alpha and Sigma Chi, 1886; Alpha Tau Omega, 1887; Delta Tau Delta, Kappa Sigma, and Phi Delta Theta, 1889; Sigma Alpha Epsilon, 1897; Delta Kappa Epsilon, 1899; Beta Theta Beta Tau, 1908.[2]

From the very beginning, one of the principal features of fraternity life, the fraternity house, was ardently desired by these student groups—not only houses, but houses on the campus. This, of course, was an impossibility on the old downtown site, but when the university was moved uptown with what at the time seemed boundless space, there was a strong demand for a fraternity row on the new campus. Sigma Chi made the first move by petitioning the administrators for authority to build on the campus. But the

[1] Chapters subsequent to 1914 were: Alpha Epsilon Phi, 1916; Delta Zeta, 1928; Beta Sigma Omicron, 1929; and Sigma Delta Tau, 1955.

[2] Later fraternities were: Delta Sigma Pi, 1916; Sigma Alpha Mu, 1920; Alpha Epsilon Pi, 1951; and Tau Epsilon (local) 1957. Medical fraternities were: Phi Chi, 1902; Alpha Kappa, 1903; Theta Kappa Psi, 1904; Nu Sigma Nu, 1910; Alpha Epsilon Iota, 1919; Phi Lambda Kappa, 1924; Phi Delta Epsilon, 1927. Honorary fraternities were: Kappa Delta Phi, 1904; Phi Beta Kappa, 1909; Alpha Omega Alpha, 1914; Beta Gamma Sigma, 1926; Omicron Delta Kappa, 1930; Order of the Coif, 1931; Sigma Xi, 1934; Tau Beta, 1936; Kappa Delta Pi, 1953; Phi Eta Sigma, 1954; Alpha Sigma Lambda, 1955.

petition ran into unexpected difficulties with the faculty, and in view of this the administrators postponed a decision until the matter could receive full investigation. The interminable delay which followed was the equivalent of a negative answer. Thus the fraternities turned to property near the university grounds for their houses. The first to buy and remodel was Beta Theta Pi at the corner of Magnolia (now Zimple) and Audubon Streets. Soon the others were following suit, but fraternity houses at Tulane were never on a grandiose scale.

Even more severe restrictions were placed upon the Newcomb sororities. The girls were not permitted to live in their chapter houses. Actually, members did not even own the houses. Alumnae members did, however, acquire property and make it available to the student groups for social occasions, but that is as far as the matter has ever gone.

Although fraternity and sorority life was important in inspiring "spirit" to university life, it was only one factor. Clubs and societies multiplied with marvelous rapidity. There were clubs devoted to debating, music, literature, the fine arts, bicycling, dancing, tennis, and almost every other phase of student interests. Even calling the roll of these would strain the reader's patience; but there is one which must be singled out because it was the oldest, the most honorable, and perhaps the most influential. This was the Glendy Burke Literary Society, formally organized in 1880. (A Glendy Burke Medal has been awarded intermittently since 1847.) Although it was never a large group its usefulness was felt throughout the university as an educational force, for it was in Glendy Burke that the issues of the day were debated. Subjects almost taboo in the classroom were given heated and at times rather thorough airings in the society's Saturday meetings. One can almost trace the evolution and change in America's great issues, particularly political issues, by consulting the minutes of the society.

For a brief period of time another society of a similar nature offered competition—the New Literary Society, founded in 1895. It was this society along with similar ones at Princeton, Harvard, Johns Hopkins, Stanford, and the University of California which awarded annually the endowed Carnot Medal given by the French government for debating and literary excellence. However, the New Literary Society soon merged with Glendy Burke and lost its separate identity. Together the two societies extended their activities throughout the region by establishing in 1897 the Gulf States Intercollegiate Oratorical Association with Louisiana State University plus colleges in the Gulf states as members.

Perhaps the most important organization of all, however, was "The Alumni Association of the Tulane University of Louisiana" founded in January 1898. For years before this, there had been alumni clubs of the various colleges. Law and Medicine had been first in this field. Then in 1889 Tulane College formed its alumni organization followed by Newcomb in 1893. These autonomous groups were earnest and sincere in their efforts to help build their colleges, and they accomplished some good, but it soon became obvious to alumni leaders that there must be a consolidated organization numerically strong and representing the entire university. Largely through the efforts of John Dymond, Jr., (B.A. 1888, LL.B. 1890) this was done. Objections, of course, were strong. The strictly college groups would lose their identity, it was argued. The proposed new organization would be too big and unwieldy, others said. But Dymond, assisted by Charles Rosen and others, explained, cajoled, argued, and finally won out. On January 20, 1898, the new organization was incorporated "for the purpose of promoting the social, literary, scientific, and educational interest of said alumni and said university, and generally to further the common interests of said alumni and university." On May 9 the administrators added their blessing by resolving that "the Administrators welcome this organization of the Alumni as an important factor in promoting the growth and development of the University." John Dymond, Jr., as might be expected, was elected the first president. Serving with him were S. P. Delaup, vice-president; Charles G. Gill, secretary; and J. H. Rapp, historian.[3]

One of Dymond's first acts was to put through the new executive committee a plan for improving the *esprit* of students and alumni alike by setting up a "Tulane Night" celebration. Such an occasion, he felt, would promote good fellowship and create a greater interest in the university by students and alumni. The first celebration of this sort was a theater party at the Tulane Theatre on Saturday night, February 25, 1899, where Otis Skinner was playing in *Rosemary, That's For Remembrance.*[4] Apparently this first theater student night went very well, but as time went on these "pit parties" became more and more boisterous until it was necessary to abandon the idea.

Another celebration, Founder's Day, was instituted about the same time. As early as 1888 a joint faculty-student movement began to advocate a holiday with appropriate exercises to honor the memory of Paul Tulane. In January 1890, the academic faculty voted to suggest to the board that a

[3] The charter members were: Bolling A. Pope, P. Arthur Thibaut, Abraham Goldberg, Armand Romain, H. G. Dupre, Grantland L. Tebault, J. W. Pearce, Alfred Raymond, C. Metessor, William Von Phul, Leon S. Scherck, Colgate Scudder, Henry M. Gill, Charles F. Buck, Jr., S. P. Delaup, C. G. Gill, I. I. Lemann, Charles Rosen, John Dymond, Jr., William Perkins, S. H. Backus, F. E. Rainold, George W. Flynn, Edward Rightor, John F. Tobin, William Bradish Forsyth, William J. Forments, John Watt, William C. McLeod, W. S. Hero, Gabriel Fernandez, Jr., J. B. Rosser, W. B. Spencer, Douglas Forsyth, C. Robert Churchill, Douglas S. Anderson, Louis G. LeBeuf, J. H. Malochee, Florence Dymond, E. D. Hurt, Eliza Graham Harral, Walter C. Peirce, and J. H. Rapp.

[4] Two theaters had been erected on the site of the old campus—the Crescent and the Tulane. Both faced Baronne but were separated from the street by a row of shops. One gained access to the theaters through an arcade.

day of remembrance be instituted. Somehow or other, however, the board did not readily get around to approving the plan. There seemed to be no real opposition, but at the same time, there was no strong sentiment for immediate action. Perhaps the board may be forgiven its lack of enthusiasm, for it was this board which had dealt with Paul Tulane's eccentricities and had felt the painful thud of disappointment over his having no will. At any event, there were no Founder's Day exercises until 1899 and no board approval until 1900.

For the first few years Founder's Day was a two-day university-wide holiday, but the two days were hardly spent by the students in solemn contemplation of the founder's virtues. Soon there appeared in the minutes of the University Council voices of protest. Dean Chaillé complained that the holiday only gave an opportunity for his medical students to have a fling in Storyville, and other deans reported on student misbehavior. Such behavior, plus that at the pit parties, came after President Johnston had passed away. Had he lived to see it, his last years undoubtedly would have been saddened, for this mass misbehavior was what he feared most. In 1892, in his annual report at commencement exercises, he had asked: "Why is it that you hear of no student riots, hazing, no breaking of rules, no lawlessness among our college students?" "It is," he replied to his own question, "because we have but one rule, 'Be a gentleman,' and to break it is to cease to be a Tulane student. It is because they are a law unto themselves, and under our system of self-government by the students, discipline is merged in self-control, and they live like other self-respecting people."

The College of Arts and Sciences did, indeed, have a system of student government based on the philosophy that "the students are presumed to be gentlemen." To implement this basic assumption the students elected annually a Board of Directors and to it was intrusted the general discipline of the college. The faculty, of course, reserved the right to act on its own in special cases and held a veto power over student actions. Just how well the system worked is a matter of some conjecture. There was frequent faculty interference, but Dean Ayres reported in 1903: "In the main, the self-government system has worked fairly well this year, although I feel the general feeling of the students toward it is not what it should be. They are somewhat prone to look upon members of the Academic Board as spies and policemen rather than as their own representatives. This makes the duties of the members of the Board not altogether pleasant."

Newcomb girls were, as might be expected in a period before the emancipation of the female student, subject to closer faculty supervision and discipline. However, in 1909, Newcomb permitted a limited form of student government and this discipline developed rapidly and effectively. In 1910, a Student Council was set up. To it was intrusted "all matters involving honor," its reports being made directly to the faculty. In 1911, a somewhat more elaborate plan of general student government was instituted, and the college announced that "the Newcomb Student Body is practically self-governing."

Of all the phases of college life mentioned previously, however, the one which came nearest absorbing the interest of every student was intercollegiate athletics in one form or another. In virtually every institution of higher learning in the country, pre-World War I years saw random physical exercise transformed into team play, and then team play assumed, in the minds of great masses of the public, an importance greater than that of professor and classroom. It is almost trite to remark that the faculties were appalled to find a situation developing where the worth of an institution was often determined in the minds of the public, including the alumni, by how many athletic games it could win. All over the country academicians slowly and reluctantly realized that American life was demanding of its universities that they provide mass entertainment for its enjoyment and its vicarious thrills.

Tulane's experience before 1914 with intercollegiate athletic competition was much the same as that of other universities. It was at first an almost spontaneous outgrowth of student demands. Students wanted it; therefore, it happened. It was in its early phases not highly organized, nor restricted to men recruited by the university for the purpose of playing a major sport. In those days any student who could afford six dollars for a uniform could "go out" for football and fight for a place on the team. There were no highly paid full-time coaches (Tulane had no full-time coach until 1914), nor were there enormous crowds every Saturday to pay for watching the spectacle. Playing schedules were on an informal basis. To the modern Tulane student, alumnus, and fan, accustomed to large coaching staffs, players subsidized for their athletic ability, great crowds in giant stadia, schedules arranged three or four years in advance, elaborate player uniforms and equipment, and all the other accouterment of big-time athletics, those early, formative years seem simple—almost primitive—a picture on a museum wall.

Organized athletics at Tulane may be said to date from 1887 with the formation of the Tulane Athletic Association composed of students who were interested primarily in track and secondarily in other sports as a part of college life. Assessing themselves 25 cents a month for dues, they elected their officers (Erasmus Darwin Fenner was the first president) and set about the promotion of a track meet in 1888 called the Spring Games. This intramural meet and successive ones until 1891 were held on the race track at the abandoned Exposition grounds at Audubon Park. In 1891 the games were shifted to the Fair Grounds race track where interest ran so high that, according to the newspapers, six thousand people attended in 1892. Track was getting to be "big time."

Other Southern institutions were also developing track teams, and it normally followed that there would be intercollegiate competition. In 1894 Tulane's team attended the spring meet of the University of Alabama, winning every event in which it competed. (Vanderbilt, Tulane, and Alabama were the three teams.) Upon their return to the campus came the inevitable third step—the demand that the university provide facilities for future meets; and this the university did. In 1895 a quarter-mile track was laid out on the campus across Freret Street just beyond the present maintenance building, and wooden bleachers seating 3,500 people were erected. Tulane had its first stadium. In 1910 the seating capacity was increased to 13,500 by moving the wooden bleachers built to accommodate the crowd which heard President Taft speak in the quadrangle back of Gibson Hall.

The Southern Intercollegiate Athletic Association formed by nineteen colleges and universities, of which Tulane was one, in 1894 began holding track meets during its first year of existence, but Tulane did not participate until 1899 when it was represented at the fifth annual meet at Nashville. Tulane sent 25 track men to the meet, their expenses being paid by the New Orleans newspapers. Encouraged by its showing (Tulane won second place) the team came home and launched a drive to bring the meet to Tulane, and was successful. The sixth annual S.I.A.A. meet was held at Tulane in the spring of 1900. But Tulane's hopes were dashed. The team came out third, behind North Carolina and Vanderbilt.

Baseball was the second major sport to develop on the campus, but it seems impossible to pin down the exact date when the first game was played. The game was being played on vacant lots by Tulane students in the 1880s, but this was hardly considered even intramural competition. It was little more than random physical exercise and sport. But baseball, like track, soon dropped its role of random activity and adopted that of coordinated team play. The intramural programs begun in 1892 aroused so much interest that a game with Louisiana State University was scheduled. On May 12, 1893, a team of Tulanians went to Baton Rouge to play what appears to have been the first regularly scheduled intercollegiate baseball game in the history of Tulane.[5] And Tulane lost 10 to 8, but the reason for the defeat, according to the Tulane team, seems to be a bit strange in view of the athletic rivalry which has developed between the two universities. The Tulane team was, it declared, greatly weakened by L.S.U.'s hospitality. There was a dance on the night before the game which lasted until 3:00 A.M. Someone, it appears, slipped a bottle or two into the festivities. Then on the day of the game there was a parade and further carryings on with the result that the team was not in the best physical trim at game time. Just why the vision of the L.S.U. team was not similarly impaired was not explained.

[5] The newspapers report, however, that a game between the two institutions was played on January 6, 1888. In those days baseball was no mere summer sport.

Baseball never attracted spectator crowds as did track, but it was popular among the students. Perhaps the fact that Newcomb girls turned out in great numbers to cheer the team was partly responsible. At any event the teams carried on, scrounging for their uniforms, for money for their trips, and for balls, bats, and other equipment. The state of the university's finances would hardly have permitted it to subsidize athletics, even had there been an inclination to do so. And as it was, the faculty tolerated baseball as long as the members of the team violated no university rules. When the team left the campus without permission, as it did in 1900 for a trip to Oxford to play Ole Miss, however, there was considerable talk among the faculty members about regulating intercollegiate athletics and bringing them under better control. This sort of talk grew as the years came and went, particularly when football came to play so important a role in campus life.

It was football, of course, which came eventually to dominate the athletic scene at Tulane. From a modest beginning, it grew to significant proportions by 1914. Tulane teams were not conspicuously nor consistently successful in the prewar period, but the sport established itself in the minds and emotions of students and the public at large almost as a *sine qua non* of university life. Baseball and track came to take secondary positions.

Football was brought to New Orleans by students who had attended Eastern universities where they had either played the game or observed it. In the late 1880s Tulane students were kicking a ball around in the small plot of ground behind the medical building on Common Street. Between 1885 and 1888 Hugh Bayne and his brother, Thomas, who had participated in football at Yale, taught these students the rules and divided them into two squads. On Christmas Day 1888, the first football game in New Orleans was played between those two groups at Sportsman's Park, then located between the New Basin Canal and Canal Street. A crowd estimated at six hundred people saw the game, and although gate receipts were small, the proceeds were donated to the Charity Hospital ambulance horse fund.

After this first game, football grew rapidly in the minds and interests of sportsmen; and at a time when athletic clubs were being formed in many Southern cities. This new game appealed to them and they promoted it. In October 1893, the Southern Athletic Club of New Orleans organized its own team and looked about for opponents. Naturally the incipient Tulane team furnished the opposition, the game being played on November 18, 1893. Hugh Bayne led the Tulanians; and his brother, Thomas, although he was coaching at Tulane then, coached the SAC team for this game. In addition, Thomas laid out the field, sold tickets, and acted as a game official. Despite the fact that Tulane's coach was in such a strategic position, the university team lost 12–0. But a week later, it redeemed itself in its first intercollegiate game.

The "Old War Skule" up the river at Baton Rouge was, like Tulane, experimenting with the new game. By 1893 it, too, had a few men who called themselves the Louisiana State University football team, and they expressed a desire to schedule games, particularly with Tulane. The two universities had little to do with it, but on November 25, 1893, these two teams met in Sportsman's Park for their first contest.

Many of the details of this game have been lost in time, but a few facts remain extant. It was characterized by the then prevailing battering ram tactics, utilizing the flying wedge and the piling on plays which resulted in so many injuries. Both teams were rather nondescript. Uniforms consisted of a pullover sweater, a pair of lightly padded khaki pants ending with a rubber drawstring just below the knee, long stockings of every hue and color, and shoes with improvised cleats. Both teams were rather light and inexperienced, and there apparently were no serious injuries on either team, although one wonders how in the absence of head guards and proper padding, the players escaped the inevitable physical effects of mayhem. The *Times-Picayune* commented on the "gentlemanly restraint" of the players, but in those days gentlemanly restraint meant that a team did not go into a game equipped with black jacks or brass knuckles.

There was no organized cheering at this game. Cheers were spontaneous or were led by students who jumped out in front of the crowd from time to time to exhort their colleagues just before or after a touchdown. (Incidentally, Tulane won 34–0.) The cheerleader was years away, seven years away to be exact; in 1900 the medical students, encouraged by President Alderman, first used the method of cheering in unison. Neither was there a band to play for the game. This feature, too, was seven years away when the medical students hired a brass band to lead a parade headed by Professor Metz to the Millsaps game. As a matter of fact this first game with L.S.U. was singularly lacking in color. Twenty-two young men went out on the field and with gentlemanly restraint tried to slug each other into insensibility. The spectators enjoyed it. That was the game.

A week later, Tulane played the University of Mississippi. A few days before the game, the team got around to selecting its colors, olive and blue; and although the new colors were stained with defeat 12–4, they did not run, and eventually the term "Greenie" emerged as the team name.

Two defeats and one victory in its first season rather set the pace for Tulane teams during the next few years. In 1895 the Olive and Blue won four and lost two; in 1899 it lost every game; in 1900 it was undefeated, untied, and unscored upon. Another good year was 1908 when the team lost only one game, but this was followed by the years of the locusts. Between 1909 and 1914 the record was dismal. Student spirit hit a new low during those years. Indeed, had it not been for the successful efforts of the indefatigable John Dymond, Jr., in raising $200 to get a band started in 1912, these years would have been barren indeed for the rah, rah student.

There were other reasons for the sagging spirit. In 1905 New Orleans had its last great yellow fever scourge, followed four years later by a smallpox epidemic, and this by an outbreak of diphtheria and mumps. Hardship resulted from the fact that Tulane had no infirmary where it could care for the sick students. On October 30, 1912, the University Council recommended to the board that an infirmary be built, but the recommendation was not acted upon. Tulane was still largely a local institution, and most of the sick students could be cared for at home.

There were other signs of a drooping morale among the students. From a heavily attended, almost rowdy celebration at Founder's Day in 1906, interest dwindled to a point where by 1912 attendance was very small in spite of the fact that thousands of invitations were sent out. There was serious discord, too, between the Tulane and Newcomb student bodies, growing out of the alleged "disloyalty" of the Newcomb girls in not supporting the team. On every hand it was becoming obvious that a winning football team was the spring from which flowed a spirited student morale and, for that matter, emotional support of the institution by large segments of the public. Football had passed from the realm of pure sport, where young college men played a game on Saturday afternoons, to a potent factor in the life and reputation of the university. However much many faculty members deplored the fact that the university was being forced to supply large-scale entertainment for masses of people wholly uninterested in higher education, the fact still remained that the university, having once waded into the stream of intercollegiate football competition, found no escape from the ever-increasing current of the waters.

Realizing this fact, universities, and even lay groups, set out to control what appeared to them to be a monster wearing the sports attire of a college student. Many groups who strongly supported intercollegiate football were aware of its problems. There was, for example, the matter of serious injuries resulting from poor protective equipment and loose rules. Although intended as humor, the *Picayune* perhaps did not exaggerate the seriousness of the situation when it paraphrased "Just Before the Battle Mother" as:

> "Farewell, mother, you may never
> Press me to your heart again;
> For I'm in the rush line, mother,
> And more likely to be slain."

Added to this were the growing faculty complaints of interrupted class work and of pseudo students who were permitted to play regardless of their class standing—"ringers" they were called. Too, there were voices to point out how much football cost; of how much went into one sport to the neglect of a basic program of physical training for all the students.

Various remedies were tried at Tulane, most of them successful to a limited degree only.

There had been a faculty committee on athletics since 1890, but it was powerless to cope with the rising football fever. In 1894 the Tulane Athletic Association advocated a regional association to enforce codes and rules designed to make the game cleaner and safer from the taint of professionalism. The result of this and similar agitation at other Southern colleges led to the formation in 1894 of the Southern Intercollegiate Athletic Association composed of 19 institutions, including Tulane. But to Tulane's great embarrassment one of the first important official acts of this body was to ban Tulane from intercollegiate competition in 1897 because Coach H. W. Baum (unwittingly, he said) had played an ineligible player in the Tulane-L.S.U. game of October 24, 1896. Tulane was restored to the fellowship of the Association in 1898, but harmonious relations with L.S.U were not restored until 1910. Between 1906 and 1910 athletic relations between the two institutions were severed completely while each hurled scholarly imprecations at the other. Football had become that powerful in institutional life.

In December 1908, Tulane tried another control device: The Tulane Athletic Association was reconstituted by the administrators. The executive body of the new group was composed of one administrator, three alumni, the chairman of the Faculty Committee on Athletics, the athletic director (when selected), and the president of the Alumni Association.[6] The board vested "control and direction of athletics and all athletic enterprises at the . . . University . . . including the financing thereof" in this group.

In general this body accomplished some better measures of control, but before it had been in business many months it made the discovery that college athletics cost money. The $15,000 spent for the cinder track and the $20,000 borrowed for construction of the gymnasium in 1912 were more than the group could finance. There was only one answer: bigger and better football teams which would attract larger and larger crowds which would pay more and more dollars at the gate.

By the end of Craighead's administration and the beginning of Sharp's term, football was more firmly intrenched than ever. Although some measure of control had been instituted, Tulane was on the verge of a period of football greatness which began with Clark Shaughnessy in 1915.

[6] In 1910 Appleton A. Mason, a Bachelor of Physical Education from the Springfield, Massachusetts, Training School, was appointed director of physical education. He was not a coach, but rather was given the task of coordinating athletic activities and of developing a well-rounded physical education program. He was not successful, however, and soon left the university.

CHAPTER 10

There is No Peace (1912-1918)

WHEN THE ADMINISTRATORS OF the Tulane Educational Fund began casting about for a successor to Edwin Boone Craighead, they were acutely aware that in spite of its progress, the administration of this man had left deep wounds which needed healing lest further infection threaten the health of the university. As something of a delaying action they looked about them and turned to a scholarly, humble, and greatly respected professor of literature, sixty-one-year-old Robert Sharp. On July 8, 1912, he was named acting president. On April 16, 1913, while out of the city, he was made president.

In many respects, slightly built, Virginia-born Dr. Sharp seemed an ideal man for the disturbed institution, for he was a man of peace who had no illusions of making over the university. "No man changes a university radically," he said at his inauguration. "Things are always shaping themselves and taking form." And this idea governed his administration. Although a man of convictions he was never compulsive, never a schismatic reformer. Rather he preferred repose to reform, scholarly pursuits to administrative duties; and he had a genuine skepticism of magic academic nostrums.

For thirty-two years, ever since he took his doctorate at Leipzig in 1879, he had taught at Tulane. He had been a part of the transition from the University of Louisiana to Tulane University. He had moved from the old campus to the new. He had seen the travail of the university as it sought to grow and expand. And all these years he had gone quietly about his work of teaching, administering the graduate school, and writing about literature. In collaboration with James A. Harrison of Washington and Lee he had edited texts of *Beowulf* and *The Fight at Finnesburh* which were widely used. He had written many critical essays and critical analyses of English masterpieces, especially Shakespeare's dramas. Too, during these years he had, quite unknown to himself, built a reputation for unostentatious integrity and true humility of spirit. Certainly one would never think of him as a man who would inspire a torchlight parade, yet he did. He had been out of the city attending an educational conference when it was announced that he had been elected to the presidency. When he returned on April 29, 1913, he was met at the railroad station by a sizable group of students, alumni, and faculty who escorted him behind a brass band to the uptown campus where a bonfire celebration was held in front of the Richardson Memorial building.

One can well imagine his surprise, perhaps embarrassment, at such a welcome, for he was a reluctant president-elect. He had no illusions about the task ahead of him. He knew the university and its problems inside out and was not sure the state of his health would permit him to do the sort of job which conditions made imperative. He would do his best, he told the crowd, but he would serve only on the condition that he be released whenever he felt he was not doing the job well. This same sentiment he later formally expressed to the administrators and added that he would have to delegate a great deal of responsibility to his deans. This, as time went on, he did, especially to Dean Dinwiddie of the College of Arts and Sciences.

The new president's pince-nez had no rosy lenses to give a false glow to the era of peace which people on every side so optimistically foretold. He felt he might restore a measure of tranquility, but many of the "things shaping themselves and taking form" in the university Sharp clearly recognized for what they were—forces which could only mean for him sleepless nights and troubled days. One does not wonder at his reluctance to accept the job. The perennial problem of finances seemed, if anything, to grow more acute as the years went by. The university had expanded out of all proportion to its resources. Many faculty members were lost, and many more were still troubled over the events of the recent past. He could not have known, of course, that hardly more than a year after he assumed office all Europe would go to war and that the shadows of this conflict would lengthen across the campus, finally becoming so dark that the spiritual and intellectual values which are the essence of a university would be, for a time, obscured.

When Sharp became acting president in 1912 he was confronted by a continuing financial problem which by now was taking on the symptoms of a chronic and malignant disease. During late 1912 and throughout 1913 the nation was sinking into the downward phase of an economic cycle. Income from rents and earnings from securities shrank, a fact clearly demonstrated by the shrinkage in the Tulane Educational Fund, invested largely in real estate, stocks, and bonds. In May 1910, the fund (not including Newcomb) had $934,595.11 in productive funds and $73,531.21 in special funds. By 1912 the productive funds had dropped to $897,644.46 and by 1916 this had further shrunk to $706,563.81. But this was only one reason for the financial distress. Another important one was that the university had expanded beyond its means. New departments had been added without adequate endowment funds to support them, and thus existed on a basis of year-to-year income from whatever source might be discovered. This state of affairs was clearly revealed in a report made by Dr. Wallace Buttrick and Dr. Abraham Flexner of the General Education Board who at the university's invitation had made an inspection in 1913–1914. They were very frank in expressing their opinion that the university had expanded in too many directions and had then unwisely attempted to finance the new departments and schools through special funds. This, the two visitors felt, endangered the entire university's financial structure. The multiplicity of special funds produced an imbalance which could do more harm than good, they said, even perhaps defeating the purposes of the donors. What the university needed to do, they reported, was to curtail its expansion, consolidate and eradicate several departments, and then seek a substantial general endowment for university-wide purposes.

The fact that there was an imbalance in funds is perfectly obvious. No better example of this can be cited than a comparison of Newcomb and Tulane funds. While Tulane was running an annual deficit, Newcomb with a much larger endowment showed annual profits running as high as $40,000 in some years. Yet Tulane could not utilize Newcomb funds to relieve the over-all distress. Other departments which had received special funds fared rather well at times while the less fortunate ones languished. To add to the financial discomfort there was the fact that enrollment was growing, necessitating a larger faculty. Since tuition charges met only a fractional part of the needs and there was no significant increase in general endowment, the result could only be lower salaries for all the faculty. University enrollment rose from 2,421 in 1911–1912 to 2,998 in 1916–1917. The number of faculty members increased from 275 in 1912–1913 to 328 by 1917. The result on faculty salaries is a matter of simple arithmetic. Two hundred and seventy-five divided into income gives one figure. Three hundred and twenty-eight divided into the same income gives a much lower result. For this and other reasons, faculty salaries, which had for full professors a range of $2,900–$4,000 in 1905 had a range in 1917 of $2,500–$3,300. Those of lower academic rank suffered an even greater salary depreciation, and this distress was acute. Appeals for salary increases to the president and the administrators brought no relief. There was no way to give relief without additional income.

The findings of the Buttrick-Flexner investigation were sound, and no one disputed their validity, yet it took time for the full impact to sink in on the minds of the administrators. They had to be prodded out of their complacency and persuaded that they should be more imaginative and vigorous in permanent fund raising. Meantime, they pursued the now almost time-honored practice of trying to meet each year's deficit through annual solicitations. For the calendar year 1913, the deficit was $42,800, and it was up to Sharp to raise it.

In early 1914 the president began the drive with an appeal in the form of a brochure entitled *Founder's Memorial*. Tulane is not a rich institution, he vigorously asserted. It is poor, and it is at a crucial period in its history. With some assistance from the alumni and New Orleans businessmen, he wiped out most of the 1913 deficit only to be confronted with a $29,000 deficit for 1914. It was discouraging, one may be sure, to make progress and then slip back again. But this was not so discouraging as the fact that President Sharp met on every hand the feeling that Tulane was a rich university and really needed no help. It was the old canard which began early in the administration of William Preston Johnston. The deplorable fact that it had not been exorcised must be laid largely at the door of the administrators. In fact, the responsibility for several unfortunate conditions must be laid there.

It would have been difficult to have found in the entire state a group of more dedicated leaders than these men who served on the board. They were men of influence, dignity, and, some of them, wealth. They were the soul of integrity and honor. But they saw no necessity for taking the public into their confidence. They were the administrators of a private educational fund responsible to no one save themselves. Therefore, they pursued a policy of dignified aloofness in the conduct of the affairs of the university, with the result that the public had no idea, or at best a nebulous and inaccurate one, of the university's financial problems. They were a self-perpetuating body and thus the new members who came on the board now and then usually conformed to the prevailing pattern of thought.[1] Moreover, most of the members were residents of New Orleans and were closely in touch with the day-by-day happenings on the campus. As a result they yielded to the temptation at times to interfere in matters which properly belonged to the president of the university or to the faculty.

[1] Membership on the board changed infrequently. This table shows the tenure of those who were members of the board in 1913:

Member	Dates of Tenure	Years on Board
Robert M. Walmsley, President	1882–1919	37
James McConnell	1882–1914	32
Charles Janvier	1894–1927	33
Edgar H. Farrar	1882–1922	40
Walter R. Stauffer	1882–1932	50
Henry Ginder	1882–1920	38
John B. Levert	1892–1930	38
Walker B. Spencer	1895–1941	46
John Dymond	1901–1932	31
Charles Rosen	1904–1954	50
Frederick W. Parham	1906–1914	8
Alfred Raymond	1908–1920	12
James H. Dillard	1908–1913	5
William R. Irby	1910–1926	16
Abraham Brittin	1910–1932	22
John Callan	1911–1924	13

These conditions were apparent to many people both within and without the university at that time. In 1913, President Sharp himself formally brought to the attention of the board the prevailing mistaken concepts about university affairs and urged that wide publicity be given to the true financial picture. But the board took no action. In 1914, Walker B. Spencer, New Orleans attorney and long-time member of the board, proposed a drastic revision of the functions of the administrators. The board, he proposed in a resolution, should consider itself as acting in a dual role. One role would be that of purely fiscal administrators of an educational fund. The other was that of an educational policy-making and public relations group. The board should, he felt, have separate meetings to consider each of these and not confuse one with the other. But this resolution died quietly in committee. In 1915, the administrators appointed a "Special Committee to Secure Financial Aid for the University." In its report, this group urged the board to build up the general endowment of the university and eventually to abandon its little piecemeal annual deficit fund-raising campaigns. In addition, the committee urged that the board inform the public of the university's true financial plight.

In June of 1915, the board made a gesture of compliance with the committee's recommendations. It unanimously voted to make a public statement of the university's finances and to make public a summary of each board meeting. On the matter of a permanent endowment fund it was silent. But apparently this gesture on the board's part was not satisfactory to everyone, for the agitation for board reform continued. The very next year a substantial group of alumni petitioned the board to abolish its self-perpetuating life tenure features and substitute an alumni election plan. This petition, along with the rest, was courteously received and quietly suffocated in committee files. Only with the coming of the war did the agitation quiet down.

Problems of faculty tenure, salaries, freedom, and retirement also became serious during Sharp's administration. The matter of lower salary schedules has already been mentioned. Added to this was the fact that the board went on record as being financially unable to make its contributions to the Carnegie pension plan. The faculty petitioned in vain for salary increases; and to its fears and misgivings over failure to secure relief there was added the problem of academic freedom.

The first serious case involving the right of a professor to write and speak on unorthodox matters had come in 1911 in the case of Professor William B. Smith, one of the university's most brilliant and versatile scholars. Dr. Smith came to the university in 1893 as professor of mathematics. In 1906, he switched to philosophy and became a full professor in that discipline. His scholarly publications were numerous and well received, particularly in European university circles. In 1910, he finished a book entitled *Ecce Deus,* a critical study of the New Testament, and its publication in 1911 stirred up rather violent controversy, especially among denominational periodicals. Soon the public, taking their cue from these, was bombarding members of the board with letters demanding the firing of Professor Smith, among other things, for denying the divinity of Christ. Professor Smith, being a man not averse to controversy, stood his ground and the matter was put squarely up to the board.

After reading all the letters of denunciation and after encountering countless people on the streets who insisted on having their say about how the professor should be punished, the board in September, 1911, appointed five of its members as a special committee to investigate the matter; but the committee never made a report. Perhaps the fact that Professor Smith was within four years of retirement plus the discovery that the book was written in German and thus practically no one, not even the committee members, could read it were mitigating factors. At least Smith was permitted to remain on the faculty until he reached retirement age in 1915.

In some respects a more explosive case was that of Dr. Gustav Mann, since 1908 a respected professor of physiology in the Medical School. In the spring of 1915, Dr. Mann made the address at annual Ivy Day exercises and took the occasion to lambaste the medical school and to arraign the university administration for permitting what he pictured as glaring deficiencies. He singled out departments and gave a bill of particulars in each case while his listeners sat aghast. While it was in some ways an intemperate speech, evidence indicates it was made without malice. But at all events, it provoked a heated controversy, and this Dr. Mann undoubtedly had anticipated, perhaps even welcomed, for there seems little doubt that he felt what he was saying was in the best interests of the medical school. The medical faculty itself was divided on the issue. Dean Dyer, however, was greatly disturbed and charged Dr. Mann with being a chronic trouble maker. On the other hand a group of New Orleans doctors presented the board with a formal document in which they declared their faith in Dr. Mann and stated the only fault they had to find with his speech was that it did not picture conditions as being really as bad as they were.

The board's method of handling the hot issue was to appoint another special committee from its own membership to consider the matter. During the early summer of 1915, while the committee was holding hearings on Dr. Mann's case, the board asked its law committee to report on just what powers the board had in the matter of faculty tenure. On June 16, 1916, the law committee reported that under the law and the charter of the board its powers in such matters were absolute. "All professors and employees of the Board hold their positions at the pleasure of the Board, and may be removed at any time . . .," the committee ruled. When this ruling was immediately adopted by the board, it became the official policy regarding tenure. Specifically applied, it resulted in the dismissal of Dr. Mann in August.

As is the case in all such controversial issues it is difficult, or even impossible, to pass final judgment on who was right and who was wrong. That there were glaring inadequacies in the medical school no one could deny. Inadequate finances and an expansion of teaching services and facilities undoubtedly had resulted in a lowering of standards in some areas. Undergraduate medicine, postgraduate medicine, tropical medicine, hygiene and preventive medicine, pharmacy, and dentistry made up a combined corps of offerings which was too much for Medicine's slim income. Too, many of the faculty members who had lifted the department to greatness were because of death, resignation, or retirement no longer on the scene. Gone before 1918 were Drs. John J. Archinard, Paul Emile Archinard, Edouard M. Dupaquier, John Barnwell Elliott, Charles J. Landfried, Ernest S. Lewis, Gustav Mann, Louis Favrot Reynaud, Edmond Souchon, and others. Their places Dean Dyer had to fill by promoting younger faculty members or by new appointments. But the dean could not guarantee much in the way of salary. He had worked and hoped for a guaranteed salary plan but had been unable to achieve it. The faculty solved the dilemma by agreeing to work for nothing or for whatever there might be left over above expenses. As for salaries, then, the medical school was back where it was in the 1880s.

Troubles came not singly but by battalions.

The School of Hygiene and Tropical Medicine, including preventive medicine, which had started with such high hopes, declined and finally was discontinued. While a large factor in the department's decline was an inadequate budget, a contributing factor appears to have been in the lackadaisical attitude of Dr. Creighton Wellman who had been appointed dean in 1913. He served only one year, but during that time seems to have caused irreparable damage through his irrational behavior. Dr. W. H. Seemann succeeded him, but the downward trend was not arrested. During Wellman's year, enrollment dropped from fifty to sixteen. In the last year of Sharp's administration only one student was in attendance. In June 1918, the department was abolished. How long Pharmacy and Dentistry would escape a similar fate was problematical.

Declining enrollment must be added to the list of Dean Dyer's problems. From a high point of 517 in 1907 the size of the medical student body dwindled to 279 in 1915. The number of graduates fell in proportion. Degrees were awarded to 104 young doctors in 1912. In 1917, 52 were awarded. And it was the same, only worse, in other Southern medical schools. Vanderbilt, Atlanta, Memphis, and Louisville each registered not more than 17 freshmen medical students in the fall of 1914. The war was having a telling effect this early.

Too, there was friction with Charity Hospital authorities over the matter of internships. Tulane had enjoyed a virtual monopoly on these internships since 1884. During 1913, Dean Dyer and his faculty were at odds with the administrators of the hospital over the matter. Finally the hospital authorities pushed a bill through the legislature in 1914 opening internships to "all other reputable and acknowledged practitioners of medicine . . . in proportion to the largest numbers of students attending said institutions respectively at any one session of the previous year." Actually, as it worked out, the act did not injure Tulane, but for several years there was the fear that Tulane graduates might not find the possibility of interning at Charity. More than anything else it was just one more matter to harass the dean and faculty. And if one wished to add other woes there was the matter of neighbors constantly complaining about the noise the dogs used for experimental purposes made in their yard outside the building. Too, limited finances made it impossible to keep the library up to date or pay the librarian a decent salary. Fortunately, none of the Dean Dyer's faculty fell down the steps and broke his neck, but it must have worried the dean that this might happen and thus make his discomfiture complete.

On the other hand, there was a brighter side to the picture. Dr. Matas added prestige and balance to the faculty when at times it showed signs of being about ready to blow up. In spite of the fact that his last years at the university were full of controversy and bickering, Dr. Metz in 1914 was elected vice-president of the National Institute of Social Sciences in recognition of his work in the field of sanitation and food and drug regulation. During this year, he, Dr. Charles C. Bass, and Dr. Charles W. Duval were the only Southerners awarded the Institute's gold medal—to Bass for his research in malaria, beriberi, hookworm, and typhoid; to Duval for his participation in research which led to the discovery of the dysentery bacillus and for his work in controling scarlet fever. In 1914, Dr. Dyer himself was honored by being elected president of the American Medical College Association. Also, there were promising younger faculty members coming along who would, in time, add to the effectiveness of the school. Dr. Marcus Feingold, first full professor of ophthalmology at Tulane, organized one of the best departments in the South. Dr. Wilbur C. Smith was attracting wide attention because of his work in gross anatomy. Other younger men were on their way up, men such as Hamilton Polk Jones, Isidore Cohn, Oscar W. Bethea, Urban Maes, Charles L. Eshleman, Isaac I. Lemann, Hiram W. Kostmayer, and others.

Out of this discouraging period when at times it seemed the tide was out and the view of the entire university was disfigured by the ugly mudbanks of inadequacies, there emerged two significant developments in the medical school—women were admitted and a new liberal arts–medicine curriculum was developed. The sentiment for admitting women to the medical school had grown rapidly during Dean Dyer's administration. On December 1,

1914, the faculty took the final action with only one dissenting vote. The decision was approved by the administrators a few days later. Two and a half years afterward Miss Lindal Hill Coleman, of Houston, Texas, received the first M.D. degree ever conferred by Tulane on a woman. By 1918, however, there were 13 women enrolled in medicine. The combined scientific-medical program was adopted by the Arts and Sciences faculty on March 2, 1917. The program led to the degree of Bachelor of Science and was intended to broaden the medical students' intellectual horizons and cultural interests. The new program was not mandatory for the student seeking admission to Medicine, but in 1918 the medical faculty approved new entrance requirements which made it necessary for the prospective student to have two full years of college work before he would be considered. The two-year course was also instituted by the College of Arts and Sciences.

The College of Arts and Sciences, of course, felt the almost numbing effects of the troubled period quite as much as the medical school. Dean Dinwiddie shared with Dean Dyer the common problem of rebuilding a faculty. Sharp had made the transition from teacher to president in 1912. In 1914, Alceé Fortier died, leaving a place in teaching and writing which no one could fill as he did. In 1915, Professor William B. Smith retired. But the full impact of faculty losses can be even better understood by noting retirements and resignations just before the Sharp era. In 1907, John W. Caldwell and John Rose Ficklen retired. Caldwell in chemistry and Ficklen in English and history had both joined the faculty in 1884. In 1911, Walter Miller, professor of classical languages and for a time dean of the College of Arts and Sciences, retired. In this same year, Ulrich Bonnell Philips in history resigned to accept another position. Professor Dillard had resigned in 1908 to accept a position with the Jeannes Fund. Professor Deiler had died in 1907. Indeed, it seemed that the college was almost beginning anew except for its retention of the three curricula (classical, literary, and scientific), almost unchanged since the early 1890s.

Faculty changes at Newcomb were not so numerous and severe. The Ordways (John Morse in biology and Evelyn Walton in chemistry) had retired in 1904 and 1905, respectively, and the irrepressible Jane Caldwell Nixon in 1907. Dixon himself had reached the retirement age, but was retained on a year-to-year basis until 1919. There were other faculty changes, but Dixon's problem between 1912 and 1918 was not one of starting over again with a comparatively new faculty but of moving the physical plant of the college from the old campus in the Garden District to the new one on Broadway. In many ways Newcomb was in a much better position during Sharp's administration than any other college in the university. As pointed out above, this certainly was true financially, for the Newcomb endowment provided amply for the college's relatively modest needs at that time. And this matter of finances was the crucial one! There was nothing wrong with the rest of Tulane that a few million dollars in general endowment would not cure.

The lack of money was also reflected in the slow growth of the library, still under the direction of Miss Minnie Bell. In 1912, the Tulane library had 37,000 volumes and in 1918, only 39,000. In the same period, Newcomb's library increased from 11,000 to 14,000. Medical students had the use of only 14,000 volumes in their own library, but they had access to some 8,000 volumes in the Orleans Parish Medical Society Library. Law was similarly situated. It had about 10,000 volumes on the campus, but it could and did use the Louisiana Bar Association Library. Of great significance for the future of the Tulane Library, however, was the rapid growth of the fine Howard Library at Lee Circle. In the six years from 1912 to 1918 it increased its holdings from 53,000 volumes to 65,000.

It was easier for the university to build a new stadium than it was to buy books. The old wooden bleachers were seriously damaged by a storm in 1915 and from all sides came a clamor of voices calling for a new stadium, this one to be of concrete and thus impervious to the weather. The *Times-Picayune* sparked a drive headed by Paul F. Jahncke to raise the funds. Friday, March 31, 1916, was designated "Realization Day," on which businessmen, students, alumni, and even faculty members made a fundraising *tour de force*, realizing some $24,000 in one day. The new concrete stadium was assured and was dedicated October 27, 1917.[2]

Except for low faculty salaries and the lack of money for new laboratory equipment, Engineering fared perhaps better than Medicine and Arts and Sciences. Law had no radical changes, either. In the fall of 1913, Professor Dudley O. McGovney, formerly of the University of Missouri Law School, was made the first full-time dean, but he held the position only one year before returning to Missouri. Charles Payne Fenner, New Orleans attorney, then became dean, but not in a full-time capacity. The *Southern Law Review* was founded in 1916, but it was a war casualty. Entrance requirements were raised to the point where at lest one year of prelegal college work was mandatory, and rendering a service similar to what it had done for medicine, the College of Arts and Sciences devised a special six-year liberal arts–legal degree program. There were small gifts to remind the law school that somebody cared, but Law, like the rest of the university, was unable to escape its financial fetters.[3] (Perhaps a postscript should be

---

[2] This was not the present "Sugar Bowl" stadium. The first concrete stadium was built immediately behind what is now the Navy building. A part of this stadium is now occupied by the maintenance department of the university.

[3] Mrs. Norma Conrad, $5,000 for the Law library; Bernard Bruenn (class of 1881), $30,000 bequest; Mrs. Benjamin Morgan Harred, $5,000. Another gift during Sharp's regime was the old French Opera House, Bourbon and Toulouse Streets, presented to the university by W. R. Irby, a member of the Board of Administrators. Mr. Irby frankly admitted the gift was a sentimental one and would bring in no income to the university. His great gift came later.

added at this point: In the fall of 1914, a red-headed, ambitious farm boy from North Louisiana, carried on the university records as Hugh Pierce Long, Jr., entered as a special student. He stayed only one year and did not complete all his courses, but this constituted the only formal law training for the extraordinary young man who later emerged as "The Kingfish"— Huey P. Long.)

The sterility of the period, however, was relieved by three significant events: the founding of the College of Commerce and Business Administration; the moving of Newcomb College to its new buildings adjacent to the main campus; and America's entrance into World War I.

It is difficult to say just *when* the idea of a school of business administration at Tulane first originated. As has been pointed out earlier, J. D. B. DeBow had tried to get such a project started as early as the 1850s; and subsequently others had given it thought. It is not difficult, however, to describe *how* the idea finally came to fruition. The College of Commerce and Business Administration was brought to life largely through the efforts of Morton Arnold Aldrich.

Aldrich was an aggressive, personable, and outspoken professor of economics at Tulane in 1914 when the new college was born. He had come to the university in 1901. Behind him was a record of excellent training —A.B., Harvard; Ph.D., Halle; plus teaching experience at Harvard and Stanford. He had not been at Tulane long before he began, at first, a quiet campaign. He and Alderman had discussed the matter of a new college from time to time, and similar conversations were held with Craighead. Both presidents had, however, approached the matter with caution in view of the strong opposition from the faculty of the College of Arts and Sciences to a "vocational" school or "business college."

What may be considered the opening gun in Aldrich's active campaign was fired on Founder's Day, 1909, by alumni orator Abraham Goldberg. "Ever since the dawn of history," he declaimed, "industry and commerce have been the forerunners of literature and civilization, and the handmaids of education." This "hue and cry against utilitarianism" set up by the faculty of the College of Arts and Sciences, he felt, was absurd. "We must establish a school of commerce and finance."

Whether or not Professor Aldrich assisted in the preparation of this oration cannot be determined, but it sounds remarkably similar to what he was preaching to anyone who would listen. Between 1909 and 1914 he was busy button-holing board members and his colleagues on the campus. He worked unceasingly with business groups in the city, especially with the Association of Commerce, of which he was a director. During these years, letters to the local newspaper editors demanding the establishment of the new college became more and more frequent until Aldrich's friends laughingly accused him of writing most of them himself. At all events, his efforts were successful. By 1913 the New Orleans Association of Commerce, through its president, Leon C. Simon, strongly endorsed the idea in a letter to President Sharp. The next year the Louisiana Society of Certified Public Accountants added its approval.

President Sharp, although not antagonistic to the plans for a new college, reminded these groups of the financial condition of the university and expressed the opinion that the matter would have to be deferred until better times should arrive. Whereupon the Association of Commerce and the accounting society secured the signatures of 104 citizens who agreed to underwrite the project for three years.[4] The Tulane board requested the guarantors to form an organization whose officers could deal with the university. When this was done, the board gave its official approval. Thus, in spite of penury and the admonitions of the Flexner-Buttrick report, the College of Commerce and Business Administration was established in 1914.

During its first year the new college had one full-time professor, Aldrich, who was also named dean. He was assisted by four businessmen who taught on a part-time basis and by one member of the Arts and Sciences faculty who also taught part time. Classes during this initial year were held at the Association of Commerce, and all the students were part time and attended only in the evening. In the following year (1915–1916), there were 13 day students enrolled and their classes were held in Gibson Hall on the main campus. Growth of day enrollment, however, was slow when compared with evening students. In 1920, after six years of operation, enrollment figures showed 86 day students and 639 in the evening.

The curriculum as adopted provided for two years of liberal arts work and two years of professional subjects leading to the degree of Bachelor of Business Administration. The implementation of the paper curriculum, however, led to controversy between strong segments of the liberal arts faculty and Aldrich. What sort of English should these commerce students take? How much credit should be given in Arts and Sciences for courses taken in the business administration curriculum? These and numerous similar questions were argued back and forth. Finally Aldrich, tiring of the haggling, went before the University Council and succeeded in pushing through a resolution which gave almost complete autonomy to the new college in curriculum matters. This actually meant another step in Aldrich's domination of the college. As time went on, it became increasingly clear that he had created it in his own image and that it bore the unmistakable stamp of his personality.

The moving of Newcomb College to its new campus was the culmination of several years of planning and delaying. References have already been made to the purchase of the new site on Broadway. But purchasing a site

---

[4] The guaranty was eventually renewed for a second three-year period. In all, 222 citizens were involved as guarantors.

and actually going through with the move were two different matters. To the Newcomb faculty and alumni the delay was galling. The Broadway property had been purchased in 1908. Newcomb opened on the new campus in September 1918. There had thus been ten years of delay. And one does not have to search very diligently to find the reason. The board was trying very unsuccessfully to outguess price trends of materials and labor.

In 1912, the board's building committee reported that the work could be started provided the cost of the new plant did not exceed $505,000, that being the amount available from the Newcomb Fund over and above that set aside for endowment. When the bids were opened, however, the lowest was $559,800, some $54,000 more than the board was willing to spend. The bid was rejected, and the board hesitated on the matter year after year. Finally, in 1916, the Newcomb Alumnae Association served notice it would not tolerate further delay. It virtually demanded that the endowment fund be further reduced, if necessary, and that construction begin at once. With this strong demand facing it, the board, having sold the old Newcomb property to the Baptists for a Bible institute for $100,000, decided to go ahead with construction. On January 9, 1917, the board authorized the immediate erection of three buildings on the Broadway campus at a cost of $767,000. The three buildings were Newcomb Hall, the administration building; the Art building; and Josephine Louise House, a dormitory. A fourth structure, the Music School, also was authorized, but this building had to wait until there was more money. So, too, did six other buildings, for the blueprints contained plans for a total of ten new buildings for the new Newcomb.

On the morning of February 24, 1917, a parade wound its way from old Newcomb to the site of the new campus. Some students walked, some rode in gaily decorated automobiles. There were laughter and cheers and banter with the townsfolks who lined the street curbs. The cavalcade turned from Washington Avenue on to St. Charles and then danced its way up the avenue to Gibson Hall and then across the Tulane campus to the gaily decorated speaker's stand which stood next to a giant pile driver. Here a crowd of some eight hundred people watched and applauded as the exercises got under way. Ernest Lee Jachncke, chairman of the board's building committee, presided. President Sharp spoke. So did President Dixon, Charles Rosen of the board, Mayor Martin Behrman, and Miss Lulie Westfeldt, president of the Newcomb student body. Then Miss Perrine Carson Dixon, granddaughter of the president and youngest member of the freshman class, pulled a lever. The great hammer of the pile driver hit the first piling with a sharp whack. To the accompaniment of ringing cheers, construction of the new Newcomb had begun. In September 1918, the buildings were completed, and the students and faculty moved in.

While the Newcomb buildings were under construction, the university was in the grip of what Dixon later described as "unreasonable hysteria." Freedom of thought and speech; freedom to seek the truth; freedom to hold unpopular opinions—all were buried under a smothering avalanche of patriotic fervor. If a university means honest inquiry, intellectual freedom, and uninhibited learning, then Tulane, along with most other American universities, ceased for a time to be a university. Never in our history, not even in the Civil War, was there such a phrenetic outgrowing of emotional patriotism. For the duration the American people, convinced they were fighting a war for the preservation of decency, righteousness, and democracy forgot all else save fighting and hating. Men's minds and spirits were mobilized along with America's physical resources.

Even before our entry into World War I, military fever touched the campus. Those Tulane students who were members of the Washington Artillery went with their unit to Lona Alta near Brownsville, Texas, in June 1916. There they did border duty with the army which was chasing Pancho Villa over hill and dale. Their release from this duty came in February 1917, just before we declared war on Germany on April 6. A number of the Tulane students, therefore, had virtually no respite between wars.

Two days after the declaration of war the administrators advised President Wilson that "Tulane University . . . places at the disposal of the constituted authorities of the Government, all of the resources of the University." Two days later at a mass meeting of students and professors a resolution offered by President Sharp was adopted to the effect that "student and members of the faculties of Tulane University of Louisiana, in meeting assembled, pledge our loyal support of our country and the President in this time of peril." The war fever spread so fast it was almost uncontrollable. Alumni and students alike rushed to volunteer their services. Rumors ran 'round the campus to the effect that any student who enlisted would receive credit for a full year's work toward his degree. Matters were about to get out of hand before anyone had the remotest idea of what the nation's needs would be for manpower. University authorities found it necessary to call another mass meeting on April 10 at which they urged the students to stay put until their services were needed. Perhaps the admonitions had some effect, but the fever did not cool perceptibly. Actually it was nearly a year before there emerged from the confusion a clearer picture of how the university could best serve the war effort.

Once a pattern emerged, however, events flowed swiftly. In August 1917, military training for all freshmen was instituted, and in January 1918, this was extended to cover all male students. (There was agitation for the same sort of training for Newcomb students, but this did not develop.) Also in January, 1918, application was made for a ROTC Unit for

Tulane; and by this time all the upper three classes of the Medical School were placed in the Medical Reserve Corps and in order to insure a steady supply of doctors for the home as well as the military front were considered as being on active duty. However, Base Hospital 24, a 500-bed Tulane Unit under the command of Major John B. Elliott, Jr., saw active service. It reached Liverpool on March 4, 1918, and six days later relieved the Yale unit at Limoges. The Tulane unit was not to see home again for more than a year, but it did its work well, and some of its officers achieved recognition. Lieutenant-Colonel Urban D. Maes served as assistant surgeon consultant of the First Army Corps, and Major Isadore Dyer, although he did not go overseas with the unit, served on the staff of the surgeon general and became president of the examining board of the Medical Reserve Corps.

In 1917, President Sharp had appointed Dean Dinwiddie as director of war emergency training, and almost immediately he was virtually submerged in the whirling chaos of mobilization. There were budgets to prepare, contracts to be approved, government and military officials to pacify, hundreds of student soldiers to be housed and fed, and a rapidly growing number of special programs to be supervised. The university had laid aside its academic nature and assumed the more primitive role of getting men and women ready for all aspects of war.

The first nonmilitary training program was the Tulane Marine Engineering School established in the School of Engineering, a program which eventually trained 855 men for the Shipping Board. There was also established in the department of physics a telegraphy course and another in radio mechanics. Then new programs hastily arranged stumbled over each other—auto mechanics, naval architecture, motor mechanics, conversational French, public speaking for war drive leaders, practical nursing, and others. At Newcomb, the young women were rolling bandages, training for Red Cross work, and engaging in other activities considered as proper for women in war times. Perhaps Newcomb's most dramatic activity was the organization of a relief unit for canteen service among American troops abroad. Ten Newcomb alumnae, financed by contributions, actually did go overseas, although not until December 1918, when the fighting was over.[5]

Tulane's most military mien, however, was afforded by the S.A.T.C.—the Student Army Training Corps, the organization authorized by Congress in august 1918 as an amendment to the Selective Service Act lowering the draft age to 18 years. Actually it was, in a way, a subsidization of the colleges and universities faced with the imminent danger of losing all their healthy male students. Under the plan, these young men could take their

[5] The ten were: Edna Danziger, Anna Many, Celeste Eshleman, Edith Dupré, Ella Hardie, Marion Monroe, May Norman, Molly Palfrey, Caroline Richardson, Dr. Lydia Lloyd Peage.

military training at selected colleges and universities instead of going to regular military training camps. Each student was given room, board, tuition, uniforms, and $30 per month with instruction being furnished by the academic faculty and military officers detailed to this duty.

In September 1918, Tulane contracted to train 6,000 men for the S.A.T.C., taking 1,200 at a time. Previously, the university had set up a training center at the Fair Grounds, called Camp Martin. Here many of the war courses were offered; but with the advent of the S.A.T.C., Camp Martin was moved to the main campus where fourteen wooden buildings were erected on the quadrangle between Gibson Hall and Freret Street. Now more than ever the university campus was a war camp, as hundreds of young men drilled, studied military tactics, and played athletic games in the daytime, and at night went to lectures and movies on physical fitness and the prevention of venereal diseases.

Hardly had these young men grown accustomed to throwing snappy salutes at their officers and to the sound of the reveille bugle, however, when the war was over. Actually little had been accomplished at Tulane, for in September and October the camp was almost paralyzed by a flu epidemic. Then in November came the Armistice and demobilization. Tulane could, however, point with some pride to her war record as a whole. Forty per cent of the medical faculty had seen active service. Some 75 per cent of the other faculties were involved in training programs or in active service. Including the S.A.T.C. Tulane had given training to 7,145 men and women. More than a thousand alumni had seen active service, and 44 of them had not come back.

Along with the actual training for service, there was, of course, another phase of the war effort which gripped the American educational institution —the channeling of men's minds into one way of thinking and the elimination of those who refused to conform. Universities everywhere were peculiarly susceptible to attack because, by and large, the professor was an individualist accustomed to taking an objective view of events and not prone to giving way to hysteria. Such things as banning German music, dropping the German language from the curriculum, renaming sour kraut "liberty cabbage" and kicking dachshunds around were to him symbolic of the fact that reason had fled and its place taken by hysterical nonsense. Pacifism, too, was strong in many universities, and in others where German or German-trained scholars were teaching there was, especially before the United States entered the war, an unwillingness to admit that Germany was wholly wrong and the allies right. When we did enter the war, many of these teachers were damned by what they had previously said.

But while many scholars might take a dim view of unreasoning patriotic emotionalism, the man in the street did not. Public sentiment forced many boards of trustees and college presidents to purge their institutions of any suspicion of pro-German sentiment among the faculties. This happened at Tulane. On January 23, 1918, the Board of Administrators went on record that "in order to remove every suspicion of disloyalty" every person connected with the university must "immediately" take the following oath: "I am a citizen of _____. I will loyally uphold the Government of the United States in the prosecution of the war against Germany and her Allies."

Anyone who knows university faculties will have no difficulty in understanding the reactions accorded the oath. Many whose loyalty was beyond question were openly indignant. Others mumbled their resentment to themselves. A few signed willingly. Of the indignant ones perhaps Professor Charlton Reid Beattie, professor of Louisiana practice in the College of Law, was the most outspoken. On February 4, 1918, he sent a stinging letter to the board denouncing the oath as an "insult" to him as a loyal American whose ancestors had defended America in every war the country had ever fought, including the American Revolution. With this letter went his resignation which the board promptly accepted.

Meantime, many faculty members were dragging their feet. On February 11, the secretary of the board reported that all but 69 had signed. He was instructed to get out another letter, and this second notice brought in the signatures of all except four—Mr. E. H. Farrar, a member of the board; Drs. J. R. Fernandez, F. R. Gomila, and F. J. Wolfe of the medical school; and, of course, Professor Beattie. Mr. Farrar was excused because he was old and ill, but the records show no action against the recalcitrant doctors. Dr. Fernandez was not listed on the medical faculty for 1919, but Drs. Gomila and Wolfe were carried in the register of the university as faculty members for several years after 1918.

However, three faculty members who did sign the oath were dismissed as a result of the report of a special board investigating committee headed by Mr. Esmond Phelps. It is impossible today to know what the evidence was in each case for there were no hearings and the committee's report was verbal, but the fact remains that George E. Beyer, professor of Botany in the College of Arts and Sciences; Heinrich H. Maurer, professor of history at Newcomb: and Anna Judge Veters, graduate assistant and high school teacher of German at Newcomb, lost their jobs. In each case the decision of dismissal was unanimous in the board except for the dissent of Charles Rosen who maintained that the defendants were entitled to a hearing.

In the midst of all the wartime confusion, President Sharp's health failed. By May 1918, it was obvious to himself as well as his colleagues that he would not find it possible to carry on much longer. On the twenty-third of that month, he submitted his resignation along with the recommendation that Dean Dinwiddie be chosen to succeed him. Dinwiddie was quickly elected to take office on October 1, 1918.

The choice of Dean Albert Bledsoe Dinwiddie obviously was a surprise to no one. Throughout the last three years of Sharp's administration he had carried the burden of university administration with conspicuous success. Those who knew him best understood the reasons for this administrative success. He was a quiet, patient man with a great capacity for detail and an analytical mind which went to the heart of a problem while most of those around him were still fumbling with preliminaries. Too, he had an excellent academic background. His undergraduate and doctoral degrees were from the University of Virginia with an extra year of graduate study at the University of Göttingen in Greek and mathematics. After serving as a preparatory school principal and on the faculty of the University School at Richmond for two years, he went to Southwestern Presbyterian University at Clarksville, Tennessee, where he remained as professor of mathematics until he came to Tulane in 1906 as assistant professor of applied mathematics and astronomy. By 1910, he was a full professor of mathematics and head of the department. In this same year he was appointed dean of the College of Arts and Sciences.

Dr. Dinwiddie was a Presbyterian, the son of a Virginia Presbyterian minister, but his Calvinism was relieved by a sly sense of humor and a love of sports, particularly of tennis, fishing, and football. He kept in good physical trim by playing tennis; he found relaxation in fishing (and he is reported to have known just where to cast for the big ones); and, whenever possible, he went with the Tulane football team on its trips. He had played football at Virginia. He did not make the team, he would admit with a smile, but would add, "I was run over by some of the best players of that day."

But he was not a frail man by any means. Although he had a tendency toward obesity in his later years, he was when elected president of Tulane a compactly built man of 180 pounds with a forehead so high it would have been the delight of a caricaturist, who would have sketched him and then probably would have labeled the sketch "big dome"; and Dinwiddie would have enjoyed the joke. He was, above all, a man completely free of bombast and pretense who took a paternal interest in students and faculty alike. Perhaps sincerity and simplicity are words which best describe his personal characteristics. Nothing better illustrates the man than an incident which happened when he was elected president. He was playing tennis in Audubon Park while the board was meeting to make its choice.[6] When the choice was known, Dr. Bechtel and Mr. Bruff rushed across St. Charles to

---

[6] The members of the Board of Administrators electing Dinwiddie were: Robert M. Walmsley, president; William R. Irby, first vice-president; Charles Janiver, second vice-president. Members: Edgar H. Farrar, Walter R. Stauffer, Henry Ginder, John B. Levert, Walker B. Spencer, John Dymond, Jr., Charles Rosen, Alfred Raymond, Abraham Brittin, John Callan, Ernest Lee Jahncke, Joseph A. Breaux, Marcus J. S. Magruder, and Esmond Phelps. Mr. Irby became president of the board shortly after Dinwiddie took office.

the courts to notify Dinwiddie. He stopped his service, thanked the two messengers very humbly, and then finished the set. "I know of nothing that was so characteristic of the man," Dr. Bechtel wrote in later years— "attention strictly to the business at hand, with an absolute horror of any pomp and ceremony."

From the standpoint of the administrators, Charles Rosen characterized Dinwiddie as "the perfect President" in that he was completely reliable and steady. "In his hands," he said, "we always felt safe." Rosen thought the chief attributes of the man were "ability," "diplomacy," "establishing proper contacts, patience to solve difficult and exacting problems."

As president, Dinwiddie would need to summon all his admirable qualities and resources, for Tulane was about to begin the metamorphosis from a small, almost local institution with limited resources to a much larger first-rate national university. As a result of the war a new world was born. The whole country was seething with a new demand for wider educational opportunities. Tulane responded to the demand, but the response was not without painful problems.

CHAPTER 11

Respite and Growth (1918-1935)

WRITERS OF FICTION, PARTICULARLY of the Western variety, have been known to write themselves into a corner to the extent that only the device of *deus ex machina* could extricate them. The familiar pattern, the reader undoubtedly knows, goes something like this: A wagon train has formed its defensive circle on the bleak and unfriendly plains. After hours of fighting, food, water, and ammunition are almost exhausted, and still the savages circle closer and closer, threatening to wipe out the band of doughty pioneers. How can these pioneers possibly be saved?

With a few strokes of his pen the author creates a regiment of U.S. cavalry which comes charging over the nearest ridge with sabers gleaming and revolvers blazing. The result inevitably is that the Indians are vanquished and the wagon train is permitted to resume its journey.

If this were a book of fiction rather than of history, the author might well be accused of creating such a convenient device for rescuing the beleaguered university, for during the Sharp administration the savages of penury and despair were closing in on the campus. Then over the horizon appeared a regiment of foundation people and private donors waving their checkbooks. Dinwiddie had slipped away and brought relief. The enemies were temporarily vanquished and the university was permitted to move on toward its destiny. Unfortunately, however, the enemy was not destroyed. He merely withdrew and thus was always a threat; but even a temporary respite was a cause for legitimate rejoicing.

There are many facets to the Dinwiddie period, but the one which must be looked at first is the fact that Tulane at long last improved its financial position. Between 1918 and 1930, endowment increased from $3,405,000 to $9,984,000, and total university assets grew from $6,895,000 to $17,886,000. These amounts, of course, seem pitifully small when compared with the resources of certain Eastern universities, but this is not the story of an Eastern university. It is an account of the development of a Southern university in a section where wealth had not accumulated to the extent it had in other parts of the country. It is the history of a university which had to accomplish a great deal with a very little. To such an institution, six and a half million dollars was the difference between despair and hope.

This new money came from several sources: (1) President Dinwiddie and the Board of Administrators organized an endowment drive in 1920 which yielded a net of some $1,700,000, largely from New Orleans. (2) Eastern foundations gave the university, the medical school in particular, about $4,000,000 for endowment, buildings, and equipment.[1] (3) William R. Irby left the university a bequest of over a million and a half dollars. (4) Numerous smaller gifts added up to a significant sum. (5) In the booming market of the twenties, many of the older securities in the endowment portfolio appreciated greatly in value.

The university's first major endowment drive, in 1920, was planned and executed rather well. Dinwiddie had hardly moved into his office in Gibson Hall before he set the wheels in motion. With the approval of the administrators he organized committees, obtained the assistance of the newspapers, and himself inaugurated a series of addresses designed to acquaint the public with the true conditions of the university's finances. For the first time in its history the university really took the public into its confidence.[2] Taking as its slogan "Keep the Doors Open" the campaign swung into action on June 21, 1920, when "General" Charles Weinberger, director of the drive, led 110 "captains" out of the old Grunewald Hotel into the streets of the city. The goal was $2,600,000. An added stimulus for the fund raisers was the fact that the General Education Board had pledged $200,000 provided the university raised $550,000. A similar offer was made by the Carnegie Corporation. Thus a campaign which raised $1,100,-000 would give the university a total of $1,550,000.

It was a whirlwind campaign aimed at achieving its goal within a few days. The newspapers carried an abundance of publicity. Thousands of citizens wore badges reading "Keep the Doors Open." Pennants and bunting were everywhere. On the banquette in front of a number of Canal Street stores large cardboard replicas of Gibson Hall were erected. The crowds walked through the open doors over which hung the legend "Keep the Doors Open." The alumni worked diligently and successfully, and the campaign yielded substantial results. Between June 21 and July 3, $1,500,000 in cash and pledges was collected. By October 1, approximately $2,000,000 was paid in or promised. (About $250,000 in pledges was never paid.)

The goal of $2,600,000 was not reached, nor were all the pledges paid, but there were results over and above the actual amount raised. The cam-

---

[1] More than half the foundation money went for buildings and equipment. This is not counted in the six and a half million endowment increase.

[2] There appeared about this time a realization of the need for a news bureau which would interpret the university to the community. In 1929, Horace Renegar was brought in from the Associated Press as publicity man for athletics. From this modest beginning there developed a full-fledged department of public relations under Renegar's direction.

paign showed a willingness and ability on the part of the university to help itself through its own efforts, and it was this sort of institution in which the foundations were interested. Just after World War I these foundations were selecting key Southern universities and assisting them financially, but the donors wanted to know that those they helped were vigorous enough to help themselves. Medical education was a major interest of these foundations, but certainly not the only one. Between 1920 and 1930 the General Education Board, Carnegie Corporation, Rockefeller Foundation, Commonwealth Fund, and the Laura Spellman Rockefeller Memorial Fund gave transfusions which enabled Tulane to survive and grow. The actual use of foundation money will be related later in this and the following chapters.

William Ratcliffe Irby died on the morning of November 20, 1926. Although a native of Virginia, he had lived in New Orleans almost all his life and had through his own ingenuity and ability made a substantial fortune in tobacco, dairy products, and banking. He was president of the Canal Bank and Trust Company until he retired to the chairmanship of the board in 1922, and during the period of his active work with the bank was a member of the Board of Administrators of Tulane. In 1920 he became president of this board, spending perhaps more time looking after the financial well-being of the university than after his own interests.

As a citizen he was deeply interested in many philanthropic endeavors, but perhaps his major concern was the preservation of the historic French Quarter. As had previously been pointed out, he had purchased the historic old French Opera House and presented it to Tulane. Likewise, he had purchased and restored the Paul Morphy house on Royal Street and given it to Tulane. He had contributed the money for the restoration and preservation of St. Louis Cathedral. He had given a swimming pool for City Park, another for Newcomb College. But no one knew of all his philanthropies for he was a modest, even secretive, man who disliked publicity. Even when he was awarded the *Times-Picayune* loving cup in 1916 as a man of the year in New Orleans, he insisted that the presentation be private.

The end of his life was in bizarre contrast to his ordinary reticence regarding publicity, for it would be difficult to imagine a more dramatic scene than that of his death. As the story was related in the newspapers, he came to his office at the bank as usual on the morning of November 20, 1926, but it was obvious that he was suffering from the heart ailment which had been getting worse year by year. However, he went out for his customary midmorning cup of coffee, and from the restaurant took a taxi to a well-known undertaking establishment where he asked the owner to show him the firm's stock of caskets. He was, he said, selecting one for a friend. Together the two men strolled among the rows of plush and satin receptacles of death, and when the banker had made his choice he asked his friend the undertaker to go downstairs and bring up the morning paper. While he was gone, Mr. Irby placed a revolver against his temple and ended his life.

Mr. Irby was survived by a son and by his former wife. Of his estate, amounting to about $3,000,000, less than half went to them and to various charities. He had made Tulane his universal legatee, and when the succession was settled the university found the book value of its share to be approximately $1,600,000 and the market value near $2,000,000. Except for Mrs. Newcomb's legacy, this was the largest single gift by a private benefactor in the history of the university to the present.

There were other smaller legacies and gifts which were most important during this period. Judge Joseph Arsenne Breaux died on July 23, 1926, leaving to the university $300,000 for scholarships. Judge Breaux was an alumnus of the university (B.A., 1857; LL.B., 1859). He had been chief justice of the Supreme Court of Louisiana, and in 1914 was elected to the Board of Administrators of the university. Samuel Zemurray made periodic gifts, adding up to more than a half million dollars by 1936.[3] In 1929 Henry Beer willed $50,000 to endow a chair in Newcomb's School of Music. In the same year $50,000 came from the estate of Mrs. Rose E. Knapp to found the Viola V. Knapp Memorial Fund for worthy Newcomb students. And still the gifts came: Mrs. Joseph Howard, $50,000 for endowment of the Law School; Charles Gouguenheim, $20,000 for scholarships; Mr. and Mrs. L. E. Schwarz, $20,000 for a medical research fund; Mrs. Maurice Stern, $12,000 for a medical periodical fund; Colonel William G. Vincent, $60,000 for tropical medicine; Chase S. Osborne, former governor of Michigan, an 800-acre island off the mouth of St. Mary's River in Lake Huron.

The log jam had been broken. After the lean years it now appeared that people of wealth were learning that it took a great deal of money to run a good university, and that the better the university the more money it took. Money from gifts and legacies such as these was never enough, and the university could hardly have existed without foundation assistance. Nevertheless, these private gifts were symptomatic of the awakening.

Just how much the university gained from a general appreciation of the securities and land markets during the twenties is difficult to determine precisely. The administrators bought and sold real estate. They sold securities at almost fabulous profits now and then, and these profits went into capital improvements at the university and into other investments. Perhaps the total gains from these transactions ran as high as four and a half million dollars during the ten-year period 1920–1930. Somehow or other the administrators outguessed the booming bull market of the twenties and sold at the right time. But the process of outguessing the market was a nerve-racking one. They could never be sure they had sold at the right time. Only the crash of 1929 revealed what skill they had employed in

[3] Subsequent donations have increased this to approximately a million dollars.

manipulating the endowment portfolios. While he lived, a great deal of the credit for success should go to Mr. Irby. After his death Esmond Phelps, who succeeded him as president of the Board of Administrators, frankly admitted that he and the board were for a time almost adrift without Irby's quiet and wise counsel in financial matters.

The amount of money raised and donated was important in itself, but even more important was the psychological "lift" it gave to the university, especially to the faculties. Early in Dinwiddie's administration, five faculty members resigned because of low salaries. The president had, of course, been aware of these low salaries because he had been a professor who received one of them. Now he insisted, even before the money was in sight, that salaries must be raised and the money found to meet the payrolls. In this, the administrators concurred, and in 1919 every person earning less than $1,500 per year was given a $300 raise. Then, on a selective basis, larger increases were made for more prominent faculty members. The extent of these increases can be determined from this brief table showing what happened to the salaries of five faculty members.

Rank	Salary, 1918–1919	Salary, 1921–1922
Professor A	$2,500	$5,000
Professor B	$2,250	$5,000
Associate Professor A	$2,100	$3,500
Assistant Professor B	$1,450	$2,750
Instructor A	$1,000	$1,800

But the matter of salaries was only one barometer of the new feeling of progress. A significant expansion of the physical plant was carried out. New departments and one new school were created. New members were added to the faculties. In retrospect, one wonders if Tulane had not again overextended itself; if the prospects and the realization of new money had not created a situation akin to that which existed all over the country during the twenties—a boom period in which few people seriously questioned the basic soundness of it all or what would be required to keep it booming.

The largest single piece of construction was the Hutchinson Memorial medical building, completed in the fall of 1930. What was originally called the Richardson medical building, on Canal Street, after nearly forty years of use had become crowded and obsolete. To replace it, Dinwiddie had at first advocated the construction of a hospital, several medical buildings clustered about it, and rows of faculty homes nearby. All this was to be on the back part of the uptown campus between Freret and Claiborne. Costs proved prohibitive, however, and the dream was abandoned in favor of a new medical unit contiguous to Charity Hospital. In 1926, the university purchased for $289,000 most of the square bounded by Tulane Avenue, Howard, Gravier, and South Liberty streets for the building. In 1928, the General Education Board gave $1,250,000 toward building and equipment, and on July 11, 1929, the first pile was driven. When the nine-story and basement brick building was completed and dedicated in December 1930, it was probably the best medical teaching unit in the country, certainly in the South. Space, equipment, faculty, and the clinical resources of Charity Hospital enabled the College of Medicine to make rapid strides not only in the training of more good doctors but in research as well.

Newcomb, too, went through a spate of building during the period under discussion. It will be recalled that when the coordinate college moved to the new campus in 1918, it had only four buildings—Newcomb Hall, the administration and classroom building; the Josephine Louise dormitory, the Art building; and the power plant. Plans at the time, however, called for numerous other buildings which, as it developed, were built in rather rapid order. In 1923, the new gymnasium was erected and through the assistance of Mr. Irby an annex containing a swimming pool was added. Under the pressure of mounting enrollment, new dormitories became a necessity. In 1925, Doris Hall, a cooperative dormitory housing 28 girls was built, a gift from Mr. Zemurray. This was followed in 1928 by the construction of a larger dormitory, Warren Newcomb House.

There were other miscellaneous additions made to the Newcomb physical plant—an athletic field, tennis courts, walks and driveways—but the climax of the building program (certainly from an emotional point of view) came in 1929 with the dedication of Dixon Hall. This was a music-auditorium-library memorial to President Dixon who had retired in 1919 and now in 1929 was ill and thought to be old. The year of 1929 marked the forty-second anniversary of his association with Newcomb. Newcomb was his child. He had fed it, protected it, nutured it, and wept over it. Now as he stood to make the dedicatory address, there were those in the audience who used their handkerchiefs to stifle the sniffles. Others let the tears flow unashamedly. Only his legs and body showed weakness. His voice had lost little of its resonance and there was still life and fire in it as he stood before the audience and recounted his years at the college and then looked ahead at what it could become. And he lived to see the future, or at least a part of it, for his amazing vitality sustained him until September 6, 1941, when he died at the age of 91 years.

The building program was in high gear. Gibson Hall had become seriously overcrowded. It housed the College of Arts and Sciences, the College of Commerce and Business Administration, the College of Law, the Graduate School, administrative offices, and the museum. In 1923, the board approved Dinwiddie's recommendation that a new science building (now Dinwiddie Hall) be erected near the downtown end of Gibson Hall. The cost of the building and its equipment was met by a $75,000 appropriation by the board and a gift of $125,000 from the General Education Board. The new building, dedicated February 22, 1924, housed laboratories and classrooms for biochemistry, botany, zoology, and geology; but it was obvious almost before the building went into use that it was inadequate. Gibson Hall was still overcrowded. Thus the board found itself in the position of having to vote another appropriation to add an annex. This it did in 1927, and when the new wing was complete there was a general exodus from Gibson Hall. The College of Law occupied the first and second floors of the new building. The biological sciences were almost crowded out by sociology, German (restored to the curriculum), and journalism on the third floor and the Middle American research department on the fourth.

Down the quadrangle toward Freret Street the roof of Stanley Thomas Hall proved defective, and while a new roof was being added in 1929, it was decided to add a fourth floor to this building and give Architecture (still a part of the College of Engineering) a home.

Beyond Freret Street there were new developments. In the fall of 1924, football fans celebrating the Tulane victory over L.S.U. began to lay plans for a new and larger stadium. Their planning was given additional impetus by the fact that the next season saw Tulane undefeated, its victims including Northwestern, one of the strongest teams in the nation. In the midst of the almost hysterical rejoicing, the campaign which raised $300,000 in two weeks was launched in December 1925. On October 23, 1926, the 30,000 capacity (45,000 with temporary seats) stadium was dedicated at the Auburn game.[4]

Then came a new gymnasium (now called the Central building) in 1932. It was a part of the by-now familiar story of inadequate facilities at Tulane. The old gymnasium had quickly become obsolete largely because it was not big enough from the very beginning. So it was with many of the buildings on the campus, a fact which is symptomatic of the lack of blue-printing of what the university's requirements might become. The policy pursued was a careful and conservative one, partially made necessary by limited funds but partially the result of an unimaginative outlook on what the university's needs in physical equipment would be over the years ahead. Too, there were those who felt that Tulane could best fulfill its role by remaining a comparatively small local institution. Even on individual buildings there were serious miscalculations. The board appropriated $150,000 for the new gymnasium, but as work progressed it became evident that this amount was insufficient. There were walls and a roof, but the interior was unfinished, the doorways lacked doors, and the empty windows were boarded up. Then ever faithful Samuel Zemurray gave the $40,000 necessary for completion.

There were other miscellaneous capital improvements. In 1922 the Uni-

---

[4] This stadium was eventually increased to a size where it seated 82,000 and came to be called the Sugar Bowl. The enlargements were made not by the university but by the New Orleans Mid-Winter Sports Association which sponsors the annual New Year's Sugar Bowl game.

versity's short-lived radio station WAAC went into operation; in 1930 Newcomb built an $80,000 laundry; in 1933 Woodward Way, the arcade connecting the Art and Gymnasium buildings at Newcomb was dedicated in honor of Elizabeth Woodward; and in 1932 the Tulane tennis stadium was dedicated.

But other phases of expansion loomed importantly during the Dinwiddie period: the creation of the School of Social Work and of the storm-tossed department of Middle American research.

The genesis of the School of Social Work goes back to 1913. In that year John M. Fletcher, professor of psychology at Newcomb; Edmund J. Glenny, a member of the Kingsley House (a community center in the manner of Hull House in Chicago) Board of Directors; and Eleanor Mc-Main, head resident at Kingsley House, successfully promoted a movement to open at Kingsley House a "school of applied sociology to train social workers." Classes began in November 1914. Three theoretical courses— "Social conditions," "Constructive social agencies," and "Relief work"— were supplemented by field trips for a first-hand study of conditions existing in various charitable and welfare agencies in the city. This was the first program in the South for the professional training of social workers, and in 1917 was formally organized as the Southern School of Social Sciences and Public Welfare.

The school was supported by limited financial contributions by local welfare groups and by a small tuition fee charged each student. By 1917, however, it was becoming obvious that the project could not support itself, and its leaders asked that Tulane take it over and develop out of it a school of social work. The request came just at a time when during the early months of the war a general awareness of the need for better-trained social workers was beginning to take place largely as a result of Red Cross efforts. Harry Hopkins, then director of this organization's field service in the Gulf division, was busy organizing Home Service Institutes for training volunteer workers. It was apparent from the very beginning of this effort that its greatest difficulties stemmed from the fact that there was a dearth of professionally trained social workers who could train the volunteers. Hopkins, therefore, added his appeal to that of the Kingsley House group.

Tulane's response was not the immediate establishment of a full-blown school of social work, but rather the creation of an emergency social work educational department. Largely at Hopkins' suggestion, Garrett Pelhemus Wyckoff, professor of sociology at Grinnell College, was invited to take, as a wartime assignment, the headship of the new department, and he accepted. He came to Tulane in 1918 and remained until 1920 when he went back to Grinnell, apparently feeling he had discharged his wartime obligations. Just as he was leaving Tulane, however, events were developing which brought him back.

The war and the wartime work of the Red Cross were over, but the organization was emerging as a great peacetime agency, and its need for trained workers was growing rather than diminishing. In the Gulf states it was apparent that the training programs for these workers ought to be centralized in one place, in one university. In June 1920, the Gulf Division of the American Red Cross designated Tulane as that central training agency. In its report there is one of the most cogent statements of Tulane's position as the leading regional institution of the Gulf area ever written. It was so forceful that it impressed and astonished the president and the administrators who could not be expected to have the objectivity possessed by an external organization.

Under the stimulus of this report, the university agreed to cooperate with the Red Cross, accepted a gift of $20,000 from it, and set up a "School of Social Science" in the fall of 1920. The school had a faculty of four full-time teachers and an ambitious program; in fact, it was too ambitious a program and during its first year showed signs of collapsing under its own weight. The more Hopkins and Dinwiddie discussed the matter the clearer it became to them that Wyckoff ought to be brought back to take charge.

Wyckoff accepted the invitation to return and in September 1921 became professor of sociology and director of the social work program. The recently established School of Social Science was discontinued, and many of the courses were divided among Arts and Sciences and Newcomb faculty members. Wyckoff himself did a great deal of teaching, and in addition was busy developing community contacts for his department. Perhaps the most important of these contacts was with the Committee on Philanthropy of the Association of Commerce. This important group headed by Charles A. Favrot had been largely instrumental in forming the Central Council of Social Agencies in 1921 and the New Orleans Community Chest in 1925. Wyckoff was liked personally and respected professionally by these groups, and thus had little difficulty in placing his students in work experience or in permanent positions.

Social work remained a department—the sociology department—until 1927 when it was given status as a full degree-granting school within the university. During these years between 1921 and 1927 Wyckoff had, as indicated above, made the sociology department into a training agency for social workers. While a great many of the courses were "farmed out" to other faculties, Wyckoff did not neglect the building of his own department. By 1926, it was composed of two full professors, three assistant professors, and one instructor. As the faculty increased in numbers and improved in competence more and more courses were offered at the graduate level, a fact which had great significance for the future of social work at Tulane.

Year by year the need for trained social workers in the South was becoming apparent to Southern businessmen and civic leaders who had been drawn into the work of the Red Cross, community chests, and other similar organizations. On every hand these men found that the administration of the comparatively new forms of organized philanthropy demanded professionally competent workers; and in March 1927, a group of Southern lay leaders, sociologists, and social workers met in New Orleans to consider the problem. They soon found that what the Red Cross had discovered in 1920 still held true. Tulane was the logical center for training Southern social workers and this fact the conference put squarely up to university authorities.

The overtures were sympathetically received, but the matter of financing the proposed new school was a matter that had to be seriously considered. In May of 1927, however, the Laura Spellman Rockefeller Fund made a grant of $93,000 to be used to support the project, and in June the administrators authorized the creation of the Tulane School of Social Work with a two-year graduate program leading to the master's degree. Immediately the school was admitted to membership in the American Association of Schools of Social Work.

In creating the new school the university was carrying out what by now appeared to be a guiding role or policy. Looked at from one viewpoint it was overextension, the creation of new departments and schools without having the money in hand to place them on a firm financial basis; and from a purely budgetary standpoint this might be considered unsound. Looked at from another viewpoint, however, one cannot but be impressed by Tulane's concept of the relationship of a private university to the public good. Was there a local or regional need basic enough and urgent enough to demand the resources of the university? If so, Tulane was likely to meet the need and then look for the money to support its program over the long pull. It seemed an almost fatalistic belief that if the university filled an urgent public necessity, the public in the long run would sustain it. The $93,000 gift was wholly inadequate but the school was founded—and it has been sustained. This was not the first time nor, indeed, the last time that Tulane acted on faith.

On October 1, 1927, the new school opened with a class of ten women. A dean was not immediately named, but Wyckoff, as might be suspected, was the director. The faculty by the next year was composed of Luther Lee Bernard and Jesse Frederick Steiner as professors; Mrs. Irene F. Conrad, Miss Grace Eleanor Kimble, and Miss Elizabeth Wisner, assistant professors; and Miss Wilmer Shields, instructor and secretary. The curriculum was arranged in three divisions—social case work, community organization, and social research. And, after much searching, a home for the school was found. It was given a portion of the third floor of the science building (Dinwiddie Hall) where the director occupied one office and the faculty members crowded into another. The stenographer sat in a corridor and the secretary, who also served as librarian, in a classroom which doubled as a library.

Despite the enthusiastic endorsement given the new school by social workers and informed lay people, the first few years were not easy ones; but somehow or other something always seemed to turn up in the way of financial aid to keep the program running. One of the major casualties was the psychiatric program inaugurated in 1928–1929 which showed signs of success until the depression year of 1932 forced the school to close it out. In fact, by 1932 the outlook was bleak for the entire school. At the most opportune time, however, the Rockefeller Foundation made a grant of $66,000 which saved the day, at least temporarily. By the time this money was utilized, the government's program of training social workers under the Federal Emergency Relief Administration was in full swing, and the increased income from a larger enrollment took up some more of the financial slack. Enrollment in normal years was never large—46 in 1931, 133 in 1933. But the FERA-swollen enrollment of 1934 was 288.

Despite the fact that the school was small, the quality of the teaching and of the product was high. Professor Wyckoff, of course, deserves a great deal of credit for this, but Elizabeth Wisner accounted for a considerable portion of it. Wyckoff retired because of ill health in 1932, and Miss Wisner was named director (made dean in 1937). Miss Wisner was a Newcomb graduate who took her master's degree from Simmons College and her Ph.D. from the University of Chicago. Under her leadership for 26 years the school acquired a national reputation. Its graduates were staffing social agencies throughout the South, and a number were established as top-flight government executives. Above all, however, the School of Social Work had further clarified the concept of Tulane as a regional institution.

In 1924 while Wyckoff was laying the foundation of the School of Social Work, another new department, the department of Middle American research, was established. Its creator was Samuel Zemurray, one of the most colorful American businessmen of the twentieth century. He had come to America in 1892—the fifteen-year-old immigrant son of a Bessarabian Jewish farmer. In Alabama, where he lived with relatives, he did odd jobs, worked with a peddler, and in the process learned two facts which started him on his career. One fact was that the people of Alabama liked bananas. The other was that at the Mobile docks one could purchase large quantities of bananas, which if shipped by ordinary slow freight would become overripe before they reached the consumer. Young Zemurray found that if he purchased these bananas and quickly sold them from cars attached to local freight trains, which stopped at nearly every village and town between Mobile and Birmingham, he could make a fast but precarious profit. He was successful, and soon formed his own company to import bananas. By 1924 he had his own fleet of ships and was carving out of the jungles of Honduras a plantation empire. Later he took over control of the vast United Fruit Company.

It was natural that Mr. Zemurray, despite his lack of academic background, should develop an interest in the cultural history of the people in the countries where his business interests lay. If for no other reason, such an interest promoted better business relations with these countries. The academic interest was supplied by his daughter, Doris, who had become fascinated by the remains of the ancient Mayan culture which she encountered on every hand hand in Honduras and Guatemala. When the Gates collection was offered for sale, therefore, it was not surprising that she and her father should have become interested in purchasing it. It is also not surprising that he abruptly notified the Tulane administrators that he was buying the Gates library and was prepared to endow a department at Tulane devoted to the study of Middle America; for Mr. Zemurray was a forceful and direct man of action. If he was going to do a thing he did it without any shilly-shallying, whether it was overthrowing a banana republic dictator, endowing a department, or peremptorily taking over control of the United Fruit Company.

The Gates collection of books, manuscripts, and artifacts dealing with ancient Mayan and Aztec life was a very valuable one. William Gates had worked almost a lifetime assembling it. Although born in Atlanta he was a descendant of the Virginia Gates family which went back to a colonial governor. A man of some wealth, he had made archeology his hobby and then his major mission in life, and at the time his collection was sold, in 1924, was president of the Mayan Society, director of archeology for the Republic of Guatemala and director of Museo Guatemalteco. Mr. Zemurray paid $60,000 for the collection and provided $300,000 for the endowment of the department. Tulane had a department of Middle American research, but, the evidence indicates, it did not have a very clear notion of what to do with it. Everyone, especially the newspapers, seemed to think a new era in Latin-American relations had begun, but beyond this generality the tasks of the department were rather vague.

Possibly as a way out of the dilemma, Mr. Gates was invited to become director of the new department. In an atmosphere of all-round cordiality and good will, he accepted and took over his duties in the late spring of 1924. Shortly thereafter, boxes and bales of codices, incunabula, printed books, artifacts, photographs and drawings of glyphs, and manuscripts began to arrive. They were hauled up to the fourth floor of the science building, and Gates began his work of unpacking and arranging. (No inventory of the collection had been made, and no part of it was catalogued, so Tulane never knew whether it got all of the collection or not. After his quarrel with the university, Gates made sales to other universities. These pieces may or may not have been parts of the collection which Tulane should have received.)

While he was puttering with his collection, the new director was also assembling a staff of assistants. He had outlined for President Dinwiddie the objectives of the new department. "I want . . . to make the Department not merely a scientific research center in linguistics, archeology, history and the rest, but a developing center of specific information useful to the Port of New Orleans, and the business that lies behind it." He clearly had in mind something in the nature of a clearing house of information which would foster friendship and understanding between Latin America and the United States and result in the strengthening of trade relations. He wished, he said, to "card-index those [Latin-American] countries."

Had conditions been different, these goals might have been reached, but the personality and lack of administrative ability of Gates plus his failure to recruit a sufficiently flexible staff caused confusion, misunderstandings, and, ultimately a state of affairs bordering on chaos.

Gates was not a good administrator. To him, budgets were merely suggestive, and he was never able to draw his staff together into a sufficiently unified group so that the general objectives might be specifically implemented. His department was not integrated with the New Orleans community nor the rest of the university. As time went on, Gates grew more and more suspicious of colleagues at the university and seemed to withdraw more and more into the shelves and cubicles of his collection where he apparently brooded over fancied wrongs to him. There were those who blamed his recurring cycles of grandeur and persecution on his fear that someone else would get the glory that was rightly his.

The beginning of Dinwiddie's disenchantment was obvious within a few months after Gates arrived, and was brought to a climax with a quarrel about Frans Blom, the golden-haired Danish archeologist whom Gates had named an associate in archeology in late 1924. Blom, Gates decided, was a trouble maker who was trying to usurp authority and run the department. Blom placed himself directly under the orders of the president and let Gates rage. When Gates became obnoxiously critical of the administrators, he was dismissed in March 1926. Thus passed the man whom the Tulane *Hullabaloo* described as "the most colossal egotist of any man we have ever observed. . . . Added to his boundless ego was, we believe, a deep seated defect in his mental make-up, a neurosis of some sort, that kept him constantly suspicious of others. . . . No man with self-respect could, we think, work harmoniously with such a man."

Meantime, in spite of his shortcomings, Gates had accomplished some things. He had assembled a fairly capable, assuredly a colorful and unpredictable staff of young archeologists, ethnologists, and anthropologists who remained in orbit about the department for a time and then began to break out like shooting stars to quench their fires in the jungles of Middle America. Blom and Oliver LaFarge, the young ethnologist just out of Harvard, led an expedition (February 1925) into southern Mexico, across the states of Tabasco and Chiapas, then into Guatemala to Guatemala City. It was a journey of more than 1,200 miles, much of it on horseback and through virtually unexplored regions. In August 1925, the two young explorers returned to the university to write their report in two volumes entitled *Tribes and Temples,* the first lengthy publication of the department. While Blom and LaFarge were cutting their way through the jungles in search of graves and gods, Gates himself headed an expedition into Tabasco. Taking with him two assistants in agronomy, he studied soil, crops, transportation, and labor in the Mexican state. He then came back to write a useful report which, among other things, pointed out the feasibility of growing rubber trees in Tabasco.

But such activities were cut short by the Gates-Blom controversy and the dismissal of Gates. Blom was not named the director immediately but was given the role of senior staff member until 1930 when he was given the title, effective as of September 1929.

The contrast in the personalities of Blom and Gates was striking. Blom was personable and affable, an excellent conversationalist and a charming host at his beautifully furnished Pontalba apartment. He wore casual clothes extremely well and seemed to make an excellent impression on everyone; and, until he himself encountered rough sailing in the late thirties, he brought a measure of stability to the department, although he was more promoter than scholar. There were numerous staff changes. LaFarge left in 1926. So did four others. But replacements were made. Included in the new staff were Dr. Hermann Beyer, world authority on Maya hieroglyphics, and Doris Zemurray Stone, who had graduated from Radcliffe in 1930 and had done graduate work in anthropology at the Peabody Museum, Harvard. Her interest was concentrated largely upon archeological research in the Ulva Valley and the eastern coast of Honduras. She also did ethnographical work in the Guatemalan highlands, publishing valuable papers on the area including "Some Spanish Entradas" and "Masters in Marble."

Even by the end of the Dinwiddie period, however, the department had not really found itself nor discovered how it might work most effectively. Its efforts were rather scattered and were lacking in scholarship, unity, and cohesion. There is also the fact that the department had not yet been integrated into the university. Its purposes and programs were only vaguely, if at all, known to the faculties. Poor communication often led many important faculty members to conclude that the goings on upon the fourth floor of the science building smacked of the esoteric or the crackbrained. It would take time and a new director to correct these impressions.

CHAPTER 12

Academic Affairs (1918-1935)

ONLY A FRAGMENT OF the whole structure of a university is visible to the casual viewer. New buildings, football games, the pageantry of graduating ceremonies when faculty and students parade across the campus in colorful academic regalia—these the public sees. But in the background dimly seen, if at all, there exists a vast accretion of less spectacular phases of university life having to do with curricula, research, faculty recruitment and development, entrance requirements, academic standards, and other matters. These at best are often esoteric, but they constitute the essence of the university and measure its effectiveness for the individual student and for society. If, therefore, one is to understand what Tulane was or was trying to be in the fifteen years after World War I, the recondite as well as the obvious must be considered.

One naturally begins the treatment of academic matters with the liberal arts colleges, for they (Newcomb and the College of Arts and Sciences) are the matrix of the university. At the same time their role was probably less well understood by the public at large than that of any of the other colleges in a university. The school of engineering turns out engineers. The school of medicine produces doctors. The school of law develops lawyers. But the liberal arts college—what does it produce? What can young men and women *do* with a liberal arts education? It is all very well to say that the liberal arts are intended to help students *be* something rather than to *do* something, but during the twenties American society on the whole was more pragmatic, perhaps more philistine, than transcendental. It was unwilling or unable completely to accept the general education role for the liberal arts. Heavy social pressures beat down upon the universities to develop the sort of education which would enable the graduate to make a living, rather than the kind which would teach him how to live. State universities probably felt the pressures more than the privately endowed institutions, but the latter received their share.

It is in this light, then, that one must consider Newcomb and the College of Arts and Sciences as they sought to become truly liberal arts colleges. They were forced to take the social pressures of the day into account. In stating the purposes of Newcomb in 1919 the college bulletin reflects this in so many words: "Instruction is offered first in what are commonly called arts and sciences; and a course of instruction in these subjects, leading to the degree of Bachelor of Arts, represents the first and most general purpose of Newcomb College. *But the college should meet the needs of the community, if possible, by more careful preparation for the specific demands of modern life. . . ."* (Italics mine.) Though not expressed as candidly as this, the aims and objectives of the College of Arts and Sciences were much the same. Both felt the pressures to become all things to all men, particularly in vocational matters. And, although some progress was made in curriculum revision, there were many false starts, and many disappointing setbacks. Actually one could cite evidence that the curricula in 1935 were in many respects more replete with vocationalism than in 1920.

During the year (1918) in which Newcomb moved to its new campus it had these programs: Bachelor of Arts, Bachelor of Arts in Education, Bachelor of Design, Bachelor of Music, a diploma in art, a diploma in music, a diploma in physical education, a diploma in household economy. This was Dean Pierce Butler's legacy from the Dixon administration. Fifteen years later there were four degree programs—Bachelor of Arts, Bachelor of Science, Bachelor of Design, and Bachelor of Music. During this period the Bachelor of Arts in Education had been dropped (1921). So had the physical education major and the various diplomas, including the one in household economy. The Bachelor of Science degree had been added. With the elimination of some of the programs, certain courses which would cause mirth in the faculty today disappeared, for example, "Embroidery S23."

In the College of Arts and Sciences there were numerous curriculum changes. In 1926 two new departments were established, one in journalism and one in geology. The department of journalism was sponsored by the New Orleans *Times-Picayune* and was headed by Professor George Simmons who had taken his training at Vanderbilt and Missouri. Geology had as its professor Reinhard August Steinmayer, an alumnus of Illinois.

Then in 1928 there was established in the College of Arts and Sciences a new degree program, the Bachelor of Education in Physical Education. Many of the liberal arts faculty members were dismayed, even angry, over the action, charging that standards were being lowered in order to produce better football teams. They could, however, console themselves with the fact that it was not the faculty of the college which had devised the program but a special committee appointed by President Dinwiddie. This committee, composed of Dean Bechtel as chairman and Professors Menuet, Mosely, ten Hoor, and Lyon as members, made its report to the University Council on May 16, 1928. The report was approved, a curriculum was adopted and then the *fait accompli* was referred to the College of Arts and Sciences.[1]

In 1935 a significant concession was made to the growing social pressure for specialization at the undergraduate level, even in the liberal arts. It will be recalled that during the Johnston era the curriculum had been largely prescribed and had aimed at a general well-rounded education. This had been altered to some extent in later years by allowing more electives, but still the philosophy of a basic education prevailed. Now the College of Arts and Sciences adopted the major-minor curriculum in both the arts and science degrees. Twenty-four hours were required for the major and twelve hours for the minor. Thus, it was hoped, the student would be better qualified to *do* something after he had completed his baccalaureate degree courses.

A breakdown of course offerings is even more revealing as to what was happening in both Newcomb and Arts and Sciences. In general, science and mathematics were surging to the front while languages, history, philosophy and education lagged or showed only slight progress.

Of these subjects, education should have special mention. The fact that Newcomb had abolished the degree of Bachelor of Arts in Education did not mean that the university was training no teachers. A department of education in which a student could get certification courses was retained at Newcomb under the direction of Professor Stuart G. Noble. The College of Arts and Sciences had no similar department, but there was the "Courses for Teachers" program, almost anomalous in nature. It was not a part either of Arts and Sciences or Newcomb, yet was supported by both. It was not a separate college, yet it granted a degree. Most of its work was offered in the late afternoons and on Saturdays, yet it was hardly an extension education activity. But whatever it was, it carried on a large part of teacher training activity in the university, especially for teachers already in service. Under the direction of Professor J. Adair Lyon the program made excellent progress, enrolling an average of some two hundred students each year and awarding as many as 28 degrees annually. It was, however, a compromise program, for the university was unable to make up

[1] The curriculum was as follows:

Physical education	60 hours
Education	17 hours
English	12 hours
Major subjects (language, history, science or mathematics)	24 hours
Speech	4 hours
Journalism	6 hours
Anatomy	6 hours
Physiology	2 hours
Hygiene	3 hours
Electives	9 hours

its mind what it ought to do about teacher education. On the subject it had waxed hot and cold. In the past there had been a "College of Education," a "Department of Education," a "Division for Teachers," and finally "Courses for Teachers." The root of the difficulty, of course, lay in the attitude of many of the liberal arts faculty members. They were afraid of the "teachers' college" type of education which included what they considered too many "professional" courses in methods without much solid content in them. The Courses for Teachers and the Summer Session at least partially made up for what otherwise would have been integral parts of the work of the two colleges throughout the regular school year.

So far as the faculty itself is concerned, it has been pointed out that the Sharp period was one of transition from the old to the new. In 1919 the College of Arts and Sciences (excluding student assistants and professors emeriti) had 19 faculty members and 261 students. In that same year Newcomb had (with the same exclusions) 52 faculty members and 529 students. Qualitatively, 39 per cent of the Arts and Sciences faculty in the same year held doctoral degrees and at Newcomb 28 per cent held the doctorate.[2] By 1935 the number of faculty members in the Colleges of Arts and Sciences had increased to 50 for 660 students and at Newcomb to 70 for 653 students. Qualitatively, 52 per cent of the Arts and Sciences faculty had the doctorate, and at Newcomb 33 per cent held the highest degree.

Faculty growth, quantitatively and qualitatively, was encouraging to the university, but not all aspects of faculty development were so inspiring. By and large neither faculty was highly productive of scholarly research and writing. Too often the senior members did not get around to this sort of thing; the younger members (of which there were many) had not yet hit their stride. Moreover, there was neither a good graduate school nor library and other research facilities to encourage them. Both colleges, then, could be classified in 1935 as moderately good undergraduate teaching institutions.

At the center of all academic matters stood Dean Pierce Butler at Newcomb and Dean Edward Ambrose Bechtel in the College of Arts and Sciences, two personalities as different as could be imagined. Dean Bechtel physically was so elfin and wispy that his long cigar seemed almost to overbalance him. Butler was tall, with a prominent nose, a blinded left eye, and the hauteur of a Roman senator. Bechtel was a Pennsylvanian who had attended Johns Hopkins and then completed his doctorate at the University of Chicago. Butler was a native of New Orleans, but his spiritual home was always Laurel Hill, the family plantation near Natchez. He had

---

[2] In academic subjects the percentages were about equal. A number of instructors in art and music, where the doctorate was very uncommon, pulled Newcomb's percentage down.

taken the bachelor's and master's degrees at Tulane and had completed the doctorate at Johns Hopkins. Interspersed between degrees were trips to Europe and study there. (On one of these trips a shipboard companion playfully tossed half a lemon at him. It hit his left eye, bruising and eventually blinding it.) He had become a teacher at Newcomb, first in the field of history; and then, switching subject matter fields, had become professor of English in 1902. As a teacher he was at times sarcastic, almost sardonic, and imagined that his students feared him. Apparently, however, they soon discovered that his bark was worse than his bite and thoroughly enjoyed his brilliant lectures. As a dean his efforts were directed toward two goals: bringing Newcomb back into the true orbit of the liberal arts and preserving and strengthening Newcomb's semi-autonomous position within the university. (In the latter activity, it might be added, many on the Tulane side of the campus considered him almost obnoxiously quixotic.)

Dean Bechtel was a modest, almost shy, lecturer on the classics with a keen sense of humor. He loved spectator sports, especially football, and on game afternoons could usually be spotted sitting in one corner of the playing field puffing furiously on his cigar and analyzing every play. He had no major reform mission in academic matters, but was excellent in administrative details. He took his job seriously, but not himself. Butler was deeply concerned about both himself and his job.

But one must turn from the liberal arts to other divisions and colleges in the university during the twenties and early thirties.

Dean Aldrich was building his College of Commerce and Business Administration with characteristic vigor and determination. And it is fortunate that the dean possessed such aggressiveness and singleness of purpose, for the going was not easy.

Throughout the period under discussion the number of evening students heavily outweighed the day students. In 1920 there were 639 students in the evening and only 86 students in the day. By 1935 the number of evening students had dropped to 362 and the number of full-time ones had increased to 186. Graduates, too, had increased from eight in 1920 to 27 in 1935. The faculty of 14, largely part time, had changed to a faculty of 13 in 1935, but most of these were full time. With the increase in the number of full-time faculty members the budget soared, and tuition fees had to be raised to meet the new costs.

But it was not budget and slow growth which presented the major problems. Rather, the matter which caused Aldrich and his faculty the greatest concern was the fact that the new college had to fight for a place in the university family of colleges. There were many members of the faculty of the College of Arts and Sciences who took a dim view of what they considered business administration's blatant vocationalism. The result was that

Dean Aldrich and the faculty were constantly on the defensive, and out of this defensive attitude the college tended to pull away from close association with liberal arts and to work out its own problems within a philosophic framework of its own. Thus Business Administration joined Newcomb in seeking to follow its own course rather than seeking closer union with the federation of colleges.

It was not the evening classes which concerned the critical members of the liberal arts faculty. These students were limited to eight courses for which they received a certificate. When it came to the day classes on the campus, there was bickering. English is English, the liberal arts man maintained. *Business English* is the need, said the business administration faculty. Mathematics should be *mathematics for business* it declared. With this the liberal arts mathematicians differed sharply. In short, the controversy was one of professionalized subject matter versus pure subject matter.

In the curriculum, which was virtually unchanged for the fifteen-year period, one may see tangible evidence of the quarrel. There were two routes by which a student might pursue a degree in business administration. If he had passed two years of strictly liberal arts courses he could take his last two years in business courses and receive a degree. If, however, he entered as a freshman in business administration he took the four-year curriculum, which was heavily weighted with professional subject matter courses and with vocational subjects.[3]

It has been said that Tulane's College of Business Administration was in the forefront of those seeking to liberalize its curriculum even before the organization of the American Association of Collegiate Schools of Business in 1916, but that statement will bear some questioning. It is true that Dean Aldrich was one of the founders of the association and served as its secretary for several years, but the liberally oriented degree program for busi-

[3] The first two years of the regular freshman and sophomore curriculum were as follows:

Freshman		*Sophomore*	
Business Economics	6 hrs.	Marketing	6 hrs.
Executive Responsibility	4 hrs.	Accounting	8 hrs.
Accounting	4 hrs.	Business Correspondence	3 hrs.
Business Talks	2 hrs.	Business Reports	3 hrs.
Business English	6 hrs.	Business Psychology	3 hrs.
Commercial Spanish	6 hrs.	Business Talks	2 hrs.
College Algebra	3 hrs.	Business Organization	3 hrs.
Business Mathematics	3 hrs.	Or physics or chemistry could be	
Physical Education	2 hrs.	taken in place of above two	
		courses.	
		Commercial Spanish	6 hrs.

The junior and senior years were entirely in the field of business administration and contained no liberal arts courses.

ness (except for the special provision made for the two-year liberal arts student wishing to enter the College of Commerce and Business Administration) did not come until comparatively recently. The curriculum of the college (now *school*) bears little resemblance to the old.

A new era was inaugurated in the College of Law in 1927. This is true for several reasons—curriculum reform, better standards, more full-time professors, and a general tightening up of all phases of operations. The date of 1927 is selected because during this year Rufus Carrollton Harris became dean; and from this time on law training underwent numerous changes. Harris was a young and vigorous Georgian, a graduate of Mercer University and the Yale Law School. When invited to come to Tulane he was dean of the Mercer University Law School where he had displayed many of the qualities President Dinwiddie felt Tulane needed to strengthen and build a stronger and better coordinated law school. This judgment was vindicated by Harris' prompt and vigorous attack on the problems which so urgently needed attention.

When he assumed his duties as dean he had a faculty of 19 men, but only three of them were full time. By 1930 the full-time faculty had doubled in size by the addition of Eugene Nabors, a Yale product; William Paul Brosman, former Mercer University professor and Yale man; and Mitchell Franklin from Harvard. By 1935 the faculty had grown to nine full-time professors.

From the number of professors one would assume that the College of Law was small, and that is true. It has never made any pretensions toward being a large college. From 50 in 1919 the student body grew to 103 in 1929, and thereafter the number hovered around this figure until 1935 except for the year 1932 when 152 students registered. Tulane's law college, therefore, had to base its claim to distinction on quality, and this became one of Harris' major objectives.

Underlying the whole structure and operations of the "new" College of Law was a new philosophy of the law, and this, too, was a product of Dean Harris' thinking. Although some had undoubtedly felt that the study of law could have ends other than preparation of men for the practice of the profession, such a feeling had never been so well expressed as it was by Dean Harris. The law, he felt, could be, and should be, a liberalizing and liberating experience for the student. In his opinion the study of law had enormous cultural significance. "The significance of law as a genuine part of the culture of a people recently has become apparent in America, though this has long been appreciated in continental Europe," he wrote. "The complicated problems of life in the XXth century must be considered in the light of the institutional devices of civilization, and it is through the study of the law that the interplay between historical culture and contemporary life becomes most fascinating, in revealing the vitality of the past and the dignity of our own time. Consequently, more and more students are entering upon the study of law, not with the view of engaging in the professional practice of law, but to understand the forces at work in the life of our time."

It is against the background of such a concept that the development of the college of law after 1927 must be viewed. Many of the achievements and problems related below are directly or indirectly related to this philosophy.

Nothing more clearly reflects the Harris concept more than curriculum revision, which took place during the period. As early as 1919 the law faculty had done away with the sharp distinction between common law and civil law instruction. Before this time, students from outside Louisiana had not been required to take courses in civil law, but thereafter all students had to follow a curriculum that was intended to be a blend of the two systems. The blend was not balanced, however, until the thirties. What resulted was a system of comparative law emphasizing what Dean Harris had called "the institutional devices of civilization." One may see this clearly by consulting the files of the important *Tulane Law Review* which was founded in 1929. Increasingly the articles dealt with the universality of the law and of the relationships between the law and human culture. Technical articles, of course, came in for their share of space, but it is clear that some new thinking on the role of law in human affairs was taking place. Comparative law had taken a place at Tulane from which it would not be dislodged. Scholarships for foreign students were established, the degree of Master of Civil Law was inaugurated, and attempts were made to form an institute for the study of comparative law.

At the same time this new emphasis was being felt there were successful efforts made to tighten admission requirements. In 1920 the requirement of one year of college as a prerequisite for the law school was adopted. In 1925 this was raised to two years, and in 1936 the law faculty increased admission requirements to 90 hours of collegiate study, or the equivalent of three years of prelegal study. Exceptions were made only for the exceptionally brilliant student who might be permitted to take only the two years of prelaw.

Recognition came to the law school—membership in the Association of American Law Schools, being placed on the approved list of the American Bar Association, recognition of the degree by the New York Board of Regents, recognition by Herbert Hoover's National Commission on Law Observance and Enforcement—but there was a constant specter which haunted faculty and dean. Some other Southern law schools had lost their accreditation because of inadequate physical quarters for classrooms, libraries, etc. The fact that Tulane did not is inexplicable. The College of Law was crowded into Gibson Hall until 1928 when it was moved to the new science building. But space here soon became cramped. The law school still retained the peripatetic role it had followed since 1847.

From the standpoint of academic matters, in faculty, in curricula and in better-trained students, however, progress was striking. Only one major issue arose to cause unpleasantness. Howard Milton Colvin, professor of law, was given a leave of absence with half pay for the year 1933–1934 and was informed that he would not be reappointed after his enforced leave. There then ensued the sort of controversy which every dean and university president greatly dislikes, to say nothing of the historian who attempts in later years to clarify the matter. The chief charge against Professor Colvin seems to have been that he was a source of constant friction in the faculty; that by his bickering and pettifogging tactics he made harmonious and effective work difficult. On the other hand he charged that Dean Harris had been misled by members of the faculty who had personal grudges and that he was being persecuted because of his liberal social and economic views.

The matter dragged out for months. Walter W. Cook, president of the American Association of University Professors, intervened in the case and in his report stated that sufficient grounds for dismissal were lacking. He felt that Dean Harris' own account of the episode indicated no more than an honest protest on policy by Colvin and suggested that Acting Dean Brosman had magnified differences of opinion into "obstructionist tactics." But the university rejected these conclusions, arguing that Colvin had been dismissed for good cause and that there had been no violation of his right to tenure. Professor Colvin was not reappointed.

Engineering changed less than any of the other colleges in the university between 1920 and 1935. Under the direction of handsome and personable Douglas Anderson who succeeded Creighton as dean in 1919 the College of Engineering (changed to that name in 1920 from College of Technology) made few changes in curricula and inaugurated no major innovations. It considered its job to be that of turning out technically trained engineers, and that it did. There was no room in the curricula for liberal subjects if the job was to be done in four years. Consequently one finds but 12 hours of the humanities in a tough 153-semester-hour degree program. There was talk now and then about a five-year program which would include more liberal subjects, and talk never reached the action stage. Most of the faculty members were technically rather than liberally educated men and thus could not be expected to have a strong devotion to the humanities and the social studies.

The degree programs were the time-honored ones of mechanical, electrical, civil, chemical, and architectural engineering. The School of Architecture thus was still included in the College of Engineering, but it was recognized that architecture was more than a skill. "Architecture is recognized as a fine art," the catalog states, "and hence a wide sympathy with every form of culture is regarded as essential. . . . It is the aim of this School to train men with a view to the ultimate practice of their profession, and the course is designed so that a just relation and balance may be maintained between the practical and the aesthetic." Actually, although it was a part of engineering, architecture was considered a separate college and its head a director. The separation, however, did not come until 1950.

With different aims it might be assumed that architecture would have an entirely different type of curriculum, and this is true. Some of the basic engineering courses such as mathematics, physics, and strength of materials were required, but the emphasis was upon architectural design with liberal amounts of architectural history and drawing. As in engineering, however, there was little of the humanities and none of the social studies in the curriculum. Again as in the case of engineering there was talk of a five-year curriculum, but it was not until 1947 that this plan was adopted.

Both Engineering and Architecture (if one may consider them separately) had able leadership in the dean and department head. Douglas Smith Anderson, dean and professor of electrical engineering, was an urbane and extremely competent man who had not only the high respect of his own faculty, but of other faculties as well. He had served as assistant professor of physics and electrical engineering under Brown Ayres from 1892, when he received his M.A. from Tulane until 1900 when he went to the University of Mississippi to organize its department of engineering. He returned to Tulane in 1901, however, as associate professor. After spending a year's leave of absence to study in Berlin and at the Zurich Polytechnic Institute in 1906–1907 he was promoted to full professor. He had filled all the ranks—assistant professor, associate professor, professor, dean, and finally in 1935 acting president. In all, he served the university for 44 years.

John Herndon Thompson became head of the School of Architecture in 1921 and served in that capacity until 1946. For four years prior to 1921 Professor Nathaniel Courtland Curtis had been head of the school, but it was Thompson who during his twenty-five years as head nursed the school through its most critical period. A native South Carolinian, he had taken his engineering and architectural degrees at the Citadel and Cornell, and was teaching at Clemson College when he accepted the position at Tulane. He was a small man with a soft Southern voice, twinkling eyes, a keen sense of humor, and a mobile face which accentuated his ability as a raconteur.

The total enrollment of the College of Technology was quite satisfactory for the available physical facilities. In 1919 there were 166 students enrolled. In 1936 there were 304. This was not a phenomenal increase, but it was symptomatic of the sort of steady but unspectacular work at the college. It pushed slowly ahead doing its best to turn out good engineers; and in general it was successful.

No such equanimity characterized the medical school during this period.

Important changes were taking place in almost every phase of its work as it advanced into new areas of research and teaching.

The progress of the department of undergraduate medicine overshadowed that of the other divisions. Under Dean Dyer's leadership the faculty constantly modified its curriculum, created new departments and expanded teaching facilities. In 1919 there were 30 professors and 100 other instructors; in 1936 the department had a teaching staff of abut 180, including 64 persons of professorial rank. Growth in physical plant and facilities was commensurate with that of the faculty, for by the end of Dinwiddie's presidency Medicine was firmly established in its well-equipped Hutchinson Memorial building on Tulane Avenue.

On October 12, 1920, the entire university received a severe shock in the death of Dean Isadore Dyer. After a two-year interval Dr. Charles Cassedy Bass was appointed to the deanship. The new dean was a slightly built, drawling Mississippian widely known for his research in bacteriology and parasitology. His major interest was tropical diseases, especially malaria. He was the first man to cultivate the malaria organism in a test tube and was preparing to follow up his discovery when he assumed the deanship. Administrative duties, of course, cut short his research activities.

Since many of the teachers were part-time employees and drew only nominal salaries, the school was able to operate within its budget. In 1936–1937, for example, income was $351,350, exceeding expenditures by $3,000. A large proportion of the revenue came from student fees, which were higher than those of other departments and which increased steadily. In 1918–1919 annual tuition fees were about $174; eighteen years later they were $400. Although operating expenses seldom matched income, the medical school had to have large donations in order to expand. Over $3,000,000 came to the school from outside sources during the Dinwiddie administration. In addition to the grants of the great foundations, there were many other gifts and funds, including The Ernest S. Lewis Student Loan Fund, the Junior League of New Orleans fellowships in obstetrics and gynecology, the Edgar Newman and Henry Dennery research funds, the Ada G. Ross bequest for a free psychiatric clinic, the Senior Medical Students' Loan Fund, and the Violet I. Hart Fund to establish the Rudolph Matas Award in vascular surgery. In 1934 Ellen H. and Hunt Henderson gave $80,000 for support of the medical school.

Increased productivity among the faculty resulted from many of these donations. The research of Dyer in dermatology, Bass in tropical diseases, Faust in parasitology, Matas in vascular surgery, and Souchon in anatomy brought recognition to the department and helped to advance the frontiers of medical knowledge. Professor Amedée Granger, director of the departments of radiology at Tulane and at the Charity Hospital, was the first Southerner to win the gold medal of the Radiological Society of North

America. In 1936 F. E. LeJeune, professor of clinical otolaryngology, was awarded the Casselberry Prize for his film, *Normal and Pathological Vocal Cords*. Professor of Clinical Surgery Carroll W. Allen distinguished himself as the author of the first thorough book in the English language on the subject of local anesthesia, and Dr. Robert Clyde Lynch claimed the honor of being the first surgeon to suture a wound in the interior of the larynx. Alumnus F. W. Parham and Professor of General Surgery E. Denegre Martin collaborated in devising a new treatment for fractures.

The Graduate School of Medicine, though outstripped by the undergraduate division, made satisfactory progress. In spite of an almost complete dependence on student fees, the graduate department grew in the quality and scope of its instruction. A vital factor in this improvement was the succession of strong deans who shaped the school's policies. Charles Louis Chassaignac served in this capacity from 1906 to 1926; Edmund Denegre Martin next filled the position, giving way to Henry Daspit in 1928. Four years later Hiram Watkins Kostmayer became dean upon the death of Daspit.

All of these men were outstanding medical authorities, and they jealously guarded their division's reputation, constantly reviewing and improving objectives and teaching methods, and, within close budgetary limits, expanding medical facilities. The result of their labors appeared in an increased national recognition, for in 1923 the chairman of the Council on Medical Education and Hospitals of the American Medical Association listed Tulane with Harvard, Illinois, Minnesota, and Pennsylvania as leaders in advancing the organization of their faculties for graduate clinical study.

A general reorganization in 1925 led Dean Martin to predict rapid growth for the graduate medical division, but his hopes fell as enrollment sagged in the mid-1920s. Within a few years conditions were made worse by the Great Depression. From a high of 317 in the 1919–1920 session, the number of students fell to 148 five years later, to 81 in 1931–1932, and to a low of 59 the following year. From that point a slow rise began, and a few sessions later the student body numbered over 100.

The College of Medicine continued to add new departments and to strengthen old ones. In 1925 the board re-established the department of tropical medicine, which soon was enlarged by the creation of a laboratory of parasitology. Under world-famous Aldo Castellani (1926–1929) and Colonel Charles F. Craig (1931–1938), the unit increased in size and advanced in quality of instruction. John Herr Musser, who came to the university in 1924, greatly strengthened the department of medicine as its full-time head. The department of surgery in 1926 acquired the full-time services of the brilliant surgeon Edward William Alton Ochsner, while preventive medicine and pediatrics became independent departments.

As new departments appeared and the curriculum broadened, an increasing number of subjects cramped the four-year program, giving rise in the 1920s to outspoken criticism from many quarters. Fred C. Zapffe, secretary of the Association of American Medical Schools, defended the nation's medical courses against the charge that they were a "hodge-podge of non-essentials." Nonetheless he confided to medical educators at Tulane and elsewhere that revision was needed in order to bring medical education into line with the progress of the profession.

A more serious accusation against the medical schools was that their lengthy, complicated courses increased student failures and arbitrarily lengthened the period of preparation. A few physicians and educators were in accord with the critics, who demanded that the training program be simplified. Tulane University's medical teachers joined with others from America's leading medical centers in attacking those whom they called advocates of "low standards." Instead of slackening requirements, they demanded increased preparation. In the spring of 1936 they cooperated with the Arts and Sciences faculty in abandoning the two-year premedical course in favor of a three-year combined scientific-medical curriculum. At the same time Dean Bass made an effort to meet complaints that the number of physicians was being unduly restricted. He presented a plan for grouping subjects into a quarterly system that would have permitted students to graduate after three years of continuous study. The board turned down the proposal, although the plan had been approved by the Association of American Medical Colleges.

All the while the medical division pressed for higher standards, setting up in 1924 a new method of evaluating credits so as to give each course a weight equal to its percentage of the total number of hours for the session. Eight years later the faculty began to administer comprehensive examinations to all seniors. As early as 1922 the college considered a proposal to give intelligence tests to all applicants for admission. Nothing was done about the idea at the time, but in 1930 it was put into effect.

Notwithstanding the steady elevation of entrance and graduation requirements, the college continued to be swamped with applicants, and as increasing numbers were turned away the clamor of criticism mounted. Especially insistent were the critics who charged that the university discriminated against candidates for admission who lived outside of New Orleans or who were not Tulane premedical students. Bass sought to forestall these complaints by placing Tulane students on an equal footing with applicants from other institutions, but the board could not accept this proposal. It reaffirmed the traditional policy of giving preference for places in the freshman medical class to local students, provided they were fully qualified.

In spite of the fact that critics here and there raised their voices against the medical division, the value of its training and the significance of the teacher's research were widely hailed. In 1926 the college became a member of the American Hospital Association, while that same year the Pennsylvania State Board of Medical Education and Licensure gave its approval to Tulane graduates. When the Louisiana State Medical Society met in New Orleans, Tulane provided a medicohistorical exhibit that drew warm praise, and in 1923 the university sent an interesting display to the Pasteur Centennial Exhibition in Strasbourg. Four years later Matas represented the medical faculty at the Lister Centennial in London and while there was awarded an honorary fellowship in the Royal College of Surgeons of England.

As a means of reducing to a minimum the administrative responsibilities of the hard-pressed medical faculty, the Board of Administrators in 1923 created an Executive Faculty within the medical school. Since that body took charge of all matters affecting the conduct and policy of the school, the other teachers quickly lost interest in general faculty meetings. The board then decided that the members of the Executive Faculty should be elected by the medical professors so as to give them greater voice in departmental affairs, and President Dinwiddie made his last appointments to the group in 1931. Three years later the administrators organized another executive body within the medical faculty, the Advisory Council. It was short-lived, however, for the complaint soon arose that it was trespassing on faculty privileges.

Faculty indiscretions and antivivisection activity sometimes embarrassed or hampered the medical school. In 1922 the old antivivisection furor broke out again, and a bill to prohibit experimentation with live animals was introduced in the state legislature. Matas rushed to Baton Rouge and spoke effectively against the measure. The university continued to be harassed by conscientious though ill-advised animal lovers. Five years later Bass had to defend his staff against charges of sadism in connection with their experiments, and in 1931 the department was falsely accused of illegally obtaining dogs from the city pound. Students also presented occasional problems, usually in connection with honor system violations. Many students had no faith in the system. The faculty, though admitting its many flaws, voted to retain it because they felt that no other plan would work any better.

More serious problems, particularly from an administrative standpoint, arose out of differences between Tulane faculty members and authorities of the Charity Hospital. In 1923 the hospital administrators, angered by criticism attributed to Dr. Charles W. Duval, professor of pathology and bacteriology, threatened to withdraw clinical facilities from the Tulane Pathology Department unless Dr. Duval and his staff would resign. It would be interesting to know how the administrators of Charity Hospital could have ousted any of Tulane's clinical services because the medical school was in Charity Hospital not by sufferance but by state law.[4] However, no legal test was made because the two institutions patched up their differences.

In 1930, however, there was much more serious trouble involving a head-on collision between the Tulane medical school and the Huey P. Long political machine which dominated Louisiana. This time the blow fell on Dr. Edward William Alton Ochsner whose appointment to succeed Dr. Rudolph Matas as head of the department of surgery was only four years old. Dr. Ochsner had made the mistake of unwittingly incurring Huey Long's wrath. He had written a letter to a doctor friend in which he was mildly critical of the "politicization" of Charity Hospital and the general political climate of the state.[5] A copy of this letter was stolen from his coat hanging on its customary peg in Charity Hospital. The copy was handed to Dr. Arthur Vidrine, superintendent of Charity Hospital, and through him was shown to the members of the Board of Administrators of Charity Hospital and to Governor Long himself. On September 13, 1930, Long called a meeting of the Charity administrators in his suite at the Roosevelt Hotel and there made it emphatically clear that "Ochsner must go." One member of the board timorously inquired if it would not be enough merely to reprimand Dr. Ochsner but, according to newspaper reports, the "King-fish" flew into a rage, declaring that acts of disloyalty must be punished. Accordingly on September 30, 1930, Dr. Ochsner received from the administrators of Charity Hospital a brief note which read:

Dear Dr. Ochsner:

At the meeting of the Board of Administrators held September 13, 1930, your appointment on the Charity Hospital staff [Senior Visiting Surgeon] was revoked.

It will be noted the letter did not state that the Tulane medical school was denied surgical clinical privileges at Charity Hospital; for these privileges, as stated above, had been established by law. Without the services of

[4] Since the Act of 1847 created the University of Louisiana, the Act of 1855 specifically provided that the medical department of the university should have access to the hospital. This was amplified by the acts of 1892 and 1914, and is presently contained in the Louisiana Statutes 46:772.

[5] Dr. Ochsner's letter read in part: "You may be somewhat surprised that I should even consider moving from Tulane, and my reason for writing to you is to get your frank opinion concerning the advisability of it. I consider it only because I feel that the outlook at Tulane as far as building up a Department is concerned is absolutely hopeless. The University is dependent upon Charity Hospital, which is a state institution and which is in the control of politics. The University is merely tolerated in the Hospital, and there is no cooperation at all. The house staff is appointed by the Hospital, and the University has no control whatever over it.

"As far as the University itself is concerned, it is perfectly free from politics, and my relations here have been very pleasant. I have an excellently equipped surgical experimental laboratory where any type or kind of experimental research may be done. However, under the present system (and apparently there is no better outlook) it is impossible to train men as surgeons."

Dr. Ochsner to direct the surgical clinical facilities, however, a crippling blow was struck at the medical school. A national news magazine reported that after the firing, Dr. Ochsner's students "cheered him lustily," but the evidence indicates Dr. Ochsner was too angry to have his spirits lifted very high by the demonstration.[6] Perhaps he was more cheered by the action of the surgical staff of the medical school. On the motion of Dr. Urban Maes, seconded by Dr. Isidore Cohn, Dr. Ochsner was given a rising vote of confidence, and deep expressions of regret were voiced. But he was out just the same.

The Tulane board solemnly and patiently considered the matter and then made an arrangement with Touro Infirmary for Dr. Ochsner's clinical activities to be held there. Dr. Mims Gage, associate professor of clinical surgery, took over the supervision of the largest segment of Tulane surgical clinical facilities, which remained at Charity.

But though Tulane was not denied all clinical facilities there ensued a period of harassment and uneasiness which lowered morale and reduced the effectiveness of medical training. Letters and telephone calls to Dr. Vidrine from Dr. C. C. Bass, dean of the medical school, from President Dinwiddie and from the Tulane board went unanswered, a circumstance which can be characterized only as studied insolence.[7] The eye, ear, nose, and throat department was put on temporary appointment. For months prior to the opening of the L.S.U. School of Medicine in October 1931, Dr. Vidrine, the first dean, had been busily engaged in trying to recruit a part of his new faculty from the ranks of the Tulane faculty, and this created additional tension.[8] Just as the L.S.U. School of Medicine was to open its doors Dr. Ambrose Storck of the Tulane surgical faculty was denied his scheduled appointment as senior house surgeon at Charity. Dr. Storck, too, had been "disloyal" to the "Kingfish." He had declined an appointment to the L.S.U. medical school, preferring to remain at Tulane.

In 1932, Governor Long moved from Baton Rouge to Washington as United States senator and his gubernatorial mantle, after flapping uncertainly for several months in the crosscurrents of state politics, fell on Oscar K. Allen, his protégé.[9] The Tulane board now concentrated its efforts on Governor Allen, and in September, 1932, almost exactly two years after

---

[6] *Time,* October 6, 1930, p. 44. It is hoped that this statement is more accurate than some others in the article.

[7] Dr. Arthur Vidrine was a devoted follower of Huey P. Long. He was a native of Evangeline Parish, a Rhodes Scholar, and a graduate of the Tulane medical school, class of 1921. It was he who performed surgery on Senator Long after he was shot on the night of September 8, 1935. The modest man shot down that night as Long's assassin was Dr. Carl Austin Weiss, also a graduate of the Tulane medical school, class of 1927.

[8] Dr. Urban Maes, professor of clinical surgery, was probably the best-known member of the Tulane faculty who resigned to accept an appointment at L.S.U.

[9] Long served as Governor from May 1928 to February 1932. He had, however, been elected to the Senate in September 1930.

Dr. Ochsner was barred and Dr. Storck denied an appointment, both were restored to Charity Hospital and an agreement was entered into between Tulane and the L.S.U. School of Medicine wherein each institution had access to the same number of hospital beds.[10] Fourteen months after his restoration Dr. Storck was again barred for a period of eighteen months because he was a member of the Judiciary Committee of the Orleans Parish Medical Society which had joined with the Louisiana State Medical Society in censuring the administration of Charity Hospital.

It would be an oversimplification, however, to think that the attacks on Dr. Ochsner and Dr. Storck were nothing more than an attack on two people. Rather, it was a convenient way to strike at Tulane University. The medical school (and the rest of the university, for that matter) bore in its body the vestigial remains of a state university which the governor found occasion to use for his own purposes. Perhaps part of his pique was an outgrowth of the fact that Tulane had refused to grant him an honorary degree and because of the fact that the Tulane Board of Administrators, Esmond Phelps in particular, was consistently opposed to him. The fact that Mr. Phelps was general counsel for the *Times-Picayune* and a director of the publishing company, Long's bête noir in New Orleans, deepened the animosity.

Long's political strategy is a matter of historical record. His success lay at least partially in his ability ruthlessly to suppress or destroy his opposition. He unfortunately saw in the Tulane medical school a rival and reasoned that he could build up his own medical school by destroying another. "Huey was determined to make L.S.U. a great medical school and as long as he was Governor of our state he was determined to do so even though it may [might] work a hardship on Tulane and particularly Dr. Ochsner, who, in his opinion, had given Tulane's Medical School a tremendous amount of prestige," writes one of Long's closest friends and advisors.

It would be easy to overemphasize the long range effects of the Ochsner-Storck incidents, however. They were merely the most serious of a series of disputes between Tulane and Charity Hospital over administrative malpractices growing out of the fact that too often "Charity" and "politics" were almost synonymous terms. The essence of the matter seemed to be its

[10] Probably no one motivating factor was responsible for the restoration of Dr. Ochsner and Dr. Storck to Charity. There appear to have been a number of factors involved: It is known that Dr. Urban Maes was reluctant to accept the position at L.S.U. until he had assurances the differences would be settled; the breach had implications for the accreditation of the L.S.U. medical school; the Isaac Delgado Grant to Charity Hospital specifically stated that Drs. Ernest Lewis and Rudolph Matas and their successors should always have access to the facilities for the use of their students. It was provided that in the event these faculty members or their successors were barred from such facilities funds from the Delgado Trust would not be given to the hospital. Accreditation of the L.S.U. medical school seems to have been the most pressing reason.

insolubility as long as the power of appointment of director and administration was with the governor. Too often administrative ability was the last qualification considered. But the Ochsner-Storck incidents were the last of the really disruptive explosions. The Tulane and L.S.U. schools of medicine learned to cooperate, especially after the appointment of Dr. William W. Frye, professor of public health and tropical medicine and assistant dean of the Tulane School of Medicine, as dean of the L.S.U. Medical School in 1949. Since this date both schools have at times been critical of some phases of Charity's activities. And no one has been fired for "disloyalty."

Although the authorities of the university were able to maintain and even to expand Tulane's major divisions during the Great Depression, they were forced through stark economic necessity to abandon the flagging departments of dentistry and pharmacy. The board closed the dental school with the greatest reluctance, for its clinic performed an invaluable public service for the poorer citizens of New Orleans. During the last years of its career, between 12,000 and 15,000 patients were treated annually, either free of charge or for a nominal fee.

The very service that so strongly justified the school's existence—the clinic's activities—was a major factor in bringing it to a close, for it pressed the division far beyond the limits of its budget. In the early 1920s enrollment was good, running between 110 and 160 annually, but the tightening of standards in 1925–1926 by inaugurating one year of predental study wiped out the freshman class and brought the number of students down to 62. Tuition fees, never adequate to the department's needs, fell even shorter of meeting operation expenses.

Treading dangerously thin financial ice was not a new experience to the dental faculty. In 1919 the school received a B rating from the Dental Educational Council of America because of unsatisfactory standards in staff and equipment. The board authorized President Dinwiddie in 1921 to undertake to raise an endowment of $500,000 for the division, but the effort failed, and the department's plight became desperate. The administrators in 1924 waved aside the president's warning of increased deficits and resolved to raise standards to meet the demands of national accrediting agencies. It was at this time that the requirement of one year of predental study was adopted, and true to Dinwiddie's warning the department ran at a loss of about $14,000 during the 1926–1927 session.

The unhappy history of the dental school in no way detracted from the professional stature of the teachers, for among them were a number of leaders in their fields of specialization. Dr. Alfred A. Leefe served as dean of the school from 1922 until it closed in June 1928, then as director of the dental clinic until ill health forced him to retire in 1930. Walter C. De Rouen then took over the post. Professor E. B. Ducasse was an authority on bridge work and dental ceramics; G. B. Crozat was prominent in orthodontia; A. B. Bland was a distinquished dental surgeon; and E. L. Fortier held wide recognition for work in prosthetic dentistry.

Faced with the prospect of an accumulated deficit of nearly $70,000 between 1925 and 1929, the board decided in July of 1926 to discontinue the school until an endowment could be obtained. The junior and senior classes were permitted to complete their training, and in June of 1928 the dental school closed its doors, though the clinic remained in operation until 1934. Funds for this useful work came from occasional donations, small charges to patients, a modest special endowment, and money from the medical school's budget.

The School of Pharmacy almost literally improved itself out of existence, for one of the major causes of its declining enrollment was the relentless drive for higher standards. In June of 1922 the faculty decided to discontinue the degree of Pharmaceutical Chemist (Ph.C.) and reaffirmed this stand almost exactly three years later. At the later date it was agreed that those taking the full three-year course were to be awarded the Bachelor of Science in Pharmacy. As early as 1925 the teachers discussed the advisability of requiring four years of study for the degree, but the matter was laid aside until two years later when the American Association of Colleges of Pharmacy began to advocate such a program. In 1929 the Medical Advisory Committee of the board recommended the adoption of the four-year course, with the first two years to be taken in the College of Arts and Sciences. This plan ultimately was approved and went into effect in the fall of 1929. The prepharmacy curriculum was almost identical with the premedical course, and the entire four-year program led to a Bachelor of Science in Pharmacy.

Over these commendable advances hung a darkening cloud of diminishing student bodies and deficit spending. Every elevation of requirements cut the enrollment figure; there were 69 students in 1921–1922, while during the last six years of the school's career it trained a total of only 78 pupils. Between 1924 and 1927 the department spent almost $10,000 more than it took in, and since these losses had to be absorbed by the medical school, they brought huffs of discontent from the parent faculty. Fees were raised from $100 to $150 and then to $165 a session, but in the absence of an endowment these gestures were futile.

The old discussion continued among the administrators as to whether they should attempt additional transfusions in the form of money from other sources, or give the ailing school the *coup de grâce* by ordering it closed. In 1930 the administrators instructed the faculty to accept no more junior students, and the decision soon followed to close the school at the end of the 1930–1931 term. Just when the pharmacy division appeared doomed, the Alumni Association, the Louisiana State Pharmaceutical Association, and the Louisiana State Board of Pharmacy came forward with assurances of financial support. The administrators altered their stand and agreed to maintain the school.

Following this new development, the board reorganized the School of Pharmacy, placing it under its own dean. Up to this time it had been under Dean Bass' authority, with Professor George Stewart Brown serving as chairman of the faculty. Professor John Felicien Simon now became dean of the school. Notwithstanding the pharmacy division's nominal independence, operating losses were still to be borne by the medical school, whose faculty protested against the continued existence of this financial umbilical cord. Reorganization failed to save the school. Adequate funds were not forthcoming, and in June of 1934 the department came to an end after performing for nearly a century the service of training competent pharmacists for the community.

CHAPTER 13

University Life Between
Two Wars (1919-1940)

FOR THE AMERICAN PEOPLE the 1920s constituted a period of frustrating change, especially in moral codes and in ways of living. The 1930s were grim depression years when our whole economic and social systems underwent profound change. Yet for the faculty at Tulane the years between World War I and World War II were for the most part unhurried years, less affected by outside turbulence than one might suspect.

There are any number of reasons why this was true. Faculties were small, and most of the members knew each other intimately. There were, until the debilitating lapse of time when there was no president, relatively few faculty cliques. Committee assignments were not burdensome. There was little pressure to publish, and thus writing could be undertaken in a leisurely manner. Salaries were not munificent even during the 1920s, but in spite of two salary cuts during the depression the faculty members' standard of living did not seriously depreciate. On the whole it was an unvexed, conservative faculty with a conservative administration functioning in an economically conservative community. This serenity was largely undisturbed until 1934–1936 when two events occurred, each of which had a disturbing impact upon the faculty.

The first of these was the illness of President Dinwiddie. On January 20, 1934, he suffered a heart attack. From this time until his death on November 21, 1935, he was unable to give his best efforts to directing affairs at the university. After his death a new president was not elected until 1937. There was thus a period of slightly more than three years when the university was without an active head. Professors Douglas Anderson and Robert L. Menuet served as acting presidents during this period, but both of these estimable gentlemen knew that their tenure would be short, and thus made no attempt to direct the affairs of the university in any positive manner. As a result of this hiatus the direction of the university's affairs was in the hands of the deans of the various colleges and the Board of Administrators. Faculty morale sagged more and more as time went on and no president was named, and then in the midst of nagging apprehensions over the presidency came charges of subversion against certain professors, an event which served further to annoy and frustrate many of the leading faculty members.

Before these charges are related, however, one must look briefly at the state of the national mind from 1932 onward for the next few years.

The country was in the grip of a devastating depression, a malady which seemed to defy therapy. Unemployment mounted; breadlines became common; and on every hand there were abundant signs that despondency had seized the minds of the American people. Many thoughtful persons began openly to question whether the democratic and capitalistic American system could continue or not. This doubt spread rapidly throughout the length and breadth of the country. Men and organizations were crying out for reform, for social justice, and for an end to want in the midst of potential plenty. Abroad, too, events were disturbing. In Spain the Loyalists were fighting for their existence against the attacks of Franco's rebels. Mussolini launched his war on Ethiopia. In Germany a roar of "Sieg Heil" responded to Adolf Hitler's impassioned oratory, and thousands of booted feet goose-stepped down Unter den Linden. On the street corners of almost every city in the world the Communists handed out their literature, and in the Kremlin evil men plotted the ideological conquest of Western civilization. The whole world seemed to be in a frightful, agonizing mess.

In the face of all this the American intellectual could not remain passive. On every side in the United States scores of organizations sprang up— Fascists, Socialists, Communists, and Liberals—each with a program. It was only through organized effort, the intellectual felt, that he could express his individual indignation. The result was that in many instances he joined or worked with organizations which had elements in them of which he would not have approved had he known the basic ideologies of some of the members.

All these reform groups came under attack by ultraconservative and superpatriotic organizations, particularly after the publication in 1934 of Mrs. Elizabeth Dilling's book *The Red Network*. This book, it will be recalled, characterized virtually every liberal and every liberal movement in the United States as subversive. Many well-meaning patriotic organizations, taking *The Red Network* as their evidence, launched attacks on college professors and other intellectuals throughout the country. One of these was against four professors at Tulane.

In the autumn of 1936 the Louisiana Coalition of Patriotic Societies, Inc., brought various charges against Dr. Mack Swearingen and Dr. Herman C. Nixon of the Tulane history faculty, Dr. Mary B. Allen of the

Newcomb history faculty, and Dr. Harlan W. Gilmore of the Tulane sociology department.[1]

The charges against Professor Swearingen were twofold: (1) "That on or about September 14, 1936, at a meeting of Socialists, Communists, and others held at 528 Bienville Street, New Orleans, for the purpose of giving help to the Socialists and Communists in Spain, and at which Negro and white men and women attended, Dr. Swearingen presided. The call for the meeting was issued by one Sidney Pailet, known to be a member of the Communist party and an organizer. At this meeting strong resolutions of sympathy with the Spanish Communistic and Socialistic government were passed and funds were collected to be sent to Spain for the furtherance of the cause." Contributions, it was stated, were to be sent to the International Ladies' Garment Workers Union "whose president is David Dubinsky known to be one of the most important Communists in the United States." Dr. Swearingen, it was charged, was in complete sympathy with the movement. (2) That when "on or about September 28, 1936, the Communist Binkley was arrested by the police and a mass of revolutionary literature seized, Dr. Swearingen called at the City Hall and protested to the mayor's assistant, Mr. Alfred Danziger, against Binkley's arrest and agitated for his release."

Against Professor Allen these charges were leveled: (1) "In the spring of this year [1936] at a meeting held in the Y.W.C.A. in New Orleans, Miss Allen acted as temporary chairman and presided at the organization meeting of a local chapter of The League against War and Fascism, a Communist organization." (2) "In the spring of 1936, Miss Allen acted as one of the leaders and sponsors in promoting a series of motion pictures held at the Happy Hour Theater on Magazine Street, this city, which for the most part attempted to place modern Red Russia in a very favorable light. These pictures lauded Lenin and endeavored to justify the acts of the Soviet rulers in murdering the *bourgoisie* in their efforts to rule Russia." (3) "We have evidence available, which can be furnished if necessary, that Dr. Allen is friendly with Communist Binkley and active in some of his organizations. We understand that Miss Allen had made frequent trips to Russia, just returning from one this summer, and it would be interesting to learn if her salary at Newcomb is sufficient to finance such visits and if not, how does she obtain the funds."

---

[1] The president of the organization was Emmett Lee Irwin, M.D. The participating organizations listed in the charter were: Sons of the American Revolution, Daughters of 1812, several American Legion auxiliaries, the Women's Auxiliary of Disabled Veterans of World War I, the American Legion, the Army and Navy Club of New Orleans, the Louisiana Colonials, and the Daughters of '98. The corporation was formed on July 6, 1936. Among its more important objects were: "To keep America American"; "to expose and combat the political and economical fallacies of any and all un-American organizations."

Dr. Nixon, it was alleged, (1) "accompanied Dr. Swearingen to the City Hall for the purpose of protesting against the arrest of Communist Binkley." (2) "Evidence has been furnished us that Binkley had Dr. Nixon as one of his white collar contacts." (3) "Dr. Nixon, in company with Dr. Swearingen, in the spring of 1936 protested violently to the commission council of the City of New Orleans against the passage of the so-called Emergency Desist Organization Ordinance, which was modeled after similar legislation adopted in cities on the west coast as a means of protecting themselves against Communist uprisings which have actually occurred in several instances. This ordinance was bitterly fought in this city by Communists and others, well knowing that it was designed to curtail their sinister plans."

Professor Gilmore was held guilty merely because he had associated with Professors Swearingen and Nixon, was friendly with them, and was "in sympathy with their subversive programs."

To the everlasting credit of the Board of Administrators it refused to be stampeded.[2] On November 12, 1936, it appointed a special committee to investigate the charges, and a few weeks later the committee made its report. The charges against Professors Nixon and Gilmore were so flimsy that these two men were not even notified by the board that charges had been preferred. On the other two persons involved the committee held six executive sessions and four lengthy private hearings. The Coalition was allowed the privilege of counsel and so were the defendants. Both sides were permitted to introduce any evidence they might have. When all the evidence was in the board reached the unanimous conclusion that "the evidence adduced does not sustain the charges." The committee added, however, that it felt Dr. Swearingen had committed "certain indiscretions" and that it believed that these were "merely thoughtless indiscretions."

A similar conclusion was reached regarding Dr. Allen. After the evidence against her was in, the committee considered the matter submitted by the Coalition, and after hearing and examining Dr. Allen, it unanimously concluded that "the evidence before it does not sustain the charges." The committee added: "It may be that Dr. Allen has been lacking in judgment, but the committee feels that this comment is sufficient in regard thereto."

With the cases thus disposed of, Mr. Walker B. Spencer, an outstanding lawyer and member of the board, asked that his views on academic freedom for faculty members be recorded. The author has not seen a more statesmanlike statement of the matter than that given by Mr. Spencer. Subversive ideologies, he felt, must not be taught in a university classroom. The classroom was no place for propaganda. On the other hand, there

[2] Esmond Phelps was president of the board at the time. He served in this capacity until his death in 1950.

came times when college professors should speak out. In such cases, he felt, they "should speak soberly and seriously and not for notoriety or self-advertisement." They should be, he thought, "under a deep sense of responsibility of the good name of the University and the dignity of their profession." Moreover, "when they speak, they should take care that they are understood to speak personally and not officially. The Administrators respect their freedom to express their sincere opinions as other citizens do, and if this be observed there will be little danger then that liberty of speaking will be misused or curtailed." The chief criticism Mr. Spencer had of Professor Swearingen, he inferred, was that Dr. Swearingen "made, facetiously or thoughtlessly, remarks which were unfortunate, and might have given ground for criticism." But, he added, he did not take the remarks seriously.

The immediate cases were thus brought to a conclusion, but the result did not halt gossip and rumor about Tulane. It has been pointed out how widespread the old canard that Tulane was a rich university catering to a rich clientele became. There was now added a second myth: that Tulane was a hotbed of radicalism. For several years after 1936 one heard this reckless and unfair statement as it circulated from mouth to ear. Perhaps it is the penalty which a university must pay for maintaining an independent position on public affairs and for allowing its professors to speak their minds.

It was the student rather than the faculty member who underwent a metamorphosis during the 1920s and early 1930s. More specifically, if one may speak euphemistically, it was the distaff side of the campus which changed so radically. The male student remained the drab figure in high collar, tight suit, and high-laced shoes he had always been. But the female blossomed out into something utterly other and frightfully modern, mad, and emancipated. The demure Gibson girl turned into the John Held, Jr., caricature of the "flapper." Off came the long tresses in favor of the short bob complete with a spit curl on the forehead. The shirtwaist and the long skirt were replaced by a short, formless sheath reaching almost to the knees, the waistline located somewhere below the hips. In the region of the knees the dress encountered daringly rolled silk stockings which were now *de rigueur*. When the young woman sat no amount of tugging made skirt and stockings meet, with the result that the Newcomb professor standing before his classes was confronted by a sea of rolled stockings and half-exposed thighs.

On the athletic field and in the gymnasium the voluminous and concealing bloomers of the turn of the century shrank to tighter-fitting and shorter garments much the same as those worn as underwear. The sweater and shorts period had not arrived, but it was well on the way. Socially, too, she defied tradition. Like her sister collegians all over the country, she parked her corset at dances, took a few drinks from a pocket flask, and danced phrenetic dances such as the "Charleston" or clung closely to her partner in the "Bunny Hug." After the dance she was likely to take a drive in her escort's automobile and to do a little necking in the moonlight. (Automobiles were just making their appearance on the campus and adding to discipline problems. To curb their speed college authorities had bunkers built across the streets, but to little avail. A student would approach a bunker, slam on his brakes and then in a swirl of dust and smoke roar away with cutout open to the next one.) In short, she seemed to do most of the things calculated to shock her elders and then after graduation to turn into a fine homemaker or career woman.

And her elders on the faculty were shocked. There was much doleful shaking of heads and clucking of tongues as faculty members attempted to meet what appeared to them to be a serious threat to manners and morals. Two approaches were made to the problem: The position of "counselor to women" was established in 1919, and Miss Anna Many, a greatly respected faculty member, was appointed to fill the post; and there was a revision and tightening of rules of conduct.

In the new rules some concessions were made to the new era and in other instances repression was attempted, especially for freshman and sophomore women dormitory students who were not permitted to attend amusement places or go walking on Canal Street on Sunday. They were limited to five minutes on the telephone and could not attend fraternity functions unchaperoned. If they did attend fraternity dances they were not permitted to dance cheek to cheek. As a matter of fact regulations required that couples be separated from each other by a distance of two inches. In 1926 Newcomb students were not permitted to smoke on the campus, in the dormitories, or anywhere in public. It was not until 1932 that the girls were allowed to smoke in designated rooms, but they were still forbidden to smoke on the campus or in the student section at the stadium. Special concessions, however, were made for seniors if their grades were satisfactory. They could take night automobile rides unchaperoned and could serve as chaperones for younger students.

In addition to faculty regulations there were also those set up by the student government. During the early 1920s this body was a powerful one. It cooperated with the faculty, performed all functions of the student body, controlled all college enterprises, fostered school spirit, and maintained the "cultural standards of the college." It had a dormitory section that acted as a self-governing body among the students residing on the campus. The executive committee of the association passed on the laws that were to be submitted to the student body for consideration, chartered all clubs and organizations, and enforced all regulations. Picked members of the association worked with a faculty committee as a court of appeals. This joint body had jurisdiction over all matters of behavior and activities of the students. Another group, the Student Council, served as an honor board. Fine as the organization sounded on paper, however, its operations were far from satisfactory. In 1933 a representative of the Women's Intercollegiate Association for Student Government made a study of the Newcomb system and reported that student government at Newcomb had a "vicious influence because immature students passed foolish and unfair regulations. The House Council was too arbitrary and respect for the faculty was undermined." This representative declared that most Newcomb students had little interest in student government and did not "care a snap for a voice in college affairs."

The rebellious or indifferent attitude of the Newcomb student had its counterpart in the male student on the other side of the campus. The student's tendency to ignore speeding and parking regulations was a part of the new rebellious attitude. The student papers lashed out at prohibition as hypocrisy and at moral reformers as insincere busybodies. In November 1927, 150 Arts and Sciences students were suspended because they refused to comply with the regulations requiring smallpox vaccinations. Drinking and gambling became serious problems. Dances were sometimes ruined by disorderly drunks. Hip-pocket flasks were carried to the football games where students and townsmen alike fortified themselves against the exigencies of the game, and sometimes the imbibing led to fights or other incidents which embarrassed university officials. Strikes, rowdyism, and pranks provoked many instances of student-faculty friction. In what appeared to have been a strike called for no reason at all except to defy authority the freshman and sophomore classes in Engineering and in Arts and Sciences absented themselves from classes on April 4, 1919. There was severe rowdyism in the physics laboratory in March 1920. In October 1920, the students staged a parade through the classrooms just before the football team departed for Ann Arbor. In February 1922, the medical classes took an unauthorized holiday to add to the one given for Mardi Gras. Two months later classes in Gibson Hall were disrupted by the ringing of bells and the throwing of stink bombs, sneezing powder, and itching powder. As late as November 1934, Campus Night was marred by the hurling of eggs and overripe fruit from the balcony of Dixon Hall. In the early 1920s a campus "painting war" broke out between Tulane and L.S.U. students. One year the L.S.U. campus would bear gallons of green decorations and the next year would find the Tulane campus artistically decorated in purple paint. A truce halted the painting temporarily, but in November, 1929, the war was renewed with even greater intensity.

It is possible, of course, to overemphasize the antics of rebellious youth during the 1920s and 1930s, for there is another view of the matter. Throughout the university there were sober and responsible students who deplored the carnival of frivolity which was so evident. In issue after issue of the *Hullabaloo* editorials lashed the students for their conduct. Religious activity through the Y.W.C.A., Y.M.C.A, and sectarian organizations grew. On the whole, however, the period of the 1920s and early 1930s was a trying one at Tulane as well as at virtually all of the other universities in the country. Rules, regulations, and appeals to reason had little effect in heading off youth who felt on all sides not only the depression but the pressures of international discord like a monster robot pushing them as if they were cattle down converging roads leading to a giant slaughterhouse. And they rebelled against this; against man's inability to create a world in which depression and war would not rob youth of its hopes for a life of usefulness and happiness. Seriously they debated the Oxford idea of refusing to fight for king and country. Half seriously and half cynically they formed a chapter of "Veterans of Future Wars." For their cynicism and pacifism they incurred the caustic criticism of the American Legion in New Orleans, thus adding to the wild rumors about subversion at Tulane. Within a relatively short period of time these same rebellious young college men were fighting as courageously on Guadalcanal and the beaches of Normandy as their critics had at Chateau-Thierry and in the Argonne forest.

It should be repeated that tension and turbulence were not the only characteristics of student life. A mere listing of additional campus activities reveals many ways in which events were in an orbit of "normalcy." The *Hullabaloo* and the *Jambalaya* were the basic campus publications. Around them revolved minor journalistic projects, most of which quickly burned out. Among the casualties was Newcomb's *Arcade* which was succeeded by *Lagniappe,* the first issue of the latter coming from the press in January 1935. Shortly thereafter the *Newcomb Alumnae News* made its appearance. Sixteen fraternities were established at Tulane and Newcomb in the period 1926–1935. Four of these were social; the balance were professional and honorary fraternities whose purpose was encouragement of scholarship and leadership. Literary clubs, debating clubs, glee clubs, and other similar organizations were active. In January 1927, the Student Council adopted olive green and blue as the official university colors. Competition for a new Alma Mater was begun in 1926, and the song written by Miss Eva Joor Williams with music by William H. Reubush was adjudged the winner in 1927 after a close vote among students and alumni. The first Homecoming Day was celebrated June 5, 1923.

These were some of the normal events which occurred in an abnormal period. It was intercollegiate athletics, however, which occupied the center of attention of campus life throughout the 1920s and 1930s. During those years Tulane teams engaged in virtually all the forms of intercollegiate sports—football, baseball, track, tennis, boxing, wrestling, golf, basketball, and rowing. Of these, football and tennis emerged as the most popular in the minds of students and citizens of the community. Most of the others were sometime things; sometimes there was a team and sometimes there was not. But football and tennis went on year after year.

In spite of rather violent ups and downs, track under coaches Forrest "Fritz" Oakes and "Big Monk" Simons made a rather creditable showing between 1920 and 1940. In the two-year period 1920–1921 Tulane won one out of three meets. Then the sport on an intercollegiate level was discontinued until 1924, during which year Tulane won one out of three meets. The team "bounced back" in 1925 and won the Southern Amateur Athletic Union championship. Between 1926 and 1929 the squad lost 12 out of 16 meets, and lost all its meets in 1930. The next year, due largely to the exploits of Don Zimmerman, champion pole vaulter, the team won the Southern Conference championship. This was the last championship for Tulane track during the period, but teams were on the path each year.

Baseball, too, was on and off. A team was organized in the spring of 1919 and won seven out of ten games, but in the following year the Athletic Council discontinued the sport because of the lack of funds. Play was resumed in 1923, but for the next few years the record was unimpressive, climaxed by the disastrous season of 1930 in which the team lost all 14 games. For seven years it remained an intramural activity. It was renewed on an intercollegiate basis in 1937, but this event failed to rescue it from the doldrums.

Tulane's basketball record during the period was much better. Claude "Big Monk" Simons coached the team during the early part of the Dinwiddie era and produced some of the finest basketball squads prior to the advent of the nationally prominent teams under Coach Cliff Wells. Up until the season of 1923–1924 the record was mediocre—breaking even or a little worse. In 1924 it lost only one game out of 22 played. In spite of its success, however, it was eliminated in the semifinals of the Southern Conference tournament. In 1924–1925 the previous year's record was almost duplicated. Tulane won 18 out of 21 games, but again was eliminated in the conference tournament. From this point until 1936 there was little to boast about. In 1937 the team won six games, lost four, but it defeated L.S.U. for the first time in five years. This, of course, made it a perfect season.

For obvious reasons tennis took and held first rank among the minor sports. From President Dinwiddie and President Harris down through the ranks of the faculty there was a favorable climate in which the sport could thrive. The construction of a small tennis stadium in 1927 added greatly in the development of the game. Above all there was an almost unbroken series of championship teams developed by Mercer Beasley, tennis coach from 1929 until 1934. This tradition of winning tennis teams has been continued under Emmett Paré, who became coach in 1934. Winning Southeastern Conference titles and developing Davis Cup players has almost become a habit at Tulane. Among the great stars developed were Clifford Sutter and his brother, Ernest, Kendall Cram, Crawford Henry, Hamilton Richardson, Pepe Aguero, Jack Tuero, and Ron Holmberg.

Intercollegiate sports at Tulane for the twenty-year period between 1920 and 1940 were under the general direction of two remarkable men: Dr. Wilbur C. Smith, athletic director, and Claude "Big Monk" Simons, who served in the capacities of trainer, baseball coach, basketball coach, track coach, and director of intramural sports. Rarely does one find men held in such high esteem for so long a period of time throughout a university and the community as were these. Dr. Smith, athletic director, nicknamed "The Bull," was professor of gross anatomy in the Tulane medical school from 1922 to 1945, when he resigned to accept the deanship of the Louisiana State University School of Medicine. He was a stern but sympathetic and effective teacher, a practical joker, a good companion, and an excellent administrator of athletic affairs. Perhaps no man on any faculty of the university was held in higher esteem than "Doc Smith." "Big Monk" Simons left a lasting imprint upon the university. His versatility and cooperativeness made a profound impression upon the entire athletic program. He was in the highest and best sense of the term a general utility man. Actually a sort of division of labor was worked out between Smith and Simons. Although Smith was in charge of all athletic programs he confined a greal deal of his attention to football, leaving to Simons much of the planning and management of other sports.

The period between 1920 and 1940 saw the flood tide of Tulane's success in football. During this time the university's team played a Rose Bowl game and two Sugar Bowl games and was conference champion or cochampion six times. Six players were named "All-America," one, Gerald "Jerry" Dalrymple, being named twice for this honor.[3] Four outstanding football coaches directed these teams: Clark Shaughnessy, 1915–1920 and 1922–1926; Bernie Bierman, 1927–1931; Ted Cox, 1932–1935; and Lowell "Red" Dawson, 1936–1941.

Clark Shaughnessy, a husky, exuberant Irishman with laughing eyes, came to Tulane from Minnesota as football coach in 1915. He ate, slept, and talked football. He managed to convey to his teams some of his own enthusiasm, and as a result they were noted for their spirit. Bernie Bierman, also from Minnesota, had been an assistant coach under Shaughnessy but in 1926 had gone to the Mississippi Agricultural and Mechanical Col-

[3] Tulane's "All-America" players between 1920 and 1940 were: Charles "Peggy" Flournoy, 1925; Willis "Bill" Banker, 1929; Gerald "Jerry" Dalrymple, 1930 and 1931; Donald "Don" Zimmerman, 1932; Claude "Little Monk" Simons, 1934; Harley Ray McCollum, 1939; and Ralph Wenzel, 1939.

lege (now Mississippi State University) as head coach. He returned to Tulane in 1927. In personality, he was the antithesis of Shaughnessy. Bierman was a taciturn, almost dour individualist who relied much more upon his assistants than had Shaughnessy.

Although Shaughnessy and Bierman differed widely in personalities and in coaching techniques they taught the same style of football. Neither of them had large squads. Indeed, during one of Shaughnessy's most successful seasons there were only 19 men on the squad. It was not until 1936 that Tulane, following the trend in other Southern universities, established a system of athletic scholarships which included board, room, and tuition. This, plus the major in physical education inaugurated in 1928, enabled coaches to have larger squads, but Shaughnessy, and to a much lesser extent Bierman, had to depend largely on nonsubsidized students who "went out for the team." Both coaches, therefore, were forced to rely on speed, spirit, stamina, and smart quarterbacking. Both coaches used the T-formation long before it was "invented" in very modern times. As a result of their coaching Tulane teams in the 1920s and 1930s were colorful and rugged. It was an era of the "iron men" who did not think it unusual to play a full sixty-minute game.

Shaughnessy's initial efforts were unspectacular. Between 1915 and 1919 he worked slowly and carefully toward the goal of developing a team capable of playing the better squads in the South. His planning began to pay off in 1919. Although there were only 19 men on the squad, Tulane won six, tied one, and lost two out of its nine-game schedule. Had it not been for the defeat at the hands of L.S.U., 27–6, the season might have been considered very successful. However, the two universities had come to the point where the true measure of a successful season was determined by which school won the annual November game.[4] Other games were relatively unimportant.

In 1920 Shaughnessy's team won six out of nine games, and this season marked Tulane's first appearance in an intersectional game. On October 30 the Green Wave invaded the North for the first time, where it was defeated by Michigan. During this same season the University of Detroit's eleven, considered one of the best in the North, won a close game at Heinemann Park (later known as Pelican Stadium) in New Orleans. Tulane's old wooden bleachers on the campus would not accommodate the crowd, and even the much larger Heinemann Park was taxed to its capacity, so much so that students complained of being discriminated against in the matter of seats. In many respects this game could be said to mark the beginning of "big-time" football in New Orleans. With this game, football began to take on some of the proportions which it assumed later.

---

[4] Between 1920 and 1940 Tulane won 12, tied 2, and lost 6 of its games with L.S.U.

A victory over L.S.U. sweetened the 1920 season but rumors that Coach Shaughnessy was about to resign injected an unpleasant note. So strong were the rumors that the *Hullabaloo* on November 19 publicly petitioned the coach to remain. "You took the 'Green Wave' when it was just a rain puddle and made it a team upon which the eyes of the entire South are turned," the paper said.[5] Coach Shaughnessy did resign, however, in order to establish a business which would supplement his slender salary of $1,500. He had been hired at a salary of $1,800. In 1916 it was increased to $2,000, but this had been trimmed by $500 during the locust years of the Sharp period.[6] It should be recognized, however, that football coaching at the time was not a year round job. The coach was paid only for the fall months.

Myron E. Fuller coached the team during the 1921 season. The two outstanding events were a game with Centre College at New Orleans and a return game with Detroit. The "Praying Colonels," fresh from their upset victory over Harvard, played the "Greenies" in New Orleans, and Bo McMillin, Centre's famous quarterback, led his team to a 21–0 victory. Detroit likewise defeated Tulane, 14–10, but the game brought into sharp focus one of the first of a long series of football heroes. Morris Legendre, Tulane fullback, averaged 65 yards in punting. On one play he punted while standing on his own five-yard line, and the ball, with a series of lucky bounces and rolls, went into Detroit's end zone.

Soon there were other heroes to proclaim, for Shaughnessy returned in 1922, but of eight games played that year the Green Wave won only four. Perhaps the distinguishing feature of this year was the organization of the first freshman team in the university's history as a result of a conference ruling against freshman participation in intercollegiate sports.

In 1923 Tulane won six, lost three, and tied one, but in the following year Shaughnessy's squad lost only one out of nine games. This 1924 team turned into a team in 1925 which won an invitation to play in the Rose Bowl. Interest in football reached a new high in New Orleans, and the community was becoming more closely involved in the ups and downs of the team. To honor the 1924 eleven and to encourage football teams of the future at Tulane, the "Side Lines Club," an organization of prominent businessmen of the city, was formed in February 1925. And it is not difficult to understand this enthusiasm. The 1924 team was full of fight and color. The "Minnesota shift," used against Tennessee for the first time that year, was so new to the South that not only were the opponents baffled

[5] The nicknames "Green Wave" and "Greenie" seemed to have originated in 1920 when E. Earl Sparling's Song "The Rolling Green Wave" was published.

[6] The university's contribution to the athletic budget in 1920 was only $8,560. This was for personnel only. Uniforms, travel, etc., were handled from a separate fund created by gate receipts and disbursed by the Athletic Council, a separate corporation.

but the referee as well. Time after time plays were called back, until the referee was given a briefing at half time. Another event which inspired enthusiasm among Tulane fans was the goal-line stand against Auburn on November 8. In this game, Tulane held Auburn for eight downs within the one-yard line, four of which were within the one-foot line, and then took possession of the ball.

With this spectacular team returning intact it was not difficult to prophesy that 1925 would be a great year; and it was. It was Shaughnessy's greatest season at Tulane, a season which produced heroes for Tulane's growing hall of football fame.

On his way to Minnesota for a visit at the close of the 1924 season, Shaughnessy went through Chicago and while in the city signed a contract with Northwestern, one of the most powerful teams of that period. There was considerable shaking of heads at Tulane, for it appeared he was getting out of his class, but on a raw, cold, fall afternoon of 1925 in Chicago Lester Lautenschlaeger, one of Tulane's greatest quarterbacks; Milton "Irish" Levy (guard); and Charles Priestley "Peggy" Flournoy (back) led Tulane to an 18–7 victory. During this same season the Greenies earned a tie with Missouri, defeated L.S.U., and had a perfect record except for the tie.

At the season's end Tulane shared with Alabama the Southern Conference championship title, and experts ranked the Greenies third in the nation. Several Tulane men made "All Southern." Flournoy was unanimously named "All American," and Levy and Lautenschlaeger received honorable mention for the mythical team. It is not surprising, therefore, that Tulane should have received an invitation from the Rose Bowl for a postseason game.[7] This invitation did come, and on December 14, 1925, the Board of Administrators declined the invitation, giving, as the reason that it was opposed to postseason games. It is pretty generally known, however, that a number of players on the squad were in danger of failing their courses. A postseason game, it was felt, would make it almost certain that these men would fail in their academic work. Nevertheless there were mutterings and mumblings of disappointment among the team, the students, and the townspeople. The ardor for a larger stadium at Tulane, however, was not cooled. The last Shaughnessy-coached team dedicated the new stadium by losing to Auburn on October 23, 1926.

There are those who feel that his disappointment over the Rose Bowl invitation was largely responsible for Shaughnessy's resignation after the

[7] The team roster was as follows: Lester J. Lautenschlaeger, captain; A. J. Odom, manager; Roy Blacklidge, Patrick W. Browne, Charles P. Flournoy, Harry P. Gamble, Jr., C. Ellis Henican, Thomas Killeen, George F. Lamprecht, Milton Levy, Alvin J. Lorio, John G. Menville, Edward C. Morgan, Walter O. Moss, David J. Norman, Pascal P. Palermo, Virgil A. Robinson, Alfred L. Stoessel, H. Horace Talbot, Reginald E. Watson, Bennett A. Wight, Gordon Wilson, and Harvey A. Wilson.

1926 season. This, however, does not appear to have been a major reason for his leaving. Rather, it seems to have been the result of several things taken together. There was alumni criticism over the loss of the L.S.U. game in 1926. There was also some bickering between him and the University Athletic Council over assistant coaches. At the time these irritating matters were being discussed an almost fabulous offer came from certain wealthy Loyola University alumni for him to cross the fence and take over football coaching duties at Loyola. Although Shaughnessy loved Tulane the fact was that the offer was doubly attractive because the business he had established (distributorship for a scale company) had not fared very well. At all events, he accepted the offer and remained at this institution for two years.

In many respects the five-year Bierman period, 1927–1931, was a time of transition from what may be termed the "old" period of football at Tulane to a "new" period. The old period was characterized by small squads, unsubsidized players, relatively small crowds, small gate receipts, and limited travel. The new period can be described in terms of much larger squads, larger coaching staffs, subsidized players, greater crowds, and thus greater revenues and much more active interest of the public and alumni in athletic affairs. Not all of this pattern was completed during the Bierman period, but it was rapidly taking shape. What the purist is likely to call "commercialized football" was peering over the stadium walls, but during the Bierman period it was held in check at Tulane. It would be too much to say that no alumnus contributed to the college expenses of a football player, but on the whole the matter of subsidization was well controlled. When the Carnegie Foundation for the Advancement of Teaching in 1929 published its study of football at 112 universities and colleges, Tulane was one of 28 given a clean bill of health.

Bierman's first outstanding team took the field in 1929, a team which added to its share of stars. Gerald "Jerry" Dalrymple, an end: Willis "Bill" Banker, believed by many to have been Tulane's greatest backfield man: and Richard O. "Dick" Baumbach at quarterback led the team to the Southern Conference title, winning all its nine games and scoring 279 points to 45 for the opposition.

The conference title was successfully defended by the 1930 team, but the championship had to be shared with Alabama, whose team went to the Rose Bowl that year. Tulane had to content itself with the satisfaction of seeing Dalrymple named "All American"—this plus the fact that L.S.U. was defeated 12–7. At this game, however, the *bête noir* of many future Tulane–L.S.U. games made his appearance running up and down the side lines, waving his arms and shouting imprecations. He was Governor Huey P. Long, "The Kingfish," whose efforts to build the greatest teams in L.S.U. history were soon to show results. Even the Kingfish could not build a team overnight, however, and there yet remained for Tulane three seasons before the evil days came when Tulane could say it had no pleasure in them. The crowning event of Bierman's career at Tulane came in 1931. In 11 regular games Tulane won them all, making 338 points to the oppositions' 45. Ole Miss, Georgia Tech, Vanderbilt, Mississippi A. and M., and L.S.U. all fell before the Greenies.[8] On the basis of this record Tulane won another invitation to appear in the Rose Bowl; and this time Tulane accepted. On January 1, 1932, in what was described by sports writers as one of the most thrilling of all the Rose Bowl games, Tulane was defeated by Southern California, 21–12. On the heels of this successful season, however, came the news that soft-spoken Coach Bierman was resigning to accept the top coaching position at Minnesota, his Alma Mater.

Bierman's line coach and also a Minnesota product, Ted Cox, began his four-year tenure in 1932 with Lester Lautenschlaeger as a backfield coach. But Lautenschlaeger was much more than an assistant coach. Actually he was associate head coach in everything but name, and to him is due credit for most of the discipline instilled into the team. Cox was a great affable hulk of a man towering well above six feet. He had a happy and infectious smile and could find something to laugh about even in misfortune. He did, however, to a remarkable degree win and hold the affection of his players.

In 1932 under Cox the team won six, lost two, and tied one. Included in the losses this year was the L.S.U. game, when an influenza-stricken Greenie team succumbed 14–0. Perhaps the conspicuous event of the year was the choice of Don Zimmerman as All-American halfback. In 1933 Tulane won six, lost three, tied one, the tie coming in the L.S.U. game. Abe Mikal, one of Governor Long's favorite protégés, threw a long touchdown pass late in the game, thereby pulling defeat out of the coals. The following year (1934) saw the Green Wave recapture some of its former success by winning nine games and losing only one. Again Tulane shared with Alabama the championship of the Southeastern Conference. Included in the victories was the L.S.U. game in which "Little Monk" Simons, by making a long punt return run in the last fifteen seconds of the game, enabled Tulane to win by the narrow margin of 13–12. This victory earned for the Greenies an invitation to the first Sugar Bowl game, January 1, 1935.[9]

[8] The roster of the Rose Bowl team was as follows: Gerald Dalrymple, captain; Ernest Eustis, Jr., manager; Claggett Upton, Donald G. Zimmerman, Lowell P. Dawson, George Haik, William Drawe, James Hodgins, Doyle Magee, William Penny, Will Pat Richardson, Floyd Roberts, William Schroeder, John McCormick, Winnie Paul Lodrigues, Elson Delaune, Calvert deColigny, Louis Boasberg, John Read, Harold Lemmon, Vernon C. Haynes, Nollie Felts, Richard Bankston, Charles Calhoun, John Scafide, Thomas Cunningham, Harry C. Glover, and Francis Payne.

[9] The roster of the 1934 Sugar Bowl team was: John E. Loftin, captain; Louis A. Mahoney, manager; Bradley C. Brownson, John B. McDaniel, Jr., Richard Page, Stanley D. Lodrigues, Bernard D. Mintz, Howard L. Bryan, Louis O. Thames, Douglas E. Johnson, James W. Henderson, Claude Simons, Jr., Farrell B. Thomas,

It seems appropriate that Tulane should have inaugurated the first of a long series of Sugar Bowl classics. The idea for a New Orleans Mid-Winter Sports Association originated in 1932. The association asked Tulane for permission to stage a postseason game at the stadium, but plans fell through for this year. It was not until 1934 that circumstances permitted the Association of Commerce and other business and civic groups to push their idea to completion. In this year the university gave its consent for the use of the stadium, and this approval has been renewed year after year until the present. In a thrilling beginning of the Sugar Bowl series All-American Claude "Little Monk" Simons led his teammates to a 20–14 win over Temple University.

In 1935, Cox's last year, the Greenies had a rather bad record, losing four out of ten games. The season was brought to a dismal close when L.S.U. mauled the Tulane team by the lopsided score of 41–0, revealing that the new emphasis on football at L.S.U. was paying off. The story of the game may be told in five words: Abe Mickal passed Tulane dizzy. But there were other repercussions. Cox and Lautenschlaeger had won 71 per cent of their games, developed a conference championship and Sugar Bowl team, and produced an All-America player; but the alumni and other sports fans now demanded the scalps of the two coaches, and got them.[10] Almost overnight the Athletic Council shifted Cox and Lautenschlaeger to professors of physical education, and they promptly resigned.

Lowell "Red" Dawson, who succeeded Cox and Lautenschlaeger, had been the quarterback on the Tulane Rose Bowl team and then had gone to Minnesota as backfield coach. He was a solemn, morose perfectionist and stern taskmaster who, at times, seemed almost to drill the heart out of his players. His teams were well coached, but there are those who feel that he sacrificed the affection of his players in the process of making them a well-oiled machine.

Viewed in retrospect Dawson's record has much to commend it. In 1939 his team was cochampion with Georgia Tech and Tennessee in the Southeastern Conference. On January 1, 1940, this team was invited to the Sugar Bowl, where it was defeated by Texas A.&M., 14–13. On the positive side also may be mentioned the fact that he developed three "All-American" players. On the negative side, he won 36 games, lost 18, and tied 4. This record probably would not have been so criticized had it not been for the fact that between 1936 and 1941 Tulane lost four of the six

John Bruno, Jr., Homer R. Robinson, Noel W. Loftin, Ernest H. Gould, Charles A. Kyle, Augustus H. Clark, Jr., Frederick Preisser, Richard Hardy, Harold G. Memtsas, Hughes Schneidau, Robert A. Tessier, Charles B. Stroble, William U. Moss, Jr., David E. Pace, Roy Delbert Ary, Marion S. Monk, Jr., Edward Poitevent, Bernard P. Evans, Charles G. Smither, George D. Tessier, and Robert L. Simon.

[10] Shaughnessy over his 11-year period won 62 per cent of his games; Bierman won 77 per cent of his games; Dawson, who followed Cox, won 62 per cent of his.

games with L.S.U. Perhaps for this reason more than any other one, Tulane alumni and other supporters became highly articulate in their criticism, with the result that Dawson resigned after the 1941 season.

As a sort of postscript to this discussion of football at Tulane between 1920 and 1940 it might be added that from 1942 through 1945 the teams were coached by "Little Monk" Simons. During this period there was a temporary eclipse of Tulane's former gridiron greatness with only 39 per cent of the games won during Simons' four-year period. But it should be quickly added that these were war years, when recruiting was difficult and when the energies of the university were being expended on a big Navy training program and other wartime activitites. With the coming of Henry E. Frnka as head coach in 1946 football again began to look up, but the Frnka regime was so characterized by excessive recruitment, excessive expenditures, and other undesirable features that the university after his resignation in 1952 began to look for the very difficult and elusive middle way. This attempt at moderation had its beginning under Coach Raymond "Bear" Wolf (1952–1954) and has continued under Coach Anton "Andy" Pilney, who succeeded Wolf, and under Coach Tommy O'Boyle.

CHAPTER 14

A University Emerges

FIFTEEN MONTHS AFTER THE death of Dr. Dinwiddie a new president of the university was elected. On February 27, 1937, Esmond Phelps, president of the board, officially notified Rufus Carrollton Harris, dean of the College of Law, that the choice had fallen upon him. On June 9, 1937, he took office.

For months prior to this event many faculty members had been talking among themselves about the type of man they felt should be selected for the presidency and the sort of program they felt should be carried out. In November 1935, just a few days before President Dinwiddie's death, a group of these faculty members submitted through channels to the Board of Administrators a document containing their observations on the matters which were being so frequently discussed informally.[1] In this letter the faculty members pointed out the important position of Tulane in Southern educational affairs, outlined the qualifications which they felt a new president should have and, perhaps more importantly, set out the nature of the program they felt should be put into effect if Tulane was to become a university in fact as well as in name.

These faculty members expressed great confidence in the future of the university. "Tulane is," they pointed out, "the one university in this section now in a position to assume leadership in solving the problems that arise from the momentous political and social changes which are already upon us." Tulane is in this enviable position, they felt, "Because of its strategic geographical location, its traditions and reputation, and its freedom from political and sectarian domination."

[1] Those signing the communication were: Marc Friedlaender, instructor in English, Arts and Sciences; George T. Kalif, instructor in English, Arts and Sciences; Harold N. Lee, associate professor of philosophy, Newcomb; Williams M. Mitchell, assistant professor of history, Arts and Sciences; Herman C. Nixon, professor of history, Arts and Sciences; Charles I. Silin, associate professor of French, Arts and Sciences; Mack B. Swearingen, associate professor of history, Arts and Sciences; Helmer L. Webb, librarian, Tulane University Library.

Other faculty members who concurred but did not sign were: John M. Fletcher, professor of psychology, Arts and Sciences; Imogen Stone, professor of English, Newcomb; Elizabeth Wisner, professor of sociology and director of the School of Social Work.

"The South," the communication continued, "must be rescued from the demagogue; it must preserve and develop its own contributions to the culture of the nation; and the exodus of southern youth of promise must be stopped. If these ends are to be attained," these faculty members felt, "southern universities that are genuine intellectual centers must be developed."

These intellectual centers, it was stated, can best be developed in the privately endowed universities. "Tulane should not and cannot compete with its sister institution [Louisiana State University] in mass education, which should remain the obligation of the State, but should produce a select and higher type of scholarship to furnish that intellectual leadership which the South so sorely needs. Because of their freedom and independence, endowed universities are the better fitted to perform such tasks."

The group then suggested a rather demanding array of qualifications which they felt the new president, whoever he might be, should possess: Skill in diplomacy, good appearance, firmness combined with flexibility, and receptivity to ideas other than his own were prescribed. Major emphasis, however, was placed upon the familiarity of a new president with the peculiar problems of the South. "He should," they thought, "have ideas on the South's educational needs and the possible lines of development."

The program which the faculty group advocated may be summarized as follows: a strengthening of the College of Arts and Sciences and Newcomb; a closer integration of Newcomb with the rest of the university, especially with respect to a freer interchange of professors and the elimination of some duplicating courses; the development of the College of Commerce and Business Administration by eliminating many vocational courses and substituting for them more liberal arts and truly professional courses; the development of more basic undergraduate courses in the social studies for prospective School of Social Work students; the development of a strong Graduate School; the creation of adequate library facilities; the addition of a business manager of the university; the development of certain features which would be of direct benefit to faculty members, such as retirement annuities, leaves, and security of tenure; and implementing the membership of the Board of Administrators so that there could be a wider geographic representation. A freer means of communication between the faculties and the board was advocated.

It is not possible to determine how much influence, if any, this faculty document had on the Board of Administrators. There is ample evidence, however, that in the negotiations between Harris and the board, prior to his election, there was a meeting of minds on the nature of the program which should be undertaken. The deficiencies were so glaring that it is difficult to understand how the board and the new head of the university could escape them. Moreover, as indicated above, the consensus of what the real needs were carried over into the ranks of deans and faculty members. Almost everyone seemed to feel that a program of strengthening existing units in the university was called for, rather than a program of expansion, and that in this process there were three important factors: improvements in the two liberal arts colleges, the building of a strong Graduate School, and the development of a first-rate library. These became the primary targets for the earlier Harris administration.

The new president took office under circumstances which were hardly auspicious. As a matter of fact many of his friends had advised him not to accept the position. They pointed out that the finances of the university would not permit the building of the type of institution which they knew was wanted. And these warnings had considerable validity. The total endowment of the university was slightly in excess of $10,000,000, but there had been no concerted fund-raising activities since President Dinwiddie's campaign in the 1920s. Moreover, the endowment fund which did exist was fragmented among various units of the university; in short, it was not a general endowment but an aggregation of separate endowments which made for inflexibility. This endowment yielded only about 20 per cent of the university's income, the balance coming largely from student fees and foundations. Added to this was the fact that in the year 1937 the country had not recovered from its depression, and no one could safely prophesy when such recovery would occur. Although plans did not call for an ambitious program of expansion, but rather for a consolidation and strengthening of the existing units of the university, even this would require much more money than was then in sight.

Added to the financial problem was that of presidential rapport with the faculties. It has been pointed out how during the three-year interregnum the faculty had somewhat fallen apart into cliques. Harris was well aware that one of his major tasks would be convincing faculty members of his ability as a leader. He had been a successful and respected dean, but there is a wide differential between the responsibilities of a dean and those of president. No one knew better than Harris that, although faculties wanted leadership, many members were likely to be extremely critical of the leader, whoever he might be.

On the other hand there were favorable aspects. President Harris had a great many very sound educational theories and was well acquainted with the role of the privately endowed university in Southern life. Moreover, he was very persuasive both in private conversation and in public addresses. He was also greatly heartened by the fact that the Board of Administrators gave him greater power and authority in the affairs of the university than any prior president had ever had. Importantly, early in his administration he was able to place men of his own choice in top administrative positions. Because of coincidental retirements, every dean in the university except one almost immediately became a Harris appointee. Paul William Brosman succeeded the president as dean of the law school; Dean Bechtel of the College of Arts and Sciences retired and his position was filled by Marten ten Hoor, professor of philosophy; Elizabeth Wisner became dean of the School of Social Work; Maxwell Edward Lapham succeeded Dean Bass in the medical school; Leslie James Buchan was named to the top position in the College of Commerce and Business Administration to replace Morton Aldrich, the retiring founder of the college; Roger Philip McCutcheon, professor of English, took over the duties of dean of the Graduate School after the retirement of John MacLaren McBryde; and Charles Frederick Hard, professor of English, succeeded Pierce Butler as dean of Newcomb. James Marshall Robert had followed Douglas Anderson as dean of the College of Engineering just before Harris became president.

In addition to these things, Dr. Harris enjoyed a fine personal and professional relationship with Esmond Phelps, president of the board.[2] Mr. Phelps headed one of the important law firms in New Orleans and exercised great influence in the community. He was a quiet, courageous, and conservative man, not given to garrulity, but rather to playing his natural role of wise counselor and good listener. He would sit for long periods of time contemplating the ash on his cigar while the new president poured out his problems to him. When the president had thoroughly covered his problem, Mr. Phelp's reply was likely to be a laconic "I'll go along with that" or "That won't work. We'll have to find another way." And his judgments were usually sound.

Since money was the fuel that powered the entire mechanism it seems logical first to discuss this phase of the Harris period.

The financial history of the Harris administration can be divided into two very distinct segments: 1937–1950 and 1950–1960. The two periods have distinct characteristics, and the dividing line is a rather sharp one.

The thirteen-year period between 1937 and 1950 was characterized by a discouragingly slow growth of university endowment, in spite of the fact that a drive in 1945 yielded $2,676,000. By 1950 the total endowment had reached a figure of $14,275,547, a growth of some $3,000,000 since Harris took office. But this meager increase was wholly inadequate, and Tulane found itself dropping behind comparable institutions. In 1928 Tulane ranked seventeenth among similar institutions in total endowment. In 1948 it had fallen to twenty-fourth place. Endowment per student had sharply declined. In 1948 Vanderbilt's endowment per student was $8,667,

[2] The members of the board at the time President Harris was elected were: Esmond Phelps, Chauncey French, Ernest Lee Jahncke, Walker Brainerd Spencer, Charles Rosen, Marcus Johns Magruder, Samuel Zemurray, Florence Dymond, Jules Blanc Monroe, James Pierce Butler, George Elliot Williams, S. Walter Stern, Charles Allen Favrot, Joseph Wheadon Carroll, Charles Leverich Eshleman, Charles Seyburn Williams, and Joseph Woodruff George.

Duke's $12,450, and Tulane's $2,287, a situation Tulane has not completely overcome even in 1965. It was clear that the university was depending more and more upon student tuition fees, foundation grants, government research funds, and other somewhat unstable sources of revenue. Income from student fees amounted to 41 per cent of total revenues when Harris took office in 1937, and the next decade showed little improvement. Periodic tuition increases failed to remedy the situation because of the spiraling cost of instruction after 1942.

It was obvious that if Tulane was to keep pace with its peer institutions there had to be a tremendous increase in income from permanent endowment. But the administrators did not feel that the times were propitious for extensive fund-raising activities. Economic horizons were blurred during the 1930s and a feeling of depression-created pessimism still gripped the minds of many people of wealth. Whereas today the Board of Administrators can rather calmly discuss a $25,000,000 campaign, that sum, or much less, would have been frightening and utterly unthinkable in 1937. Being cautious as individuals they, acting collectively, yielded to the spirit of the times and became *conservant* rather than *entreprenant,* but in managing the university's funds the board showed marked ability, and the returns from investments were much higher than the average at other universities. It bought and sold real estate almost always at a good profit.[3] It shuffled its securities portfolio to take advantage of prevailing conditions, but there was no substantial increase in the university's general endowment funds from which a predictable and adequate income could be realized. It was not until 1945, approximately twenty-five years after the Dinwiddie drive, that the board approved a campaign aimed at raising sufficient funds to match a $500,000 offer from the General Education Board. But then fund-raising activities slumped.

In view of conditions as they existed, President Harris had no choice but to cut the garment to fit the cloth. He and the board wasted no time putting into effect fiscal and administrative reforms aimed at eliminating outmoded practices and thus creating greater efficiency of operation. Every department of the university came under scrutiny, and economy became the

[3] Among the more prominent real estate deals were the sales of commercial property at 536–538 Canal Street in 1938, the sale of the Tulane-Newcomb building on Camp Street in 1941, the sale of a valuable piece of property on the Airline Highway to the Borden Company in 1946, the sale of most of the block of ground at Canal and South Claiborne in 1949 to the company which built the Claiborne Towers apartment building. In 1949 the old campus fronting Common Street was leased for 99 years to a corporation which built the present Shell Oil–Roosevelt Hotel building. Under the terms of the lease Tulane would realize $150,000 a year for the first few years, the scale going up to a minimum of $245,000 a year during the last few years of the lease. In 1938 the university had purchased the uptown lake corner of University Place and Common Street where a large parking garage now stands.

password. The university's policy on scholarships was given a thorough review, and substantial improvements were made. Salaries were maintained at a level which makes one wonder how Tulane was able to hire and keep good men. Even utility bills for heat and light were reviewed and reduced. By 1947, however, it was apparent that the university's fiscal operations had reached a point of magnitude where centralization of control was necessary. Dean Leslie J. Buchan had been for several years the president's adviser on administrative affairs, but it had become obvious that he could not carry on this function and that of dean at the same time. In 1947 Dr. Clarence Scheps, a trained and experienced specialist in university fiscal affairs, was named comptroller (since then named vice-president). In the face of some apathy and some opposition from a limited number of deans and department heads, Dr. Scheps instituted a centralized system of control in the business affairs of the university. With remarkable efficiency and without any cataclysmic upheavals he instituted the new system which involved operations making it possible to eliminate waste and loose practices. In the matter of budgets and the construction of new buildings, as well as in matters of accounting practices and purchasing, his advice and assistance have proved invaluable.

The year 1950 was truly a year of demarcation marked by the confluence of three important factors: (1) The economy of New Orleans, due to the coming of new industries and the development of the oil resources of the region, reflected far greater wealth than it had ever known in the past; (2) several new and aggressive members were added to the Board of Administrators to replace older members who had died, retired, or resigned; and (3) Joseph Merrick Jones became president of the board.

Each of these factors was intimately related to the other.

Traditionally, New Orleans had been a commercial city. Income from its port and merchandising operations had been basic in its economy. This type of economy had afforded a comfortable income for many of the citizens, but, on the whole, it had not been conducive to the accumulation of large aggregations of wealth which could be tapped for university educational purposes. Between 1945 and 1955 the development of industries which were largely the result of South Louisiana's abundant supplies of gas, petroleum, sulphur, and water changed its economy radically. New Orleans became the center of a vast industrial as well as commercial empire. During this time the composition of the Board of Administrators was radically altered.[4] The new members were, on the whole, younger, more

---

[4] Members of the board were: Ernest Lee Jahncke, Jules Blanc Monroe, Clifford Freret Favrot, Charles Leverich Eshleman, George Shepherd Farnsworth, Darwin Schriever Fenner, Leon Irwin, Jr., Lester Joseph Lautenschlaeger, Joseph McCloskey, Joseph West Montgomery, Isidore Newman II, Ashton Phelps, Marie Louise Wilcox Snellings, Edgar Bloom Stern, George Angus Wilson, Samuel Zemurray, and Joseph Merrick Jones.

aggressive, more imaginative, and more cognizant of what was involved in building a great university than had been many members of the old board. Between 1950 and 1955 eight new members, all Tulane alumni, were elected to the board. In 1951 Clifford Freret Favrot, George Shepherd Farnsworth, and Marie Louise Wilcox Snellings took office. In 1953 Lester Joseph Lautenschlaeger and Darwin Schriever Fenner were added. In 1954 Isidore Newman II was elected to membership, and in 1955 Leon Irwin, Jr., and Ashton Phelps, son of Esmond Phelps, became members. In many respects it became an almost ideal board because there remained on it enough of the older and more conservative members to give it balance.

After the death of Esmond Phelps, in 1950, the members of the board elected as president Joseph Merrick Jones, a member of the board since 1947 and head of one of the city's leading law firms. Under his leadership there were some rather sharp breaks with previous board policies. The matter of public relations, for example, received a new emphasis. "Let people know what the university's problems are," Jones said over and over again, "and they will help solve them."

Another sharp break with the past was the board's willingness to budget an amount which would be sufficient for the university to grow and then to go out and try to raise the money necessary to cover whatever deficit might exist. For three or four years this deficit amounted to approximately a million dollars annually, and much of this amount was raised each year through annual giving. This was a striking contrast to the policies of previous boards which had insisted that the university live within its income regardless of consequences. This, of course, is often considered sound practice for an individual, but at the university it meant that low salaries were causing serious erosion in the ranks of the faculty. In fact, the matter of faculty salaries had become acute. In 1950 Dean McCutcheon of the Graduate School, who was not given to loose statements, advised the president as follows:

> Our salary scale competitively is too low and has failed to increase with the increased cost of living. There is a growing discontent in our faculty, a feeling that nobody is particularly active in attempting to secure funds for faculty salaries. We have a young and ambitious faculty; a faculty which with proper encouragement could make tremendous academic history for our whole region. We have a considerable edge on other institutions in our region, but we cannot much longer get by with a holding operation only. Tulane's opportunity is at present enormous; it may be gone forever in the near future. This is no time for further hesitation. The time has come for action.

President Harris and the board were aware of the urgent need for higher salaries, but until additional funds were secured they had to curb the impatient demands of the deans, each of whom saw clearly the pressing needs of his own division. Under the circumstances the president could do little more than admonish the deans to keep within salary scales, patiently explaining, as he did to Dean Wisner in May 1950, that "there is a point beyond which I cannot go in the allotment of funds. The university and its colleges, like a family, must scale its pattern of living to its income."

It was the matter of low faculty salaries more than any other single factor which stimulated the administrators to inaugurate a long-range fund-raising program, the initial phase of which began in 1951. The board did not, however, plunge precipitately into a long-range program, but led up to it gradually. In 1948 Joseph Chandler Morris, head of the physics department, was made a vice-president of the university with a rather general assignment of duties, part of them being in the field of fund raising. Dr. Morris did not give up his academic work but rather added the vice-presidential duties to his regular load. The board had, therefore, only a part-time director of fund raising.

In 1950, a united effort carried out at the direction of the board raised $2,069,000. This was known as "Phase One" of the Tulane Educational Advancement Program in which Albert Barnett Paterson a board member, played such a prominent part. The campaign was also marked by contributions of faculty, staff, and students in excess of $115,000. Also associated with the first phase of this program was an Esmond Phelps Memorial Fund in which friends of the late board president raised $155,000. Mr. Paterson died shortly after the first phase of the campaign closed, but the second phase was carried to a successful conclusion under the leadership of Clifford F. Favrot, who now emerged as a leading figure in the fund-raising activities of the university. By December 31, 1952, the second phase of the Advancement Program yielded $1,200,000 which earned an award of an additional $1,200,000 from the General Education Board.

By 1953 it was perfectly apparent to the board that fund raising could not be a part-time, sporadic activity but, rather, required a full-time staff devoting its entire time and attention to the university's financial needs. With this objective in mind the board in 1953 set up a Division of Development. Vice-President Morris's duties were shifted, and the board appointed Robert Warren French, dean of the School of Business Administration, vice-president in charge of development. Dr. French set up a full-time staff and began to lay plans for a continuing program of solicitation embracing wills and trusts, annual giving, alumni giving, large individual gifts, and related activities. He, however, resigned as vice-president in 1956 to become the director of the Port of New Orleans and was succeeded by Alvin Lyons, a professionally trained fund raiser. The groundwork had been laid by Morris, Gibson, Favrot, and French, and there were favorable signs that more money would be forthcoming. Especially encouraging was the growth of alumni giving. This phase of university support had begun with small amounts as early as 1940 when Hale Boggs was director of alumni activities, but enjoyed its greatest growth under Beatrice Field, who became director of alumni activities in 1942. In 1948–1949 alumni gifts were $38,637; the next year it grew to $44,598. Each year thereafter showed a steady growth of alumni giving, reaching an all-time high of a half a million dollars in 1964–1965.

There were, of course, other significant gifts which have not been enumerated. In 1951 the university received $1,000,000 from the General Education Board. The Graduate School has also received $550,000 for scholarships, fellowships, and research. Total gifts by the Ford Foundation up to 1964 for general endowment, medical education, and law amounted to $4,866,000. In short, it would seem that by 1957–1958 there was every reason for optimism over Tulane's financial picture. Endowment had grown from approximately $13,000,000 in 1937 to a book value of $27,-138,000 in 1957 with a market value of $43,468,000. During the same period income of the university had grown from slightly over $1,000,000 to nearly $11,000,000, but when these over-all figures are broken down a sobering picture emerges. For the fiscal period 1956–1957 only 13.9 per cent of the university's income was from endowment. From student fees the university realized 30.2 per cent of its income; 10.1 per cent from annual giving; 21.8 per cent from auxiliary enterprises such as bookstore, food services, etc.; 1.9 per cent from income from the endowed scholarships; 2.5 per cent, miscellaneous income and 19.6 per cent from the federal government, foundations, and corporations for special research largely in the field of medicine. In brief, approximately 50 per cent of Tulane's income for 1956–1957 was from student fees and restricted gifts and grants for research, and only 13.9 per cent from endowment. In the treasurer's report for 1956–1957 fourteen large pages are required to list the special grants for research. These grants were, of course, not permanent. Although they were extremely valuable, one must face the fact that they do not in the long run take the place of permanent endowment.

Against the background of the financial condition of the university one can, perhaps, see in sharper relief Harris's attempts to strengthen the liberal arts program, the graduate program, and library facilities.

Strengthening of the liberal arts program may be considered both quantitatively and qualitatively. Purely from the quantitative standpoint one may see enormous progress. In 1936–1937 the faculty of Arts and Sciences numbered 65. In 1956–1957 there were 243 members on this faculty. At Newcomb during the same years there were 76 and 136 faculty members, respectively. In 1936–1937 there were 184 courses offered in the College of Arts and Sciences. In 1956–1957 there were 527. At Newcomb during the same period there were 248 and 426, respectively. These figures represent a growth in total faculty of the liberal arts colleges over the twenty-year period of 169 per cent. In course offerings the increase was approximately 123 per cent. Growth in enrollment was similarly impressive. Over the twenty-year period 1936–1937 to 1964–1965 total enrollment in the two liberal arts colleges increased by approximately 70 per cent.

These figures, particularly those dealing with increases in faculty and courses offered, reflect the quantitative strengthening of the liberal arts curricula. But behind these statistics are the faculty members who teach the courses and in them is the essence of the new strength. The demand for new faculty can best be understood when one considers the across-the-board increase in course offerings both at Newcomb and in the College of Arts and Sciences. There were a dozen new courses in anthropology where none had been offered when Harris took office. A new department of theater and speech was established, and psychology grew to be an important department. The physical sciences grew into much larger and stronger departments. In the biological sciences zoology and botany were separated, thus creating two strong departments, now merged again into one. Likewise history and political science were reorganized into separate departments, and both were soon thriving. Mathematics offerings were increased, and the department became undoubtedly the strongest in the South. Modern language offerings, especially in Spanish, grew enormously. Departments of education were organized. A committee for Latin-American studies was set up and a cooperative plan developed between it and the reorganized and revitalized Middle American Research Institute under the direction of Robert Wauchope who, after an interval, had succeeded Frans Blom. The Urban Life Research Institute was created to study the problems of urban life in the South. The degree program in physical education was abolished, and football players took the same courses as other students. (The Harris program of moderation in football was met by responses ranging from vigorous applause to derision. One football-minded alumnus remarked: "The football coaches at Tulane must be developing a lot of character for they certainly are not winning games.")

All this expansion of course offerings would have been meaningless unless there was excellent instruction, and, on the whole, this excellent instruction was provided, although it was a constant source of wonder how Tulane held so many good faculty members on a relatively low salary schedule; and the university did hold most of its top-ranking teachers. The fact that Tulane was able to do this was a subject of comment from many quarters. There were, to be sure, some regrettable faculty losses, but there seemed to be something about the atmosphere of the university which held many, even though other campuses might appear more lush. Gradually, as time went on, the university was able to offer the faculty periodic and substantial salary increases; to develop a much better retirement program; to offer fringe benefits such as insurance and hospitalization; and, perhaps above all, to put into effect a tenure policy which the faculties themselves developed.

A tightening up of academic traces was obvious in both liberal arts colleges. In 1948 Newcomb adopted the policy of requiring College Entrance Board examinations for admissions. This plan, however, was not adopted until 1956 by the College of Arts and Sciences. In its entrance requirements the university had made a complete circle. In 1890 admission to the university was almost wholly by examination. Then it went all out in support of the Carnegie Unit System as secondary schools were developed in the South. Experience through the years, however, taught the university that high school graduation with 16 units did not necessarily mean that a young student was ready for college. In both colleges, curricula were made a subject of intensive study and changes were instituted designed to bring offerings more in line with the modern educational philosophy held by the university. In general, the trend was away from an earlier concept of specialization in the liberal arts toward a broader role. The major-field-of-study plan was not dropped, but the minor field of concentration has given way to a plan under which the semester hours ordinarily utilized in a minor field may be used to broaden the student's program. The trend in both colleges also has been in the direction of eliminating a multiplicity of degree curricula and concentrating largely on the Bachelor of Arts and the Bachelor of Science programs and retaining the Bachelor of Fine Arts degree.

One of the significant achievements in the tightening up of academic affairs is the present plan of university-wide departments which cut across college lines. Under this plan there is a rotating system of university departmental chairmen who coordinate the activities of a department regardless of college lines. For example, there is a university chairman of English. This chairman is responsible for the functioning of an English program throughout the university—at Newcomb, University College, Engineering, Business Administration, Architecture, and Arts and Sciences. The same is true with other major departments, with the result that there is a better utilization of faculty time, the elimination of many overlapping courses, and a generally better accommodation of the needs of students. It is quite the ordinary experience of a professor to find in his course or courses students from every undergraduate college and school in the university. In addition, this plan has greatly expedited the creation of a more uniform system of grading, intercollege transfers of students, methods of computing quality points, and the determination of criteria under which students are denied readmission because of academic deficiencies. Complete uniformity in these matters has not been achieved, but a big step has been made in this direction.

One of the most significant steps taken by President Harris to strengthen academic standards was the appointment of Fred Carrington Cole as academic vice-president in 1954. Dr. Cole came to Tulane from L.S.U. in 1946 as professor of history. The next year he was made dean of the

College of Arts and Sciences, succeeding Dean ten Hoor who had resigned to accept a similar position at the University of Alabama.[5] After seven successful years as dean, Dr. Cole was moved into a position where he could work directly with deans and faculties on their academic problems. It has been said of President Harris that one of his strongest points as an administrator was his ability to select good men for top administrative positions. Certainly this was true in the case of the academic vice-president.

It is interesting to note that the changes made by Harris met with singularly little overt faculty opposition. It is true, of course, that shortly after he took office the history department made headlines by resigning en masse (if one may characterize the resignation of three men as en masse), but this incident was the result of a condition which the president had inherited from the previous administration. For three or four years before the death of President Dinwiddie, Professors Herman C. Nixon, Mack B. Swearingen, and Williams M. Mitchell of the history department had reflected a chronic lack of confidence in the Board of Administrators, the president of the university, and Dean Bechtel; and, it might be added, this lack of confidence apparently was reciprocated. The three men did not find the new president-dean combination of Harris and ten Hoor any more palatable, and thus they resigned in a huff.

Among the Newcomb alumnae and faculty there were those who continued to look with suspicion on any change in the *status quo* such as that inherent in the departmental reorganization plan. Some older faculty members and graduates had perpetuated the fear that there existed a latent conspiracy to deprive Newcomb of its autonomy and to take from the college portions of its endowment funds for general university purposes. This fear that Newcomb would lose its identity began as early as the last years of Mrs. Newcomb's life, was kept alive during Dixon's administration, and then was fanned into periodic blazes by Dean Butler. The flare-up over Harris's policy of mild centralization came shortly after Dean Logan Wilson was appointed to succeed Dean Hard, who had resigned to accept the presidency of Scripps College.[6] Major resentment seems to have grown out of the old fear that the administrators would take over Newcomb's endowment. To refute this idea Dean Wilson published in 1949 a brochure entitled *Some Facts About Newcomb College Finances*. Patiently he explained that Mrs. Newcomb's original donations had totaled $3,574,-391.79. This endowment made Newcomb the wealthiest independent college for women in the country prior to World War I. However, this favorable financial picture became blurred. In 1923, $1,325,707.59 of New-

---

[5] Professor George Simmons of the journalism department was acting dean, 1944–1947.

[6] Miss Anna Many served as acting dean between the time of Hard's resignation, in December 1943, and the arrival of Dean Wilson, July 1, 1944.

comb's endowment principal was transferred to the physical plant fund to pay for Newcomb's new buildings and grounds, and very little was added to the principal of the capital endowment after this transfer was made. As late as June 30, 1951, the book value of the Newcomb endowment fund was slightly less that $2,500,000. Newcomb had slipped from first to twelfth place, and in explaining this descent Dean Wilson rather pointedly rebuked the alumnae. The reason Newcomb had slipped, he wrote, was not due to any meddling on the part of the administrators but to the failure of the alumnae and friends of Newcomb College to make contributions which would boost the endowment fund. He pointed out that the administrators had been scrupulously careful in preserving Newcomb's endowment. He also pointed out another significant fact: The Newcomb endowment no longer produced a sufficient income to support the college and the deficits were being met out of general university funds. Centralization of financial control, he asserted, was bringing each year an income of approximately $250,000 from general university funds which Newcomb would not receive without centralized fiscal controls.

The general mumblings of discontent among the alumnae died down, but the almost unreasoning fears of many individuals were not allayed. However, President Harris, with the assistance of the deans of Newcomb since Pierce Butler's retirement, accomplished a great deal in the way of bringing Newcomb into the union without destroying the individuality of the college. This was forcefully pointed out by Dean Hubbard in an address to the Board of Visitors on April 12, 1957, when he gave unqualified approval to a 1954 agreement entitled "A Plan to Further Coordination Between Departments in Newcomb College and The College of Arts and Sciences."

This significant document presents seven points of contact. The first three of these deal with the university chairman, outlining his duties and responsibilities in the graduate program, in Summer School, and in University College, and with his responsibility to eliminate duplication of courses at all levels. The other four points concern recruitment of faculty personnel, promotions, salaries and teaching loads, budgets, and the library.

In commenting on the plan Dean Hubbard said,

I would suggest that never before in the history of the university has there been such a thorough elimination of the wasteful duplication of effort and resources and so conscious a spirit of cooperation toward common objectives. . . . Newcomb never has been, no matter how intensively some people may have desired it, an independent institution. . . . In the beginning there was the physical separation of facilities and precious little communication between Newcomb and other divisions of the university. . . . Gradually, however, the university began to grow together physically, and the intervening spaces were filled with new buildings and spiritually, as a community of interests was established. . . . So it was that the distance between Newcomb Hall and Gibson seemed to grow shorter and shorter. . . . Neither college can afford to think exclusively in terms of its own corporate makeup; coordination in its true sense must supplant competition if we are to gain the most from our resources.

While the strengthening of the liberal arts colleges was going on and an amicable adjustment with Newcomb was being worked out President Harris was giving a great deal of time and attention to the building of a first-rate graduate school.

It has been pointed out previously that the university had what is called a graduate school since the days of William Preston Johnston, but by the wildest stretch of the imagination it could not be called a first-rate graduate school. It had a series of deans and conferred graduate degrees, but it was lacking in so many ways that the university can take no pride in it prior to 1937.

The emergence of an excellent graduate school dates from the appointment of Roger Philip McCutcheon as dean in 1937. McCutcheon was a Harvard-trained professor of English when President Harris asked him to take over the office of dean, succeeding John MacLaren McBryde, who had retired.[7]

Conditions in the Graduate School when McCutcheon took over were deplorable, not because other graduate deans had not made a sincere effort to build the division but because no real assistance had been forthcoming from the previous administrations which recognized but dimly the part which graduate education played in a modern university. The dean had little authority, no spearate budget, and not even a secretary. The graduate courses were few in number, were on a different time schedule from the Arts and Sciences courses, and the tuition was considerably lower than that for undergraduate courses. Graduate faculty meetings were formal and unimpressive affairs since, in the absence of any funds with which to operate, the departments got very little except kudos from the Graduate School. The Ph.D. programs were very limited, being confined largely to subjects in the medical sciences. There were no fellowships of any real worth.

McCutcheon began his work in a small office (but it was *his* office) in Gibson Hall with a secretary, a small budget, a great deal of energy and idealism, and the strong support of President Harris. Within two years changes were becoming obvious, and by 1945 there were substantial improvements. By 1951 McCutcheon's efforts flowered, and the university began to speak of its Graduate School with pride. Slowly many of the defects had been remedied. Tuition for graduate courses was raised better

---

[7] Previous deans of the Graduate School were: Brown Ayres (1900–1904); James Hardy Dillard (1904–1908); Robert Sharp (1908–1912); Alcée Fortier (1912–1914); Pierce Butler (1914–1919); John Madison Fletcher (1919–1923); and John MacLaren McBryde (1923–1937).

to correspond with similar charges in the College of Arts and Sciences. The Graduate School budget was slowly increased from meager university funds to include small amounts for fellowships and scholarships, for outside lecturers, for travel, and for support of research. In 1951, as previously mentioned, the Graduate School received $2,000,000 in endowment and shortly thereafter a $300,000 grant from the General Education Board for fellowships and scholarships. This, and subsequent financial assistance, was, of course, invaluable in building a graduate school.

Perhaps no phase of the development received closer scrutiny than the admission policy. Instead of admission on the basis of an undergraduate degree only, McCutcheon set the standard of requiring for admission a B average in the student's major subject; and, it should be added, nothing added more to the dean's tribulations than this policy. Almost daily there were unpleasant interviews with students who did not meet admission standards. The result was, of course, that McCutcheon acquired a reputation of being "hard-boiled," but he stuck to his position because he knew that a superior graduate school could not be built with inferior material. He probably would have been the first to admit to being inflexible about admissions. Many of his reports to the president reflect his distaste for the role of dictator, but he was in no sense apologetic. The end justified the means.

In 1950 there were 679 applications for admission to the Graduate School and 292 of these were refused, but even with this high percentage of rejections the Graduate School was growing rapidly in enrollment. There were 199 students enrolled in 1937–1938 and 373 in 1951–1952. By 1956–1957 the number enrolled was 453, and this grew to 1,476 in 1964–1965. Even more interesting is the change which took place in origins of students. In 1944 only 30 per cent of the graduate students came from outside Louisiana. In 1951, 53 per cent came from states other than Louisiana. By 1956 the percentage of students from outside the state had grown to 59 per cent from 130 different colleges and universities. The number of graduate degrees increased correspondingly, as did the fields of graduate study. In 1936, 36 graduate degrees were awarded; in 1942 there were 49; in 1949 there were 89; by 1965 the number had grown to 257, of which 92 were the Ph.D.[8] By 1950 work toward the Ph.D. degree was offered in anatomy, bacteriology, biochemistry, chemistry, English, French, German, history, mathematics, parasitology, pharmacology, physiology, psychology, Spanish, and zoology. In 1951 German was deleted from the list and then restored six years later. Other fields have been added: political science,

---

[8] In addition to the 257 graduate degrees offered in the graduate school there were in 1965 a total of 160 graduate degrees in social work, medicine, law, and business administration. This, then, would mean that a grand total of 417 graduate degrees were awarded.

classical languages, theater and speech, biostatistics, chemical engineering, geology, mechanical engineering, engineering, physics, and music.

One might also cite statistics to show the growth in the number of graduate faculty members and other factors to indicate the quantitative growth of the graduate program. McCutcheon, however, was wholly uninterested in mushrooming figures which reflected how big the graduate school was getting to be. His whole emphasis was on quality, the development of which required time, discrimination, and patient work with the faculties in indoctrinating them in what superior graduate work really meant. Perhaps no better example of this can be cited than McCutcheon's experience in establishing a Graduate Council to assist him in the development of the program. He had expected that the council would be made up of members elected by the faculties, but he soon found that he had to appoint the members, with the approval of the president, because some of the faculties appeared to have only a faint concept of what a graduate council and a graduate faculty ought to be. Appointments to the graduate faculty were often made by deans purely on the basis of the faculty members' seniority rather than by using the criteria of research, publication, and the direction of graduate students' programs. In persuading faculties and deans that membership on the graduate faculty must be based upon solid achievement in the graduate field rather than on seniority, Dean McCutcheon rendered one of his most conspicuous services to graduate education at Tulane. By the time he retired in 1954 there was a clear understanding of what membership in the graduate faculty represented. It should be pointed out here also that the insistence upon achievement as a basis for membership in the graduate faculty was a potent stimulus to faculty research and publication. Before McCutcheon's time there had been only slight emphasis placed upon this function of the faculty member. Within a few years scholarly production had grown enormously, and in 1941, when the first bibliography of scholarly writing at Tulane was published, it showed 709 separate items of faculty publications. The 1954–1956 biennial report showed 1,286 published research items of which 936 were articles in learned journals and 23 were books.

There was no end to McCutcheon's probing of weaknesses. In order to find out what went on in oral examinations he began to attend these, and almost immediately there was a distinct improvement in the caliber of the examinations. He began to check closely on graduate theses, sometimes reading them and insisting upon revision even though the particular piece of research was outside his scholarly competence. If he could not get the revision done by the department or the student he sometimes did it himself. In this phase of investigation he found some very interesting anomalies, one of which was a 23-page typewritten article on the poetry of Robert Burns which had been presented for a graduate degree in engineering. This one he silently overlooked in his compilation of thesis titles. In 1944 the Graduate Record Examination, already in use by prominent Eastern graduate schools, was instituted at Tulane, and shortly thereafter all entering graduate students were required to take the tests. Encouragement of faculty research was further undertaken in the establishment of the *Tulane Studies in English, Tulane Studies in Philosophy, Tulane Studies in Political Science*, and *Tulane Studies in Zoology*. Another significant step in the encouragement of scholarly publication was the transfer of the *Mississippi Valley Historical Review* from Iowa to Tulane in 1947. Professor Wendell Holmes Stephenson was the editor of this journal from 1947 to 1953. From 1953 to his retirement in 1963 Professor William Campbell Binkley edited the journal.

As the historian looks at the achievements of Dr. McCutcheon in laying the foundations for the Tulane Graduate School, he becomes conscious of two very important facts: (1) The Graduate School was not developed in isolation but rather in cooperation with similar movements in other Southern universities and, (2) although solid foundations were laid by McCutcheon the task was by no means complete by the time of his retirement. These two points should be set alongside the splendid achievements from 1937 to 1954.

During the 1940s and early 1950s there was a general recognition among educational leaders and the foundations that the development of graduate education in the South was of primary importance if this region was to take its proper place in the cavalcade of educational progress. In 1950 Southern universities in a region comprising one-third of the nation's population awarded only one-twelfth of the nation's doctoral degrees. All too often educators saw fine young graduate students go to universities outside of the South for their advanced graduate degrees and never return. This, of course, meant that the South was constantly being drained of its top research and teaching scholars.

In order to combat this trend several significant steps were taken cooperatively by several of the more prominent Southern universities interested in graduate work. In 1944 the Conference of Deans of Southern Graduate Schools was established with the aim of raising standards and exploring ways and means of expanding graduate education in the South. In 1945 McCutcheon and Philip G. Davidson, then graduate dean at Vanderbilt, advanced the idea that the strengthening of graduate education could be significantly increased by the development at strategic points in the South of a few centers of high-quality graduate work, research, and scholarship. This plan found favor with the great foundations, especially with the Carnegie Corporation and the General Education Board, which were willing to invest money in the development of graduate centers at Duke, North Carolina, Texas, Tulane, and Vanderbilt. They also fostered the appointment of distinguished visiting professors and the development of regional conferences on graduate education. Dean McCutcheon remarked many times on the almost incalculable benefits of the work of these foundations.

The idea of regional cooperation in the matter of graduate education was further expanded in 1952 by the organization of the Council of Southern Universities, comprising Tulane, Duke, Emory, Vanderbilt, Rice, North Carolina, Texas, and Virginia. One of the primary objectives of this organization was "to give the developing region better scientists, college teachers, and organized research." To accomplish this the council planned to search for superior talent and to curb the drain of promising young scholars from the South. In order to accomplish this the participating universities had to face the twofold necessity of strengthening their graduate offerings and of offering scholarships and fellowships which would attract the most promising young scholars.

These two goals are on their way toward realization. The universities themselves have substantially increased their graduate school budgets from their own funds and have found the foundations willing to supplement with grants the universities' individual efforts.

At Tulane the further development and strengthening of a graduate program went forward under the administration of Robert Mayer Lumiansky, who succeeded McCutcheon as dean of the Graduate School in 1954. Dean Lumiansky, like Dean McCutcheon, is an English scholar, and like McCutcheon, he showed a comprehensive grasp of the problems of present-day graduate education and what they will be within the next decade or so; but the programs of the two men differed considerably.

The essence of Lumiansky's plans may be summarized as: (1) the development of a comprehensive program of graduate education for teachers; (2) a model plan of guidance and financial assistance for graduate students through the Ph.D. degree; (3) a search for talent at the undergraduate level at Tulane and the encouragement of this talent.

When Dean Lumiansky entered upon the duties of his office, he, the Graduate Council, and various departments agreed that, since the Graduate School had by then reached almost the full curricular breadth that had been originally envisioned, the next ten years should be devoted mainly to raising the established curricula to the highest possible quality. In keeping with this determination not to spread the educational jam too thin, the Graduate School's present objective is to increase its student body moderately without making any further extensive additions to the curricula.

At a time when the entire nation is increasingly concerned about the present quality of education and the possibility that the impending teacher shortage may lead to lower teaching standards, the Tulane Graduate School's progress in teacher education is an encouraging positive factor.

Graduate programs put heavy emphasis on preparing students for teaching in colleges and universities. It is in the institutions of higher learning, Dean Lumiansky felt, that the coming teacher shortage is likely to be most critical, since no "crash program," such as might meet the emergency in the lower schools, can possibly turn out professors of genuine scholastic attainment and teaching ability. But under his leadership, Tulane faculties concentrated considerable effort on interesting superior students in the profession of teaching at all levels. A faculty committee on teacher preparation was established even before the Center for Teacher Education came into being. Following the principle that preparing teachers is the responsibility of the whole university rather than of any one department, this committee included both members of the education department and representatives from the various other departments. Two new graduate degrees for teachers, the Master of Arts in Teaching and the Master of Education, were established. On the surface this does not appear exciting, but in view of Tulane's past record of somewhat neglecting teacher training it is almost revolutionary.

Other committees interviewed the above-average students at various stages of their undergraduate work and acquainted them with the opportunities and advantages in academic careers. Students recommended by committee members as good prospects were interviewed individually by Dean Lumiansky in their junior years and offered the chance to take certain graduate courses during their senior years, with the understanding that if they entered graduate school they could transfer the credits for these courses from undergraduate to graduate.

In addition, Tulane has adopted a particularly effective system of financial assistance to graduate students. "One of the most frequently heard criticisms of graduate work in this country is that too many years are required for earning the Ph.D. degree," Dr. Lumiansky said in an address describing the Tulane loan system. "In many cases the process drags out to five, seven, or more years and many graduate schools have a collection of perennial Ph.D. students who will probably never complete the degree."

Since the delay in most cases is a result of the student's struggle to pay his way by part-time teaching, Tulane has, for one thing, established a loan fund to enable its graduate students to keep their first and fourth years free to devote full time to their studies. "The student should work as a part-time teacher or research assistant only as long as his professors feel this is needed to give him the necessary experience in teaching and research procedures." Dr. Lumiansky said "The situation to be avoided is having the student teach half-time or more year after year and fail to complete his degree."

The university considers that the ideal four-year pattern for study toward the Ph.D. degree will allow the first year for full-time study, the second and third years for half-time study and half-time teaching or research assisting, and the fourth year for full time on the dissertation. To help the students achieve this pattern, the school offers long-term loans repayable on a five-to-ten-year basis, with no interest charged. This is not to say that Tulane has abandoned teaching fellowships. Rather it has increased them. National Defense Education Act fellowships, Woodrow Wilson fellowships, and other forms of student aid, of course, help the situation.

In offering its loans, the Graduate School makes these two points as to why it is to the student's educational, financial, and psychological advantage to borrow from the load fund: (1) The student who borrows money to finish his degree several years earlier will come out much better financially than if he continues to teach part time for those several years or works full time at a lower salary than he will receive with the degree; (2) since salaries for Ph.D. holders are rising, the repayment of the loan over a long period, it is felt, will not be a great financial burden. "The graduate dean and the departments can, by planning with each student, work out a financial plan for the student's whole career in graduate school which will turn him out in a relatively short time as a thoroughly competent teacher-scholar," Dr. Lumiansky stated. "By this method we have a chance of demolishing forever the traditional image of the impoverished graduate student with frayed cuffs routinely teaching two or more sections year after year at a low salary while he tries to complete his doctoral dissertation in his spare moments."

If space in this book were unlimited other recent developments in the Graduate School might be discussed. Tulane's election to membership in the Association of American Universities is partly, if not largely, the result of the excellent showing made by the Graduate School.[9] Interesting experiments were tried in a combined Doctor of Medicine–Master of Science and a Doctor of Medicine–Doctor of Philosophy program. Work progressed toward the raising of several departmental offerings from the master's level to that of the doctorate. One plan, however, cannot be dismissed by mere mention of it. This is the faculty-leave program and policy.

The university has developed what appears to be for it a good system for leaves of absences, the University Council on Research being the executive agency for this system. Any faculty member may apply at any time for a research or study leave often at full salary to cover whatever period is needed for his project. He may, in some cases, also receive a modest financial grant from the council. The departments and deans concerned make recommendations and the council decides on matters touching the leave. At

<hr>

[9] In 1958 Tulane also accepted membership in the Association of International Universities.

first, members of the council had considerable doubt that this system could work, given human frailty. In practice, however, it has been found that the departments are setting up flexible rotation schemes which give everyone his fair chance. There is rather general agreement that the strength of the system is that it depends upon careful judgment of individual cases and not upon automatic rules. There seems to be little doubt that the system is working well and that it is bringing substantial results in research output and teaching effectiveness.

The graduate program is, of course, not without its problems, the chief one being financial. In addition to the amounts raised during McCutcheon's administration the university has increased its budget for graduate education and some $3,00,0000 has been received from foundations and the federal government for general support of graduate education and for fellowships. Still the budget is very short of the actual needs. If Tulane was to continue its substantial contributions to Southern education, Dean Lumiansky estimated that by 1965 the Graduate School would need $150,000 a year for scholarships, $100,000 a year for loans, and $100,000 annually for research grants; and these amounts have been exceeded. In addition he pointed out three other acute needs: (1) the establishment of a university press with the highest quality of professional direction; (2) adding the necessary strength to raise a number of master's degree programs to the Ph.D. level; and (3) strengthening of the library, particularly in its research facilities.

Dean Lumiansky's concern for the strengthening of the libraries calls to mind the important steps which were taken during the Harris administration in building up this important factor in the university's academic life.

Before 1937 Tulane's libraries were weak and fragmented. The major units were the Newcomb Library, the Law Library, the Tilton Library, the Commerce Library, the Medical Library (including the Orleans Parish Medical Society Library), and the Middle American Research Institute Library. These had a total of some 239,000 volumes, excluding pamphlets. This fragmentation was administratively indefensible, but before it could be corrected there had to be constructed a central building large enough to accommodate the proposed united libraries and to provide for future expansion.

Faculty discussions of the problem of fragmentation had taken place in 1936 and 1937, but it was not until 1938 that definite steps were taken to correct the situation. In this year several important decisions were made. A university committee on libraries was set up, a general library budget was instituted, the decision was made to consolidate the Newcomb and Tilton libraries, and, of transcendent importance, the Board of Trustees of the Howard Memorial Library agreed to merge this excellent reference library with that of Tulane, provided the university would construct an adequate building.[10] Not only did the Howard collection add 107,000 volumes to the Tulane Library but it also provided an annual income of approximately $25,000. More importantly, perhaps, it was a direct stimulus to the immediate construction of a new library building.

Studies were made of other university libraries, and in 1939 construction of the present air-conditioned building was begun, the Board of Administrators appropriating some $700,000 out of capital funds to pay for it. In January and February 1941, the Newcomb, Tilton, and Howard libraries were moved to the new building, and in March 1941, the consolidated libraries were opened.

From 1938, when the consolidation of the Tilton and Howard libraries was agreed upon, Robert James Usher, who had been the Howard librarian since 1927, was appointed to the same position in the Howard-Tilton Library. Much of the physical consolidation took place under his direction, but actual integration of the two libraries was a rather involved and drawn-out activity. Actually there were two libraries under one roof with separate shelving and catalogs for the Tilton-Newcomb holdings and the Howard collection, and Mr. Usher did not live to see the completion of the task of integrating the entire collections; for it was not until 1947 that substantial progress had been made in this direction. Even as late as 1950 the process of unification still presented problems. Garland Forbes Taylor, who was named director of libraries in 1944, found that encouraging progress had been made but saw the necessity for other steps. What had been done up to that date, he maintained, was only of limited effectiveness so long as the catalog lacked logical as differentiated from mere physical unity. Accomplishment of this logical unity, with the assistance of foundation grants, became a major aim of Dr. Taylor, an aim which has been realized.[11]

Physical integration was a necessary first step in making the library useful for university purposes, but it was only a first step. Large purchases of books and archival materials had to follow, and in this, the university has made some progress. Tulane's main library holdings have increased from about 20,000 volumes in 1900 to approximately 800,000 volumes. During the same period recorded circulation has increased from roughly 15,000 to 238,000. Law, Commerce, the Middle American Research Institute, and the medical libraries have also enlarged their holdings to a total

[10] Members of the Board of Trustees of the Howard Memorial Library in 1938 were: Esmond Phelps, president; Henri T. Howard, Edgar B. Howard, Charles E. Fenner, Mrs. Laura H. Howard, Paul Villere, Mrs. Elise Mason Smith Howard, Leonard K. Nicholson, Edgar B. Stern, Moise H. Goldstein, Stamps Farrar, Mrs. Flores Howard Sussdorf, John P. Labouisse, Chapman H. Hymans, Jr., Burt W. Henry, Brandt B. V. Dixon, and Dr. Abraham L. Metz.

[11] Dr. Taylor was succeeded in 1960 as director of libraries by Robert L. Talmadge, a professionally trained and experienced university librarian.

of approximately 227,000 volumes. Under the provisions of the will of the late Rudolph Matas the library of the medical school will be enormously increased.

At the present time the Howard-Tilton Library is not a first-class research library, although it is reaching in that direction. The medical library, however, has perhaps the most valuable collection in existence on the history of medicine in Louisiana and the South.

Although there was some interest in collecting of historical manuscripts before the merger of the Howard, Tilton, and Newcomb collections, the principal activity in this area has occurred since 1940. Very inadequate space has been assigned to the archives, and one of the most persistent problems in library administration at the present time is adequate space for the growing collection of manuscripts.

Resources for the purchase of collections are limited. To this must be added the fact that the university has not made a sustained effort to search out and acquire outstanding collections which might be had for a very small price. With special assistance a few fine purchases have been made, however, and some collections of real importance have come through donation or long-term deposit. At the present time some 405,000 pieces are available for use. The George W. Cable Collection is first rate. So is the Lafcadio Hearn Collection. There is a distinguished group of early Louisiana historical documents and family papers in the Favrot Papers, notably seconded by the Kuntz Collection, both of which contain books as well as manuscripts. The papers of the Louisiana Historical Association, numbering some 100,000 pieces, are one of the large Civil War collections still awaiting extensive use. The Grima Papers and the Bouligny-Baldwin Papers both go back to colonial Louisiana, and the Colonel Andrew Hynes Papers stretch back to the period of American control. Other holdings include the Kenneth Urquhart Papers with its collection of Confederate sheet music; the John McDonogh Collection; the William Preston and Albert Sidney Johnston Papers; the New Orleans Municipal Papers; and others less extensive in nature.

Microfilming began shortly after the formation of the Howard-Tilton Library, and today Tulane has holdings of the more common microfilms, with films predominating, microprint coming second, and microcards last. Various newspaper files constitute the largest single block of film holdings, including several entire colonial newspapers, portions of the *New York Times* and *Herald-Tribune*, the London *Times*, and the New Orleans *Times-Picayune*. The library is at present occupied with the task of filming the entire run of the New Orleans *Bee*. There are other miscellaneous microfilm collections, including collections of early federal censuses of Louisiana and Mississippi. Microfilming, the university feels, is a large part of the answer to the problem of space and the acquisition of collections.

Leaving manuscript collections and other research materials out of consideration, a major problem of the Howard-Tilton Library is space. The handsome building is bulging at the seams. What seemed adequate in the way of a building a few years ago is now recognized as being lamentably insufficient. But no one foresaw, not even President Harris himself, that the university would grow and expand as rapidly as it has within the past twenty years. Now, in 1965, a new library is assured—a most heartening thing for the entire university.

CHAPTER 15

Intimations of Maturity

WHILE STRENGTHENING AND EXPANDING the liberal arts programs, developing a first-rate graduate school, building a good library, and tightening up general administrative practices were basic in the Harris administration, these are by no means the only major accomplishments. There are many important phases of the university's growth which have come into being as a result of maturation rather than as part of an original blueprint.

Two new colleges, University College and the School of Architecture, for example, were created. These were the result of needs which arose out of the growth of the university, and more than likely they complete the academic organization. The enormous building and plant rehabilitation programs likewise were manifestations of the university's new requirements for space for both living and instructional purposes. Too, the various schools and colleges have, in many instances, modified their programs to meet the needs of a changing society. The university has reached a point in its life where it may take a more mature view of its proper roles.

Located as it is in a large urban center, Tulane must look in two directions. It must look to the needs of the region, or indeed of the nation, but at the same time it does not overlook the needs of its immediate urban community. University College, the evening and adult education division created in 1942, is one of the university's responses to the educational needs of metropolitan New Orleans, needs which are not easily met through the day divisions. The new college is the culmination of more than a half-century of adult education activities which began early in the administration of William Preston Johnston and which have steadily increased in scope. There were the adult drawing classes and the adult lecture series under Johnston and his successors. Then came the program for teachers, the classes being held in the late afternoon and on Saturdays. With the organization of the College of Commerce and Business Administration in 1914 hundreds of business people, old and young, flocked to the college's evening classes in business subjects.

By 1940 it had become evident that an administrative division devoted entirely to adult evening college education ought to be created. In late

1941 the administrators authorized the creation of such a division, to be called "University College"—so named because its offerings cut across university lines. The first courses in the new division were offered in the fall of 1942 with 685 students registering. Of this number 91 were teachers, 30 were members of the university staff or faculty, and the balance were business students. The students, Dean McCutcheon reported, were "well worthwhile," "They are mature and earnest people," he added.

Dr. McCutcheon was one of the leading figures in the organization of the new college and served during the formative years from 1942 to 1946 as acting director. In 1946 he was succeeded by Professor Ross Trump of the College of Commerce and Business Administration, who served for one year. In 1947, Thomas Theron Earle, professor of botany and director of the Summer School, was appointed interim director and acted until July 1, 1948. By this time the growth of University College required the appointment of a full-time director. John Percy Dyer, historian and former radio executive and government civil servant, was named to the position on July 1, 1948. The title of "director" was changed to "dean" in 1952.

During the first few years the curricula were credit oriented. Two degree programs, one in liberal arts and one in the field of commerce, were set up, and at the annual university commencement on May 31, 1944, the first four degrees, all Bachelor of Arts, were awarded. It was not until 1948 that a degree in commercial science was awarded. Subsequently, degree programs in nursing and in medical technology were added, and then the nursing degree program was dropped.

Significant additions have been made to the curricula of the college in the past few years. Without any slackening of efforts to build first-rate degree programs an important series of noncredit offerings has been added. These courses represent an effort on the part of the college to reach a large group of adults who are not interested in credits and degrees but who are interested in continuing their educational experience. Many of these people already possess college degrees but are coming back in ever increasing numbers because they realize that education is a lifelong process. The major emphasis in the noncredit programs is in the field of liberal education, but topics in business and finance are not neglected. A grant of $71,500 from the Fund for Adult Education assisted materially in the development of a new type of program in which larger problems of a national and international nature are approached through a study of the background and problems of New Orleans itself. Enrollment in both credit and noncredit programs has grown substantially. The average enrollment runs around 3,000. In 1965 eighty-seven degrees were awarded.

In 1950 Architecture was separated from Engineering and made into a separate school with Buford Lindsay Pickens, an alumnus of the University of Illinois and the University of Chicago, as the first director. This move had been anticipated for several years, particularly since 1946 when the program was expanded from four years to five. It was generally understood also that administrative and accreditation problems could not be solved as long as architecture was a part of the engineering program. In 1945 an inspection team from the National Architectural Accrediting Board examined the department and reported unfavorably, with the result that it was removed from the accredited list on which it had been registered since 1937. Dean Robert of the School of Engineering and his faculty, the president of the university, the Board of Administrators, and local architectural groups were, as might be expected, greatly disappointed, for they all recognized the need of a first-rate school of architecture in the Deep South area. The way to achieve it was clearly through a separate school with an adequate faculty.

While still a department of engineering, architecture had made substantial contributions especially to the city of New Orleans itself. With a separate administration and a greatly expanded faculty its contributions became even more noteworthy not only in New Orleans but in the region. Assistance received from the New Orleans chapter of the American Institute of Architects was most encouraging, especially the work of a committee composed of Moise Goldstein, H. Mortimer Favrot, Arthur H. Feitel, Douglass V. Freret, and Richard Koch. This committee secured the services of Walter R. McCormick, former dean of architecture at the Massachusetts Institute of Technology, and with him made a comprehensive study of the school's needs. Pickens displayed great vigor in carrying out the recommendations of this group. By necessity he was so engrossed in the organization and administration of the new school that he had far too little time to devote to a study of what the school's discrete contributions ought to be. He had to obtain clerical and administrative help for the office, reorganize the library, expand the faculty and encourage it in carrying on original work, revise the curriculum, and perform scores of other basic duties.

When a committee of the National Architectural Accrediting Board reviewed the college in March 1952, the report was favorable to a degree that was encouraging and stimulating. The report established Tulane as one of the 39 accredited schools among 60 collegiate schools of architecture in the United States. The committee commented most favorably upon the improvements made since 1947, but pointed out that a further enlargement of the teaching staff and a raising of salary scales were needs that had to be met if continued progress was anticipated. The committee also suggested that Tulane should exploit its geographical position, not only to serve the domestic region but also to become the dominant center in the Caribbean area for architectural study.

Pickens resigned in 1953 to become head of the school of architecture at

Washington University and was succeeded by John Ekin Dinwiddie, a foremost practicing architect as well as a teacher of architectural subjects. As alumnus of Michigan and a student of Eliel Saarinen, Dinwiddie had won twenty-three national awards for his work by the time of his appointment as dean on September 1, 1953. Under him, numerous changes took place. The faculty was augmented, enrollment rose to an optimum level for the physical facilities, a new building is being planned, and other changes of a physical nature can be observed. The most conspicuous changes, however, are in basic philosophy, goals, and directions. Perhaps these may be summarized under three heads:

1. The curriculum has been humanized and liberalized by the inclusion of work in the social studies such as anthropology, sociology, and cultural history. In the revision of the curriculum a compulsory first-year course dealing with the history of American culture has been introduced. In the third year this will be reinforced by a similar type of course dealing with Western civilization and its development. It is expected that these courses together with the other work in the social studies will make the architectural student more aware of the cultural forces and values of the milieu in which he will live and build as a practicing architect.

2. Following a prevailing trend, the school is returning to basic principles derived from universal experiences rather than doing servile obeisance to any one school of architecture, particularly the Bauhaus school. Indoctrination of the student in any one phase of architecture is avoided. Rather, it is expected that the student will be taught how to distill an essence from man's age-long experiences as a builder and that this essence will be utilized in meeting the cultural and utilitarian needs of any given geographic area.

3. Of great importance in carrying into effect the new directions is the fact that the faculty accepts the new philosophy and is unified in its belief that one of the basic aims of the school is to place the attainment of full maturity of the student as a human being who deals with other human beings as they live and work above mere technical proficiency.

By and large these trends are being carried forward by Dean John W. Lawrence, who succeeded to the deanship upon the death of Mr. Dinwiddie in 1959. Architecture is not merely technical training. It is related to people and society.

A discussion of architecture brings to mind the enormous building program at Tulane during the period of Harris's presidency and since.

The old grad who has not visited the campus since 1935 will still recognize Gibson Hall and other portions of the St. Charles Avenue sector of the campus. Beyond this, however, he probably will have great difficulty in finding his way around, but in his confusion he undoubtedly will have a feeling of pride in what has happened to the physical plant. The *Hullabaloo* reported that physical changes on the Tulane campus were the major topic of conversation at the annual 1958 homecoming celebration. According to the student paper "remarkable," "marvelous," and "astonishing" were words used by former graduates to describe what was happening to the face of the campus. "Many," the paper reported, "spent Saturday afternoon wandering around the campus looking for familiar landmarks that they found had given way to modern buildings."

When Harris assumed the presidency the campus was bleak and barren, the few buildings standing out naked against the horizon. Poor drainage resulted in puddles of mud and water scattered here and there over all the area from St. Charles Avenue to the stadium. The absence of flowers and shrubs was conspicuous; only a few live oaks relieved the unpleasant monotony. This condition Harris set out to improve. At his insistence shrubs, trees, and flowers were planted, roads were paved, nearly 5,000 feet of widewalks were laid, a drainage system was installed, the low spots were leveled by the filling in of thousands of cubic feet of earth. Grass was planted, and ivy began to craw up the bare walls of the buildings. This beautification provided the setting for a much larger building and rehabilitation program.

One by one vacant areas on the Tulane and Newcomb campus were filled with new buildings. In 1938 Mrs. Amelie McAlister Upshur of San Marino, California, gave the university a sum of money for the construction of an auditorium in memory of her mother. In April of 1940 the great domed McAlister Auditorium was dedicated. Early in 1938 a city-wide drive for funds to be used in the construction of a student center building was inaugurated. The people of the community contributed a sufficient amount so that the center could be dedicated in 1940. Also in 1940, the university built a modest brick observatory with money donated by Mrs. Grace S. Cross in memory of a family friend, Thomas F. Cunningham, late president of the Mississippi Shipping Company. In the summer of 1940 President Harris reported that Mrs. Norman Mayer had left the university a sizable sum of money in memory of her husband for the construction and maintenance of a combined classroom and library building for the College of Commerce and Business Administration. The classroom portion of the Norman Mayer building was completed in 1942, but the library portion had to wait until after World War II. The complete structure was dedicated on May 11, 1949.

These were the buildings constructed with funds from gifts and bequests, but the university was doing a significant amount of construction out of capital funds. Between 1937 and 1953 Tulane spent a total of approximately $6,500,000 for capital improvements.

The construction of the new library building has already been mentioned. In addition to this improvement there was other building and renovation. In 1948 the old academic dormitory was remodeled and converted into the social work building, and the next year the Richardson Memorial dormitory was thoroughly renovated and renamed Alcée Fortier Hall for the use of University College, the Summer School, and the modern language department. In 1947 the university obtained war surplus material out of which was erected the History Building, a cafeteria, and a large number of "barracks" for the use of married students and faculty members. Two years later a new building for mechanical and chemical engineering was completed.

One of the most significant building projects of the period under discussion was the addition to the Hutchinson Memorial medical building on Tulane Avenue. In 1951 the National Heart Institute granted Tulane $485,000 for a cardiovascular laboratory. The original intention was to build a four-story wing to the Hutchinson Memorial building, but in September 1952, the board decided to fulfill a long-cherished plan of bringing all divisions of the Medical School together and to erect a ten-story annex for this purpose. To the funds donated by the National Heart Institute, the administrators added approximately $2,000,000 advanced from the Medical School's endowment. Work was begun on the new structure late in 1952, and four years later the ten-story addition was completed, at a cost of some $8,000,000, making it possible to move the second year of medicine from the main campus to the Tulane Avenue campus. Since that time another wing has been constructed at a cost of $8,000,000. Approximately $2,225,000 was contributed toward the building fund from the United States Department of Public Health. With the new structure completed the entire medical school is housed on Tulane Avenue rather than being divided between this site and the main campus.

Newcomb, too, shared in the building program. The college since 1940 had consistently been forced to refuse admission to more than 200 applicants annually because it had no place for them to live. By 1949 the situation had become so serious President Harris reported that "The question is no longer whether Newcomb can afford to construct additional dormitory facilities, but whether we can afford not to do so." A drive for funds among friends and alumnae of Newcomb was inaugurated in 1949 and yielded some $200,000. Construction of a new dormitory was begun in 1954 and completed a year later. This modernistic building, christened Johnston Hall in honor of William Preston Johnston, houses 84 students. Since its completion two other women's residence halls, Butler and Doris, have been completed. In addition a new air-conditioned dining room building has been put into use. A new health services building to serve the needs of the entire university was completed in 1959.

On the Tulane side of the campus other major construction projects for living and recreational purposes have been completed. Four new men's residence halls, Samuel Zemurray, Jr. Memorial Hall, Phelps House, Irby House, and Paterson House were in use before 1960. Since 1960 two other residence halls have been completed, Sharp and Monroe, the latter rising twelve stories. On the Claiborne Avenue end of the campus a new seven-story air-conditioned apartment building, Rosen House, was completed in 1959. It accomodates 179 families of graduate students and faculty members. Between it and the stadium is the new Favrot Field House for intramural sports, given to the university by Clifford Favrot. Adjacent to the stadium on Willow Street the Alumni Association has occupied its new quarters in a handsome renovated home. Nearer Freret Street a $2,500,000 University Center was completed in 1959, a building which is indispensable to the university's new social and recreational programs; and one wonders how the university ever got along without it. To complete the present era of student facilities, construction of a new food services building for men, Bruff Commons, was completed in 1963.

Dramatic as is the story of the expansion of the physical plant through 1958, this does not tell the whole story. New buildings for law, architecture, the library, and science are in the planning state. In addition the university has completed a $6,000,000 rehabilitation program. Many of the older buildings have been thoroughly renovated and modernized, and a central heating and air-conditioning plant has been completed. Ultimately it is expected that most of the buildings on the campus will be served by this plant.

This vast building and renovation program has been financed in three ways: by a limited number of individual gifts such as the Favrot Field House; by dipping into university capital funds; and by loans from the federal government. The rehabilitation and renovation program has been paid for out of university capital funds. The $14,500,000 for new construction has been obtained from government loans.

This building program has dramatic significance for the university in ways other than providing additional living and working space. Perhaps the most significant results may be summarized under three heads:

1. The fact that there are now approximately 2,400 students (exclusive of those in fraternity houses) living on the campus and that this number will steadily increase as additional residence halls are completed, whereas ten years ago there were hardly more than 400, marks the beginning of a very radical change in the nature of the university. To put the matter succinctly it means that Tulane has changed from an institution with a definitely local orientation to one which attracts students from all parts of the country. This change did not meet with complete approval from all people concerned with the university; nevertheless it has occurred and the Tulane of today is not the Tulane of even fifteen years ago. This development of a substantial residential community on the campus has brought

with it many problems and opportunities which the old Tulane did not have. Social and recreational problems naturally have arisen, and the university finds itself in the position of having to devise more adequate programs along these lines.

2. The willingness of the Board of Administrators to obligate the future of the university in the form of government loans marks another sharp break with the practices of former boards. This new attitude reflects the enormous confidence which the Board of Administrators has in the future of the university and its determination that the institution will not lack the necessary physical facilities for developing into greatness. There were, of course, individual members of previous boards who were willing to commit the university to something like its present course, but the major sentiment was for maintaining of *status quo* and not going into debt, especially to the federal government, even though this new course showed every indication of success.

3. The new program of expansion has brought to university officials and faculties the necessity for careful planning both in academic matters and in plant expansion. The processes of this planning have, in turn, brought the faculties, the deans, other administrative officials, and the Board of Administrators into a coordinated and cooperative situation which bodes great good for the future. The fact that this planning is a cooperative venture should be emphasized. The expansion is not the product of thinking of any one individual or group of individuals. Vice-president Clarence Scheps has been in the forefront of physical plant financing and planning. Vice-president Fred Cole played an equally important part in putting emphasis on academic planning. But these two phases of planning are not mutually exclusive; rather they are parts of the same problem. Neither of these two phases of planning can go forward to fruition without due consideration of financial problems, and this involves the Development Office and the Board of Administrators. The result is the planning indicated above, one of the healthiest and most promising aspects of the greater Tulane.

Not only has the Board of Administrators sought the cooperation and assistance of faculties and university administrators but it has turned to prominent people throughout the country for advice in the solution of the university's problems. At first this was on a more or less random and informal basis, but in 1954 the Board of Administrators brought into being a Board of Visitors, a formal organization of advisers composed of both alumni and nonalumni members. This new board is necessarily extralegal, since membership on the Board of Administrators itself is limited to citizens of Louisiana. Nevertheless, the administrators have found that this newly formed group is rendering conspicuous service to the university. Ordinarily the Board of Visitors meets annually in the spring, and at its meetings reviews the problems of the university and offers its advice in the solution of them.

The matter of specific planning, of course, is based on the question of what the university will need in the way of physical facilities, and this depends upon an accurate projection of what the university's enrollment and academic offerings will be at any given time within the foreseeable future. This objective look into Tulane's future has brought into focus three mature and basic questions: (a) What is Tulane now? (b) What role should Tulane as a privately endowed university play in the life of the South and the nation in the forseeable future? (c) What sort of institution should Tulane become and what facilities will it need in order to play its most effective role?

It is not easy to arrive at the answers to these questions, as the entire university has discovered. Nevertheless substantial progress is being made in the direction of tentative answers. Perhaps at no time in the university's history have deans, the president, and the faculties been so acutely aware of the necessity of projecting the schools and colleges into the future.

Fruitful results of these investigations are already being experienced. Perhaps the best way to reveal some of the new developments is to take a brief view of developments which are projected or are under way in the various units which make up the university.

Some of the significant aspects of growth at Newcomb and in the College of Arts and Sciences have been related in the previous chapter. There are other matters which could be dealt with at some length if space permitted. A better system of student orientation and counseling has been developed in both colleges. A modern language laboratory with the newest in electronic equipment has been installed to serve the entire university. The honors programs have encouraged superior students. In Arts and Sciences a faculty group with the long name of "Committee on Programs for Students of Superior Preparation" counsels and encourages students who may, out of their interests and intellectual curiosity, wish to investigate topics not ordinarily dealt with in the formal curricula. These topics may have a range as great as that from the nocturnal habits of Cro-Magnon man to the multiple integrals of vector analysis. But whatever the field may be, the student is encouraged to use his own ingenuity in placing together bits of human knowledge into a meaningful pattern. Newcomb has inaugurated a plan whereby well-qualified young women may, under supervision, take their junior year at a European university and then return to the college for their senior year. The College of Arts and Sciences was not long in adopting the plan.

All these and other developments have taken place within a relatively few years and under the direction of a small group of administrative officials. Frederick Hard, dean of Newcomb from 1938 to 1943, was a dawn man in the transition from the Newcomb of Dean Pierce Butler to a college less lavishly devoted to a veneration of the *status quo*. This process was not complete during Hard's period, but by the time of Dean Logan Wilson (1943–1951) the faculty was beginning to show signs that it might be willing to consider some degree of modernization. Actually, much of the transition from the old to the new was accomplished under Wilson, who resigned in 1951 to accept the vice-presidency of the consolidated University of North Carolina, going from there to the presidency of the University of Texas and then to the presidency of the American Council on Education. For a period of two years Miss Anna Many served as dean, and in 1953 Dr. John Randolph Hubbard, of the history faculty of the College of Arts and Sciences, was named head of the college; and under him Newcomb has taken large strides forward.

The transformation from the old to the new took place in the College of Arts and Sciences at about the same time as at Newcomb. In retrospect one may see that this transition dates from the appointment of Dr. Fred Carrington Cole as dean in 1947. Although Dean Cole was named academic vice-president in 1952, he did not until after a lapse of three years give up entirely his work as dean. During this time when he was serving in a dual capacity Dr. Russel Mortimer Geer, the W. R. Irby Professor of Classical Languages, was acting and associate dean. In 1955 William Wallace Peery, from the English department of the University of Texas, became the dean of the college which, it might be added, is still very much in the midst of change.

The School of Engineering, under the direction of Dean James M. Robert (1937–1950), devoted itself with a singleness of purpose to the education of a limited number of good engineers; and the term "engineer" is used in its technical sense. There were few innovations in the curricula. Little or no attempt was made to inject any humanizing or liberalizing subjects into the courses of study. Every year the school turned out 40 to 60 graduates well trained in engineering skills, but with little else. In 1950 Lee Harnie Johnson, former dean of the school of engineering at the University of Mississippi, succeeded Dean Robert, who had retired. Although the desideratum of humanized engineer has not been reached, significant changes in thinking have been taking place during the past five years or more. This new thought is in keeping with the general trends in engineering education toward emphasis on a broader and more basic type of education as contrasted with the more specialized.

Changes in the undergraduate curricula include the eliminations of former options in the electrical and mechanical engineering curricula, more emphasis on mathematics and analysis, blending of theory and practice of engineering into introductory courses, more emphasis on the humanities and social studies, greater flexibility among electives in the junior and senior years, and reduction of time devoted to descriptive material and techniques. Courses in nuclear engineering have been introduced.

In the past five years masters' degrees in all four engineering departments have been offered, and the enrollment of graduate students has risen from 15 to as many as 49 graduate students in 1957–1958. The number of graduate courses has been increased, and the schedules have been so arranged that engineers in practice may take advantage of opportunities for graduate study. There are now available several scholarships in the School of Engineering for graduate students, where formerly there were none. The departments now offer the Ph.D. degree.

The faculty of the school has consisted primarily of young men who have become increasingly active during this period as teaching loads have been reduced and opportunities for research and development have presented themselves. Three department heads have retired or resigned and have been replaced by younger men. The fourth department head will retire at the end of this year. Thus during the five-year period the faculty has become almost entirely a youthful group with great energy and zeal which is looking forward to making significant contributions in teaching and research. Several holders of the Ph.D. degrees have been added, and there has been increased interest in taking leaves of absences to work on advanced degrees.

The undergraduate enrollment of the School of Engineering has remained relatively constant during the past four or five years, remaining in the vicinity of 500 students. The physical facilities of the school, however, have been greatly improved. The Board of Administrators made available over $100,000 in 1957 for replacing old equipment and obtaining new equipment and instruments. The buildings of the School of Engineering were renovated during 1958, and a small additional shop building was constructed at the north end of Stanley Thomas Hall. The chief features of the remodeling are the shop building; new additional offices, classrooms, and research laboratories on the first floor of Stanley Thomas Hall; a revised and expanded suite of electrical engineering offices on the second floor of Stanley Thomas Hall; a new suite of civil engineering offices on the second floor of the building; and revision of the side entrance of the Chemical Engineering building to make available additional interior space.

In 1940, Frans Ferdinand Blom, the blond, personable Dane who did much to popularize archaeological knowledge of Middle America, left the university with the administrative affairs of the Middle American Research Institute in something less than first-rate condition. In the interim period between directors, Arthur Gropp, the institute librarian, and Maurice Ries, a research associate, were jointly in charge. The research program, because of World War II conditions, was at a standstill; and this afforded an opportunity to remodel the old-fashioned museum into a modern and attractive gallery. Dr. Robert Wauchope of the University of North Carolina was brought in as director in 1942, but within a few months went on leave to enter the armed services, which, with other government agencies, claimed all other members of the staff except one. By the end of the war, two staff members had died, two had resigned to enter government work, and one had become director of maintenance at the university. Dr. Wauchope thus had an entire new staff to build, and with it a new program.

Since 1945, research associates of the institute have been, for the most part, Latin-American studies specialists on the university faculty, assigned to the institute staff part time for research. Less stress is placed on museum activities, an expensive and time-consuming program, and although the museum gallery is still open to students and public, there is no curatorial staff. Instead, the library staff has been increased, and the scope of research has broadened. In addition to a staff of archaeologists and anthropologists, there are now for the first time research associates in sociology, history, political science, resources, art history, language, and literature. The research program centers around selected themes, with staff members (and often graduate students) from these various disciplines bringing to bear on common problems their different points of view, methods, and experience. The research staff discusses these matters and reports on progress at staff seminars, which are recorded and mimeographed so that the results of this interplay of minds can be filed for future reference by each person in the program.

The results of this new multidisciplinary research are perhaps best seen in the institute's publications. Volumes are built around themes, with staff and graduate students, as well as outside scholars, contributing monographs. Final sections in each volume synthesize the results. The research themes change gradually, as the associates turn to new interests or as developments lead them into new aspects of old topics. For example, one volume is devoted to *Foreign Influences on Native Religious Ideology*, another to *Applied Enlightenment: 19th Century Liberalism* (its marks on legal codes, politics, foreign colonization, economic development and trade, and political philosophy), and a third centers on *Indian Influences on the Folk Theater* and related subjects. Instead of concentrating on the Mayan area of Central America, which was once the announced intention of the institute, studies now range from native Indian situations there to urban social structure, modern government, and industry throughout Middle America. Another interesting project is devoted to studies in *Frontier Hispanic Americanism*, including subjects located in Texas, New Mexico, and the Spanish southern United States.

Archaeological and anthropological research continue on a large scale. A five-year study of modern Indian, German, and Guatemalan culture in the Alta Verapaz region of Guatemala was completed in 1956. Archaeological excavation and exploration were carried on in the Guatemala highland and on the east coast of Quintana Roo and Yucatan. In 1957, the institute, in cooperation with the National Geographic Society, began intensive excavations and restoration at the Mayan ruins of Dzibilchaltun in Yucatan. Over $100,000 was raised for this project, including substantial grants by the National Science Foundation and the American Philosophical Society. In 1958 the National Science Foundation awarded the institute a grant of $140,700 to begin a ten-volume encyclopedia of Middle American Indians, their archaeology, ethnology, linguistics, physical anthropology, and ethno-history.

Paul William Brosman, who succeeded President Harris as dean of the law school in 1937, was a successful dean, adept in public relations as well as internal administration. Unfortunately, however, World War II interfered seriously with the law school, Dean Brosman himself going on active military duty in 1942. For three years Professor Robert Joseph Farley of the law school faculty acted as dean, and in 1945 Brosman returned. The school was further handicapped by paucity of finances which prevented fully effective faculty recruitment and necessary additions to the library. However, substantial improvements were made. Of tremendous importance was the fact that the law school at last found a permanent and, for the time being, adequate home for itself. When it moved from Dinwiddie Hall to the recently vacated Tilton Library building in 1941, this was the first time it had its own building since the university moved from the old downtown campus in 1894. There was some curriculum modification, but perhaps the outstanding innovations were the development of the comparative law program and the establishment of a law-science program. Dr. Hubert Kinston Smith, who headed the latter program, possessed unusual qualifications for supervising a program intended to bring law and medicine in closer juxtaposition. Dr. Smith possessed both the degree of Doctor of Medicine and Bachelor of Laws, and although he resigned to accept a similar position at the University of Texas after two years at Tulane, his program has not lost its influence.

Dean Brosman resigned in 1951 to accept a judgeship on the United States Court of Military Appeals and was serving in this capacity when he died suddenly in 1955. Professor Clarence James Morrow acted as dean during 1951–1952 until the appointment of William Ray Forrester in 1952. Dean Forrester had previously taught at the Tulane law school, but immediately prior to his appointment at Tulane was dean of the law school at Vanderbilt University.

During the past ten years there have been significant developments in the law school. The size and over-all strength of full-time faculty has increased substantially.

The program in the field of comparative law has been strengthened and enlarged with the assistance of grants from the Ford and Rockefeller foundations totaling nearly a half a million dollars. As a result of these grants

Mr. Rodolfo Batiza of Mexico City was appointed associate professor of Latin-American legal studies and associate director of the Institute of Comparative Law. The graduate program of the Law School has grown rather rapidly, bringing to the campus students from areas as widely separated as Germany, Chile, and Taiwan. In addition to the degrees of Master of Laws and Master of Civil Law, a new program leading to the degree of Doctor of Juridical Science in Comparative Law has been established.

A plan has been developed under which distinguished visiting professors come to the law school from all parts of the world. During recent years, they have included professors from Oxford University, the University of Paris, the University of Montevideo, the University of London, the University of Rennes, the University of Grenoble, the University of Aberdeen, the University of Wales, and the National University of Korea.

A system of professional study was inaugurated in 1953 to afford an opportunity for practicing attorneys to supplement their daily experiences with formal courses in newly developed areas of law. Under this plan many of the upperclass courses in the regular curriculum are made available to members of the bar, and in addition, forums, institutes, and conferences devoted to specific subjects of current interest are sponsored. These range in content from the practical, as represented by the Institute on Real Estate, to the philosophical "Law and Morals in the 20th Century." At the same time a reciprocal plan of assistance has been developed in the community in which the district attorney's office and the Legal Aid Bureau give opportunities for law students to interview clients, conduct investigative work and legal research, and work closely with attorneys in the handling of litigation.

Admission requirements have been raised, and the curriculum has undergone extensive revision. The Law School Admission Test is now required of all applicants. In order to be considered for admission an applicant must have completed at least three years of college work with an average grade of C or better. The entering class is selected from those who are permitted to apply under these basic minimal standards. Notwithstanding this process of selection, however, the size of the student body has increased from 174 students in 1953 to 274 in 1958.

The curriculum in law has been reviewed and augmented during recent years. Additional courses have been offered as the size of the faculty has increased. Particular attention has been given to the strengthening of the common law curriculum and to the offering of additional seminars in the fields of civil and comparative law. A program in legal research and writing has been inaugurated in an attempt to improve the training of law students in this important area. It has been found that a great weakness with many students coming into the law school is their incapacity to express themselves fully and completely in written and oral English. This program is not one of remedial English but rather one which attempts to show the student the necessity for rich expression not only in legal terms but also in complementary usage.

Elizabeth Wisner, dean of the School of Social Work, retired in 1958 and was succeeded by Walter Lewis Kindelsperger, who had served for several years as professor of group work under Dean Wisner. Dean Wisner had played a major part in founding the school and had been almost solely responsible for the direction it had taken and for the recognition it had achieved. Dean Kindelsperger has a solid foundation upon which he can build.

The recent period of the School of Social Work, beginning in 1950, has produced faculty activity which reflects the growing preoccupation with curriculum revision in the light of contemporary knowledge in the social sciences and contemporary learning theory. Various members of the faculty continue to be active on national committees and research projects concerned with this emphasis.

This decade has seen the growing recognition of theory-based knowledge derived from research, and a greatly accelerated interest in the contribution of the social and biological sciences to the understanding and solution of major problems dealt with by social welfare programs.

In terms of curriculum, the faculty is more and more preoccupied with the question of appropriate research training at the master's level and with an awareness of the need for increased intellectual content in the classroom and laboratory experience. Parallel to this atmosphere of questioning, revising, and seeking new knowledge is the effort to try to define more precisely the function of the School of Social Work in a private university. Schools of social work sponsored by both public and private sources have, in general, reached a point of adequate geographical coverage and of minimum competence.

In determining Tulane's role in the future, there has been a growing realization that the freedom of the private university enables it to move forward in developing the student with special capacities for leadership, scholarship, and teaching. For Tulane, this involves the faculty responsibility of developing a third-year clinical residency program and a full program of training at the doctorate level. The geographical location of Tulane, combined with the traditions and qualities of the University, makes this a natural development in the future of the School of Social Work.

The School of Social Work for many years has maintained a high-quality master's degree program (terminal professional degree) and consequently has successfully laid the basis for the development of the doctorate program. It is logically anticipated therefore that the next decade will see the school launched in this new and additional responsibility for training of the scholar-teacher for the schools of tomorrow, paralleled by increasing productivity in the areas of social welfare knowledge and theory.

Dean Morton Aldrich of the College of Commerce and Business Administration[1] retired in 1939. Since 1914 he had wrestled with the problems of a new school seeking identity and status in the university complex. As is customary in such situations a developmental period is likely to be characterized by some internal friction. Dean Aldrich established excellent rapport with business and industry in the community, but his efforts were not so successful in relation to other colleges in the university, particularly the College of Arts and Sciences. This college rather generally felt that the school of business was strongly vocationally oriented and that this sort of orientation was undesirable in a university such as Tulane. And one may easily see the liberal arts point of view. In 1930, sixteen years after the school of business was founded, only 13 hours out of a total of 130 hours required for graduation could be considered liberal subjects. The only student who had any basic general education was the one who transferred to the school of business from the College of Arts and Sciences at the end of his second year. The student who entered the College of Commerce and Business Administration as a freshman was given little opportunity to be exposed to courses in the liberal arts. This situation continued throughout Dean Aldrich's administration and was a constant source of criticism by the liberal arts faculty members. Dean Aldrich's reaction to this was a natural one. More and more he and his faculty tended to withdraw within the walls of their school and there to commiserate with each other on the persecution they were experiencing.

Dean Leslie James Buchan, who succeeded Aldrich in 1939, did little to dissipate the defense mechanism which Aldrich had built up. Dean Buchan was trained as an accountant and had taught under Aldrich. Since there was no immediate curriculum revision, criticism from the liberal arts faculties did not diminish. New faculty members soon caught the old spirit of academic autonomy and acquired the feeling of being discriminated against by liberal arts.

By 1948, however, more liberal subjects were creeping into the curriculum. A standard course in English composition replaced "English for Business," and there still was no liberature offered. The regular course in college mathematics replaced "Mathematics for Business." Foreign language was introduced into the curriculum by Buchan and his faculty. Slowly they yielded to the pressure for a more liberal curriculum.

They were reluctant to see a new evening division established in the university which would take from the day college its evening students; and these evening students were by no means an unimportant part of the business school's enrollment. In 1930, for example, there were 189 day students and 457 evening students. In 1942, when University College was formed, there were 289 day students and 607 evening students. Day enrollment continued to grow year by year, however, and the loss of the evening

[1] The official name is now the School of Business Administration.

students was felt less keenly as time went on. In 1949 Buchan resigned to accept the deanship of the School of Business Administration at Washington University, St. Louis. Robert Warren French, a Michigander via the University of Texas, was selected to fill the vacant position; and with French new tides began to run through the school. French was a very personable and flexible individual who took little stock in the isolationist view of many of the older faculty members. Perhaps his philosophy can best be told in this quotation from one of his messages to his faculty:

> Whatever the stated objectives, the fundamental task of a college of business administration is to provide training for meeting the business and economic problems of its day. Its task is therefore dynamic and ever-changing. The college must be alert to trends in the business economy, to social thinking, to developments in other collegiate schools of business, and to shifts in its own position within the institutional framework of the university of which it is a part. The college must adapt its program of activities to these changes. Only in this way can it fulfill its mission.

He set in motion certain reforms which, had he continued in office, undoubtedly would have reflected great credit upon him. He began a process of curriculum revision, instituted a graduate program, brought in new faculty members, and encouraged research. Hardly had he adjusted himself to his office in the Norman Mayer building, however, when he was called upon to organize a privately financed institution known as the Public Affairs Research Council, dedicated to an investigation of economic affairs in Louisiana especially as those affairs touched state government. He took a year's leave of absence for this work and shortly after his return to the university was named, in 1953, a vice-president in charge of the development program. He remained in this position until 1956 when he was appointed director of the Port of New Orleans.

For two years Paul Victor Grambsch, professor of management, served as acting dean and in 1955 was named dean. He carried out a number of the basic reforms instituted or suggested by French, but he added a number of his own ideas.

Undoubtedly the most significant development under Grambsch was the integration of the curriculum into the university liberal arts pattern. All of the work in the first two years of business administration, with the exception of accounting, is now taken in the liberal arts colleges, and the faculty of the School of Business Administration has set as the first goal of undergraduate instruction the acquisition of a general education. Within the work of the third and fourth years there was a gradual movement to introduce analytical material and to minimize the time spent on description. From the standpoint of the curriculum, therefore, the school moved to a point where it was drawing on the rest of the university for the best it had to offer, and in addition, was developing a much higher professional-level program in the field of business administration.

Within the past ten years the graduate division made a start toward reaching its full potential. The curriculum was overhauled along the lines of some of the leading graduate schools of business, and the increasing number of students attest to the degree of attention which the program is attracting. In 1963 the decision was made to phase out the undergraduate program and to devote its energies entirely to the graduate school.

During this same period of time the school has conducted a growing number of institutes and short courses. The Tulane Tax Institute and the Institute on Foreign Transportation and Port Operation have achieved nationwide standing, and they have attracted the finest talent available in these fields. The other short courses, dealing mainly with management problems of various industries, undoubtedly will continue to grow.

The faculty has undergone considerable transition, and in the period of the past five years a number of senior members have retired. This has brought the opportunity to add new members to the faculty, many of whom have had a different outlook in the field of business administration. Starting in an excellent position with forty-four years of high-quality education, the school will be able to realize a much greater potential in the years to come. The recognition needed for academic leadership among the schools of business in the South, and in the nation as a whole, is steadily being obtained. In continuing to advance the field of business administration by looking closely at all areas of learning and their potential contribution to the business field, there is no question that the school can aid in the university's march toward its goals.

Dean Bass of the School of Medicine retired in 1939 effective in January 1940. Maxwell Edward Lapham, a Pennsylvanian who had taught obstetrics in the medical school since 1937, was named to the vacant position. Before he could really get hold of the job, however, he was called into military service which lasted for more than three years. During the interim period Hiram Watkins Kostmayer served with exceptional proficiency in the capacity of dean. As might be expected no significant innovations occurred during this period, but the mature organization which Bass had handed on to Lapham was held together by Kostmayer in a notably efficient manner.

It was not until 1945, therefore, that Dean Lapham had an opportunity to incorporate into the structure of the medical school his ideas of how it could best train outstanding medical scientists as well as practicing physicians. Within a few years he altered considerably the organic structure of the school, setting up clearly defined departments headed by outstanding men who not only taught medicine but did medical research themselves and supervised numerous programs in their respective fields. Although not differing completely from the organization of the Bass period the new plan divided the school into two parts. The undergraduate division offers a course of study leading to the degree of Doctor of Medicine. The Division of Graduate Medicine offers formal and informal postgraduate courses of a general or specialized nature to medical graduates and occasionally to other workers in the health field, such as speech therapy and nutrition. Basic science review programs and long-term training in the clinical fields are also emphasized. Selected clinical fellows and residents may register for the Master of Medical Science degree, while a fully developed curriculum in public health offers programs of study leading to the Master of Public Health, the Master of Public Health (Tropical Medicine), and the Doctor of Public Health degrees. In addition, the departments of anatomy, biochemistry, microbiology, parasitology, pharmacology, and physiology offer advanced studies in these special fields leading to the degree of Doctor of Philosophy, this degree being offered through the Graduate School rather than through the School of Medicine. In order to facilitate administration of the new organizational plan two new officials were added: Dr. Clifford Grosselle Grulee, Jr., as associate dean of the School of Medicine and director of the Division of Graduate Medicine; and Dr. Harold Cummins as the assistant dean. Since that time Dr. Grulee has resigned, and Dr. Cummins has retired.

In order for the layman to understand how the School of Medicine carries on its programs it is necessary to note the departmental organization. The departments are anatomy, biochemistry, microbiology, obstetrics and gynecology, ophthalmology, otolaryngology, pathology, pediatrics, pharmacology, physiology, psychiatry and neurology, surgery, and tropical medicine and public health. These departments, each headed by a departmental chairman, serve both the undergraduate and graduate divisions in the training of doctors, but this function is paralleled by extensive programs of research carried on by the department head or under his direction. Without exception every one of the departments has one or more major research projects under development and without exception every department has made notable contributions to the field of medical knowledge.

Emphasis upon research has presented the school with problems as well as progress. It has, for example, meant funds for research have been increasingly available from the federal government, voluntary health agencies, and foundations. In 1963–1964 these grants amounted to nearly $3 million. On the other hand, valuable as these grants are, they do not add to the basic endowment of the medical school. Thus they cannot be considered as permanent additions to funds necessary for the financial security which will enable the school to carry out its role of training practicing physicians. Other major consequences of these research programs are heavy pressures for additional space and a substantial increase in research and technical personnel. Above all, perhaps, it is the fact that the school has constantly to be on guard lest its research functions overshadow its teaching role.

There have been substantial additions to the basic endowment of the medical school in recent years. In 1931 Miss Sarah H. Henderson gave approximately $123,000 for the Henderson Educational Fund for Medicine; in 1938 she gave an additional $216,000 for the William Henderson Chair in Surgery; and in 1945 she bequeathed approximately $1,075,000 for the William Henderson Chair for Prevention of Tropical and Semi-Tropical Diseases. In 1945 another substantial gift was received in the Henry E. and Henrietta Nenage gift of $100,000 in endowment for research in dermatology. In 1948 Mrs. Doris Wise Joachim made available $100,000 to endow the Otto Joachim Chair of Otolaryngology. In 1939 the General Education Board gave $450,000 for endowment which was matched by the university. In 1957 the Ford Foundation made a grant of $2,300,000, and in 1958 Dr. Rudolph Matas bequeathed the major portion of his estate, valued at some $1,500,000, as an endowment particularly for the medical school library. These and other smaller gifts when added together come to a substantial sum; but over against this must be set the rising cost of medical education and the fact that it has been necessary for the Board of Administrators to dip into capital funds to finance new construction and purchase of land.

The Tulane School of Medicine is one of the first-rate medical schools in the country. Every year it turns out approximately 125 doctors of medicine in addition to training a number of physicians and others in graduate medicine and public health. Its research activities touch almost every phase of human disease and disorder. It has long since passed from the position of a regional to that of a national institution. Although its primary orientation remains Southern its reputation has spread throughout the United States and particularly in tropical medicine and public health, through Southeast Asia, the Orient, and Latin America. Research and service programs are underway from Peru to the Belgian Congo to Singapore. Approximately 25 per cent of the students are from the state of Louisiana; about 60 per cent are from the South, including Louisiana; about 40 per cent are from areas outside the South. Yet this school which plays so large a part in the well being of this and other countries finds itself constantly haunted by the specter of financial want. So great are the costs of medical education today that the medical school accounts for approximately 35 per cent of the entire budget of the university. Its expenditures for all items for the academic year 1963–1964 amounted to approximately $8,809,502, a sum which would have made Dean Dyer's and Dean Bass' eyes pop out on stems. However, $6,254,490 of this amount came from gifts and grants of the federal government and from foundations large and small.

CHAPTER 16

The Mid-Sixties

ON THE MORNING OF April 17, 1959, President Harris read to a joint meeting of the Board of Administrators and the Board of Visitors a brief statement announcing his intention to retire. He expressed the belief that after twenty-two years in the position he ought to resign so that the board could find a younger man (President Harris was at the time sixty-two years of age) for the chief executive's job. He also stated that personally he welcomed an opportunity to do some long-postponed reading, writing, lecturing, and thinking.[1]

Almost immediately the Tulane board with the assistance of a faculty committee began the search for a new president.[2] On December 17, 1959, Joseph M. Jones, president of the Board of Administrators, announced the acceptance of Herbert Eugene Longenecker, vice-president of the University of Illinois at the Medical Center. The effective date of the appointment was September 1, 1960.

The forty-seven-year-old new president, known to his friends as "Herb," is a native of Lititz, Pennsylvania. In 1936 he married Marjorie Jane Segar and in that same year received his Ph.D. degree from Pennsylvania State University where he had taken his undergraduate work. The Longeneckers have four children—a daughter and three sons. Since 1936, his rise in the academic world has been almost meteoric. As a biochemist he was awarded in 1936 a National Research Council Fellowship for advanced study at the University of Liverpool, the University of Cologne, and at Queen's University, Kingston, Canada. Upon his return to the United States in 1938 he joined the chemistry faculty at the University of Pittsburgh. In the short space of six years he was promoted to full professor, in

---

[1] This program he was not able to carry out, however. A few months after his retirement the trustees of Mercer University persuaded him to accept the presidency of that institution, his Alma Mater.

[2] The faculty committee (an innovation at Tulane) was composed of Professor Charles Silin of the French department, chairman; Professors Arthur O. Kastler, medicine; John W. Lawrence, architecture; Leonard Reismann, sociology; Howard G. Schaller, economics; John M. Scott, chemistry; and Elsie M. Watters, business administration.

which capacity he served from 1944 until 1955. During this period, however, he followed the path taken by so many promising scholars. He became an administrator—first as dean of research in the natural sciences at Pittsburgh and then as dean of the Graduate School at the same institution He was filling these positions when he was named vice-president of the University of Illinois in 1955.

His participation in national and regional educational affairs through his work on commissions and committees can be described only as prodigious. Even an abridged listing of these is too long for the space here. Not only is the list a long one but it is notably varied, reflecting the wide range of his educational interests. And in New Orleans his activities in local cultural, social, and economic organizations have been equally conspicuous. It is small wonder that he has been so well received by the New Orleans community, for it is quite clear that he and the board intend to form a new and more effective partnership between the city and the university.

A change in the presidency of a major university is likely to be accompanied by changes in general administration and even at professorial levels. The transition was made easier at Tulane, however, because Dr. Harris stayed on for a year after his retirement and fully cooperated with the new president not yet in residence. But there were changes. Dr. Fred Cole, vice-president for academic affairs, resigned, effective September 1, 1959, to accept the presidency of Washington and Lee University. On January 4, 1960, Dean Robert Lumiansky of the Graduate School was named to the newly created position of provost, still retaining his position as dean. On April 1, 1960, when Dr. Harris actually left the university, Dr. Maxwell Lapham, dean of the medical school, became acting president. But as time went on there were more resignations, new appointments, and retirements, as will be related below, most of these being in the making before the new president arrived.

President Longenecker took a minimum of time to get acquainted, for there were problems so pressing they could not be set aside for a leisurely period of orientation. At the heart of the entire university, as might be expected, was the question of finances. It was not a new problem. It was the replaying of an old record with the volume turned up. Desegregation daily became a more pressing problem. Intercollegiate athletics, particularly football, had been a headache for years. There was an urgent need for settling the matter of teacher education. A science center, a new library, additions to the medical school plant, and other building needs were weighty. Purely academic questions demanded consideration, raising problems of balance between graduate and undergraduate instruction, addition of new faculty, creation of new programs, and building up the library.

As has been indicated in previous chapters, the basic financial bind at Tulane grows out of a decision made in 1953 by the president and the board to develop a really first-rate university. The feeling was that Tulane must grow or wither; there was no standing still. Financial resources from unrestricted endowment income, annual giving, and student fees fell woefully short of making this possible. Therefore there seemed to be no alternative except to increase student fees, increase the unrestricted endowment, seek new sources of restricted grants, and resort to financing by digging into undesignated assets. It was a calculated risk that new funds would be forthcoming to compensate for the withdrawals.

Tulane did grow and expand its usefulness, and new funds did come in, but never in sufficient quantities to eliminate a depedence upon undesignated assets. Alumni giving went up appreciably, foundation support increased, tuition fees were raised, federal government research grants rose significantly—but still there was not enough and the ambitious programs of the university were soaring in response to regional and national needs.[3]

When President Longenecker arrived in 1960 Tulane was almost desperately in need of money, not small sums but millions of dollars, especially in the category of unrestricted endowment. The university was fast approaching the point where further deficit financing was dangerous, and operating budgets, especially for faculty salaries, still had of necessity to continue their upward trend.[4]

Buildings which could be handled on a self-liquidating basis did not constitute as great a problem as academic buildings and salaries. Dormitories, food-dispensing buildings, and similar structures could be built with funds borrowed from the United States government or private lenders. But plant renovation, a new heating and cooling plant, and a new wing to the medical school had to be paid for largely out of funds already in hand or in the form of annual gifts. During 1963–1964 the campus renovation program amounted to the cumulative total of $6,500,000. In addition the new medical school wing cost nearly $7,000,000 and the addition to the new heating and cooling plant ran almost a million.[5] Buildings constructed with the proceeds of loans came to $14,500,000. Thus the university spent over a seven-year period approximately $29,000,000 on buildings. And still the necessary new library and science complex were not provided for. When these are completed the total will rise to almost $47,000,000.

To President Longenecker and the Board of Administrators there was only one course open—there had to be new money and, as stated previously, lots of it for salaries, academic buildings, maintenance, new faculty, and new programs. The results of their deliberations and efforts are proving successful. An ambitious fund-raising drive, "The Tulane Forward

[3] For the fiscal year 1963–1964 the chief sources of Tulane's $24,909,177 income were: Student fees, 27.8 per cent; endowment, 7.0 per cent; restricted gifts and grants, 34.8 per cent; auxiliary enterprises, 16.4 per cent.

[4] Average faculty compensation rose from $8,107 in 1959–1960 to $11,348 for 1964–1965. The A.A.U.P. index grade rose from D to B.

[5] The university requires elaborate air-conditioning equipment in order that it may utilize its physical plant twelve months out of the year.

Fund," is now under way, aimed at raising $24,400,000 from gifts of a voluntary nature over a three year period, $12,000,000 of which will be used to match a Ford Foundation challenge grant of $6,000,000; and to this campaign the president is devoting almost all his time. It is a nation-wide drive, and assistance is coming in from all over the country, but managers of the campaign are particularly gratified over the local response. During the first year the Board of Administrators gave $2,000,000, the faculty without any pressure whatsoever gave $175,000; the New Orleans alumni contributed $500,000; local foundations, businessmen, corporations, professional men, and just plain citizens are adding daily to the total sum desired.

Private gifts and government grants have been most important in the building program as well as in restricted research and in other areas. In 1963–1964 restricted gifts and grants from the federal government, foundations, and corporations amounted to $8,675,397—34.8 per cent of the university's total income. In 1964 Percival Stern, prominent New Orleans businessman, pledged $3,000,000 toward the construction of the proposed science complex. The federal government has allocated nearly $2,000,000 for the new library and, in addition, contributed some $2,200,000 for the new medical wing.

All this talk and writing about millions of dollars going to Tulane has had the unfortunate effect of recreating in the minds of many persons the old myth that the university is rich, when the opposite is true.[6] Tulane is not affluent, and nothing approaching affluence can be reached until many more millions of dollars have been added to the unrestricted endowment. It is no small job Tulane has created for itself, and no small amount of money will get it done. And when by the standards of some it may appear to have reached affluence it will not have. New needs calling for new programs will lift its sights. The dynamics of modern society make it impossible for a good university to become static or complacent.

The first formal step in the desegregation of Tulane took place on April 12, 1954, at a meeting of the faculty of the Graduate School. At this meeting Professor James K. Feibleman, chairman of the department of philosophy, requested that a full discussion be given to the matter of admitting Negroes to the Graduate School. The faculty resolved itself into a committee of the whole where a free discussion took place. Upon arising from the committee of the whole Dr. Fred C. Cole, dean of the College of Arts and Sciences, proposed this resolution:

In view of the great need of our Southerners for opportunities to receive specialized training, the Faculty of the Graduate School recommends that steps be taken to clarify the policy of admission to the Graduate School in order that admission of Negroes may be facilitated.

[6] Endowment in 1963–1964 is given as $29,162,545, with a market value of $49,698,075.

The resolution was unanimously adopted and sent through channels with the approval of President Harris to the Board of Administrators.

Almost exactly a month later, May 17, 1954, came the historic Supreme Court decision on segregation—*Brown et al.* v. *Board of Education of Topeka et al.* The result was, as history has recorded, confusion and resistance throughout almost all of the lower South. At Tulane, however, there were no disturbances and many of the faculty joined groups working for a full implementation of the Supreme Court decision. Others adopted a more cautious and patient attitude. The division of opinion within the Board of Administrators was never fully revealed, but it is known that some of the members were opposed to the integration of Tulane and Mr. Jones was determined that when and if integration should come it would be by the unanimous vote of the board.

This division of opinion among members of the board, however, was not the chief impediment. There were limitations in the gifts of Paul Tulane, Mrs. Newcomb, the charter of the university, and Act 43 of 1884, which limited admission to white students. Competent legal advisors wrestled with the problem and came up with the conclusion there was nothing the board could do without court sanction which would legally permit the admission of Negroes. Thus the board was faced on one hand with its responsibilities as trustees to honor the conditions of the gifts made to them and on the other hand a necessity to take account of changing social and economic conditions that had developed since the time the gifts were made. There seems to be no doubt that the board felt that the restrictions were inhibiting factors in its responsibility to build a great university, but because of their legal position as trustees the members could not take the initiative in a court action which might serve to change the terms of the trust.

The board felt that it could do no more than announce a policy decision, which it did on April 12, 1961. This statement was as follows:

The Administrators of the Tulane Educational Fund met Wednesday and voted that Tulane University would admit qualified students regardless of race or color if it were legally permissible.

Times have changed since the university was founded. To meet these changes and the obligations to create and maintain a great university, it was decided to establish this policy. This course of action was taken in the knowledge that Tulane University must move ahead and assume its rightful place of leadership among America's outstanding universities.

But this policy statement did not alter the legal restrictions growing out of Mr. Tulane's act of donation and Mrs. Newcomb's will. Even as the statement was being issued, however, Mrs. Pearlie Hardin Elloie applied for admission to the School of Social Work and Miss Barbara Marie Guillory for admission to the Graduate School. Pursuant to the board's policy statement Dean Walter Kindelsperger of the School of Social Work advised

Mrs. Elloie that her application for admission had been found acceptable but that it was not legally possible for the university to admit Negroes. Simultaneously Dean Lumiansky of the Graduate School gave the same information to Miss Guillory.

On July 11, 1961, John P. Nelson, a local attorney, advised legal counsel for the board that he represented the two women and indicated that he expected to file suit. The board employed John Pat Little as special counsel and Wood Brown III as his assistant to represent the administrators. Thus both sides squared away from the litigation necessary to clear the atmosphere one way or another.

In September 1961, the suit was filed by Mr. Nelson in the court of Federal District Judge J. Skelly Wright. It was contended that because Tulane had been the recipient of property from the University of Louisiana, had been granted special tax exemptions, had the governor, the mayor of New Orleans, and the state superintendent of education as ex officio members of the board, and had received governmental money in support of the institution, the university was in effect a state agency amenable to the provisions of the Fourteenth Amendment of the United States Constitution which prohibits discrimination by state or federal agencies. The plaintiffs asked for a motion for summary judgment before any answer was filed by the university. Over the objections of the university in March 1962, Judge Wright rendered his opinion in which he stated in part that one might question whether any school or college could ever be so private as to escape the reach of the Fourteenth Amendment. Education, he said, was a matter of the greatest public interest and the private college often does the work of the state in place of the state. He held that Tulane was so impressed with public interest that it was amenable to the term of the Fourteenth Amendment and could not restrict its admission to whites only. And that appeared to be that.

Shortly thereafter Judge Wright was named as judge of the Circuit Court of Appeals for the District of Columbia and Judge Frank Ellis was appointed in his stead. The university applied for a stay of Judge Wright's decision and for a new hearing based on the facts in the case rather than on a summary judgment. The board was aware that Tulane would project an image throughout the country of a Southern university which was forced to integrate, to say nothing of being legally declared a state agency. Too, there were unresolved questions of fact which could only be brought out in a new hearing. In April 1962, Judge Ellis granted the motion for a stay and a new trial and his decision was upheld by the Circuit Court of Appeals for the Fifth Circuit. The new trial was held August 3–7, 1962, with Tulane presenting all phases of the matter which seemed to demand judicial determination. Counsel for the Tulane heirs were in court along with counsel for the Newcomb heirs. Mr. Harry Gamble intervened to represent all other persons who had made donations to the university. It short, Mr. Little gave attention to every possible aspect of the case which might be a subject for future litigation. On December 5, 1962, Judge Ellis rendered what for Tulane was a momentous decision. He stated that Tulane could voluntarily admit Negroes, since it would be unconstitutional to compel discrimination. He also held that Tulane was not so significantly impressed with a public interest as to be amendable to the Fourteenth Amendment, and that by the same token Tulane could not be compelled to admit Negroes.[7] One week later Tulane was voluntarily desegregated by the Tulane board.

This is an outline of the formal and legal steps taken to desegregate Tulane University, but the human side is significant and impressive. The first registration in which Negroes were involved was at the beginning of the spring semester, 1963. In order to insure that no unpleasant incident might take place, maximum security measures were taken, measures which it was soon demonstrated were not needed. Negroes who presented themselves for registration went by their counselors' tables, took their place in queues, paid their fees, and walked out of the gymnasium to the coffee shop where they joined white and nonwhite students from all over the world. There was not a raised eyebrow among the white students in the gymnasium where registration took place nor on the campus; nor has there been a single unpleasant incident over integration since that time. A Tulane student is a Tulane student. It has been that simple.

Monday, March 13, 1963, brought shocking news to New Orleans and the university. Joseph M. Jones and his wife had died as a result of a disastrous fire which swept their handsome home in suburban Metairie. The exact cause of the fire has never been determined, but it apparently started in the attic somewhere near 1 o'clock in the morning and swept downward into the bedroom area on the second floor. Mrs. Jones was asphyxiated and Mr. Jones was taken in critical condition to a nearby hospital where he died at 5:50 A.M.

On street corners, in clubs, in bars and restaurants little clumps of men, leaders of the community, gathered with sad faces and hushed voices. "Joe Jones is dead," they mumbled and almost in disbelief shook their collective heads. This fifty-nine-year-old, casually dressed man with a bulldog face and hesitant voice had for years been in a position at the center of civic and social leadership in New Orleans. The sociologist undoubtedly would characterize him as being near the top of the power structure, which he was, but he was never pretentious nor stuffy. "With the death of Joe

---

[7] The full text of the decisions in the case of *Guillory* v. *The Administrators of the Tulane Educational Fund* may be found in 203 Fed. Supp. 855 and in 212 Fed. Supp. 674.

Jones," his successor as president of the Board of Administrators remarked to the author, "an era in the life of Tulane University ended."

To succeed Mr. Jones the board chose modest, soft-spoken Darwin Schriever Fenner, a partner in the investment firm of Merrill Lynch, Pierce, Fenner and Smith. Mr. Fenner worked himself up from the bottom to a partnership, displaying along the way, a contemporary said of him, the same agility and footwork he possessed as a welterweight boxer on the Tulane team of the late twenties. In his maturity he has come to take a prominent and exacting part in civic affairs not only in New Orleans but in the entire state; and for his activities he has received numerous trophies and testimonials from civic organizations.[8] Mr. Fenner needed no warm-up period for his job, for he had been acquainted with Tulane's problems since 1953, when he was elected to the board. Finance, fund raising, and investments, of course, have taken much of Mr. Fenner's time, but there is no phase of the university's activities, from the dilemma of undergraduate-graduate education to intercollegiate sports, which has not had his interest.

Previous chapters have shown that Tulane has had programs for training elementary and secondary teachers almost from the beginning. These programs have carried different titles through the years—Teacher's College, Courses for Teachers, Extension Division, and Division for Teachers. In 1942 the Division for Teachers and the evening division of the School of Business Administration were merged into University College, and from this date for the next fifteen years Tulane had a tripodic type of teacher education. The College of Arts and Sciences had a small education department and a curriculum; Newcomb College had a small education department with a curriculum different from that in Arts and Sciences; and University College had a curriculum different from either of the other two. On top of this there was no one person to coordinate the teacher education program.

In 1956 President Harris set up a committee of deans to deal with the problem, and this group brought to the campus Dr. George Barton, a philosopher of education from the staff of the Center for the Study of Liberal Education for Adults in Chicago. Dr. Barton was a firm believer in teacher education, with deep roots in the liberal arts; and thus his theories found great favor with the liberal arts faculties. They looked with disfavor on the "educationists" and with favor on Barton, but they could not agree on what a liberal education for teachers should be. There were faculty groups

---

[8] New members of the board elected since 1959 are: Richard West Freeman (1959), Gerald Louis Andrus (1960), Jacob S. Landry (1960), Edgar B. Stern, Jr. (1960), Arthur L. Jung, Jr. (1961), Sam Israel, Jr. (1962), and Harry B. Kelleher (1963).

and splinter groups; but they had two things in common: an adamant belief in the liberal education of teachers and an almost unreasoning fear that a school of education would be established. Perhaps this fear of a school of education was the chief inhibiting factor in the implementation of Dean Lumiansky's ideas. He himself did not see the necessity for centralized administrative control of teacher education.

This was the situation when Dr. Longenecker became president. Almost immediately he and the Board of Administrators took a firm position on teacher education and began to urge the committee of deans to get something done. Morever the Division of Certification of the State Department of Education was making it clear that Tulane's teacher education program was in danger of losing accreditation if the university could not put its house in order.

Under the prodding of the president the committee came up with an administrative compromise, a Center for Teacher Education. The center was neither a school of education nor merely a university-wide department. It had some autonomy, its own budget, a director, a small professional faculty and, it hoped, the full cooperation of representatives from the liberal arts faculties—known as "associates." As this change was being made Dr. Barton transferred full time to the Department of Philosophy, and the committee, in September 1962, brought in Dr. Thomas E. Jordan from St. Louis University as director of the center. But Dr. Jordan was unable to reconcile the warring factions, and in August 1963 he resigned. The committee then turned to Dr. Gaither McConnell, head of the department of education at Newcomb. She became acting director of the center in September 1963 and has been able to make a viable organization of it. It has added to its faculty, adopted uniform liberal arts curricula, and provided centralized administrative machinery and responsibility for teacher education. In April 1964, it received approval from the State Department of Education, and thus any threat of disaccreditation was removed. Meantime the training of college teachers in the Graduate School goes on.

On January 21, 1965, the Board of Administrators made what was for many people a dramatic announcement: *"Tulane University will withdraw from the Southeastern Conference in June, 1966,* in order to broaden its football schedule making patterns."

In a clarifying statement President Longenecker stated that the change in policy was made only after much consideration and with reluctance but "Tulane University has changed in the past two decades from an institution drawing its students mostly from this area to one attracting students from all states of the nation. The purposes of the University, for this reason, will be better served by scheduling intersectional games. We also wish to have freedom to design schedules that will improve our competitive position and avoid the overload situation Tulane has experienced in recent years." The president indicated Tulane would play some Southeastern Conference teams, but added the names of Notre Dame, Stanford, Illinois, Pittsburgh, Miami (Fla.), and others.

Behind this decision of the board lie fourteen years of uncertainty and disputation over what the university's athletic course should be. There were strong factions pulling in different directions. There were alumni, sports writers, and members of the public who looked back to what they remembered as Tulane's days of glory on the football field. There were some faculty members who wanted it abolished, some who merely wanted to contain it, and perhaps a few who would take the glory road.

After the end of the Frnka period (1951) and the abandonment of the physical education degree program Tulane's football fortunes hit new lows. Raymond "Bear" Wolf tried his hand at the coaching job for two years and gave it up. Anton "Andy" Pilney succeeded Wolf and remained for eight years, and he in turn was succeeded by Tommy O'Boyle in 1962. But Tulane teams were lacking in depth and were no match for other more powerful Southeastern Conference teams. It became almost a jest to speculate on which team, Vanderbilt or Tulane, would end the season in the Conference cellar.

There are, of course, some basic reasons for Tulane's hapless situation. Although probably an oversimplification one faculty member summed it up rather neatly: "You can't have Ivy League academic ideals and successful Southeastern Conference football. The two are incompatible."

More specifically the problem breaks down into at least three facets: (1) Unless a student athlete possesses a great deal more than physical prowess his chances of academic survival are slim. There are no easy programs for athletes. (2) This factor limits recruitment especially when confined to the Southern region (3) Rigidity of scheduling in the Southeastern Conferences (at least six games each season must be against Conference opponents) pits Tulane against much more powerful teams week after week with no breathers. The sheer physical beating which team members take is devastating.

Both coach Tommy O'Boyle and Athletic Director Dr. Rix N. Yard are well aware of the situation and are most cooperative with the efforts being made to put football into proper perspective in the academic scene. A more selective plan of recruitment has been put into practice with the result that academic mortality for athletes has been greatly reduced. A new spirit of optimism seems to pervade the players, and during the 1964 football season Tulane actually won three games, defeating Duke, Vanderbilt, and Virginia Military Institute. The full effects of the withdrawal from the Conference, of course, will not be known for several years.

Of far greater importance, however, is the matter of balance between undergraduate and graduate education. This problem, of course, is not unique nor does Tulane claim to have solved it. Most of the forty-one of Tulane's fellow members of the Association of American Universities are to a greater or lesser degree encountering their own dilemmas, to say nothing of the hundreds of universities and colleges not in this organization. Every year increasing thousands of young men and women apply and are admitted to already overcrowded ivy halls. "How are these people to be taught?" is the harassed cry of deans, faculties, and presidents. And at precisely the same period of time pressures for research and graduate-level education have become so great the universities can curtail them only at their own peril and the peril of society. Business, industry, government, and the universities themselves are demanding the well-trained specialist, preferably with the Ph.D. degree.

For the affluent university (and there possibly are a few) the answer is a simple one: expand both the undergraduate and the graduate programs and thus meet society's needs. For the less affluent such as Tulane the answer is more difficult.

In seeking a solution Tulane has resorted to two basic assumptions which apply alike to undergraduate and graduate education: (1) It cannot even approach anything resembling mass education. Thus it must be selective in its admission of students and in its curricula and programs. (2) It should use its resources for educational programs that are calculated to produce a multiplying effect. That is to say, if Tulane produces a well-qualified Ph.D. who becomes a teacher in a Southern college or university and teaches two hundred students a year then the multiplying effects are enormous. Or if a doctor takes a graduate degree in public health or tropical medicine he may well influence the well being of an entire community or region.

With its thirty-five hundred undergraduate students (exclusive of Medicine and University College) Tulane has only about 6 per cent of the total undergraduate enrollment in the state of Louisiana, a potent argument that a quantity job is out of the question. Tulane must, then, as it has for many years, follow its twofold policy of almost annually raising its entrance requirements, hoping thereby to select potential "multipliers" and offering special inducements and programs for the superior student. The honors programs and the Scholars and Fellows plan are examples. The junior year abroad is an added inducement for the excellent student. This is not to say, of course, that Tulane completely neglects the "average" student. It merely means that if Tulane is to justify its being and make the best use of its resources it must constantly be engaged in the search for excellence.

Graduate education follows a general philosophy similar to that just mentioned. Again there is a limited enrollment and standards devised to challenge the superior student. Actually there are several divisions of graduate education. The general graduate school, concerned largely with work in the sciences, humanities, engineering and social studies had an enrollment in 1964–1965 of 1,476 students; Medicine had 390; Social Work (exclusively graduate) enrolled 270; Business Administration, which is phasing out its undergraduate program and will be completely graduate by 1968, had 157; Law had 15.[9]

Any adequate qualitative evaluation of the graduate programs is impossible within the space limitations of this chapter. Cognizance of its own inadequacies, however, is the beginning point of strength; and of its deficiencies the university is acutely aware. Tulane gets, on the whole, good graduate students, but it is unable to compete for the best in the country largely because of limited financial resources for fellowships and grants. It has been ranked twenty-fourth among the top forty-five universities in the country in the humanities and social studies but fell below the 45th place in the sciences. The faculty does a great amount of research and writing, yet it can claim few scholars of large national repute. But in spite of this the university constantly faces the threat of losing some of its best scholars because of higher salaries and better facilities elsewhere. University research grants are limited, but foundation and government research projects are not in short supply. An encouraging number of National Defense Education Act fellowships are allocated to Tulane, but too large a number of excellent Southern students go to graduate schools outside the South. Tulane is completely desegregated, but the number of Negro students who meet admission standards, graduate or undergraduate, is discouragingly small.

One might pursue such an evaluation almost indefinitely. Perhaps it is a valid general summary that Tulane has good undergraduate and graduate programs with a high potential for excellence. From this observation perhaps the medical school should be excluded for it has, in spite of financial limitations, achieved a high degree of excellence.

What the casual visitor ordinarily does not see is the fact that Tulane now has four campuses: There is the main uptown campus with its sparkling new buildings; the downtown medical school with its towering monolithic structure and hotel now being refurbished as a residence hall; the Primate Center; and the Riverside Research Laboratories. Tulane also has a major operation overseas at Cali, Columbia, South America, where its International Center for Medical Research and Training is located. The Delta Regional Primate Center was established in 1962 with support by the National Institutes of Health on a beautiful 500-acre tract near Covington,

---

[9] Total enrollment for 1964–1965 is as follows: Full-time students in all categories, 7,401; University College (parttime credit students), 2,575; University College (noncredit, seminars), 1,311; *total*: 11,287. This does not include the hundreds of individuals who have attended short courses, institutes, workshops, etc.

Louisiana, across Lake Pontchartrain north of New Orleans. The center is under the administration of Tulane with several universities in the region associated in the research programs. Over a million dollars per year are spent in support of this modern campus of laboratories, offices, and lecture rooms where research in the areas of infectious diseases; chronic metabolic and degenerative diseases; genetic, developmental, and embryological diseases; behavioral sciences; and environmental health. Work is done primarily with chimpanzees, monkeys, and other primates.

The campus for the Riverside Research Laboratories is in the process of development. This center for advanced graduate study and research is located on some 400 acres of land immediately across the Mississippi River from downtown New Orleans. It came to the university in 1963 as a federal government gift through the Department of Health, Education, and Welfare. Tulane must develop and maintain this former ammunition depot with its bunkers, warehouses, and miscellaneous smaller buildings; and at the present time is spending half a million dollars cutting roads, installing utilities, and driving out snakes. Eventually it will provide specialized research facilities for many of the disciplines, especially biology and engineering.

Returning alumni, too, discover that many familiar faces of deans and professors are missing. Since 1960 Tulane has lost through death, retirement, or resignation thirty-eight professors and five deans. Twelve professors retired, sixteen (including part-time professors in Law and Medicine) resigned, and death took ten. The professorial loss is about par for the five-year period in an institution the size of Tulane, but the turnover in deans is a bit on the high side.

The polite and dignified academic game of musical chairs among the deans began with the resignation in 1960 of Dean Paul Grambsch of the School of Business Administration, who accepted the deanship of the University of Minnesota School of Business Administration. Dr. Howard Schaller, professor of economics, took his place but by agreement for a limited time only. In 1963 he resumed his position as professor of economics and shortly thereafter joined the faculty of the Indiana University School of Business Administration. Charles Jackson Grayson of the business faculty was named to succeed Schaller, but he had a year's leave coming up so Clinton A. Phillips acted as dean for a period of one year.

William Ray Forrester decided in 1963 to accept the deanship of the Cornell University School of Law and was succeeded by Cecil Morgan, former judge and corporation lawyer; and still the changes went on. In this same year of 1963, Robert M. Lumiansky resigned as dean and provost to accept a position as professor of English at Duke University. His job was broken down into its component parts with Maxwell E. Lapham, M.D., dean of the medical school becoming provost and Charles C. Sprague,

M.D., of the medical school faculty succeeding him. The deanship of the Graduate School went to John L. Snell, professor of history in the university.

In 1964 Alvin Lyons, director of development, resigned to return to his company, whose business is fund raising. In a reorganization plan Vice-President Fred R. Cagle, formerly in charge of research projects and planning, had added to his office university development, public relations, planning, and related areas of the university's activities. Under the new plan Provost Lapham concerns himself with academic affairs and relations with the deans while Dr. Cagle administers the phases just indicated.

In the College of Arts and Sciences Dean William W. Peery died April 30, 1964. The next month Joseph E. Gordon, former assistant dean of University College, associate director of admissions, and director of the Scholars and Fellows program was named acting dean. In October of 1964, he was made dean.

Chronic crisis has been Tulane's lot through its history, and there is every indication that crises will become more frequent and more acute as time goes on. This is inevitable in a socially conscious institution located in a changing and dynamic South. Tulane has chosen not to attempt a detailed blueprint of its future but rather to lay down certain broad assumptions as guide lines which point the way toward its future:

1. *Tulane owes a special obligation to the area in which it is located.* In the lower South quantitative educational requirements doubtless will be reasonably well met by public colleges and universities. The pressing need not being adequately filled is for education of high quality, offered by strong faculties that are enabled to develop their scholarship and to impart it to students who share the goal of free inquiry. All this can be done, the university feels, without excessive parochialism and without interfering with its national and international goals.

2. *Tulane's immediate region will continue for some time to lag economically in relation to the rest of the country.* This time lag can be shortened by the development of quality in higher education. A special problem for the South in its efforts to attain economic and educational parity with the rest of the country is to provide adequate opportunities for Negroes. It is especially important that they be encouraged and given every opportunity to develop competence, especially for careers in teaching and research.

3. *Despite the absolute and relative growth of graduate education in the South during recent years, an increasing proportion of superior students of the region are going elsewhere for advanced study.*

4. *Tulane should use its resources for educational programs that are calculated to produce a multiplying effect.*

5. *Tulane will be called upon for increasing involvement in international affairs.* The strength Tulane has developed in its Latin-American relationships has led to a succession of expectations for (a) qualified consultants to advise governments, foundations and private business organizations, (b) willing and available faculty members for service on governmental missions or in teaching assignments abroad, (c) library service in support of less-developed institutions, and (d) assistance in developing whole institutions abroad.

6. *Cooperation among institutions is desirable in defining and sharing the educational tasks of the area.*

7. *Effectiveness in instruction is dependent upon the competence, motivation, and freedom of the faculty.*

8. *Although Tulane has a selective admissions policy, a significant range of differences in ability is likely to persist in the undergraduate student body through at least the decade 1965–1975.*

9. *The instructional objective of Tulane's undergraduate programs is to help students develop into enlightened, fully participating citizens of their communities, their countries, and their times.*

10. *Tulane must improve its programs for adults, including those who receive adequate or even superior education in regular college or university curricula.* Continuing adult education, of growing importance in modern life, is an increasing responsibility of urban universities.

11. *Tulane must exploit new educational techniques to increase the efficiency of instruction.* Experimentation with television and programed learning is essential if a faculty of limited size is to be utilized to its best advantage.

12. *Research and university teaching are not only compatible and complementary activities but are two aspects of the same function.*

13. *Increasing government support of technology and the natural sciences imposes additional financial burdens on the university that restrict the availability of funds to support scholarship in the humanities and the arts.* This statement gives emphasis to the fact that the university must give more adequate support to humanities scholarships.

14. *Tulane faces an increasing pressure to produce information and knowledge, a pressure by the offer of research support by organizations external to the university.* Tulane views the availability of these funds as a challenge, but at the same time realizes that overemphasis in this direction may frustrate the basic functions of a university.

15. *Tulane desires to become a center of excellence in research and graduate training. Such excellence cannot be attained unless the university can provide opportunities for interdisciplinary attacks on major problems.*

16. *The exponential growth in publication will not level off perceptibly.*

But new systems will aid the university in furnishing materials required by its scholars. Tulane plans to utilize any system that promises to provide improved information flow. But until such systems are operative, emphasis must still be placed on the improvement of traditional library services and resources.

APPENDIXES

Appendix I

CHARTER

ADOPTED JUNE 25TH, 1882, AND AS AMENDED UP TO JULY 8TH, 1955.

United States of America
State of Louisiana
City of New Orleans

Be it known, that on this twenty-ninth day of the month of May, in the year of our Lord one thousand eight hundred and eighty-two, and of the independence of the United States of America the one hundred and sixth,

Before me, Charles G. Andry, a Notary Public, duly commissioned and sworn, in this city and the Parish of Orleans, State of Louisiana, therein residing, and in the presence of the witnesses hereinafter named and undersigned.

Personally came and appeared, the several persons whose names are hereunto subscribed, who declared, that availing themselves of the provisions of the statutes of this State relative to the organization of corporations for literary, scientific, religious and charitable purposes, they do by these presents organize themselves into a body politic and corporate, with the view of carrying out the wishes, intentions and suggestions of Paul Tulane, Esq., formerly of the said city of New Orleans, and now residing in Princeton, in the State of New Jersey, as the same are expressed and set forth in a letter to them, the present appearers, by the said Paul Tulane, dated the second day of May, 1882, the original of which letter is hereunto annexed, and is transcribed herein for reference and explanation, and is in the following words, to wit:

Princeton, May 2, 1882

To Messrs. Randall L. Gibson, Chas. E. Fenner, James McConnell, T. G. Richardson, M.D., Edward White, E. H. Farrar, P. N. Strong, B. M. Palmer, D.D., Hugh Miller Thompson, D.D., Chas. A. Whitney, Sam'l Kennedy, Walter Stauffer, Cartwright Eustis, Henry Ginder, John T. Hardie, R. M. Walmsley, and Wm. O. Rogers:

GENTLEMEN—A resident of New Orleans for many years of my active life, having formed many friendships and associations dear to me, and deeply sympathizing with its people in whatever misfortune or disasters may have befallen them, as well as being sincerely desirous of contributing to their moral and intellectual welfare, I do hereby express to you my intention to donate to you by an act of donation *intervivos,* all the real estate I own and

301

I am possessed of in the said city of New Orleans, State of Louisiana, for the promotion and encouragement of intellectual, moral and industrial education among the white young persons in the city of New Orleans, State of Louisiana, and for the advancement of learning and letters, the arts and sciences therein, my intention being that the benefits shall be applied and expended in the city of New Orleans.

By the term education, I mean to foster such a course of intellectual development as shall be useful and of solid worth, and not be merely ornamental or superficial. I mean you should adopt the course which, as wise and good men, would commend itself to you as being conducive to immediate practical benefit, rather than theoretical possible advantage. I wish you to establish or foster institutions of a higher grade of learning where the young persons to be benefitted shall, upon due examination, be found competent and qualified for admission, both by age and previous training, to receive the benefits of a more advanced degree of educational culture.

Intellectual advancement should be unfettered by sectarianism, but the profound reverence I entertain for the Holy Scriptures leads me to express here the hope, that the educational development intended by this gift, should never antagonize, but be in harmony with the great fundamental principles of Christian truth contained in them.

I express to you now my formal intentions in order to suggest to you the advisability, should you determine to aid me in my purposes, that you should take such steps as may be necessary under the laws of Louisiana to enable you to accept the donations when made, thus giving me the assurance that my purpose, when executed, will be carried out with fidelity, and be rich in bountiful results.

The fact that property donated for educational purposes is at this time liable to taxation in the State of Louisiana, has occasioned me much embarrassment, as I should like to feel that the citizens of that State, who are to be the beneficiaries of this donation, should enjoy its advantages to the full measure of the value of the property donated. There are other States whose laws do not, by taxation, repel such gifts in aid of education, whose wise example, I am assured, will be followed by the State of Louisiana and the city of New Orleans in such instance; and I earnestly urge that you make immediate effort to secure the exemption of this property from taxation, and be constant in so doing until your efforts are successful.

The character of the property donated is to remain unchanged. It cannot be mortgaged, and it cannot be sold nor incumbered in any way, except at the end of not less than fifty years, as hereinafter stated. Mortgaging it or selling it, and the investment of the proceeds in stocks, bonds or other securities, might and probably would lead to disaster, owing to the uncertain and fluctuating nature of the value of securities of every description. On the other hand, the real estate, the title to which I intended to donate to you, is well located, and can not fail to increase in value as the city shall become prosperous.

You must keep the property well insured in solvent offices and in good repairs, so that the best rental possible may be realized.

The plans and details of any organization, corporate or otherwise, must of necessity be left to your own judgment; but I desire to communicate to you my wishes in such manner as to enable you more fully to enter into the motives which impel me, thereby enabling you completely to enter into my thoughts and purposes.

Of course, whatever I may determine to donate to you, should you conclude to organize, will be (whilst leaving you the absolute owners of the property) with the object of enabling you, in your discretion, to use the revenues for the purpose already by me mentioned.

I suggest and recommend—1. That in your organization, whatever form it may assume, that my friend, Gen. Randall Lee Gibson, be your chairman or president, and that Judge Chas. E. Fenner and James McConnell may be vice presidents or vice chairmen. 2. That you provide for the filling of any vacancies in your number by death, resignation or otherwise, by election. 3. That whilst my desire is that you shall continue my purpose for more than fifty years, nevertheless I would consider it no violation of these wishes should you, when organized, determine, after fifty years, no longer to perform the duties incident to the ownership of this property which I may donate, and the income of which, I have expressed the desire, that you administer, as aforesaid; in that event, I suggest that you distribute the property, or the proceeds from the sale thereof, among such educational or literary institutions, or for such educational purposes as you may determine, in the city of New Orleans, as are contemplated by this donation. 4. In order that there shall be no doubt in regard to my intentions, I will say it is not my desire to bind you to distribute the incomes or benefits of the fund or property to any particular school, college or institution of learning, or to create any claim on the part of any school, college or institution of learning, to any distributive share; nor do I design to subject you collectively or individually to any responsibility to those intended to be benefitted, or to any individual responsibility of any sort for the management of the property and fund, which may be by me donated.

I have entire confidence that you will carry out with wisdom, equity and fidelity my expressed suggestions. It would be personally agreeable to me if you would retain the services of Mr. P. N. Strong, of New Orleans.

In order to prevent misapprehension, I desire to say you should, of course, make such disbursement as you may deem it fair to expend in the employment of any necessary agent or otherwise, and especially to keep the property well insured, and in a proper state of repair.

With devout gratitude to our Heavenly Father for enabling us to perform these plans, and invoking His divine blessing upon you and your counsels, and upon the good work proposed among the present and future generations of our beloved Crescent City.

I remain, with great respect,

Your friend and humble servant,

PAUL TULANE.

ARTICLE I

And the said appearers further declared that the corporation of which the organization is contemplated by this act shall be known and designated as "the Administrators of the Tulane Educational Fund." Its domicile is hereby fixed in the City of New Orleans, Parish of Orleans, State of Louisiana, and it shall exist and continue during ninety-nine years from the date hereof.

ARTICLE II

The corporate powers of this corporation shall be exercised by the following named incorporators, who shall constitute a perpetual Board of Administrators, to-wit:—Randall Lee Gibson, Charles Erasmus Fenner, James McConnell, Tobias Gibson Richardson, M.D., Edward Douglass White, Edgar Howard Farrar, Paschal Neilson Strong, Benjamin M. Palmer, D.D., Hugh Miller Thompson, D.D., Charles Augustus Whitney, Samuel Horton Kennedy, Walter Robinson Stauffer, Cartwright Eustis, Henry Ginder, John Timmons Hardie, Robert Miller Walmsley, William Oscar Rogers. In case of the death or resignation of any of the seventeen administrators above named, the vacancies which shall thereby be created will be filled by such other persons as may be chosen or elected by a majority of the remaining administrators at any regular or special meeting after the said vacancy shall have occurred; provided, that due notice of such election shall be given in writing to the said remaining administrators.

ARTICLE III

The objects, purposes and powers of this corporation are hereby declared to be: To hold property, both real and personal, by purchase or by donation, for educational purposes, and to use and dispose of the same upon the terms and conditions upon which the said property is or may be donated or acquired.

ARTICLE IV

The officers of the corporation shall be a Chairman of the Board, a President, three Vice Presidents, a Treasurer and a Secretary, both of which last named offices may, in the discretion of the Board, be filled by one person. The Chairman of the Board, the President and the Vice Presidents shall have such administrative powers as shall be determined by the Board, and as specified in the By-Laws to be adopted, and shall exercise their functions during life or until they shall have resigned. In case of death or resignation of any one of the said officers the vacancy which may occur shall be filled by an election to be held thirty (30) days after due written notice shall have been given to the members of the corporation. The Treasurer and Secretary shall be elected by the members of the corporation, in such manner as may hereafter be specified by its By-Laws.

The President is hereby declared to be Randall Lee Gibson, Judge Charles E. Fenner shall be the First Vice President, and James McConnell, Esquire, the Second Vice-President. The President and Vice Presidents shall have such administrative powers as shall be determined by the Board and specified in the By-Laws, to be adopted, and shall exercise their functions during life, or until they shall have resigned. In case of death or resignation of any one of the said officers, the vacancy which may occur shall be filled by an election, to be held thirty days after due written notice shall be given to the members of the corporation. The Treasurer and Secretary shall be elected by the members of the corporation, in such manner as may hereafter be specified by its By-Laws.

ARTICLE V

Citations and other legal process shall be served on the President or in his absence on either of the Vice Presidents.

ARTICLE VI

A general meeting of the administrators will be held at least once a year, on the second Tuesday in May.

The rules and regulations for the conduct and management of the business of the corporation, and the administration of its property, shall be provided for by By-Laws, to be adopted by a meeting of the incorporators or administrators, called for that purpose, within sixty days from the date hereof; and said By-Laws shall be subject to amendment at any general meeting of the corporation by a majority of the members of the corporation.

Thus done and passed in my office, in the City of New Orleans aforesaid, on the day, month, and year first above written, in the presence of Messrs. Edgar Grima and George Grima, competent witnesses, both of this city, who hereunto sign their names with the said appearers and me, the said Notary, after due reading of the whole.

The original is signed: Randall Lee Gibson, Chas. E. Fenner, James McConnell, Tobias G. Richardson, E. D. White, Edgar Howard Farrar, Paschal Neilson Strong, Hugh Miller Thompson, Samuel H. Kennedy, Cartwright Eustis, Henry Ginder, William O. Rogers, B. M. Palmer, Walter R. Stauffer, Chas. A. Whitney, John T. Hardie, R. M. Walmsley, Edgar Grima, George Grima, Charles G. Andry, Notary Public.

Having examined the foregoing Act of Incorporation, I am of the opinion that the purposes and objects of the same, as specified therein, are legal, and that none of the provisions therein contained are contrary to law. I therefore approve the same.

JOSHUA G. BAKER
Asst. Dist. Attorney, Parish of Orleans.

New Orleans, June 12th, 1882.

I, the undersigned, Recorder of Mortgages in and for the Parish of Orleans, State of Louisiana, do hereby certify that the above and foregoing Act of Incorporation of the "Administrators of the Tulane Educational Fund" was this day duly recorded in my office, in Book 226, Folio 122.

(Signed)   GEO. GUINAULT, *Deputy*

New Orleans, June 12th, 1882.

A true copy of the original, extant and of record in my office.

CHAS. G. ANDRY
Notary Public.

Appendix II

ACT NO. 43
OF THE GENERAL ASSEMBLY, SESSION OF 1884,
establishing
THE TULANE UNIVERSITY OF LOUISIANA
AN ACT

To foster, maintain and develop the University of Louisiana, to that end to make the Board of Administrators of the Tulane Education Fund, as presently constituted, with the addition of the Governor, Superintendent of Public Education, and Mayor of the city of New Orleans, as ex-officio members thereof, the Administrators of the University of Lousiana, which shall hereafter be known as the "Tulane University of Louisiana"; to invest said Tulane Board with all the powers, privileges, franchises and immunities now vested in the Board of Administrators of the University of Louisiana; and with such other powers as may be necessary or pertinent to develop, control, foster and maintain it as a great university in the city of New Orleans. To give to the Administrators of the Tulane Educational Fund the control, management and use of all of the property of the University of Louisiana, in the city of New Orleans, for the purposes aforesaid: To exempt, in consequence of the terms of this act and the dedication of its revenues to the purposes stated in this act, all the property, real and personal, present and future, of the said Board of Administrators of the Tulane Educational Fund, from all taxation, whether State, parochial or municipal: To make a contract, irrevocable and conclusive, between the State and Administrators of the Tulane Educational Fund, covering the provisions of this act: To enable the said Board of Administrators of the "Tulane Education Fund" to decline to accept the provisions of this act, unless the same, in all its provisions, be ratified and approved by a constitutional amendment, to be submitted at the next general election: To give said Board of Administrators of the "Tulane Education Fund," upon the adoption of the said constitutional amendment, not only the full powers of administration over the University of Louisiana conferred by this act, but also the power to create, develop and maintain a great University in the city of New Orleans, which University so to be created shall perpetually be under their full and complete control: To enable said Board, should they act under the provisions of this act, pending the submission of the said constitutional amendment, to withdraw and relieve themselves from all the effects of said action should said proposed con-

306

stitutional amendment be rejected, and to provide for the submission of a constitutional amendment ratifying the provisions of this act to the people of the State at the next general election;

WHEREAS, Paul Tulane, Esq., formerly a resident of this State, and now of Princeton, New Jersey, with the beneficent purpose of fostering higher education in this State, did, in May, 1882, express to certain citizens of this State his intention to donate for such purposes valuable real estate to him belonging, situated in the City of New Orleans; and,

WHEREAS, The citizens to whom the intention of Paul Tulane, Esq., were expressed, did, by act, before Charles G. Andry, a notary public in the city of New Orleans, organize themselves into a corporation, under the name of the "Administrators of the Tulane Education Fund," with the objects and purposes specified in said act of incorporation; and,

WHEREAS, Since the formation of said corporation, Paul Tulane, Esq., in the execution of his previously expressed intentions, has donated to said Administrators of the "Tulane Education Fund" nearly one million dollars, the revenues whereof are to be used for the promotion and encouragement of intellectual, moral and industrial education, and has expressed his intention to largely increase said donation should this act be adopted; and,

WHEREAS, The said Board of Administrators of the "Tulane Education Fund," in order to make their work fruitful in results, have expressed their desire to take charge of the University of Louisiana, in the city of New Orleans, and to devote the revenues of the property now owned, or hereafter to be owned, by said Board, to its expansion and development; and upon the adoption of a constitutional amendment to that end, to apply all the revenues of property now owned, or hereafter to be acquired by them, to the creation and development in the city of New Orleans of a great University, whereby the blessings of higher education, intellectual, moral and industrial, may be given to the youth of the State; and,

WHEREAS, Under the terms of this action, as proposed by said Board, the property of said Board, and the revenues thereof, will not be used for the purpose of private or corporate income or profit, but will be exclusively dedicated to school purposes, and to the service of the State in maintaining and developing the University of Louisiana, an institution recognized in the Constitution, therefore entitling the said property of said Board to exemption from all taxation, both State, parochial and municipal; therefore,

BE *it enacted by the General Assembly of the State of Louisiana,*

Section 1. That the Board of Administrators of the University of Louisiana shall hereafter, instead of the Board appointed as provided by section thirteen hundred and fifty-one (1351) of the Revised Statutes, consist of the seventeen administrators of the "Tulane Education Fund," with power, perpetually, to fill any vacancy in their own number; *provided* that the said Board shall, on the passage of this statute, recognize by formal notarial act the Governor of the State, the Superintendent of Public Education and the Mayor of the City of New Orleans, as *ex-officio* members of said Board.

Section 2. *Be it further enacted, etc.,* That the Board of Administrators of the "Tulane Education Fund," as administrators of the University of

Louisiana shall have all the rights, powers, privileges, franchises and immunities, now vested in the Board of Administrators of the University of Louisiana by existing laws. That they shall further have full direction, control and administration of the University of Louisiana, now established in the city of New Orleans, in all its departments as also of all the property belonging to the State of Louisiana, and now dedicated to or used by the University of Louisiana as well as of all property controlled or used by the said University of Louisiana and for the purposes thereof, and Board of Administration of the University of Louisiana are hereby empowered and directed to turn over to the Board of Administrators of the "Tulane Education Fund" all the property rights, books, papers and archives now under their administration or control; *provided,* that if the custody of the State Library should be transferred to the Tulane University of Louisiana, as herein established by the consolidation of the University of Louisiana at New Orleans with the Board of Administrators of the "Tulane Education Fund," as herein provided for, through the University of Louisiana, at New Orleans, as it now exists, or otherwise, it shall be on the express condition and agreement that the State of Louisiana, may resume the custody and control of said State Library, whenever, it may be deemed advisable; *and provided further,* that after the establishment of the "Tulane University of Louisiana," as herein provided for, and after the transfer of the custody of the State Library, thereto, as aforesaid, if the custody thereof shall be transferred to the "Tulane University of Louisiana," as herein established, then and in that event, the State of Louisiana shall be relieved of and released from all obligations to pay the salary or compensation of the State Librarian or his assistants as is now or may hereafter be fixed by law, during the period the said State Library may remain in the custody of said "Tulane University of Louisiana"; but that during said period the salary or compensation of said State Librarian shall be paid by the "Tulane University of Louisiana." An inventory shall be made of all property, movable and immovable, belonging to the University of Louisiana, and transferred by this act to the control and administration of the Administrators of the Tulane Education Fund, by two appraisers to be appointed for that purpose by the Governor of the State and sworn, which appraisement shall be filed in the office of the Secretary of the State, as evidencing the description and appraised value of the property so transferred, and also in order that the liability of the said Administrators of the Tulane Education Fund may not be extended, in any contingency; *provided further,* that the property so transferred, may not be sold or disposed of, except under Legislative sanction; *provided further,* that if the "Tulane University of Louisiana," as herein established, should cease to use the property, and exercise the privileges, franchises and immunities, now under the control of administration of, and enjoyed by the University of Louisiana, as now constituted and transferred by this act, for the exclusive purpose intended by this act, then and in that event the State of Louisiana shall have the right to resume the custody, control and administration of said property, and the exercise of said privileges, franchises and immunities.

Sec. 3. *Be it further enacted, etc.,* That the said Board of Administrators of the "Tulane Education Fund" shall perpetually as Administrators of the University of Louisiana, as above provided, have full and complete control of all the property and rights, and now vested in the University of Louisiana. The said Board shall have the powers above provided in addition to those conferred by its charter, by act passed before Chas. G. Andry, Notary Public, in the city of New Orleans, on the 29th day of May, Anno Domini 1882, including the power to hold and own all real and personal property, now to said Board belonging, or hereafter to be by it acquired, during its corporate existence, for the purposes and objects of its being, or the revenues whereof are to be solely applicable to such purposes.

Sec. 4. *Be it further enacted, etc.,* That in honor of Paul Tulane and in recognition of his beneficent gifts and of their dedication to the purposes expressed in this act, the name of the University of Louisiana be, and the same is hereby changed to that of the "Tulane University of Louisiana," under which name it shall possess all the powers, privileges, immunities and franchises, now vested in said University of Louisiana, as well as such powers as may flow from this act or may be vested in said Board, under the terms of this act, from the adoption of the Constitutional Amendment hereafter referred to. The purpose of this act, being, to invest the Board of Administrators of the "Tulane Education Fund" with all the rights now vested in the University of Louisiana; to give said Board moreover complete control of said University in all its departments, and in every respect, with all the powers necessary or incidental to the exercise of said control. To enable said Board, besides the powers designated by this act, to have irrevocably upon the adoption of said Constitutional Amendment, full power with the rights hereby conferred, to create and develop a great University in the city of New Orleans, to be named as aforesaid. Said University to be established by the said Board of Administrators of the "Tulane Education Fund," to be dedicated to the intellectual, moral and industrial education of the youth of the State, in accordance with the Charter of said Board of Administrators of the "Tulane Education Fund."

Sec. 5. *Be it further enacted, etc.,* That in consideration of the agreement of said Board to develop and maintain the University of Louisiana, and thereby dedicate its revenues not to purposes of private or corporate income or profit, but to the public purposes of developing and maintaining the University of Louisiana, all the property of the said Board, present and future, be and the same is hereby recognized as exempt from all taxation, State, parochial and municipal; this exemption to remain in force as long as the revenues of the said Board are directed to the maintenance of the University of Louisiana, as aforesaid, or until said Constitutional Amendment be adopted. That adoption of said amendment shall operate such exemption in consideration of the said Board in expending their revenues as aforesaid, or creating, maintaining and developing a great University in the city of New Orleans; *provided,* that the property exempted from taxation by this act shall not exceed in value five million dollars, invested in real estate not otherwise exempted, which said value shall be determined in the mode required by law for the assessment and valuation of property subject to taxation, it being the true meaning and intent hereof, that all the property of the Tulane University of Louisiana, of whatsoever character, shall be exempted from taxation, State, parochial and municipal, except the excess of real estate belonging thereto, over and above the value of five million dollars as above stated.

Sec. 6. *Be it further enacted, etc.,* That in consideration of the vesting of the administration of the University of Louisiana in the said Administrators of "Tulane Education Fund," of the transfer of the rights, powers, privileges, franchises and immunities of the said University to said Administrators, and of the exemption from all taxation as hereinabove provided, the said Administrators hereby agree to bind themselves, with the revenues and income of the property heretofore given them by Paul Tulane, Esq., as well as from the revenues of all other property, real, personal or mixed, hereafter to be held, owned or controlled by them, for the purposes of education, to develop, foster and maintain, to the best of their ability and judgment, the University of Louisiana, hereafter to be known as the "Tulane University of Louisiana," and upon adoption of the Constitutional Amendment aforesaid, to perpetually use the powers conferred by this act, and all the power vested in them for the purpose of creating and maintaining in the city of New Orleans a great University, devoted to the intellectual, moral and industrial education and advancement of the youth of this State, under the terms of the donation of Paul Tulane, and the previous provisions of this act. The said Board further agree and bind themselves to waive all legal claim upon the State of Louisiana for any appropriation, as provided in the Constitution of this State, in favor of the University of Louisiana. Besides the waiver of the claim, as aforesaid, as an additional consideration between the parties of this act, the said Board agrees to give continuously, in the academic department, free tuition to one student from each Senatorial and from each Representative district or parish, to be nominated by its members in the General Assembly from among the *bona fide* citizens and residents of his district or parish, who shall comply with the requirements for admission established by said Board. The meaning of this provision being that each member of the General Assembly, whether Senator or Representative, shall have the right of appointing one student, in accordance with the foregoing provisions. The free tuition herein provided for shall continue until each student has graduated from the academic department, unless his scholarship has ceased from other causes. Whenever a scholarship becomes vacant, from any cause, the Senator or Representative, who, appointed the previous student, or his successor, shall, in the manner prescribed by this section, immediately name a successor.

Sec. 7. *Be it further enacted, etc.,* That this act, in all its provisions be and the same is hereby declared to be a contract between the State of Louisiana and the Administrators of the "Tulane Education Fund," irrevocably vesting the said Administrators of the "Tulane Education Fund" with the powers, franchises, rights, immunities and exemptions herein enumerated and hereby granted, and irrevocably binding said administrators to develop, foster and maintain as above provided, the University as aforesaid in the city of New Orleans, subject to and in accordance with the terms of this act.

Sec. 8. *Be it further enacted, etc.,* That this act, in all its terms, provisions and stipulations, without in any manner affecting the validity thereof, or casting any doubt upon its constitutionality, be submitted for ratification at the next general election by a constitutional amendment, as hereinabove and hereinafter provided.

Sec. 9. *Be it further enacted, etc.,* That upon the passage and promulgation of this act the said Administrators of the "Tulane Education Fund," shall have the right to avail themselves of the provisions of this act pending the submission of the constitutional amendment aforesaid. In case they should so elect to do, the said Administrators upon the passage and promulgation of this law thereof, shall give notice of such intention to his Excellency, the Governor of this State, which notice shall authorize said Board to act under the provisions of this act and to exercise all the powers, privileges, franchises, immunities and rights which this act confers, and to undertake the performance of the duties by it imposed. In case the said Constitutional Amendment as aforesaid be not ratified, the said Board shall not in any way be held bound by its said action, but shall have the right to relieve itself of all liability growing out of such action by turning over to the Governor of the State, any property received by it from the State, or from the Administrators of the University of Louisiana, under the terms of this act, which to the extent of its imposing any obligation on the said Administrators of the "Tulane Education Fund," shall by said return, become null and void, *provided,* that the said Board may in the event of the defeat of said Constitutional Amendment continue to execute and to avail themselves of the provisions of this act to the full extent that, the same are legal without Constitutional enactment.

Sec. 10. *Be it further enacted, etc.,* That sections 1357, 1362, 1363, 1365, 1366, 1367, 1370, 1372, 1373, and 1374 of the Revised Statutes, be and the same are hereby repealed, and that all laws and parts of laws conflicting in any manner with the terms of this act, be and the same are hereby repealed.

Sec. 11. *Be it further enacted, etc.,* That at the next general election to be held in this State, there shall be submitted to the people of the State, the following amendment to the Constitution: (The terms of the act. No. 43 adopted at the session of the Legislature in the year 1884, are hereby ratified and approved; and all provisions of the Constitution of 1879 repugnant thereto, or in any way impairing the passage thereof, are hereby repealed so far as the operations of said act are concerned.)

Sec. 12. *Be it further enacted, etc.,* That the electors who desire to vote at said election for said amendment, shall write or print upon their ballots the words "For the Tulane University amendment," and all electors who desire to vote at said election against said amendment shall write or print upon their ballots the words "Against the Tulane University amendment."

H. W. OGDEN
Speaker of the House of Representatives.
CLAY KNOBLOCH,
Lieut. Governor, and President of the Senate.
S. D. MCENERY,
Governor of the State of Louisiana.

Approved 5th of July, 1884

Appendix III

WILL OF JOSEPHINE LOUISE NEWCOMB
New Orleans, May 12, 1898

Aware as I am, of the uncertainty of life, I, Josephine Louise Newcomb, widow of Warren Newcomb, do make this my last will and testament:

FIRST: I have resided of late years in different places but I have made the City of New Orleans my permanent home, because I here witness and enjoy the growth of the "H. Sophie Newcomb Memorial College," a department of the Tulane University of Louisiana, which I have founded, and has been named in honor of the memory of my beloved daughter.

I have implicit confidence that the "Administrators of the Tulane Educational Fund" will continue to use and apply the benefactions and property I have bestowed and may give, for the present and future development of this department of the University known as the "H. Sophie Newcomb Memorial College" which engrosses my thoughts and purposes, and is endeared to me by such hallowed associations.

SECOND: I have no forced heirs; I have no debts; and I hereby revoke all wills of a date anterior to this.

I hereby make the following special legacies and bequests:

To the Greenwood Cemetery, a corporation organized and existing under and by virtue of Chapter 298 of the laws of the State of New York passed in 1838, the sum of Two Thousand (2,000) Dollars for the care of lots numbered 17,036 and 17,037, and it is my desire that at my death my remains may be placed with the loved ones there at rest.

To Alice Bowman of New Orleans, Five Thousand (5,000) Dollars.

To William Robertson of Charleston, South Charleston, South Carolina, One Thousand (1,000) Dollars.

THIRD: With the exception of the special legacies and bequests herein above stated and made, I hereby give and bequeath to the "Administrators of the Tulane Educational Fund" of New Orleans, the whole of the property real, personal, and mixed of which I am now possessed or which I may leave at the time of my death, and to that end and purpose I do hereby name and constitute the said "Administrators of the Tulane Educational Fund" to be my universal legatee.

I appoint my cousin and friend, Joseph A. Hincks, and my friend B. V. B. Dixon, to be Executors, giving them seizin and detainer of my estate and requiring no bond from them.

Thus wholly have I written, dated and signed this my last will and testament at New Orleans, Louisiana, this 12th day of May, 1898.

(Signed) JOSEPHINE LOUISE NEWCOMB
Ne Varietur,
Apl., 8, 1901
(Signed) T. C. W. ELLIS, *Judge*.

Appendix IV

THE ADMINISTRATORS OF THE
TULANE EDUCATIONAL FUND

	Date of Election	Date of Death or Resignation
Randall Lee Gibson*	May 2, 1882	Died, Dec. 14, 1892
Charles Erasmus Fenner*	May 2, 1882	Res., Aug. 13, 1906
James McConnell	May 2, 1882	Died, Dec. 14, 1914
Tobias Gibson Richardson	May 2, 1882	Died, May 26, 1892
Edward Douglass White	May 2, 1882	Res., Dec. 13, 1897
Edgar Howard Farrar	May 2, 1882	Died, Jan. 6, 1922
Paschal Neilson Strong	May 2, 1882	Died, Mar. 13, 1892
Benjamin Morgan Palmer	May 2, 1882	Died, May 22, 1902
Hugh Miller Thompson	May 2, 1882	Res., Dec. 9, 1884
Charles Augustus Whitney	May 2, 1882	Died, Oct. 29, 1882
Samuel Horton Kennedy	May 2, 1882	Died, Nov. 7, 1893
Walter Robinson Stauffer	May 2, 1882	Died, July 30, 1932
Cartwright Eustis	May 2, 1882	Died, Dec. 2, 1900
Henry Ginder*	May 2, 1882	Res., Mar. 8, 1920
John Timmons Hardie	May 2, 1882	Died, Apr. 10, 1895
Robert Miller Walnsley*	May 2, 1882	Died, Dec. 26, 1919
William Oscar Rogers	May 2, 1882	Res., Nov. 11, 1884
William Forrest Halsey	Jan. 9, 1883	Res., Feb. 8, 1887
John Nicholas Galleher	Feb. 10, 1885	Died, Dec. 7, 1891
Joseph Chandler Morris	Feb. 10, 1885	Died, Aug. 3, 1903
Charles Morgan Whitney	Mar. 12, 1889	Res., Feb. 11, 1892
George Quintard Whitney	Mar. 14, 1892	Res., Feb. 12, 1903
Leonard Matthews Finley	Apr. 11, 1892	Died, June 7, 1894
John Baptist Levert	Apr. 11, 1892	Died, Oct. 15, 1930
Charles Jasper Bickham	Mar. 13, 1893	Res., Oct. 19, 1896
Walter Chew Flower	Mar. 13, 1893	Died, Oct. 11, 1900
Charles Janvier	Dec. 12, 1894	Died, Jan. 21, 1927
Ashton Phelps*	Dec. 12, 1894	Res., Oct. 11, 1909
Walker Brainerd Spencer	June 11, 1895	Died, Mar. 15, 1941

* President of the board.

Beverley Ellison Warner	Jan. 10, 1898	Res., Feb. 13, 1905
Walter Denis Denegre	Jan. 10, 1898	Res., Oct. 12, 1908
John Dymond, Jr.	Feb. 11, 1901	Died, Nov. 12, 1932
Daniel C. Scarborough	Jan. 13, 1903	Res., Feb. 12, 1912
John Westley Castles	Jan. 13, 1903	Res., Jan. 20, 1904
Gustaf Reinhold Westfeldt	June 8, 1903	Res., Dec. 3, 1910
Charles Rosen	Mar. 28, 1904	Res., Apr. 21, 1954
Ernest B. Kruttschnitt	Mar. 28, 1904	Died, May 17, 1906
Beverley Ellison Warner	Apr. 10, 1905	Died, Dec. 3, 1910
Frederick William Parham	Aug. 2, 1906	Res., Oct. 10, 1914
Alfred Raymond	Nov. 11, 1908	Died, Feb. 9, 1920
James Hardy Dillard	Nov. 11, 1908	Res., Oct. 13, 1913
William Ratcliffe Irby*	Dec. 3, 1910	Died, Nov. 20, 1926
Abraham Brittin	Dec. 12, 1910	Died, July 31, 1932
John Callan	Jan. 16, 1911	Died, Jan. 14, 1924
Ernest Lee Jahncke	Aug. 13, 1914	Died, Nov. 16, 1960
Joseph Arsenne Breaux	Aug. 13, 1914	Died, July 26, 1926
Marcus Johns Magruder	Aug. 13, 1914	Res., Jan. 15, 1946
Esmond Phelps*	June 14, 1915	Died, Oct. 18, 1950
Paul Hill Saunders	Feb. 9, 1920	Res., July 7, 1936
Samuel Zemurray	Mar. 8, 1920	Died, Nov. 30, 1961
Arthur Devereaux Parker	Apr. 12, 1920	Res., May 15, 1922
Florence Dymond	Feb. 13, 1922	Res., Jan. 9, 1951
Chauncey French	Nov. 20, 1922	Died, Apr. 30, 1938
Frederick William Parham	July 13, 1925	Died, May 6, 1927
Jules Blanc Monroe	Dec. 13, 1926	Died, Apr. 20, 1960
James Pierce Butler	Dec. 13, 1926	Res., May 16, 1940
John Barnwell Elliott	June 14, 1927	Res., Nov. 13, 1935
George Elliott Williams	Nov. 14, 1927	Died, Sept. 8, 1947
S. Walter Stern	Nov. 18, 1932	Died, Dec. 16, 1943
Charles Allen Favrot	Nov. 18, 1932	Died, Mar. 10, 1939
Joseph Wheadon Carroll	Jan. 10, 1933	Res., Dec. 9, 1947
Charles Leverich Eshleman	Apr. 7, 1936	Res., Nov. 11, 1959†
Charles Seyburn Williams	Apr. 7, 1936	Res., Oct. 15, 1946
Joseph Woodruff George	Nov. 12, 1936	Res., May 8, 1961
Albert Barnett Paterson	June 14, 1938	Died, Aug. 6, 1952
Bernard Henry Grehan	Apr. 9, 1940	Died Dec. 15, 1952
Samuel A. LeBlanc	June 25, 1941	Died, July 8, 1955
Alfred Bird Freeman	Feb. 15, 1941	Res., Mar. 9, 1955
Edgar B. Stern	Feb. 14, 1941	Died, Aug. 24, 1959
Joseph W. Montgomery	Apr. 17, 1947	
Joseph Merrick Jones*	Apr. 27, 1947	Died, Mar. 11, 1963
George A. Wilson	Mar. 25, 1948	
Joseph McCloskey	Mar. 25, 1948	
Clifford F. Favrot	Mar. 8, 1951	

* President of the board.

Mrs. George M. Snellings, Jr.	
(Marie Louise Wilcox)	May 30, 1951
George S. Farnsworth	May 30, 1951
Darwin S. Fenner*	Jan. 14, 1953
Lester J. Lautenschlaeger	May 13, 1953
Isidore Newman, II	Dec. 8, 1954
Leon Irwin, Jr.	May 18, 1955
Ashton Phelps	Dec. 15, 1955
Richard West Freeman	May 13, 1959
Gerald Louis Andrus	Jan. 21, 1960
Jacob S. Landry	Feb. 10, 1960
Edgar B. Stern, Jr.	Oct. 12, 1960
Arthur L. Jung, Jr.	Feb. 8, 1961
Sam Israel, Jr.	Feb. 12, 1962
Harry B. Kelleher	Apr. 18, 1963

* President of the board.
† Elected advisory administrator

Appendix V

THE BOARD OF VISITORS

Jack R. Aron	1959–
John Chalmers Baine	1957–1959; 1960–1964
William Oliver Baker	1963–
Chester Irving Barnard	1953–1955
The Very Rev. Cosam Julian Bartlett	1964–
Stanhope Bayne-Jones	1953–1964
Detley Wulf Bronk	1960–
Bruce Keith Brown	1953–1964
Leonard Carmichael	1959–
William Hodding Carter	1954–1963
David Blackshear Hamilton Chaffe, Jr.	1955–1956
Arden Watson Chapman	1956–1960
Hollis Hobson Crosby	1956–
Gayle L. Dalferes	1964–
Benjamin Cornwell Dawkins	1954–1956
Michael Ellis DeBakey	1965–
John Winton Deming	1964–
George Summey Dinwiddie	1953–1964
Streuby Lloyd Drumm	1965–
Mayo Lowndes Emory	1958–1961
Marion Jay Epley, Jr.	1960–
Frank Cyril Fisher	1960–
William Henry Walter Fitzpatrick	1953–1964
Douglass Vincent Freret	1954–
George Shelby Friedrichs	1953–1954
Parrish Fuller	1953–
Harry Pollard Gamble, Jr.	1957–1958
James McMillan Gibson	1964–
Ben Goldsmith	1953–1960
Kathryn Claire Briede Gore	1953–1961

317

Lawrence Randolph Hafstad	1955–1961; 1963–
William Mumford Haile	1962–
Charles Frederick Hard	1953–
Caryl Parker Haskins	1956
Theodore V. Hauser	1963–
The Rev. Theodore Martin Hesburgh	1965–
James Johnston Hicks	1963–
John Cunyus Hodges	1960–
Etta Hodgins	1953–1959
John Erik Jonsson	1962–
Arthur Louis Jung, Jr.	1954 (only)
James R. Killian, Jr.	1960–
Lawrence A. Kimpton	1961–
Robert Archibald Lambert	1953–1956
Jacob Segura Landry	1956–1957
Monte M. Lemann	1953–1959
Gustave Lahman Levy	1956–
Jesse Talbot Littleton	1953–1955
Carolyn Stubbs Lynch	1953–1960
Charlton Havard Lyons, Sr.	1959–
Everett Patrick McCloskey	1960–1963
Norris Cochran McGowen	1953–1955
Earl Maron McGowin	1962–
Armand Theodore Mercier	1953–1957
Lisette Sylvia Moore Meyers	1957–1958
Cecil Morgan	1953–1963
Lillie Hozey Nairne	1953–1960
Isidore Newman II	1953–1954
Whitney Jennings Oates	1959–1964
Francis Cameron Payne	1956–1957
Ashton Phelps	1953–1955
Emanuel Rubin Piore	1965–
LeDoux Roger Provosty	1953–1964
Donald Joseph Russell	1963–
Julian Lloyd Samuel	1958–1960
Mortimer Silvey	1962–
Robert Louis Simpson	1953–1960
Howard Kingsbury Smith	1960–1964
Charles Gabriel Smither	1957–1958; 1963–
John Ewart Wallace Sterling	1961–
Earl Place Stevenson	1953–

Vernon F. Taylor 1962–
William Homer Turner 1963–

Mordelo Lee Vincent, Jr. 1953–1960

Arthur Joseph Waechter 1959–1964
Woollen Hands Walshe 1956–
Herman B. Wells 1965–
Langbourne Meade Williams 1953–1960
Logan Wilson 1963–
Louis Booker Wright 1965–

Appendix VI

PRESIDENTS AND ADMINISTRATIVE OFFICERS OF THE UNIVERSITY

PRESIDENTS

Francis Lister Hawks	1847–1849
Theodore Howard McCaleb	1850–1862
(The university was closed on account of war)	1862–1865
Thomas Hunt	1865–1867
Randell Hunt	1867–1884
William Preston Johnston	1884–1899
William Oscar Rogers (Acting)	1899–1900
Edwin Anderson Alderman	1900–1904
Edwin Boone Craighead	1904–1912
Robert Sharp (Acting)	1912–1913
Robert Sharp	1913–1918
Albert Bledsoe Dinwiddie	1918–1935
Douglas Smith Anderson (Acting)	1935–1936
Robert Leonval Menuet (Acting)	1936–1937
Rufus Carrollton Harris	1937–1960
Maxwell Edward Lapham (Acting)	Apr. 1–Aug. 31, 1960
Herbert Eugene Longnecker	1960–

PROVOSTS

Robert Mayer Lumiansky	1960–Feb. 1, 1963
Maxwell Edward Lapham	1963–1965

VICE-PRESIDENTS

Joseph Chandler Morris	1948–
Robert Warren French	1953–1956
Fred Carrington Cole	1954–1959
Clarence Scheps	1958–
Fred Ray Cagle	1963–

ASSISTANTS TO THE PRESIDENT

Leslie James Buchan (in Finance Administration)	1944–1947
Ross Myron Trump (executive assistant)	Jan.–June 1947
Clarence Scheps (executive assistant)	1947–1949
Kathryn Davis	1951–
Horace Calvin Renegar	1961–

DEANS OF THE SCHOOL OF LAW

Henry Adams Bullard	1847–1850
Randell Hunt	1850–1862
(The university was closed on account of war)	1862–1865
Christian Roselius	1865–1872
Carleton Hunt	1872–1883
William Francis Mellen	1883–1888
Henry Carleton Miller	1888–1897
Harry Hinckley Hall	1897–1906
Eugene Davis Saunders	1906–1913
Dudley Odell McGovney	1913–1914
Charles Payne Fenner	1914–1920
Rufus Edward Foster	1920–1927
Rufus Carrollton Harris	1927–1937
Paul William Brosman	1937–1942
Robert Joseph Farley (Pro tem)	1942–1945
Paul William Brosman	1945–1951
Clarence James Morrow (Acting)	1951–1952
William Ray Forrester	1952–1963
Cecil Morgan	1963–

DEANS OF THE COLLEGE OF ARTS AND SCIENCES

Claudius Wistar Sears	1850–1860
(College closed)	1861–1878
Richard Henry Jesse	1878–1884
(Office discontinued)	1884–1892
James Hardy Dillard	1893–1900
Brown Ayres	1900–1904
James Hardy Dillard	1904–1907
Walter Miller	1907–1911
Albert Bledsoe Dinwiddie	1911–1918
Edward Ambrose Bechtel	1918–1937
Marten ten Hoor	1937–1944
George Evans Simmons (Pro tem)	1944–1947
Fred Carrington Cole	1947–1955
William Wallace Peery	1955–1964 (Died 4/30/64)
Joseph Elwell Gordon (Acting)	May–Oct. 1964
Joseph Elwell Gordon	Oct. 19, 1964–

Deans of Newcomb College

Brandt Van Blarcom Dixon*	1887–1919
Pierce Butler	1919–1938
Frederick Hard	1938–1943
Logan Wilson	1943–1951
Anna Many	1951–1953
John Randolph Hubbard	1953–

Deans of the School of Engineering

Brown Ayres†	1893–1904
James Hardy Dillard†	1904–1907
Walter Miller†	1907–1911
William Henry P. Creighton	1911–1919
Douglas Smith Anderson	1919–1937
James Marshall Robert	1937–1950
Lee Harnie Johnson	1950–

Deans of the Graduate School

Brown Ayres‡	1900–1904
James Hardy Dillard‡	1904–1908
Robert Sharp	1908–1912
Alcée Fortier	1912–1914
Pierce Butler	1914–1919
John Madison Fletcher	1919–1923
John MacLaren McBryde	1923–1937
Roger Philip McCutcheon	1937–1954
Robert Mayer Lumiansky	1954–1963
John Leslie Snell	Feb. 1, 1963–

Deans and Directors, Division of Graduate Medicine

Charles Louis Chassaignac (Dean)	1906–1925
Edmund Denegre Martin (Dean)	1925–1928
Henry Daspit (Dean)	1928–1932
Hiram Watkins Kostmayer (Dean)	1933–1937
Hiram Watkins Kostmayer (Director)	1937–1949
Roscoe Leroy Pullen (Director)	1949–1952
Clifford Grosselle Grulee, Jr. (Director)	1952–1962
Walter George Unglaub	1963–

Deans of the School of Business Administration

Morton Arnold Aldrich	1914–1939
Leslie James Buchan	1939–1949

* President.
† Dean of the College of Arts and Sciences and the School of Engineering.
‡ Vice-chairman of the faculty of the Graduate Department.

Robert Warren French	1949–1955
Paul Victor Grambsch	1955–1960
Howard Graham Schaller	1960–1963
Charles Jackson Grayson, Jr. (leave of absence)	1963–1964
Clinton Adam Phillips (Acting)	1963–1964
Charles Jackson Grayson, Jr.	1964–

DEANS OF THE SCHOOL OF ARCHITECTURE

Nathaniel Cortlandt Curtis (Head)	1916–1921
John Herndon Thompson (Head)	1921–1946
Buford Lindsay Pickens (Head)	1946–1950
Buford Lindsay Pickens (Director)	1950–1953
John Ekin Dinwiddie (Dean)	1953–1959
John William Lawrence (Acting Dean)	1959–1960
John William Lawrence (Dean)	1960–

DEANS AND DIRECTORS, SCHOOL OF SOCIAL WORK

Garrett Pelhemus Wyckoff (Director)	1927–1937
Elizabeth Wisner (Director)	1932–1939
Elizabeth Wisner (Dean)	1939–1958
Walter Lewis Kindelsperger (Dean)	1958–

DIRECTORS AND DEAN OF THE UNIVERSITY COLLEGE

Roger P. McCutcheon (Director)	1942–1946
Ross M. Trump (Director)	1946–1947
Thomas T. Earle (Acting Director)	1947–1948
John P. Dyer (Director)	1948–1952
John P. Dyer (Dean)	1952–

DEANS OF THE SCHOOL OF MEDICINE

Thomas Hunt	1834–1835
Charles A. Luzenberg	1835–1836
Edward H. Barton	1836–1840
John Hoffman Harrison	1840–1841
James Jones	1841–1842
John Hoffman Harrison	1842–1844
Augustus H. Cenas	1844–1845
William M. Carpenter	1845–1846
Alexander John Wedderburn	1846–1848
James Jones	1848–1849
Gustavus Adolphus Nott	1849–1852
Thomas Hunt	1852–1862
(Closed on account of war)	1862–1865
James Jones	1865 (only)
Tobias Gibson Richardson	1865–1885

Stanford Emerson Chaillé	1885–1908
Isadore Dyer	1908–1920
Albert Bledsoe Dinwiddie (Acting)	1920–1922
Charles Cassedy Bass	1922–1940
Maxwell Edward Lapham	1940–1942
Hiram Watkins Kostmayer	1942–1945
Maxwell Edward Lapham	1945–1963
Charles Cameron Sprague	1963–

DEANS OF THE SCHOOL OF DENTISTRY AND DIRECTORS OF THE DENTAL CLINIC

Andrew G. Friedrich	1909–1914
Wallace Wood, Jr.	1914–1922
Alfred Archinard Leefe (Acting)	1922–1925
Alfred Archinard Leefe	1925–1928
Alfred Archinard Leefe (Director, Dental Clinic)	1928–1930
Walter Clarence DeRouen, Jr. (Director, Dental Clinic)	1930–1933

DEAN OF THE SCHOOL OF PHARMACY

John Felicien Simon	1931–1934

DIRECTORS OF THE MIDDLE AMERICAN RESEARCH INSTITUTE

William Gates	1924–1926
(Office discontinued)	1926–1929
Frans Ferdinand Blom	1929–1940
Arthur Eric Gropp*	1940–1942
Maurice Ruddell Ries*	1940–1942
Robert Wauchope	1942–·

DIRECTORS OF THE SUMMER SCHOOL

Edwin Boone Craighead	1908–1910
Albert Bledsoe Dinwiddie	1911–1922
Edward Ambrose Bechtel	1923–1937
James Adair Lyon	1938–1941
Roger Philip McCutcheon	1942–1945
Joseph Edward Gibson	1947–1947
Thomas Theron Earle	1948–

DIRECTOR OF PERSONNEL

Robert John Stone, Jr. (Officer of Personnel)	1957–1959
Robert John Stone, Jr. (Director of Personnel)	1959–

* Acting jointly for the director.

DIRECTORS OF PLACEMENT

Johnie Ervin Branch (Placement Officer)	1950–1957
James David Schneider (Placement Officer)	1957–1960
James David Schneider (Director of Placement)	1960–1965
James Mason Webster, Sr. (Director)	1965–

DIRECTORS OF DEVELOPMENT

Robert William Elsasser (special assignment)	1946–1947
Joseph Chandler Morris (Vice-president for Development)	1948–1953
Robert Warren French (Vice-president for Development)	1953–1956
Alvin L. Lyons (Director of the Development Office)	1956–1965

DIRECTORS OF THE SCHOOL OF ART, NEWCOMB COLLEGE

Ellsworth Woodward	1895–1931
Lota Lee Troy (Acting)	1931–1935
Lota Lee Troy (Director)	1935–1940
Robert Durant Feild (Director)	1940–1949
Alice Stirling Parkerson (Acting)	1949–1950
John Edwin Canaday (Director)	1950–1953
Alice Stirling Parkerson (Acting)	1953–1955
George Warren Rickey (Director)	1955–1958
Alice Stirling Parkerson (Acting)	1958–1959
Roberta Murray Alford Capers (Director)	1959–

DIRECTORS OF THE SCHOOL OF MUSIC, NEWCOMB COLLEGE

Leon Ryder Maxwell	1909–1953
Peter Sijer Hansen	1953–

MEDICAL OFFICERS AND DIRECTORS OF UNIVERSITY HEALTH SERVICE

William Alvin Love (Medical Officer)	1914–1920
Muir Bradburn (Medical Officer)	1920–1922
James Clifton Cole (Medical Officer)	1922–1924
Frank Lee Cato (Medical Officer)	1924–1926
Edmond Lawrence Faust (Medical Officer)	1926–1942
Edmond Lawrence Faust (Director)	1942–1946
Lloyd John Kuhn (Acting Director)	1942–1943
Lloyd John Kuhn (Director Pro tem)	1943–1946
Lloyd John Kuhn (Clinical Executive Officer)	1946–1950
Lloyd John Kuhn (Director)	1950–1959
Charles Pelot Summerall III (Director)	1959–1961
Paul Carey Trickett (Director)	1961–

LIBRARIANS AND DIRECTORS OF LIBRARIES

William Oscar Rogers (Librarian)	1884–1891
Charles G. Gill (Librarian)	1891–1895
Ernest J. Villasavo (Librarian)	1895–1896
Minnie Marie Bell (Librarian)	1896–1929
Helmer Lewis Webb (Librarian)	1929–1936
Ralph Wendell McComb (Acting Librarian)	1936–1938
Robert James Usher (Librarian)	1938–1944
Garland Forbes Taylor (Acting Librarian)	1944–1945
Garland Forbes Taylor (Librarian)	1945–1948
Garland Forbes Taylor (Director of Libraries)	1948–1960
Robert L. Talmadge (Director of Libraries)	1960–

DEAN AND DIRECTOR OF ADMISSIONS

Forrest Una Lake (Dean)	1945–1956
Cliff Waldron Wing (Director)	1956–

DIRECTORS OF ALUMNI ACTIVITIES

Lewis Farrington Wakeman (Alumni Secretary)	1923–1924
John Randolph Foote (Alumni Secretary)	1924–1927
George Frederick Lamprecht (Alumni Secretary)	1927–1930
Francis Xavier Armstrong (Alumni Secretary)	1930–1934
Charles Murrah Rucker (General Manager)	1934–1937
Thomas Hale Boggs (General Manager)	1937–1940
Thomas Hale Boggs (Director)	1940–1941
Kendall Hutchinson Cram (Director)	1941–1942
Beatrice McMillan Field (Director)	1942–

SECRETARY-TREASURERS OF THE BOARD OF ADMINISTRATORS

Joseph Anatole Hincks	1892–1911
Lawrence Andre Wogan	1911–1952
Anthony Percy Generes	1952–

DIRECTORS OF PUBLIC RELATIONS

John Hampden Randolph Feltus	1938–1941
Horace Calvin Renegar (Acting Director)	1941–1945
Horace Calvin Renegar (Director)	1945–1961

PURCHASING AGENTS OF THE UNIVERSITY

Daniel Frank Layman	1918–1927
Victor Buerkle (Acting)	1927–1928
Victor Buerkle	1928–1948
Victor Buerkle (Assistant)	1948–1950
Jesse Berry Morgan	1950–1958

William Thomas Haywood, Jr.	1958–1960
Lawrence Joseph Guichard	1960–

BUSINESS MANAGER OF THE UNIVERSITY

Jesse Berry Morgan	1958–

BURSARS OF THE UNIVERSITY

Benjamin Crump	1912–1922
Lawrence Charles Daigre	1922–1952
Emanuel Francis Livaudais	1952–

REGISTRARS OF THE UNIVERSITY AND DIRECTOR OF STUDENT RECORDS AND REGISTRATION

Richard Kearny Bruff (Registrar)	1914–1927
Ernest Carl Miller (Registrar)	1927–1928
Glenn Brown Hasty (Acting)	1928–1929
Glenn Brown Hasty (Registrar)	1929–1941
Florence Wintz Toppino (Assistant)	1941–1945
Florence Wintz Toppino (Registrar)	1945–1963
Endicott Appleton Batchelder (Director of Student Records and Registration)	1961–

DIRECTOR AND GRADUATE MANAGERS OF STUDENT ACTIVITIES (Dean of Students)

Albert Elliot Holleman (Director)	1926–1929
Frederick Hewitt Fox (Director)	1929–1930
John Barkley (Manager)	1930–1932
Calvert de Coligny (Graduate Manager)	1932–1935
John Hampden Randolph Feltus (Graduate Manager)	1935–1937
Maurice H. Born (Graduate Manager)	1937–1938
Kendall Hutchinson Cram (Graduate Manager)*	1938–1942
Beatrice McMillan Field (Graduate Manager)*	1942–1948
Claude Simons, Jr. (Director)	1948–1949
John Henry Stibbs (Director)	1949–1951
John Henry Stibbs (Dean of Students)	1951–

PRESIDENTS OF THE TULANE ALUMNI ASSOCIATION

1898–1901	John Dymond, Jr., B.A., 1888; LL.B., 1890
1901–1903	Johnston A. Armstrong, LL.B., 1888
1903–1904	Charles Rosen, A.B., 1892; LL.B., 1894
1904–1907	William M. Perkins, B.S., 1893; M.D., 1897
1907–1910	I. I. Lemann, M.D., 1900
1910–1911	Warren B. Reed, B.S. (Engr.), 1891

* While serving as director of alumni activities.

1911–1912	J. Blanc Monroe, B.A., 1899; LL.B., 1901
1912–1914	Douglas S. Anderson, M.A., 1892; LL.D., 1937
1914–1915	George H. Terriberry, B.A., 1898; LL.B., 1900
1915–1917	Frank William Hart, B.A., 1904; LL.B., 1906
1917–1918	Michel B. Provosty, LL.B., 1912
1918–1919	J. Phares O'Kelley, M.D., 1893
1919–1921	Henry W. Robinson, LL.B., 1891
1921–1923	J. Birney Guthrie, B.S., 1896; M.D., 1900
1923–1925	Charles E. Dunbar, Jr., A.B., 1910; LL.B., 1915; LL.D., 1935
1925–1927	Lucien H. Landry, M.D., 1907
1927–1928	S. Walter Stern, B.A., 1905
1928–1930	Rudolph J. Weinmann, B.A., 1914; LL.B., 1916
1930–1932	Cuthbert S. Baldwin, LL.B., 1914
1932–1934	Edmond L. Faust, M.D., 1918
1934–1936	Louis Rosen, LL.B., 1923
1936–1938	Joseph L. Killeen, LL.B., 1916
1938–1939	Clifford F. Favrot, B.E., 1919
1939–1940	Walter M. Barnett, Jr., LL.B., 1925; M.A., 1925
1940–1941	Alva P. Frith, A&S, 1907 (not a graduate)
1941–1942	Edward S. Bres, B.E., 1910; C.E., 1931
1942–1943	Frank S. Cannon, LL.B., 1907
1943–1944	Richard O. Baumbach, B.B.A., 1926
1944–1945	George T. Walne, B.B.A., 1926
1945–1946	Lester J. Lautenschlaeger, LL.B., 1925
1946–1947	Walter O. Moss, M.D., 1927; M.S., 1931
1947–1948	E. Claggett Upton, Jr., B.B.A., 1932
1948–1949	A. Watson Chapman, B.E., 1927; B.S., 1927
1949–1950	Clayton L. Nairne, B.E., 1924
1950–1951	Francisco L. Figueroa, LL.B., 1934
1951–1952	Gerald L. Andrus, B.B.A., 1928
1952–1953	Arthur F. Hoge, M.D., 1909
1953–1954	G. Shelby Friedrichs, B.B.A., 1933
1954–1955	Jesse T. Littleton, M.A., 1908
1955–1956	D. B. H. Chaffe, B.E., 1912
1956–1957	Jacob S. Landry, A.B., 1926; LL.B., 1927
1957–1958	Harry P. Gamble, Jr., LL.B., 1926
1958–1959	John Chalmers Baine, B.E., 1927
1959–1960	Mayo Lowndes Emory, M.D., 1940
1960–1961	Vance M. Strange, M.D., 1934
1961–1962	Ernest B. Mason, B.B.A., 1926
1962–1963	Arthur J. Waechter, LL.B., 1936
1963–1964	John C. Hodges, A.M., 1912
1964–1965	Woollen H. Walshe, LL.B., 1932

TEACHER EDUCATION

Teachers College

(B.A. in Educ. conferred 1908–1915)

Joseph M. Gwinn (Director)   1908–1910

Extension Division
J. Adair Lyon (Chairman) | 1910–1915
Courses for Teachers
J. Adair Lyon (Chairman of the Committee on Courses for Teachers) | 1915–1938
Division for Teachers
J. Adair Lyon (Director of the Division for Teachers) | 1938–1942
George Estes Barton (Director, Teacher Training Program) | 1956–1962
Thomas Edward Jordan (Director, Center for Teacher Education) | 1962–1963
Gaither Abigail McConnell (Acting Director, Center for Teacher Education) | 1963–1965
Melvin L. Gruwell (Director, Center for Teacher Education) | 1965–

DELTA REGIONAL PRIMATE CENTER

Arthur Jean Riopelle (Director) | 1962–

UNIVERSITY NEWS SERVICE

Quentin Ault (Director) | 1961–

BUSINESS MANAGER—HOUSING

Francis Manson Radford | 1958–

SECURITY OFFICER

Robert Arthur Scruton | 1959–

DIRECTORS OF PHYSICAL PLANT

Herman Fair Hustedt (Superintendent, Buildings and Grounds) | 1918–1938
Ellis Robbert (Director of Maintenance and Supply) | 1938–1945
Salo K. Lowe (Superintendent of Physical Plant) | 1945–1955
George Johnson (Director, Physical Plant) | 1955–

Appendix VII

PROFESSORS OF THE UNIVERSITY SINCE 1847

Professors are listed by the latest titles held, and their service as professors emeriti is not included. Divisions or colleges are not indicated, the titles being self-explanatory, except in the case of professorships held at Newcomb College, which are so indicated. Dates given are those which include the professor's tenure as a full professor rather than the entire period of his service to the university.

Adams, Richard Perrill, Ph.D., English	1960–
Adams, St. Clair, LL.B., Law	1924–1928
Adriani, John, M.D., Surgery (Anesthesiology)	1952–
Ainsworth, Walden Lee, B.S., Captain, U.S. Navy, Naval Science and Tactics	1938–1940
Albrecht, Erich August, Ph.D., German (Newcomb)	1963–1965
Aldrich, Morton Arnold, Ph.D., Economics and Employment Management	1905–1939
Alldredge, Rufus Henry, M.D., Sc.D.Med., Clinical Orthopedics (Surgery)	1960–
Allen, Carroll Woolsey, M.D., Clinical Surgery and Clinical Anesthesia	1919–1926
Allen, James Harrill, M.D., M.S., Ophthalmology	1950–
Amsel, Abram, M.A., Ph.D., Psychology (Newcomb)	1956–1960
Anderson, Douglas Smith, A.M., D.Sc., Electrical Engineering	1907–1936
Anderson, Nola Lee, Ph.D., Mathematics (Newcomb)	1936–1938
Ané, Joseph Novell, M.D., Radiology	1943–1964
Archinard, Enolia Bradsher, M.A., M.S.W., Social Work	1964–
Archinard, John Joseph, A.M., M.D., Clinical Microscopy and Bacteriology	1906–1909
Archinard, John Joseph, Jr., B.S., M.D., Clinical Medicine	1960–
Archinard, Louis Doumeing, D.D.S., Operative Dentistry and Dental Pathology and Therapeutics	1909–1912
Archinard, Paul Emile, A.M., M.D., Diseases of the Nervous System	1907–1912

Arrowsmith, William Rankin, B.S., M.D., Clinical
Medicine   1960–
Assad, Thomas Joseph, Ph.D., English   1964–
Augustin, Marie, French (Newcomb)   1890–1910
Ayres, Brown, B.Sc., Ph.D., Physics and Astronomy   1880–1904

Bach, L. Matthew N., Ph.D., Physiology   1959–
Baer, Clara Gregory, Physical Education (Newcomb)   1899–1929
Bahn, Charles Adolph, M.D., Ophthalmology   1920–1928
Bailey, Raymond Victor, Ph.D., Chemical Engi-
neering   1950–
Bailkey, Nels Martin, Ph.D., History   1961–
Baillif, Ralph Norman, Ph.D., Anatomy   1958–
Baker, Newman Freese, A.B., M.A., LL.B., J.S.D.,
Law   1928–1930
Ballard, Edward Goodwin, Ph.D., Philosophy   1958–
Bamber, James Monroe, M.D., F.A.C.P., Clinical
Medicine   1938–1939
Bancroft, Huldah, Ph.D., Biostatistics   1949–1958
Barnett, Samuel Jackson, Ph.D., Physics   1905–1911
Barton, George Estes, Jr., Ph.D., Philosophy   1963–
Bass, Charles Cassedy, M.D., D.Sc., LL.D., F.A.C.P.,
Experimental Medicine   1912–1940
Bass, Mary Elizabeth, M.D., Clinical Laboratory
Diagnosis   1920–1937
Batiza, Rodolfo, B.S., LL.B., Latin-American Legal
Studies   1963–
Bayon, John Henry, A.M., M.D., Applied Anatomy   1918–1925
Beacham, Woodard Davis, B.A., B.S., M.D.,
F.A.C.S., Clinical Obstetrics and Gynecology   1949–
Bean, Robert Bennett, B.Sc., M.D., Gross Anatomy   1914–1916
Beattie, Charlton Reid, B.L., Louisiana Practice Law 1914–1918
Beaver, Paul Chester, Ph.D., William Vincent Pro-
fessor of Tropical Diseases and Hygiene   1953–
Bechtel, Edward Ambrose, Ph.D., Classical Languages   1912–1937
Beckjord, Philip Raines, B.S., M.B., M.D., M.P.H.,
Dr.P.H., Public Health Administration   1960–
Bel, George Sam, M.D., Clinical Medicine; Theory
and Practice of Medicine   1909–1924
Bemiss, Samuel Merrifield, M.D., Theory and Prac-
tice of Medicine and Clinical Medicine   1866–1884
Bennett, Granville Allison, B.S., M.D., Pathology
and Bacteriology   1943–1944
Benson, Lawrence K., LL.B., Law   1962–1964
Bernard, Luther Lee, B.S., A.B., Ph.D., Sociology
(Newcomb)   1927–1928
Bernhard, Robert, M.D., F.A.C.P., Clinical Medicine   1949–1956

Bethea, Oscar Walter, M.D., M.Ph., Ph.G., F.A.C.S.,
F.A.C.P., Clinical Medicine   1919–1943
Bettison, Ulric, Mathematics (Newcomb)   1890–1899
Beutel, Frederick Keating, A.B., LL.B., S.J.D.,
Thomas Pickles Professor of Law   1928–1935
Beyer, George Eugene, Biology   1912–1918
Bierman, Bernie William, B.A., Athletic Training   1927–1932
Bilodeau, Edward Alfred, A.B., M.S., Ph.D., Psy-
chology   1960–
Bilodeau, Ina M., Ph.D., Psychology (Newcomb)   1965–
Binkley, William Campbell, Ph.D., History   1953–1963
Blackshear, Stephen Mertle, M.D., Clinical Otology,
Rhinology, and Laryngology   1917–1930
Blain, Hugh Mercer, Journalism   1923–1925
Bland, Archie Button, D.D.S., Operative Dentistry   1922–1928
Blessey, Walter Emanuel, B.E., C.E., Civil Engi-
neering   1956–
Bliss, Sidney William, B.S., Ph.D., Biochemistry   1929–1945
Bloom, Charles James, B.S., M.D., F.A.C.P.,
F.A.A.P., Pediatrics   1919–1937
Blum, Henry Nathan, B.Sc., M.D., F.A.C.S., Clinical
Ophthalmology   1927–1929
Boles, William McDonald, M.D., Clinical Ophthal-
mology   1959–
Bolle, Louis Frederic, Doctor of Letters, French   1962–
Bollier, Ernest Philip, Ph.D., English   1964–
Bonnett, Clarence Elmore, Ph.D., Economics   1920–1950
Bosch, Walter Christian, M.S., Physics   1943–1959
Boyce, Frederick Fitzherbert, B.S., M.D., F.A.C.S.,
Clinical Surgery   1952–
Boyd, Julian Deigh, B.Sc., M.Sc., M.D., Research
Professor of Pediatrics   1952–1954
Boyer, Harriet Amelia, Domestic Science (Newcomb)   1914–1922
Bradburn, William Plummer, Jr., B.S., M.D.,
F.A.C.S., Clinical Surgery   1938–1942
Breed, Warren, Ph.D., Sociology   1963–
Bresler, Emanuel Harold, B.S., M.D., Clinical
Medicine   1963–
Brittain, Thomas Baldwin, B.S., Commander, U.S.
Navy, Naval Science and Tactics   1941–1943
Brosman, Paul William, A.B., LL.B., J.S.D., Law   1929–1955
Bross, Robert Warren Leute, Colonel, U.S. Marine
Corps, A.B., Naval Science   1963–
Brown, Charles Lafayette, B.S., M.D., Clinical
Otolaryngology   1941–1956
Brown, George Stewart, M.Ph., M.D., Pharmacy   1913–1925
Brown, Marion Earle, M.D., Ophthalmology   1927–1936

Brown, Samuel Wood, A.B., LL.B., J.S.D., W. R.
Irby, Professor of Law 1943–
Brown, William Burlie, B.A., LL.B., M.A., Ph.D.,
History 1961–
Browne, Donovan Clarence, B.S., M.D., Clinical
Medicine 1955–1962
Bruns, Henry Dickson, M.D., Diseases of the Eye 1906–1919
Buchan, Leslie James, B.S., M.S., Ph.D., C.P.A.,
Accounting 1933–1949
Buchanan, Herbert Earle, Ph.D., LL.D., Mathematics 1920–1950
Buchanan, James J., B.A., M.B.A., Ph.D., Classical
Languages 1964–
Buddington, Ralph Wells, A.B., M.D., Psychiatry 1964–
Buechner, Howard Albert, B.S., M.D., Medicine 1963–
Buffington, Wiley Ross, M.D., Ophthalmology 1926–1940
Bullard, Henry Adams, Civil Law 1847–1850
Burch, George Edward, B.S., M.D., William Hen-
derson, Professor of Medicine 1947–
Burdick, Charles Kellogg, A.B., LL.B., Law 1909–1912
Burks, James Willis, Jr., A.B., M.D., M.S., Clinical
Medicine (Dermatology) 1960–
Burns, Edgar, M.D., Clinical Urology 1943–
Burns, Kenneth Franklin, D.V.M., D.V.Sc., Ph.D.,
Veterinary Medicine 1962–
Burns, Louis Henry, LL.B., Law 1926–1928
Butler, Mary Williams, Drawing and Design (New-
comb) 1934–1937
Butler, Pierce, A.M., Ph.D., English (Newcomb) 1902–1938
Butterworth, William Walton, M.D., Diseases of
Children 1908–1930

Cagle, Fred Ray, B.Ed., M.S., Ph.D., Zoology 1949–
Cajori, Florian, M.S., Applied Science 1886–1888
Caldwell, Benjamin Palmer, A.B., Ch.E., Ph.D.,
Chemistry 1911–1916
Caldwell, Guy Alvin, B.S., M.D., Clinical Surgery
(Orthopedics) 1938–1956
Caldwell, John Williamson, A.M., M.D., Chemistry
and Geology 1884–1907
Calongne, W. F., Jr., B.Arch., Architecture 1965–
Canaday, John Edwin, M.A., Art (Newcomb) 1950–1953
Capers, Gerald Mortimer, Jr., A.B., Ph.D., History
(Newcomb) 1948–
Capers, Roberta Murray Alford, A.B., Art (New-
comb) 1959–
Cardwell, Guy Adams, Jr., Ph.D., English 1944–1945
Carlson, Philip G., D.E.S., Operations Research 1965–

Carnes, Hugh Byron, A.B., M.A., Doctor en Letras, Foreign Trade and Business Communications   1938–

Carpenter, William M., Materia Medica and Therapeutics   1844–1848

Carroll, Joseph Wheadon, LL.B., Civil Law   1913–1922

Carter, Thomas, A.B., B.D., Greek   1897–1902

Cassidy, Helen Elizabeth, B.A., M.S.W., Social Work (Field Instruction)   1964–

Castellani, Aldo, M.D., F.R.C.P., Tropical Medicine   1925–1929

Cazenavette, Lionel Louis, M.D., Neurology and Psychiatry   1917–1938

Cecchetti, Giovanni (Laurea) Doctor's degree, Italian   1963–1965

Cenas, Augustus H., M.D., Obstetrics and the Diseases of Women and Children   1834–1866

Chaillé, Stanford Emerson, M.D., Physiology, Hygiene, and Pathological Anatomy   1868–1908

Chase, Gilbert Culmell, D. of Litt., Music (Newcomb)   1961–

Chassaignac, Charles Louis, M.D., Genito-Urinary and Rectal Diseases   1906–1925

Chilton, Richard H., Geology   1850–1852

Christian, Mildred Gayler, Ph.D., English (Newcomb), Pierce Butler Chair of English   1948–

Clark, Samuel Marmaduke Dinwiddie, B.Sc., M.D., F.A.C.S., Gynecology and Clinical Obstetrics   1911–1925

Clark, William Burton, M.D., Ophthalmology   1940–1963

Clark, Wallace Henderson, Jr., B.S., M.D., Pathology   1961–1962

Clarke, Thomas Allen, Common Law and Equity Jurisprudence   1870–1878

Claverie, Louis Barbot, A.B., LL.B.   1961–

Clifford, Alfred Hoblitzelle, A.B., Ph.D., Mathematics (Newcomb)   1955–

Clo, J. Harry, Ph.D., Physics   1916–1920

Cobb, Percy Wells, B.S., M.D., Research Professor of Psychology   1939–1940

Cocks, Reginald Somers, A.M., Ida A. Richardson Professor of Botany and Pharmacognosy   1908–1926

Cocram, Henry Sula, B.Sc., M.D., Gynecology and Obstetrics   1906–1924

Cohn, Isidore, B.Sc., M.D., F.A.C.S., Clinical Surgery   1919–1938

Colbert, Roy Jefferson, A.B., Social Technology   1920–1921

Cole, Fred Carrington, Ph.D., History   1947–1959

Cole, Henry T., English Language and Literature   1858–1859

Cole, James Clifton, A.B., M.D., F.A.C.S., Clinical Laboratory Diagnosis   1920–1927

Collins, Conrad Green, B.S., M.D., M.S., F.A.C.S., Obstetrics and Gynecology   1945–

Collins, Jason Haydel, B.S., M.D., Clinical Obstetrics
and Gynecology 1960–
Colvin, Howard Milton, A.B., LL.B., J.S.D., Law 1927–1934
Conrad, Paul F., Ph.D., Mathematics (Newcomb) 1961–
Copeland, Donald Eugene, Ph.D., Zoology 1959–
Cortner, Clarence Edward, B.S., Captain, U.S. Navy,
Naval Science 1953–1955
Countiss, Eugene Hendrix, B.S., M.D., Obstetrics
and Gynecology 1958–
Cox, Albert Brooks, A.B., J.D., Law 1923–1928
Craig, Charles Franklin, M.D., F.A.C.S., F.A.C.P.,
Colonel, U.S. Army, Tropical Medicine 1932–1938
Crandall, Lathan Augustus, Jr., M.D., Ph.D., Clinical
Psychiatry 1962–
Crebbin, John Thomson, M.D., Diseases of the Eye,
Ear, Nose and Throat 1920–1927
Creech, Oscar, Jr., B.S., M.D., William Henderson
Professor of Surgery 1956–
Creighton, William Henry P., U.S. Navy, Mechani-
cal Engineering 1894–1932
Cronvich, James Anthony, B.E., M.S., S.M. in E.E.,
Electrical Engineering and Biophysics 1949–
Cross, James Lucius, A.B., Mathematics 1878–1893
Crozat, George Bernard, D.D.S., Orthodontia 1917–1922
Crumpler, Thomas Bigelow, Ph.D., Chemistry 1943–
Cummins, Harold, Ph.D., Anatomy 1932–1964
Curtis, Nathaniel Cortlandt, Ph.B., B.S., Architecture 1912–1917

Dalzell, William Campbell, A.B., J.D., Thomas
Pickles Professor of Law 1921–1928
Danhof, Clarence Hendy, Ph.D., Economics 1953–1961
Danna, Joseph Anthony, M.D., Ph.D., F.A.C.S.,
Clinical Surgery 1926–1931
D'Antoni, Joseph Steven, M.D., Clinical Tropical
Medicine 1946–
Daspit, Henry, M.D., F.A.C.P., Neurology and
Psychiatry 1920–1932
Davis, Charles Till, D.Phil., History 1964–
Davis, William D., M.D., Medicine 1965–
Dean, Leonard Fellows, Ph.D., English 1947–1948
de Bordes, Andre Beziat, Ph.D., French (Newcomb) 1908–1916
De Bow, J. D. B., M.A., Political Economy 1850–1855
De Buys, Laurence Richard, B.S., M.D., F.A.C.P.,
Pediatrics 1916–1929
de Castro e Silva, Egydio, Music (Newcomb) 1964–
Deener, David Russell, Ph.D., Political Science 1958–
Deiler, John Hanno, German 1880–1907

Delaup, Sidney Philip, B.S., M.D., Surgery of the
Genito-Urinary Organs and Rectum   1907–1923
De Laureal, Boni James, M.D., Clinical Medicine   1960–
de Milt, Clara Marie, Ph.D., Chemistry (Newcomb)   1930–1953
Denis, Henry, B.L., Civil Law   1884–1906
Denis, Willey, Ph.D., Biochemistry   1924–1929
Derbes, Vincent Joseph De Paul, M.D., Medicine
(Dermatology)   1954–
Derickson, Donald, C. E., Civil Engineering   1914–1946
de Tornos, J., Spanish Language and Literature   1851–1853
De Verges, Paul, D.D.S., Orthodontia   1909–1915
Dillard, James Hardy, M.A., D.L., LL.B., Latin   1891–1908
Dinwiddie, Albert Bledsoe, A.M., Ph.D., LL.D.,
Mathematics   1910–1935
Dinwiddie, John Ekin, B.S.(Arch), Architecture   1953–1959
Dinwiddie, William, M.A., LL.D., Mathematics   1918–1919
Ditchy, Jay Karl, A.M., Ph.D., French   1929–1952
Dixon, Brandt Van Blarcom, A.M., LL.D., Philoso-
phy (Newcomb)   1886–1919
Dock, George, A.M., M.D., Theory and Practice of
Medicine and Clinical Medicine   1908–1910
Dowling, Oscar, M.D., F.A.C.P., Public Health   1919–1931
Dubos, Louis Joseph, B.A., M.D., Clinical Medicine   1947–1957
Ducasse, Edward Bernard, D.D.S., Crown and Bridge
Work and Ceramics   1914–1926
Duchamp, Charles Augustus, A.M., Civil Law   1920–1921
Dufau, Louis, M.A., Mental and Moral Philosophy   1858–1859
Dufour, Horace Generes, B.E., LL.B., Civil Law   1915–1918
Dunbar, Charles Edward, Jr., A.B., LL.B., LL.D.,
Law   1923–1946
Duncan, William C., A.M., Greek and Latin Lan-
guages and Literature   1850–1854
Dunlap, Archibald Lee, B.S., M.E., Mechanical
Engineering   1945–1960
Dunlap, Charles Edward, A.B., M.D., Pathology   1945–
Dupaquier, Edouard Michel, B.Let., B.Sc., M.D.,
Tropical Medicine and Acute Infectious Diseases   1906–1917
Durel, Lionel Charles, Ph.D., Romance Languages
(Newcomb)   1928–1950
Durel, Wallace, Joseph Eugene, M.D., Clinical
Medicine   1916–1935
Duren, William Larkin, Jr., Ph.D., Mathematics   1943–1955
Duval, Charles Warren, A.B., M.D., F.A.C.P.,
Pathology and Bacteriology   1909–1942
Dyer, Isadore, Ph.B., M.D., Diseases of the Skin   1907–1920
Dyer, Isadore, B.S., M.D., F.A.C.S., Obstetrics   1950–
Dyer, John Percy, Ph.D., History   1955–

Earle, Thomas Theron, Ph.D., Ida A. Richardson
    Professor of Botany   1946–
Echols, Dean Holland, M.D., Clinical Neurosurgery   1943–
Edmonson, Munro Sterling, Ph.D., Sociology and
    Anthropology   1960–
Eggler, Willis Alexander, Ph.D., Botany (Newcomb)   1959–
Elliott, Daniel Stanley, Ph.D., W. R. Irby Professor
    of Physics   1920–1944
Elliott, John Barnwell, A.B., M.D., Ph.D., Theory
    and Practice of Medicine   1877–1914
Elliott, John Barnwell, Jr., A.M., M.D., Theory and
    Practice of Medicine and Clinical Medicine   1907–1920
Ellis, Thomas Cargill Warner, A.B., LL.B., Ad-
    miralty and International Law   1898–1906
Elsasser, Robert William, A.B., M.C.S., Economics
    and Management   1927–1942
Englekirk, John Eugene, Jr., Ph.D., Spanish   1940–1958
Eustis, Allen Chotard, B.S., Ph.B., M.D., F.A.C.P.,
    Clinical Medicine   1916–1936
Eustis, James Biddle, Civil Law   1884–1885
Eves, Edward Thomas, B.S., Captain, U.S. Navy,
    Naval Science   1949–1953; 1955–1958
Ewan, Joseph Andorfer, A.B., Botany   1957–

Fagley, Thomas Fisher, Ph.D., Chemistry   1961–
Fair, Marvin Luke, Ph.D., Economics and Trans-
    portation   1948–1959
Farber, Emmanuel, M.D., Ph.D., American Cancer
    Society Research Professor of Pathology and Bio-
    chemistry   1959–1961
Faris, Ellsworth, Ph.D., Sociology (Newcomb)   1930–1931
Farley, Robert Joseph, A.B., LL.B., J.S.D., Law   1936–1946
Faust, Ernest Carroll, A.B., A.M., Ph.D., Parasitol-
    ogy; William Vincent Professor of Tropical Dis-
    eases and Hygiene   1928–1961
Fearn, J. Walker, B.A., Spanish   1884–1885
Feibleman, James Kern, Philosophy   1946–
Feild, Robert Durant, B.A., Art (Newcomb)   1940–1958
Feingold, Marcus, M.D., F.A.C.S., Ophthalmology   1907–1925
Fenner, Charles Payne, B.S., LL.B., Civil Law   1912–1920
Fenner, Erasmus Darwin, A.B., M.D., F.A.C.S.,
    Orthopedics and Surgical Diseases of Children   1907–1927
Ferguson, Edward Bernard, Jr., B.S., M.D., Clinical
    Medicine   1963–
Fernandez, J. A., Spanish   1884–1886
Ferrata, Chevalier Giusseppe, Mus.D., Piano and
    Composition (Newcomb)   1909–1928

Ficklen, John Rose, B.Let., English, History and
   Political Science   1884–1907
Findley, Thomas Palmer, Jr., B.A., B.S., M.D.,
   Clinical Medicine   1949–1954
Fingerman, Milton, Ph.D., Zoology   1963–
Fletcher, John Madison, Ph.D., Psychology (New-   1914–1924; 1928–1938;
   comb)   1942–1944
Fogle, Richard Harter, Ph.D., English   1950–
Forrester, William Ray, A.B., J.D., W. R. Irby Pro-
   fessor of Law   1943–1949; 1952–1963
Fortier, Alcée, D.Lit., Romance Languages   1880–1914
Fortier, Eugene Louis, D.D.S., Operative Dentistry   1914–1926
Fossier, Albert Emile, A.M., M.D., Clinical Medicine   1919–1924; 1933–1940
Foster, Rufus Edward, LL.B., Law   1921–1927
Fox, Frederick Hewitt, B.E., W. R. Irby Professor of
   Civil Engineering   1946–1959
Fox, John Perrigo, M.D., Ph.D., M.P.H., William
   Hamilton Watkins Professor of Epidemiology;   1949–1959
     Visiting Professor of Epidemiology   1960–
Franklin, Mitchell, A.B., LL.B., S.J.D., W. R. Irby
   Professor of Law   1930–
French, Robert Warren, Ph.D., Economics and Busi-
   ness Administration   1949–1956
Friedman, Lorraine, B.A., M.P.H., Ph.D., Micro-
   biology   1964–
Friedrichs, Andrew Gaiennie, M.D., D.D.S., Oral
   Hygiene   1906–1918
Friedrichs, George John, M.D., D.D.S., Operative
   Dentistry   1909–1912
Frnka, Henry Edward, B.A., M.A., Physical Educa-
   tion   1945–1952
Frotscher, Lydia Elizabeth, Ph.D., German (New-
   comb)   1931–1943
Frye, William Wesley, B.A., M.D., Ph.D., Tropical
   Medicine and Public Health   1948–1949
Fueg, John William, B.A., Lt. Colonel, U.S. Army,
   Military Science   1959–1963
Fuller, Hoffman Franklin, LL.B., Law   1964–

Gage, Idys Mims, M.D., F.A.C.S., Clinical Surgery   1945–1957
Gammon, George Davis, A.B., M.D., Neurology   1963–1964
Garcia, Manuel, M.D., Clinical Radiology   1952–
Garrey, Walter Eugene, B.S., Ph.D., M.D., Physi-
   ology   1916–1925
Geer, Russel Mortimer, Ph.D., W. R. Irby Professor
   of Classical Languages   1937–1961
Gelpi, Maurice Joseph, A.B., M.D., F.A.C.S., Clini-
   cal Surgery   1927–1931

Gelpi, Paul Joseph, A.M., M.D., Genito-Urinary
Diseases and Cystoscopy 1917–1925

Gentil, J., M.A., French and Spanish Languages and
Literature 1858–1859

Gerall, Arnold Abraham, B.S., M.A., Ph.D., Psychology 1963–

Gessner, George, Ph.D., Greek and Latin Languages
and Literature and German Language 1858–1859

Gessner, Herman Bertram, M.A., M.D., F.A.C.S.,
Clinical Surgery 1909–1936

Gibson, Joseph Edward, M.A., Education 1936–1947

Gicovate, Bernard Echeverz, B.A., Dr.F.L., M.A.,
Ph.D., Spanish 1960–1965

Giffin, Cyril Guy, M.B.A., Banking and Business
Finance 1926–1927

Gilmore, Harlan Welch, Ph.D., Sociology 1955–1959

Glick, Clarence Elmer, Ph.D., Sociology 1946–1949

Goldsmith, Grace Arabell, B.S., M.D., M.S., Medicine 1949–

Goldstein, Harris Klotz, D.S.W., Social Work 1962–

Gore, Benjamin Levi, D.D.S., Dental Surgery 1917–1921

Gould, Harley Nathan, Ph.D., Biology (Newcomb) 1924–1952

Grace, John Daniel, Law 1923–1928

Grambsch, Paul Victor, B.A., M.A., D.B.A., Management 1959–1960

Granger, Amédée Bercier, M.D., O.d'A., F.A.C.R.,
Radiology 1915–1931

Gray, Robert F., Ph.D., Anthropology 1965–

Grayson, Charles Jackson, Jr., D.B.A., C.P.A. 1963–

Gregory, Richard V., Captain, U.S. Navy, Naval
Science 1958–1962

Gregory, William Benjamin, M.M.E., Experimental
Engineering and Hydraulics 1908–1938

Griffin, Max Liles, Ph.D., English 1951–1953

Griffith, William Joyce, Ph.D., History 1955–

Grulee, Clifford Grosselle, Jr., B.A., B.M., M.D.,
Pediatrics 1956–1962

Guthrie, James Birney, B.Sc., M.D., F.A.C.P., Clinical Medicine 1911–1930

Hack, Marvin Howard, Ph.D., Histochemistry 1962–

Hale, Mark Pendleton, M.A., Social Economics 1947–1948

Hall, Gladys E., M.A., Child Welfare 1947–1961

Hall, Harry Hinckley, Criminal Law, Law of Evidence, and Practice under the Code of Practice of
Louisiana 1888–1906

Halley, Donald MacDougall, A.B., A.M., Economics
and Finance 1932–

Halsey, John Taylor, M.D., Pharmacology	1904–1937
Hamburg, Carl Heinz, Ph.D., Philosophy	1960–
Hampton, John Kyle, Jr., Ph.D., Physiology	1960–
Hanley, Patrick Henry, M.D., Surgery	1964–
Hansen, Peter Sijer, Ph.D., Music (Newcomb)	1953–
Hard, Frederick, Ph.D., English (Newcomb)	1938–1944
Hardesty, Irving, A.B., Ph.D., D.Sc., Anatomy	1909–1933
Hardin, George Leon, B.S., M.D., Clinical Ophthalmology	1937–1938
Harding, Edward Coles, A.M., Greek	1879–1880
Harkness, Mary Leal A.M., Ph.D., Lit.D., Latin (Newcomb)	1890–1921
Harris, Edward Hooper, B.S.(C.E.), B.S.(E.E.), M.S., Mechanical Engineering	1964–
Harris, Rufus Carrollton, A.B., LL.B., Jur.D., LL.D., Litt.D., D.C.L., Law	1927–1960
Harris, William Herbert, A.B., M.D., Pathology	1918–1937
Harrison, John Hoffman, Physiology and Pathological Anatomy	1838–1849
Hatch, Edward Sparhawk, M.D., F.A.C.S., Orthopedics	1927–1937
Hathaway, Edward Sturtevant, Ph.D., Zoology	1926–1952
Hava, Walter Chavigny, D.D.S., Dental Surgery	1923–1925
Hawthorne, Frank, Obstetrics and Diseases of Women and Children	1868–1875
Hayes, Harry Gordon, Ph.D., L.H.D., Economics	1952–1958
Heaney, George Francis, Jr., B.S., Colonel, U.S. Army, Military Science and Tactics	1947–1950
Heard, T. J., M.D., Materia Medica and Therapeutics	1876–1877
Heath, Robert Galbraith, B.S., M.D., D.M.Sc., Psychiatry and Neurology	1948–
Heck, Harold Joseph, M.A., M.B.A., D.C.S., Business Administration and Finance	1947–1959
Heller, Max, M. L., Hebrew	1912–1927
Hendrickson, George Windsor, B.A., M.F.A., Theater and Speech	1957–
Hennen, Alfred, Common and Constitutional Law and Equity Jurisprudence	1855–1870
Hill, Arthur Middleton, B.E.(M.E.), S.M., Mechanical Engineering	1945–1956
Hill, David Spence, Ph.D., Psychology and Education	1911–1913
Hines, Merrell Odom, B.S., M.D., Surgery (Clinical)	1964–
Hodes, Robert, Ph.D., Neurophysiology	1948–1953
Hofmann, Carl H., Ph.D., Mathematics	1965–
Hogan, William Ranson, Ph.D., History	1950–
Holbrook, Charles Shute, B.S., M.D., F.A.C.P., Clinical Neuropsychiatry	1931–1953

Hopkins, Ralph, A.B., M.D., Dermatology	1926–1941
Hostetler, Paul S., Ph.D., Theatre and Speech	1965–
Howard, Lawrence Vaughan, Ph.D., Political Science	1947–
Howerton, Dorothy Kellogg, Ph.D., Social Work	1961–1965
Hrubecky, Henry Francis, Ph.D., Mechanical Engineering	1961–
Hubbard, John Randolph, Ph.D., History	1958–
Hubert, Leon Dayries, Jr., B.A., LL.B., Law	1953–
Hughes, Harold, Ph.B., Jur.D., Economics	1947–1949
Hughes, William Lee, LL.B., Dental Jurisprudence	1917–1920
Hume, John Raymond, M.D., Otolaryngology	1931–1938
Hume, Joseph, Ph.B., M.D., F.A.C.S., Genito-Urinary and Venereal Diseases	1917–1930
Hummel, Edward Morton, M.D., Diseases of the Nervous System	1915–1918
Hunt, Carleton, LL.D., Admiralty and International Law	1869–1884
Hunt, Randell, LL.D., Commercial and Criminal Law and the Law of Evidence	1847–1889
Hunt, Thomas, M.D., Physiology and Pathology	1850–1867
Hurt, Ashley D., A.M., LL.D., Greek	1884–1897
Husband, John Dillon, B.S., M.A., Ph.D., English	1958–
Hutton, Mary Louise Marshall, Medical Bibliography	1949–1959
Irion, Arthur Lloyd, Ph.D., Psychology	1952–
Ivey, Joseph Nettles, A.M., LL.B., Ph.D., Mathematics and Astronomy	1907–1909
Jacobs, Sydney, B.S., M.D., Clinical Medicine	1962–
James, Francis Godwin, Ph.D., History	1957–
Jamison, Stanford Chaille, M.D., Clinical Medicine	1929–1945
Janvier, George, LL.B., Law	1935–1953
Jesse, Richard Henry, Latin	1878–1890
Johnson, Arnold Waldemar, B.B.A., M.B.A., C.P.A., Accounting	1942–1947
Johnson, Chapman Gordon, M.D., Clinical Obstetrics and Gynecology	1952–
Johnson, Hamilton McKee, Ph.D., Geology and Geophysics	1958–
Johnson, Harry Miles, Ph.D., John Madison Fletcher Research Professor of Psychology	1938–1950
Johnson, Lee Harnie, M.A., S.M., Sc.D., Civil Engineering	1950–
Johnson, Sydney L., Common and Constitutional Law and Equity Jurisprudence	1852–1855
Jonassen, Hans Boegh, Ph.D., Chemistry	1952–
Jones, Alexander Hugh, D.D.S., Orthodontia	1912–1916

Jones, James, M.D., Obstetrics and Diseases of
Women and Children   1839–1874
Jones, Joseph, M.D., LL.D., Chemistry and Medical
Jurisprudence   1868–1896
Jones, Philip Harold, Jr., B.A., M.D., Ph.D.,
F.A.C.P., Clinical Medicine   1948–1961
Joor, Joseph F., M.D., Botany   1885–1892
Jordan, Thomas Edward, Ph.D., Education   1962–1963
Julian, M. P., French Language and Literature   1878–1880
Jung, Rodney Clifton, M.D., Ph.D., Tropical Medi-
cine   1963–

Kahle, Pierre Jorda, B.A., M.D., Urology   1924–1931
Karnes, Thomas Lindas, Ph.D., History   1964–
Kastler, Arthur Ordway, B.E., M.S., Ph.D., Bio-
chemistry   1956–
Keller, Frank Leuer, Ph.D., Resources (Economics)   1957–
Kendall, John Smith, M.A., W. R. Irby Professor of
Spanish   1929–1939
Kennedy, Thomas Seilles, M.D., Diseases of Children   1906–1912
Kindelsperger, Walter Lewis, M.A., Ph.D., W. R.
Irby Professor of Social Welfare Policy   1947–
King, Alfred Clinton, M.D., F.A.C.S., Clinical
Surgery   1924–1933
King, Arden Ross, Ph.D., Anthropology (Newcomb)   1957–
King, Edward Lacy, A.B., M.D., F.A.C.S., Obstetrics   1927–1950
King, Gordon, M.D., Diseases of the Ear, Nose and
Throat   1907–1910
Kirgis, Homer Dale, Ph.D., M.D., Clinical Anatomy
and Neurosurgery   1964–
Kirk, Richard Ray, A.M., English   1937–1943; 1945–1947
Kittredge, Willoughby Eaton, Jr., B.S., M.D., Clini-
cal Urology (Surgery)   1959–
Klein, Maynard Jacob, B.S., M.M., Choral Music
(Newcomb)   1947–1948
Kohlmeyer, Hermann, Ph.D., German Language
and Literature, Hebrew and other Oriental Lan-
guages   1850–1854
Kolb, William Lester, Ph.D., Sociology (Newcomb)   1951–1959
Kostmayer, Hiram Watkins, A.B., M.D., F.A.C.S.,
LL.D., W. R. Irby Professor of Clinical Gyne-
cology   1925–1949
Krementz, Edward Thomas, B.A., M.D., Surgery   1961–
Ktsanes, Thomas, Ph.D., Sociology   1964–
Kuypers, John, A.B., Music   1961–

Laguaite, Jeannette Katherine, Ph.D., Otolaryngology
(Audiology and Speech Pathology)   1961–

Lake, Forrest Una, B.S., Captain, U.S. Navy, Naval
Science 1942–1946
Lamar, Rene, A.M., Agrégé de l'Université (Sorbonne), French 1924–1928
LaMeslee, Alphonse Marin, B. ès L., A.M., French 1916–1921
Landfried, Charles John, M.D., Otology, Laryngology and Rhinology 1907–1916
Lang, Samuel, B.A., LL.B., Law 1961–
Langmaid, Stephen Ives, A.M., LL.B., Law 1916–1921
Lapham, Maxwell Edward, M.D., F.A.C.S., W. R.
Irby Professor of Obstetrics 1939–
Larremore, Thomas Armitage, A.B., LL.B., Law 1921–1922
Larue, Felix Alphonse, A.M., M.D., Operative and
Clinical Surgery 1906–1925
Laurens, Henry, A.B., A.M., Ph.D., Physiology 1926–1944
LaViolette, Forrest Emanuel, Ph.D., Sociology 1949–
Lawrence, John William, B.S. in Arch., M.S. in Arch. 1960–
Lawrence, Marjorie, Voice (Newcomb) 1956–1962
Lawson, Edwin Hugh, B.S., M.D., Clinical Medicine 1943–1963
Leary, Daniel Bell, A.M., Education (Newcomb) 1917–1918
Lee, Harold Newton, Ph.D., Philosophy (Newcomb) 1943–1965
Leefe, Alfred Archinard, D.D.S., Dental Pathology
and Therapeutics 1918–1928
Lefevre, Albert, A.B., Ph.D., Philosophy 1903–1905
LeJeune, Francis Ernest, B.S., M.D., M.S., Otolaryngology 1931–1959
Lemann, Bernard, B.Arch., B.S., M.A., Ph.D.,
Architecture 1960–
Lemann, Isaac Ivan, B.A., M.D., F.A.C.P., Clinical
Medicine 1914–1937
Lemann, Monte Mordecai, A.B., LL.B., LL.D., Law 1912–1938
Lennox, Robert Henry, B.Sc., M.D., C.M., D.T.M.,
Child Health and Pediatrics 1962–
Lerch, Otto, A.M., Ph.D., M.D., Medical Diagnosis
and Treatment 1906–1919
Leucht, I. L., Hebrew 1889–1891
Levy, Arthur Herbert, B.Arch., Architecture 1957–1962
Levy, Walter Edmond, B.S., M.D., F.A.C.S.,
Obstetrics 1933–1937
Lewis, Ernest Sidney, B.S., M.D., LL.D., General
and Clinical Obstetrics and Diseases of Women
and Children 1875–1912
Lewis, James Leon, M.D., Clinical Medicine 1919–1936
Lewis, James Mackey, B.S., Commander, U.S. Navy,
Naval Science and Tactics 1940–1941
Lewis, Mary Evelyn, M.A., Public Welfare Administration 1961–

Lewis, Robert Frank, B.S., M.P.H., Ph.D., Biostatistics	1962–
Lief, Harold Isaiah, A.B., M.D., Psychiatry	1960–
Lippman, Monroe, Ph.D., Theater and Speech	1947–
Llewellyn, Raeburn Carson, A.B., M.D., Neurosurgery (Surgery)	1960–
Loeber, Maud, M.A., M.D., F.A.C.P., F.A.A.P., Clinical Pediatrics	1930–1948
Logan, Samuel, M.D., Surgery	1873–1885; 1890–1893
Loria, Frank Leo, B.S., M.D., Physical Education	1958–1962
Lumiansky, Robert Mayer, Ph.D., English	1948–1963
Luzenberg, Chandler Clement, B.S., LL.B., Law	1923–1924
Lynch, Robert Clyde, M.D., F.A.C.S., Otolaryngology	1911–1931
Lyon, James Adair, Jr., A.M., D.Sc., W. R. Irby Professor of Physics; Astronomy (Newcomb)	1900–1949
Lyons, Randolph, A.B., M.D., F.A.C.P., Clinical Medicine	1921–1946
Lystad, Robert Arthur, B.A., B.D., Ph.D., Anthropology	1960–1961
McAfee, Samuel Harrison, D.D.S., Operative Dentistry, Dental Pathology and Therapeutics	1911–1914
McBryde, John MacLaren, Jr., Ph.D., Litt.D., English	1919–1938
McCaleb, Theodore H., LL.D., Admiralty and International Law	1847–1862
McClure, Matthew Thompson, Jr., M.A., Ph.D., Philosophy (Newcomb)	1918–1921
McConnell, Gaither Abigail, Ph.D., Education	1964–
McCutcheon, Roger Philip, A.M., Ph.D., W. R. Irby Professor of English	1925–1954
McGovney, Dudley Odell, A.M., LL.B., Law	1908–1914
McIlhenny, Paul Avery, M.D., F.A.C.S., Orthopedics	1920–1938
McLaurin, James Walter, B.S., M.D., Otto Joachim Professor of Otolaryngology	1949–
McLean, Lee Davidson, B.A., M.D., Clinical Dermatology	1962–
McPeek, Gwynn Spencer, B.S., M.M., Ph.D., Music (Newcomb)	1959–1964
McPheeters, Dean William, B.S., M.A., Ph.D., Spanish	1964–
Macdonald, Frank Whitmore, B.E.(C.E.), S.B.(Pub. Health), C.E., D.P.H., Public Health (Sanitation), Civil Engineering	1960–
Maes, Urban, M.D., F.A.C.S., Clinical Surgery	1919–1932
Magruder, Howard Pierce, D.D.S., Prosthetic Dentistry and Crown and Bridge Work	1909–1914

Mallet, J. W., Chemistry	1865–1868
Mann, Arthur Seldon, M.D., M.S. (Med.), Clinical Medicine	1962–
Mann, Cecil William, B.A., M.A., Ed.D., Psychology	1946–1961
Mann, Gustav, B.Sc., M.D., Physiology	1908–1915
Many, Anna Estelle, A.M., Mathematics (Newcomb)	1939–1954
Marcoux, Harvey Lee, A.M., English	1931–1949
Marks, Sumter Davis, Jr., A.B., LL.B., Louisiana Practice	1929–1957
Marr, Robert Harden, A.M., LL.B., Law	1924–1926
Marshak, Alfred George, Ph.D., Pathology	1964–
Martin, Edmund Denegre, M.D., LL.D., F.A.C.S., Surgery	1906–1932
Martin, Melvin Albert, Ph.D., Psychology (Newcomb)	1923–1936
Mason, Henry Lloyd, Ph.D., Certificate, Academy of International Law, The Hague, Political Science	1961–
Mason, John Angus Campbell, A.M., History (Newcomb)	1911–1914
Matas, Rudolph, M.D., LL.D., D.Sc., F.A.C.S., F.R.C.S., General and Clinical Surgery	1895–1927
Matthews, Edward de Saunhac, B.S., M.D., Clinical Medicine	1960–
Maurer, Heinrich Herman, Ph.D., History (Newcomb)	1915–1918
Maxfield, William Streeter, B.A., M.D., Clinical Radiology	1964–
Maxwell, Leon Ryder, A.M., Virginia Beer Professor of Music (Newcomb)	1909–1953
Mayer, George Alfred, M.D., F.A.C.S., Clinical Obstetrics	1937–1950
Mayer, John King, M.S., Mechanical Engineering	1948–
Mayerson, Hymen Samuel, B.A., Ph.D., Physiology	1945–1965
Mellen, William Francis, Common Law and Equity Jurisprudence	1878–1888
Menage, Henry Edward, M.D., M.P.H., Dermatology	1907–1927
Menuet, Robert Leonval, B.E., W. R. Irby Professor of Mathematics	1927–1943
Menville, Leon John, M.D., Radiology	1934–1948
Merrill, Aaron Stanton, B.S., Captain, U.S. Navy, Naval Science and Tactics	1941–1942
Merton, Robert King, Ph.D., Sociology (Newcomb)	1940–1941
Metz, Abraham, Louis, M.Ph., M.D., Chemistry and Toxicology	1896–1919
Meyer, George Wilbur, Ph.D., English (Newcomb)	1946–
Meynier, Alphonse Charles Bernard, D.D.S., Crown and Bridge Work and Ceramics	1926–1928

Michinard, Paul, M.D., Obstetrics and Gynecology   1906–1925
Miles, A. B., M.D., General and Clinical Surgery   1886–1895
Miles, Henry Harcourt Waters, B.S., M.D., Clinical
Psychiatry   1965–
Miller, Charles Jefferson, M.D., D.Sc., F.A.C.S.,
Gynecology   1906–1936
Miller, Henry Carleton, Admiralty and International
Law   1882–1899
Miller, Hilliard Eve, M.D., F.A.C.S., Gynecology   1936–1944
Miller, James Albert, Jr., Ph.D., Anatomy   1960–
Miller, Oscar Neal, Ph.D., Biochemistry and Medi-
cine   1960–
Miller, Walter, A.M., Classical Philology   1902–1911
Mitchell, Harry Adam, A.B., M.B.A., Marketing   1930–
Mogabgab, William Joseph, B.S., M.D., Medicine   1962–
Monroe, Frank Adair, Law   1888–1909
Monroe, Thomas B., LL.D., Common and Constitu-
tional Law and Equity Jurisprudence   1847–1851
Montgomery, R. B., Penmanship and Commercial
Course   1878–1880
Mooney, Rose LeDieu, Ph.D., Physics (Newcomb)   1941–1954
Moreno, Arthur Alphonse, A.B., LL.B., Louisiana
Code of Practice   1917–1918
Morgan, Cecil, LL.B., LL.D., Law   1963–
Morphos, Panos Paul, Ph.D., French   1953–
Morris, Harry Dunlap, B.S., M.D., Clinical Ortho-
pedics   1960–
Morris, Joseph Chandler, Ph.D., Physics   1941–
Morrissey, John Joseph, B.A., A.M., Music   1947–
Morrow, Clarence James, B.A., LL.B., J.S.D., Law   1947–
Moseley, Hal Walters, M.S., A.M., Chemistry   1927–1941
Mosley, Kirk Thornton, B.A., M.D., Epidemiology   1946–1950
Musser, John Herr, B.S., M.D., F.A.C.P., Medicine   1924–1948

Nabors, Eugene Augustus, A.B., LL.B., J.S.D.,
Thomas Pickles Professor of Law   1933–1959
Nadler, Samuel Bernard, Ph.D., M.D., Clinical
Medicine   1952–
Negus, Norman C., Ph.D. Biology   1965–
Nelson, Ervin Ellis, Ph.D., M.D., Pharmacology   1937–1944
Newell, Kenneth Wyatt, M.B., Ch.B., D.P.H., Wil-
liam Hamilton Watkins Professor of Epidemiology   1961–
Newman, Jacob Warren, Ph.D., M.D., F.A.C.S.,
Obstetrics   1918–1933
Newton, Robert Russell, Ph.D., Physics (Project
Director)   1954–1957
Nice, Charles Monroe, Jr., A.B., M.D., M.S., Ph.D.,
Radiology   1958–

Nieset, Robert Thomas, M.A., B.S.E., Ph.D., Physics
and Biophysics 1953–1962
Nixon, Herman Clarence, Ph.D., History 1930–1938
Nixon, Jane Caldwell, English and Rhetoric (New-comb) 1890–1907
Noble, Stuart Grayson, Ph.D., W. R. Irby Professor
of Education (Newcomb) 1924–1952
Northrup, Ann Hero, A.M., Chemistry (Newcomb) 1905–1926
Northrup, Elliott Judd, A.B., LL.B., Law 1911–1926
Nott, Gustavus Adolphus, M.D., Materia Medica
and Therapeutics 1849–1862; 1866–1867
Nott, Josiah Clark, Anatomy 1857–1858
Nunn, Walter Melrose, Ph.D., Electrical Engineering 1963–

Oakes, Forrest Edward, Physical Education 1946–1964
Ochsner, Edward William Alton, B.A., M.D., F.A.-C.S., William Henderson Professor of Surgery 1927–1961
Oechsner, John Frederick, M.D., F.A.C.S., Ortho-pedics and Surgical Diseases of Children 1907–1926
O'Kelley, James Phares, M.D., F.A.C.S., Clinical
Otology, Rhinology, and Laryngology 1916–1933
Oppenheim, Leonard, B. A., LL.B., M.C.L., M.A.,
S.J.D., Law 1956–
Ordway, Evelyn Walton, B.S., Chemistry (Newcomb) 1890–1905
Ordway, John Morse, A.M., Biology (Newcomb) 1884–1904
O'Rourke, John Bernard, Jr., B.M., Air Science 1959–1963
Orr, Henry B., Ph.D., Biology 1890–1899
Owens, Arthur Neal, B.S., M.D., Plastic Surgery
(Clinical Surgery) 1943–

Paine, J. F. Y., M.D., Materia Medica and Thera-peutics and Hygiene and Clinical Medicine 1884–1886
Parham, Frederick William, M.D., General and
Abdominal Surgery 1915–1924
Parry, Carl Eugene, A.M., Ph.D., Foreign Trade 1919–1922
Paterson, John Cargill, B.Sc., M.B., Ch.B., M.D.,
William Henderson Professor of the Prevention of
Tropical and Semi-Tropical Diseases and Hygiene 1958–
Paterson, Ruth Doreen, B.A., M.D., Medicine and
Neurology 1963–
Patterson, Claude Allan, B.A., M.A., Design (New-comb) 1928–1929
Patton, George Farrar, M.D., Practice of Medicine 1906–1920
Peacock, Charles LeRoy, A.B., M.S., Ph.D., Physics 1962–
Pearce, J. W., A.M., Ph.D., English and Mathematics 1891–1895
Peebles, Florence, Ph.D., Biology (Newcomb) 1915–1916
Peery, William Wallace, Ph.D., English 1955–1964
Pelz, Victor H., A.M., Marketing 1922–1924

Penfound, William Theodore, Ph.D., Ida A. Richardson Professor of Botany   1940–1947
Penick, Rawley Martin, Jr., Ph.B., M.D., Clinical Surgery   1948–1963
Penn, George Henry, Ph.D., Zoology   1957–1963
Perkins, William Harvey, M.D., Preventive Medicine   1931–1941
Perkins, William Martin, B.Sc., M.D., Clinical and Minor Surgery   1907–1921
Peters, Lawrence, Ph.D., M.D., Pharmacology   1953–1955
Pettis, Billy James, Ph.D., Mathematics   1948–1957
Peyronnin, Chester Arthur, Jr., B.E., M.S., Mechanical Engineering   1964–
Philips, Alfred, Admiralty and International Law   1865–1869
Phillips, Clinton Adam, B.A., Ph.D., Business Administration   1964–
Phillips, Ulrich Bonnell, A.M., Ph.D., History and Political Science   1908–1911
Phillips, William David, B.Sc., M.Ph., M.D., Operative Gynecology   1917–1925
Pickens, Buford Lindsay, B.S.(Arch.), A.M., Architecture   1946–1953
Pickering, Donald Everett, M.A., M.D., Developmental Biology (Pediatrics)   1963–1964
Pierce, William Arthur, Jr., B.A., M.S., Ph.D., Microbiology   1961–
Pipkin, Willis Benton, B.S. (Commerce), M.B.A., Business Finance   1931–1933
Pizer, Donald, B.A., Ph.D., English (Newcomb)   1964–
Platou, Ralph Victor, B.S., M.D., M.S., Pediatrics   1944–
Polumbo, Fred Albert, LL.B., Lt. Colonel, U.S. Army, Military Science and Tactics   1955–1959
Postell, William Dosite, M.S., B.S. in L.S., Medical Bibliography   1959–
Power, Henry Douglas, B.S., Captain, U.S. Navy, Naval Science   1945–1949
Pratt, John Galbraith, M.D., Urology   1934–1949
Pullen, Roscoe LeRoy, B.A., M.D., Graduate Medicine   1949–1952

Quigley, Frank Douglas, Ph.D., Mathematics   1964–

Rankin, Hugh Franklin, Ph.D., History   1964–
Ransmeier, John Christian, A.M., Ph.D., German   1912–1920
Reck, Andrew Joseph, Ph.D., Philosophy   1964–
Reed, Adrian Faragher, Ph.D., M.D., Anatomy   1953–1956
  Medicine   1962–
Reed, Francis Santry, A.B., M.B.A., Marketing   1927–1962

Reed, Lyman C., A.B., A.M., English	1884–1893
Reeder, Robert Patterson, LL.M., Law	1920–1921
Regenos, Graydon Wendell, Ph.D., Classical Languages	1959–
Regensburg, Jeannette, Ph.D., Social Casework	1943–1947
Reissman, Leonard, Ph.D., Charles A. and Leo M. Favrot Professor of Human Relations (Sociology and Anthropology)	1957–
Reuter, Edward Byron, Ph.D., Sociology	1920–1921
Reynaud, Louis Favrot, M.D., Materia Medica, Therapeutics, and Clinical Medicine	1893–1904
Rials, Grady Ford, Colonel, U.S. Army, B.A., M.B.A., Military Science	1963–
Richardson, Caroline Francis, Ph.D., English (Newcomb)	1931–1932
Richardson, Tobias Gibson, M.D., Surgery	1860–1862; 1866–1889
Ricker, Claire William, S.B., S.M., M.E.E., W. R. Irby Professor of Electrical Engineering	1928–1956
Rickey, George Warren, M.A., Art (Newcomb)	1954–1962
Riddell, John Leonard, M.D., Chemistry	1837–1862
Riddell, W. P., M.A., M.D., Chemistry and Natural Sciences	1856–1857
Riedel, Ernest Henry, Ph.D., Classical Languages	1941–1945
Robbins, Isidore Leon, M.D., Clinical Medicine	1959–1964
Robert, James Marshall, B.E., W. R. Irby Professor of Mechanical Engineering	1917–1950
Robertson, Donald, Ph.D., Art History (Newcomb)	1965–
Robin, Ernest Alexis, B.Sc., M.D., Diseases of the Eye	1906–1920
Robinson, Gustavus Hill, A.B., LL.B., Law	1914–1916
Rogers, Wynne Grey, LL.B., Louisiana Code of Practice	1920–1925
Rogers, Winfield Heyser, Ph.D., English	1945 (only)
Rohrer, John Harrison, Ph.D., Psychology	1951–1957
Roland, Charles Pierce, Ph.D., History	1960–
Roppolo, Joseph Patrick, Ph.D., English	1964–
Rose, S. Meryl, Ph.D., Anatomy (Experimental Embryology)	1961–
Roselius, Christian, LL.D., Civil Law	1851–1862; 1866–1872
Rotty, Ralph McGee, B.S.(E.E.), M.S.(M.E.), Ph.D. (M.E.), Mechanical Engineering	1958–
Roux, Marc, French Language and Literature	1850–1854
Rugan, Henry Fisler, Mechanic Arts	1915–1916
Ryland, Gladys, B.S., M.Ed., Group Work	1954–1957
Samuel, Ernest Charles, M.D., Radiology	1931–1937
Saunders, Eugene Davis, B.L., Law	1899–1914

Schales, Otto, D.Sc., Biochemistry — 1952–1964
Schaller, Howard Graham, Ph.D., Economics — 1960–1964
Scheps, Clarence, A.B., M.S., Ph.D., Accounting — 1954–
Schlegel, Jorgen Ulrik, Ph.D., M.D., Urology — 1959–
Schmidt, Charles Edward, Admiralty and International Law — 1881–1882
Schmidt, Ernest Albert, M.D., Clinical Radiology — 1948–1950
Schmitt, Hans Adolf, Ph.D., History — 1962–
Schoell, Frank Louis, Ph.D., French — 1923–1924
Schueler, Fred Warren, B.A., M.A., Ph.D., Pharmacology — 1956–1964
Schulhofer, Edith, LL.D., M.S., Social Casework — 1961–
Schwarz, Ralph Jacob, A.M., LL.B., Commercial Law — 1912–1929
Seago, Dorothy Wilson, B.A., Ph.D., John Madison Fletcher Professor of Psychology (Newcomb) — 1936–
Sears, Claudius Wister, Mathematics and Natural Philosophy — 1850–1860
Seavey, Warren Abner, A.B., LL.B., Law — 1914–1916
Seemann, William Henry, A.B., A.M., M.Ph., M.D., Hygiene — 1911–1938
Segaloff, Albert, M.S., M.D., Clinical Medicine — 1963–
Semmes, Thomas J., LL.D., Constitutional Law, Common Law and Equity Conflict of Laws, with Jurisdiction and Practice of the United States Courts at Law and in Equity — 1888–1899
Shaffer, Morris Frank, D.Phil., Microbiology — 1947–
Shands, Garvin Dugas, LL.B., LL.D., Law — 1906–1909
Sharp, Robert, A.M., Ph.D., LL.D., English — 1880–1918
Shaughnessy, Clark Daniel, Athletic Training — 1924–1926
Shaw, Elliott Nathan, Ph.D., Biochemistry — 1961–
Shaw, William Wesley, Ph.D., Political Science — 1960–
Sheerer, Mary Given, Pottery and China Decoration (Newcomb) — 1903–1931
Shelley, Lillian, Domestic Art (Newcomb) — 1914–1924
Sheppard, Harry Edwin, Commerce — 1920–1922
Silin, Charles Intervale, Ph.D., French — 1945–1961
Silvert, Kalman Hirsch, Ph.D., Political Science — 1960–1963
Simmons, George Evans, B.Jour., A.M., Times-Picayune Professor of Journalism — 1937–1964
Simon, John Felicien, M.Pharm., Ph.D., Pharmacy and Pharmacology — 1925–1934
Simon, Sidney Kohn, A.B., M.D., Gastroenterology — 1925–1936
Simons, Claude, Sr., Physical Education — 1940–1943
Simons, Claude, Jr., B.A., M.A., Physical Education — 1943–1950
Siporin, Max, D.S.W., Social Work — 1965–
Skinner, Hubert C., Ph.D., Geology — 1962–

Smith, Chester Howard, A.B., LL.B., S.J.D., Law 1926–1927

Smith, Florence Ambrose, M.A., Physical Education (Newcomb) 1944–1962

Smith, Gertrude Roberts, Water-Color Painting and Decoration of Textiles (Newcomb) 1903–1934

Smith, Hubert Winston, A.B., M.B.A., LL.B., M.D., Law and Legal Medicine 1949–1951

Smith, J. Lawrence, M.D., Chemistry and Mineralogy 1850–1852

Smith, Margaret Hamilton Donald, M.D., Pediatrics and Epidemiology 1961–

Smith, Ralph Grafton, M.D., Ph.D., Pharmacology 1943–1950

Smith, Victor Conway, M.D., F.A.C.S., Clinical Ophthalmology 1920–1926

Smith, Wilbur Cleveland, B. A., M.D., D.Sc., Gross Anatomy 1918–1919; 1921–1945

Smith, William Benjamin, A.M., Ph.D., LL.D., Philosophy 1893–1917

Smith, William F., Ph.D., Spanish 1965–

Smither, William J., Ph.D., Spanish and Portuguese (Newcomb) 1965–

Smythe, John, Jr., M.D., F.A.C.S., Clinical and Oral Surgery 1915–1927

Snell, John Leslie, Jr., Ph.D., History 1959–

Snyder, Christopher Harrison, A.B., M.D., Clinical Pediatrics 1964–

Sodeman, William Anthony, B.S., M.D., F.A.C.P., William Henderson Professor of the Prevention of Tropical and Semi-Tropical Diseases and Hygiene 1941–1953

Sogandares-Bernal, Franklin, Ph.D., Biology 1965–

Sogin, Harold H., Ph.D.(M.E.), Mechanical Engineering 1960–

Sommers, Charles, B.S., Colonel, U.S. Air Force, Air Science 1955–1959

Soniat, Theodore Louis Lucien, M.D., M.S., Clinical Neurology 1963–

Souchon, Edmond, M.D., Anatomy and Clinical Surgery 1884–1907

Souers, Philip Webster, Ph.D., English 1938–1945

Spencer, Adelin Elam, M.A., M.S., Geology 1934–1936

Spencer, Mary Cass, A.B., M.S., Mathematics (Newcomb) 1898–1931

Sperry, Claude J., M.S., Electrical Engineering 1965–

Sprague, Charles Cameron, B.S., B.B.A., M.D., Medicine 1962–

Steg, James Louis, M.F.A., Art 1964–

Steiner, Jesse Frederick, A.B., A.M., Ph.D., Sociology
(Newcomb)   1927–1931
Steinmayer, Reinhard August, B.S., Geology   1942–1957
Stephenson, Wendell Holmes, Ph.D., Litt.D., South-
ern History   1946–1953
Sternberg, William Howard, B.A., M.D., Pathology   1955–
Stevens, William Harrison Spring, A.M., Business
Organization and Management   1916–1917
Stevens, Will Henry, Art (Newcomb)   1945–1947
Stibbs, John Henry, Ph.D., English   1958–
Stone, Ferdinand Fairfax, B.A., M.A., B.A. in Juris.,
B.C.L., J.S.D., Thomas Pickles Professor of Law   1946–
Stone, Imogen, A.M., English Literature (Newcomb)   1920–1938
Stone, Warren, M.D., Surgery   1837–1862; 1865–1872
Storck, Ambrose Howell, B.S., M.D., M.S., F.A.C.S.,
Clinical Surgery   1947–
Storck, Jacob Ambrose, M.Ph., M.D., Gastro-
enterology   1906–1932
Strong, Robert Alexander, M.D., F.A.A.P., Pediatrics   1920–1923; 1929–1944
Struppeck, Julius, B.F.A., M.A., Art   1958–
Suthon, Walter Joseph, Jr., LL.B., Civil Law   1924–1956
Suttkus, Royal Dallas, Ph.D., Zoology   1960–
Sweeney, James William, Ph.D., Industrial Manage-
ment   1960–
Swinney, John Bayly, A.B., Marketing   1917–1918
Sytz, Florence, A.B., M.S.S., Social Casework   1939–1962

Tabb, Harold Granberry, B.S., M.D., Otolaryngology   1958–
Tatro, Clement Austin, B.A., M.S., Ph.D., Mechani-
cal Engineering   1962–
Taylor, Aline Mackenzie, B.A., M.A., Ph.D., English
(Newcomb)   1956–
Taylor, Dick, Jr., Ph.D., English   1959–1962
Taylor, Francis McBryde, Ph.D., Chemical Engi-
neering   1945–
Taylor, Garland Forbes, Ph.D., English   1946–1959
Taylor, Paul Canaday, B.S. in Commerce, M.S. in
Accountancy, Ph.D., C.P.A., Accounting   1938–1965
ten Hoor, Marten, Ph.D., W. R. Irby Professor of
Philosophy   1926–1944
Terhune, Thornton Powell, B.A., M.A., Docteur de
l'Université de Toulouse (Lettres), European
History   1945–1950
Terris, Milton, A.B., M.D., M.P.H., Epidemiology   1958–1960
Tew, Susan Dinsmore, Ph.D., Classical Languages
(Newcomb)   1902–1938
Theard, Delvaille Henry, A.B., LL.B., Civil Law   1919–1935

Thomas, Edward Perry, B.A., M.D., M.S., Clinical
Gynecology 1949–1962
Thomson, John Herndon, B.S., B.Arch., Architecture 1923–1957
Threefoot, Sam Abraham, B.S., M.D., Medicine 1963–
Towles, John Ker, A.M., Ph.D., Business Organiza-
tion and Management 1916–1918
Treuting, Theodore Francis, B.S., M.D., Medicine
and Psychiatry 1963–
Treuting, Waldo Louis, B.S., M.D., M.P.H., Public
Health 1948–1958
Trivigno, Pat, B.S., M.A., Art (Newcomb) 1960–
Troy, Lota Lee, B.S., Art (Newcomb) 1931–1940
Trump, Ross Myron, B.S., M.B.A., Administration 1946–1947
Tsai, Loh Seng, B.A., M.S., Ph.D., Psychology 1950–
Turck, Charles Joseph, A.M., LL.B., Law 1917–1920
Turner, Roy Hope, B.Sc., M.D., Medicine 1946–1961
Tyrone, Curtis Hartmen, M.D., F.A.C.S., Clinical
Gynecology 1949–

Unglaub, Walter George, B.A., M.D., Medicine 1963–

Van Gelder, David W., M.D., Pediatrics 1965–
Van Kirk, Jay Calvin, B.S., M.B.A., C.P.A., W. R.
Irby Professor of Accounting 1927–1961
Van Studdiford, Martin Thomas, B.S., M.D., Clini-
cal Dermatology 1941–1953
Van Wart, Roy McLean, A.B., M.P., Psychiatry 1917–1925
Vincent, Richard Wiltz, B.S., M.D., Clinical Plastic
Surgery 1960–
Viosca, Rene Adams, A.B., LL.B., Civil Law 1921–1956
Vliet, Daniel, Ph.D., Electrical Engineering 1965–
Vokes, Harold Ernest, A.B., Ph.D., Geology 1956–
Volpe, Erminio Peter, Ph.D., Zoology 1960–
von Langerman, B.S., M.D., Medicine 1962–
Voorhies, Norton William, B.S., M.D., Clinical
Medicine 1962–

Waechter, Arthur Joseph, Jr., B.A., LL.B., Law 1961–
Wagner, William Alfred, M.D., F.A.C.S., Clinical
Otolaryngology 1940–1963
Walbillich, Charles Arthur, M.D., Clinical Gyne-
cology 1924–1928
Walker, Arthur Judson, M.D., C.M., D.T.M., Para-
sitology 1951–1960
Walker, Joseph Clay, Ph.D., W. R. Irby Professor
of German 1932–1946
Wallace, Alexander Doniphan, Ph.D., Mathematics 1947–1963

Wallace, Sebon Rains, Jr., Ph.D., Psychology — 1946–1947
Walsdorf, Edward Henry, Administrative Pharmacy — 1925–1928
Waring, William W., M. D., Pediatrics — 1965–
Warren, Gerald Emery, Ph.D., Economics — 1950–1958
Watters, Theodore Albert, B.S., M.D., Neuropsychiatry — 1942–1946
Wauchope, Robert, A.M., Ph.D., Anthropology — 1947–
Weaver, Neill K., M.D., Medicine — 1965–
Webb, Byron Benjamin, Colonel, U.S. Air Force, Air Science and Tactics — 1950–1954
Wedderburn, A. J., M.D., Anatomy — 1843–1856
Wedderstrandt, John C. P., Anatomy — 1856–1857
Weed, John Conant, B.S., M.D., M.S., Clinical Obstetrics and Gynecology — 1960–
Weis, Joseph Deutch, M.D., Tropical and Clinical Medicine — 1914–1922
Weiss, Marie Johanna, Ph.D., Mathematics (Newcomb) — 1938–1952
Weiss, Thomas E., M.D., Medicine — 1965–
Weissman, Irving, M.A., M.S.W., Social Research — 1948–1963
Wellman, Creighton, M.D., Tropical Medicine and Hygiene, including Preventive Medicine — 1911–1914
Wendel, William Bean, B.S., Ph.D., Biochemistry — 1945–
Wespy, Frederick, Ph.D., German (Newcomb) — 1895–1917
Westerfield, William Weeks, LL.B., Louisiana Practice — 1926–1928
White, Alan George Castle, Ph.D., Biochemistry — 1960–
White, Melvin Johnson, Ph.D., History — 1916–1931
Whittemore, Robert Clifton, Ph.D., Philosophy — 1963–
Wickstrom, Jack Kenneth, B.A., M.D., Lee C. Schlesinger Professor of Orthopedics — 1955–
Wilde, Richard H., Constitutional and Common Law and Equity — 1847 (only)
Wilde, Walter Samuel, Ph.D., Physiology — 1952–1956
Wilkinson, Levi Washington, M.Sc., Industrial and Sugar Chemistry — 1897–1913
Williams, Thomas Edwin, M.A., Colonel, U.S. Marine Corps, Naval Science — 1962–1963
Williamson, Charles Samuel, Jr., M.S., Chemical Engineering — 1918–1946
Williamson, Gladys Richarda, M.B., Ch.B., D.P.H., F.A.C.P., F.A.A.P., Clinical Pediatrics — 1945–1956
Wilson, Julius Lane, B.S., M.D., F.A.C.P., Clinical Medicine — 1948–1952
Wilson, Logan, Ph.D., Sociology (Newcomb) — 1941–1951
Winston, James Edward, M.A., Ph.D., History (Newcomb) — 1918–1939

Wirth, Willard Ralph, B.S., M.D., Clinical Medicine	1952–1956
Wisdom, John Minor, A.B., LL.B., Law	1939–
Wisner, Elizabeth, Ph.D., W. R. Irby Professor of Public Welfare Administration	1934–1958
Wissner, Howard William, Ph.D., Economics and Industrial Relations	1957–
Wogan, Daniel Spelman, Ph.D., Spanish	1951–
Wood, Frank Lee, M.A., Lt. Colonel, U.S. Army, Military Science and Tactics	1948–1951
Wood, Wallace, Jr., D.D.S., Operative Dentistry	1914–1922
Woodman, John Duncan, A.B.A., Lt. Colonel, U.S. Army, Military Science and Tactics	1953–1955
Woods, William Sledge, Ph.D., French (Newcomb)	1951–
Woodward, Ellsworth, Drawing and Painting (Newcomb)	1885–1931
Woodward, William, Drawing and Painting (Newcomb)	1884–1922
Woody, Norman Cooper, B.S., M.D., Pediatrics	1965–
Wright, Fred Boyer, Jr., Ph.D., Mathematics	1962–
Wyckoff, Garrett Polhemus, A.B., LL.D., Sociology	1922–1937
Yost, Lowell Allen, M.S. in Eng'g., Colonel, U.S. Army, Military Science and Tactics	1950–1953
Young, Alexander Norman, C.A., Accounting	1914–1915
Young, Gail Sellers, Jr., Ph.D., Mathematics	1959–
Zardoya, Maria Concepcion, Ph.D., Spanish (Newcomb)	1956–1963
Ziskind, Morton Moses, B.S.S., B.S., M.D., Medicine	1962–

Appendix VIII

DIRECTORS OF ATHLETICS

Appleton Adam Mason	1910–1913
Clark D. Shaughnessy	1915–1922
Wilbur C. Smith	1922–1945
Horace C. Renegar	Aug. 1945–Jan. 1946
Claude Simons, Jr.	1946–1948
Horace C. Renegar (Director of Public Relations)	1948–1952
Richard O. Baumbach	1952–1960
Horace C. Renegar (Acting)	1961–1962
Rix Nelson Yard	1963–

ATHLETIC COACHES

Football

1893–1894	T. L. Bayne	1909–1910	Robert Brown
1894–1895	Fred Sweet	1910–1913	A. A. Mason
1895–1896	Porter Parker, and T. L. Bayne	1913–1914	A. C. Hoffman
		1914–1915	T. R. Sweetland
1896–1897	H. W. Baum	1915–1921	Clark Shaughnessy
1898–1899	John E. Lombard	1921–1922	Myron Fuller
1899–1900	H. T. Collier	1922–1927	Clark Shaughnessy
1900–1902	H. T. Summersgill	1927–1932	Bernie Bierman
1902–1903	Virginus Dabney	1932–1936	Ted Cox
1903–1904	Charles Eshleman	1936–1942	Lowell Dawson
1904–1905	Thomas A. Barry, and John Janvier	1942–1946	Claude Simons, Jr.
		1946–1952	Henry Frnka
1905–1906	John Tobin, and Harry Ludlow	1952–1954	Raymond Wolf
		1954–1962	Anton Pilney
1906–1907	John Russ	1962–1965	Thomas O'Boyle
1907–1909	Joe Curtis		

Basketball

1905–1906	Silas Hickey
1912–1913	A. A. Mason
1913–1914	Carl Hanson
1914–1915	T. R. Sweetland
1915–1917	Clark Shaughnessy
1918–1919	M. A. Moenck
1920–1927	Claude Simons
1927–1930	Bernie Bierman
1930–1931	Claude Simons
1931–1933	George Rody
1933–1938	Ray Dauber
1938–1942	Claude Simons, Jr.
1942–1945	Vernon Haynes
1945–1962	Clifford Wells
1962–1964	Theodore Lenhardt
1964–	Ralph Pedersen

Baseball

1894–1895	Jack Dowling and T. L. Bayne
1896–1897	F. B. Morris
1899–1900	H. T. Summersgill
1900–1901	"Home Run" Smith
1906–1907	J. Richard
1911–1917	Bruce Hayes
1919–1920	John Gondolfi
1922–1923	Bruce Hayes
1923–1927	Claude Simons
1928–1929	Ted Bank
1929–1930	Charles Flournoy
1937–1938	Claude Simons
1938–1941	Claude Simons, Jr.
1941–1942	Robert Kellogg
1942–1949	Claude Simons, Jr.
1949–1951	John Read
1951–1954	Dennis Vinzant
1954–1957	Bernard Abadie
1958–1959	Mel Parnell
1959–1960	Bob Whitman
1960–1962	Jack Orsley
1962–1963	Doug Hafner
1963–	Bernard Abadie

Track

1904–1905	Rev. H. W. Foote
1907–1908	Dr. Charles Eshleman
1911–1912	A. A. Mason, and M. J. White
1912–1913	Tad Gormley
1915–1920	Clark Shaughnessy
1920–1923	Claude Simons
1923–1925	Bernie Bierman
1925–1929	Forrest E. Oakes
1959–	John S. Oelkers

Tennis

1929–1933	Mercer Beasley
1933-1942	Emmett Paré
1943–1945	Ernest Sutter (part time)
1945–	Emmett Paré

Golf

1930–1931	Prof. Frederick Hard
1934–1935	Prof. George Simmons
1936–1942	George Turpie, Jr.
1942–	Innes Millar

Swimming

1961–	Lowell Damonte

Index